D0712271

*This book was donated to
the Richmond Public Library
by the Friends of the Richmond Public Library*

The Birth of
BLACK
AMERICA

The Birth of BLACK AMERICA

THE FIRST AFRICAN AMERICANS AND THE PURSUIT OF FREEDOM AT JAMESTOWN

~ *Tim Hashaw* ~

CARROLL & GRAF PUBLISHERS
NEW YORK

THE BIRTH OF BLACK AMERICA

The First African Americans and the Pursuit of Freedom at Jamestown

Carroll & Graf Publishers
An Imprint of Avalon Publishing Group, Inc.
245 West 17th Street, 11th Floor
New York, NY 10011

AVALON

Library of Congress Cataloging-in-Publication Data is available.

ISBN-13: 978-0-78671-718-7
ISBN-10: 0-7867-1718-1

9 8 7 6 5 4 3 2 1

INTERIOR DESIGN BY PAULINE NEUWIRTH, NEUWIRTH & ASSOCIATES, INC.

Printed in the United States of America
Distributed by Publishers Group West

To the related
Gowens, Goins, Goyens,
Goynes, and Guynes in all
their countless variations,
and to the Johnsons

· CONTENTS ·

The Birth of
BLACK
AMERICA

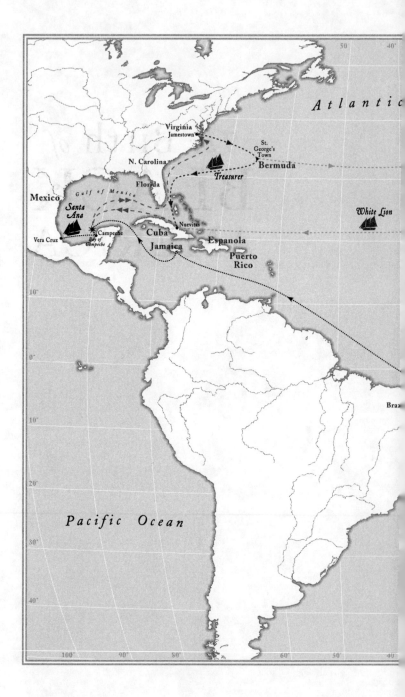

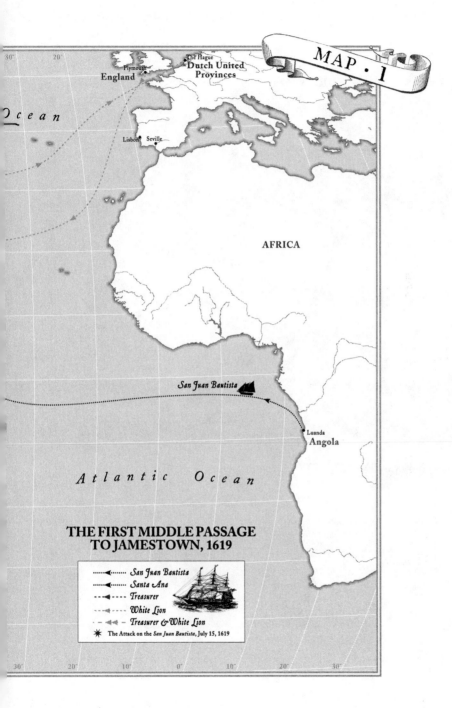

MAP · 1

30°   20°

England
Plymouth

The Hague
Dutch United
Provinces

Ocean

Lisbon   Seville

AFRICA

San Juan Bautista

Luanda
Angola

Atlantic   Ocean

THE FIRST MIDDLE PASSAGE
TO JAMESTOWN, 1619

San Juan Bautista
Santa Ana
Treasurer
White Lion
Treasurer & White Lion
✳ The Attack on the *San Juan Bautista*, July 15, 1619

30°   20°   10°   0°   10°   20°   30°

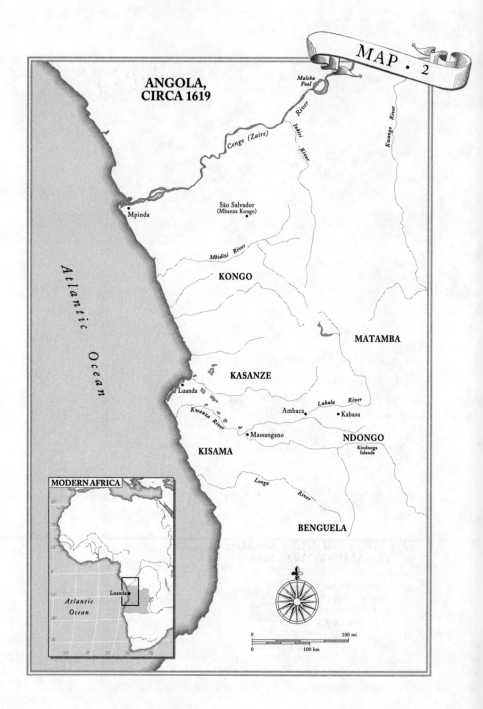

MAP · 2

ANGOLA,
CIRCA 1619

Maleba Pool

Congo (Zaire) River

Inkisi River

Kwango River

Mpinda

São Salvador
(Mbanza Kongo)

Mbidizi River

KONGO

MATAMBA

Atlantic Ocean

KASANZE

Luanda

Lukala River

Ambaca

Kabasa

Kwanza River

Massangano

NDONGO

KISAMA

Kindonga
Islands

Longa River

BENGUELA

MODERN AFRICA

Atlantic Ocean

Luanda

0   100 mi

0   100 km

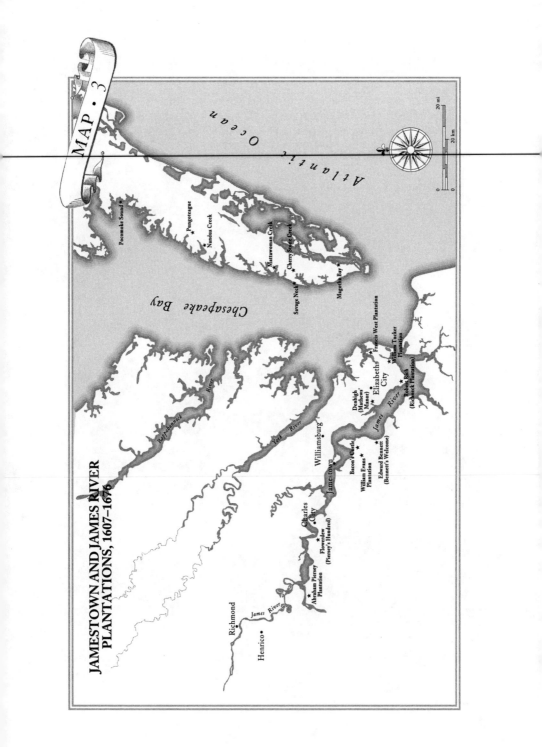

MAP · 3

JAMESTOWN AND JAMES RIVER PLANTATIONS, 1607–1676

Richmond

Henrico●

James River

Abraham Piersey Plantation

Charles City●

Flowerdew (Piersey's Hundred)

Jamestown

Williamsburg

York River

Rappahannock River

Bacon's Castle ★

William Evans Plantation ★

Edward Bennett (Bennett's Welcome) ★

Denbigh (Mathews' Manor) ★

Francis West Plantation ★

William Tucker Plantation ★

Elizabeth City

Robert Bruce (Richneck Plantation) ★

James River

Chesapeake Bay

Pocomoke Sound ★

Pungoteague ★

Nandua Creek ★

Mattawoman Creek ★

Cherry Stone Creek ★

Savage Neck ★

Magothe Bay ★

Atlantic Ocean

20 mi
20 km

THE "BLACK MAYFLOWER" voyage of 1619 and the Jamestown experiences of the first Africans are documented in seventeenth-century records of the Virginia Company of London, the Bermuda Company, the British High Court of Admiralty, the Public Records Office in London, the New England Council, the king's Privy Council, the Ferrar Papers, the Manchester Papers, the Rich Papers, Library of Congress, published pamphlets, Spanish and Portuguese shipping records, and Angolan oral traditions; as well as in colonial American land deeds, historical registers, probated wills, escheats, abstracts, letters, shipping lists, headright applications, edicts, assembly acts, court orders, militia musters, marriages, baptisms, and numerous other records and private papers. There is no imagined dialogue, no fictional characters or scenes in this story. For clarity, archaic seventeenth-century Jacobean ("Jacobean" meaning "of the age of James I") English has been modernized.

No one ship can claim the title "Black Mayflower" for, as it happened, three vessels were instrumental in bringing the first Africans from Angola to English-speaking America in 1619. The Spanish slave frigate *San Juan Bautista* left Africa with 350 slaves and crossed the Atlantic to be captured in the Gulf of Mexico in the summer of 1619 by two English pirate ships—the *White Lion*, carrying a Dutch letters of marque, and the *Treasurer*, which had an expired Italian license. The *Bautista* was destroyed in that attack before she could reach her intended destination of Vera Cruz, Mexico. Continuing the voyage, these two pirate vessels brought some sixty of the *Bautista*'s stolen Africans to Virginia and Bermuda to complete the epic adventure of the Black Mayflower.

Concerning the identification of the very first Africans and the date of their arrival in English America, the author is certainly familiar with the Virginia census discovered in the Ferrar Papers by paleographer William Thorndale, who in 1995 published in the *Magazine of Virginia Genealogy* an article entitled "The Virginia Census of 1619." Thorndale claimed the muster shows the presence of Africans in Jamestown "in the beginning of March 1619"—that is, five months *before* the arrivals of the *White Lion* and the *Treasurer* at the "latter end of August" 1619.

However, in "An Early Virginia Census Reprised," published in the *Quarterly Bulletin of the Virginia Archaeological Society* in 1999, Martha W. McCartney presents a convincing case that the census was actually taken in 1620, not 1619. Thus, the Africans listed in the Ferrar census in fact *are* the roughly two dozen *White Lion* Africans of August 1619 who were traded to Governor George Yeardley and cape merchant Abraham Piersey, along with an additional half dozen or so that her consort, the *Treasurer*, delivered within days to a handful of anti-Yeardley settlers before she fled to Bermuda to trade the rest of her captives there. While the Ferrar-Thorndale census is important in determining the sex and number of the Africans delivered by those two corsairs, it still stands that the first Africans in English North America were those pirated in 1619 by the *White Lion* and the *Treasurer* from the Spanish frigate *San Juan Bautista* in July, and delivered to Jamestown six weeks later at the latter end of August.

• PREFACE •

I N SEARCH OF a Confederate ancestor, an investigative journalist unexpectedly finds he is a descendant of Africans who arrived in America under a veil of mystery one year before the Pilgrims' *Mayflower* left England. Behind the mystery is a secret Puritan conspiracy at the highest levels of seventeenth-century Europe. Languishing in obscurity for four centuries, here at last is the true story of intrigue, scandal, pirates, kings, slavery, freedom, and war surrounding the 1619 voyage of the Black Mayflower and the founding of African America at the dawn of English-speaking America.

The four-hundredth anniversary of the founding of Jamestown—the first English colony in America—offers a new generation the opportunity to ask questions never raised by previous generations. One century ago, most Americans considered the Jamestown adventure of the first African Americans to be a historical footnote—if they considered it at all. In 1907, some historians challenged established traditions surrounding Pocahontas, the Pilgrims, and Thanksgiving that were engraved in the nation's sentiment after the American Civil War, but no one reexamined the story of the Africans who came before the Pilgrims and before that first legendary Thanksgiving feast.

Ironically, the previously ignored Jamestown African story emerges as *the* most significant early event in the shaping of the original thirteen colonies. The author presents primary evidence that an international scandal over the Black Mayflower broke the Virginia Company's monopoly on North America, allowing competing colonies to be founded in the following years. Those diverse colonies became the framework of the nation born in the American Revolution a century and a half later.

Furthermore, the pre-Jamestown history of the first African-American generation destroys early historical contentions that they were "crude savages." In less than two decades after arriving, many of this skilled and intelligent first generation of Jamestown Africans were free and had established their own farms and communities in Tidewater Virginia. The early promise they showed in colonial America, however, was eclipsed by the shadow of racism, a shadow fully grown shortly before the seventeenth century ended. Jamestown, Virginia, was in fact the birthplace of two African Americas—one free and one slave.

This book is the first to present the important story of the black founding of America from 1619 to 1676, a story as essential to our national identity as those of John Smith, Pocahontas, and Jamestown; the Dutch of New York; the Pilgrims of Plymouth; the Quakers of Pennsylvania, and the Catholics of Maryland.

The Birth of
BLACK
AMERICA

PART I

The Founders of Black America Leave Africa

Somewhere in a creek off Chesapeake Bay rests the four-hundred-year-old undiscovered remains of a pirate ship that was built in the age of Atlantic exploration, when Francis Drake circumnavigated the globe and Protestants challenged Catholics for supremacy of the seas. Beneath a blazing comet early in 1619, a cold north wind sent this corsair from the young colony of Jamestown on a forbidden voyage to the West Indies to join in consort with another infamous privateer. Riding a wicked storm in the Gulf of Mexico, the two errant ships attacked a Spanish frigate described by the Persian pirate John Martyn as an "Angola ship." In the belly of the frigate were more than three hundred Bantu prisoners bound for a lifetime of bondage in the silver mines of Mexico. After the battle, the victorious thieves left the Spanish slaver smoking and sixty Africans lighter and sailed north.

Violating the delicate treaty between England and Spain and implicating a prince, this act of piracy on July 15, 1619, created a diplomatic furor in London, Lisbon, and Seville, and instigated an international manhunt covering all Atlantic ports. Soon after the event, the widowed husband of Pocahontas reported to London that a mysterious corsair had traded Africans to planters in Virginia. But before an enraged king could fulfill his vow to send the renegades to the gallows, the pirates quietly vanished in the mists of Chesapeake Bay. A few months later, on a cold gray morning of stinging sleet in early 1620, the phantom shape of a badly battered ship was seen gliding close to the Virginia shore. In a lost creek, somewhere between the James and York rivers, her crew abandoned her and faded into the forest.

This was supposed to be the end of the scandal, but it was not. The repercussions over the pirated Africans were far reaching and, though the beached vessel never sailed again, nine months later the ripple effect caused by her role in the piracy would send a leaking channel tub packed with Pilgrim Separatists westward to establish a new colony that would be called Plymouth. The international fallout over the stolen Africans would also allow the king of England to dissolve the Virginia Company of London and end its monopoly over North America, thereby opening the way for thirteen diverse colonies where once there had been only one.

In the opening chapter of part 1, we attend a play in which a new king launches a new empire poised to begin colonizing America, and we accompany the first Europeans to visit the homeland of the Africans who are destined to be the original founders of English-speaking black America. In chapter 2, we find resistance in England and Angola to the imperial dreams of kings. In chapter 3, we meet an aristocratic English actor who secretly becomes a buccaneer, and the Spanish lord who connives to send him to the gallows over a shipload of stolen Africans. In chapter 4, we sail with the African founders of America on the harrowing maiden Middle Passage voyage of the Black Mayflower to America in 1619. In chapter 5, that voyage that will be interrupted by piracy.

Masquerade

T HE FOUNDING OF English-speaking African America in 1619 is closely intertwined with a sensational theatrical play that premiered on the London stage fourteen years earlier. Called a *masque*, or *masquerade*, this play, performed for the king and queen, for the first time featured white actors in blackface as Africans. The plot parallels a real-life drama that began when one of the actors, a genuine pirate, seized a slave ship in a conspiracy that would eventually topple a king and shape the destiny of English America at its birth.

Following the death of Queen Elizabeth I in 1603, England offered the crown to her middle-aged cousin James Stuart, then king of Scotland. The historic coronation united for the first time under one monarch the countries of England, Scotland, Wales, and part of France as well as divided Ireland. Though Elizabeth had persistently declined to name her successor during her reign, James's accession to the throne was a moment long contemplated, prearranged backstage by England's power brokers to ensure a smooth transition. Therefore, even before the royal procession left Edinburgh for London on horseback, James had already determined how he would rule his diverse kingdoms. Of momentous importance in the development of the English-speaking world was his plan to merge the separate countries into one superstate. As James would inform the English Parliament a few months later, "What God hath conjoined then, let no man separate. I am the Husband, and all the whole Isle is my lawful Wife." This marriage of the island kingdoms into one state is known as "the Union." At that time, England was three years away from planting its first colony in North America.

James I was an avid hunter and, as the plague was then creeping through London, he was in no rush to greet his new subjects. As the royal entourage leisurely rode south from the Scottish border through the English countryside, they were met by a stream of English lords, ladies, knights, and wealthy merchants coming ahead to swear loyalty. Among the first was a longtime friend, Penelope Rich, an actress said to be the most beautiful woman in England. In addition to seeking favors from the new king, these courtiers were curious to learn how he intended to govern. James, contemptuous of the English system of parliament, informed his new subjects that he would rule under an old notion recently resurrected by the French monarchy to limit the power of the Catholic Church. The notion was called *absolutism*—the divine right of a monarch to rule by decree—a right he viewed as superior to constitutions or consent of parliaments.

Those flocking to his side also wanted to know how he planned to turn around the English economy that had soured in the latter part of Elizabeth's reign. James blamed the country's economic problems on the queen's long and bitter sectarian wars against Catholic countries, especially against Spain, and he vowed to prod England out of its proud self-isolation and transform it into an international power on par with Spain, France, and Italy. What Elizabeth had failed to achieve through war and privateering, James boasted he would accomplish through peace and trade with those Catholic nations.

As the plague ravaged London, the king stayed in the castles and country manors of English noblemen who, though eager to court his favor, found the honor extremely expensive. James introduced England to conspicuous consumption and, during his reign, for example, guests described such costly entertainment as the disposable visual banquet in which wealthy hosts would adorn sideboards with dishes as high as a tall man could well reach, filled with the choicest and dearest viands Sea or Land could afford: And all this once seen, and having feasted the eyes of the invited, was in a manner thrown away, and [a fresh banquet] set on to the same height, having only this advantage of the other, that it was hot.

To mark his coronation, James, upon entering London after the plague subsided, commissioned the playwright Ben Jonson in 1604 to produce for the royal stage a dazzling pageant that would be called *Masque of Blackness*. A fantasy about African princesses coming to England, the play was to feature actors in disguise, dancing, choirs, orchestras, lavish scenery, and a sumptuous banquet and was to be performed in the great hall of London's glittering Whitehall Palace overlooking the snowy banks of the Thames River on Twelfth Night, January 7, 1605.

Reaching the height of popularity during the times of Elizabeth and James, masques were privately staged plays performed in palaces and great manor houses exclusively for the entertainment of favored aristocrats, the wealthy gentry, and foreign dignitaries. Stately and formal, Queen Elizabeth's previous masques had been pastoral plays touting rustic English values sung by choirs of cherubic boys—wholesome patriotic entertainment. The Jacobean *Masque of Blackness*, by contrast, featured African characters in blackface for the first time on the royal London stage, and the starring actress in blackface was to be James's blond, fair-skinned consort, Anne of Denmark. The visibly pregnant Queen Anne was to enter the stage at Whitehall as the African goddess Euphoris, draped in a diaphanous costume, her flesh slathered in black paint except for her two tiny white ankles daringly exposed. For Londoners, the earthy, Renaissance-influenced Stuart style would be a startling change from formal English Tudor provincialism.

In keeping with his lectures on internationalism, James broke with Elizabethan politics by promoting Catholic talent. Catholics were then the best theatrical producers in Europe, and James hired Italians and Italian-trained Englishmen as artists and technicians to produce *Masque of Blackness*. The playwright Ben Jonson had converted to Catholicism after landing in prison for killing an actor in a duel in 1598 and, in a pairing that would soon make both men famous, was joined backstage by the Italian-trained Catholic Englishman, Inigo Jones. Alfonso Ferrabosco, a Catholic Englishman of Italian descent, scored the musical arrangement and the costumes came from a book drawn by yet another Italian Catholic. Since the death of Queen Mary Tudor, a.k.a. Bloody Mary, James's masque provided Catholics their first positions of prominence in fiercely anti-Catholic London, on a stage other than the executioner's platform.

With this neglected talent unleashed, *Masque of Blackness* would be the most revolutionary and expensive artistic and technical production ever staged in London up to that time. On opening night Inigo Jones unveiled marvelous engineered wonders from the Mediterranean world that would afterward become staples in the London theater: the Italian "picture-stage" in which English actors appeared for the first time on a framed stage with curtains; changeable sets on movable runners, and intricate machinery that allowed "six huge sea-monsters" to swim in a moving ocean. Queen Anne and her ladies in their African caricature and exotic costumes sailed onto the stage on gilded faux clam shells, while levers and pulleys had gods descending and ascending heavenward. The whole effect, set to a grand orchestra, was spectacular and cutting edge for its time. Inigo Jones's production team threw in nearly every Italian innovation that had bypassed Protestant England in the past half century. And to the utter shock of all, *Masque of Blackness* was the very first London play in which men and women danced together. Actors and actresses in blackface chose partners from out of the white audience and swirled together to music across the dance floor. As a whole, *Masque of Blackness* was an audacious cultural invasion.

The casts of Jacobean masques frequently included members of the English nobility. The fairest of the titled daughters of the realm appeared in these private plays several decades before Margaret Hughes was allowed as the first professional actress on the London public stage in 1660, in the role of Desdemona, wife of the Moor Othello. To appear in a royal masque was a rare social coup that revealed the special favor in which the king and queen held that person. Anne's English ladies-in-waiting excelled in grace, beauty, talent, and intellect, and among the starlets made up as Africans for *Masque of Blackness* that night in 1605 were Lady Mary Wroth and the woman who had welcomed James and Anne at the Scottish border in 1603, Lady Penelope Devereaux Rich.

Lady Wroth, whose poetry was published and widely read at a time when men dominated literature, portrayed an African nymph named Baryte, which means "weight" or "intellect" in Latin.

Said by some to have been Shakespeare's "Dark Lady," lovely Lady Penelope, who, with her red hair, dark eyes, many lovers, and recent divorce from Baron Robert Rich, was the most scandalous noblewoman in England, was cast as the African goddess Ocyte, meaning "swiftness," for her wit. The inspiration for many poets, including the great Sir Philip Sidney, the poised Penelope Rich was fluent in French, Spanish, and Latin, and she had corresponded through letters with James since 1586, when he was only king of Scotland. James was exceptionally impressed with Lady Penelope's missives and "commended much the fineness of her wit, the invention and well-writing." He also favored her because she was the sister and unrepentant supporter of the Earl of Essex who, for attempting to bring James to the English throne prematurely in Queen Elizabeth's old age, had lost his head to the ax. In his confession before his execution, Essex, to his discredit, claimed that above all others, his headstrong sister was responsible for goading him into rebelling against Elizabeth on James's behalf.

Appearing in the masque with Lady Penelope was her teenage son Robert Rich II. By casting in his play specifically those of the English nobility who, for their association with Essex and Philip Sidney, had been persecuted for their loyalty to him while he waited impatiently in Scotland for Elizabeth to die, James was making a statement to the Old Guard supportive of the former queen. The new king, who was about to reach out to the international community, would not tolerate English statesmen seeking to continue past isolationist policies; and he would require absolute obedience to the new course that he, by divine right, alone would set. The casting of *Masque of Blackness* in 1605 was the first sign that the willful new king would have a controversial reign.

The plot of the masque concerns twelve African princesses—daughters of the river god Niger—who have been defamed by an envious poet as being not as attractive as European women. Their remedy lies in a land newly named "Britannia," and they must journey to its shore to be "made beautiful" by its unique sun that never sets:

> Britannia, whose new name makes all tongues sing . . .
> Whose beams shine day and night, and are of force
> To blanch an Æthiop, and revive a corpse.

Though the genius was provided by Ben Jonson, the masque's thinly veiled political content came from the new king. The allegorical play's glorious "sun" symbolized James. Unused for centuries, Britannia was the ancient Roman name for the island kingdoms. Seeing himself as the new King Arthur, destined to reunite the British Isles, James became the first monarch to style himself "king of Great Britain." To James, Britannia was not merely England, Scotland, and Wales, for the sun's beams do not "shine day and night" in only that tiny corner of the world. Britannia would include faraway parts of the globe that James was planning to colonize. On the night when *Masque of Blackness* premiered, he was already eying the idle charter of Virginia, which he would renew a few months later in hope of emulating Spain's success in finding American gold.

When he'd commissioned the masque one year earlier, King James had also petitioned the English House of Commons to officially abolish the terms "English" and "Scottish," and have all of his subjects known collectively as "Britons," united as a single state under a single all-powerful monarch. Also in 1604, as promised to those who had met him at the Scottish border, he had immediately after reaching London signed a treaty with Spanish King Philip III that ended decades of war between England and Spain. *Masque of Blackness* was meant to convey allegorically the policies that James optimistically planned to introduce during his reign: absolutism, a united government centralized at his throne, colonization, and international peace and trade. As James's inaugural speech, the forward-looking masque, with its invitation for African goddesses to journey to Britannia and bask in its glorious new healing sun, announced the birth of the British Empire.

❂

THOUGH THE UNDERLYING political message originated with James, the novel African theme for the entertainment was Queen Anne's idea. According to Ben Jonson, she personally instructed him to feature her and her noble companions as not simply Moors (North African Muslims), but as *blackamoors*, daughters of the African god Niger:

Hence, because it was her majesty's will to have them blackamores at first, the invention was derived by me, and presented thus.

The previous year, Shakespeare had presented *Othello, The Moor of Venice*, which James and Anne had seen, starring Richard Burbage in the title role, but without the blackface. For *Masque of Blackness*, Anne wanted the actors painted black because she, like her husband, wanted the new court to exude a continental flavor. Black West African dignitaries were then coveted as guests of honor at royal courts in Catholic southern Europe. Their exotic presence personified the international cosmopolitan society into which Anne wished to transform the provincial backwater nation of sheepherders and rustic bumpkins that she considered England to be.

At this time, black skin was the idealized expression of beauty. Europeans, for example, depicted the goddess of love and beauty, Venus, as a black African. Therefore, the political subtext that required African goddesses to be "made beautiful" was thematically confusing. Forced to take conflicting input from the masque's two royal executive producers, Jonson did the best he could under the circumstances.

Anne's interest in Africana had been fanned by a wave of recently translated publications about the mysterious continent of which English merchants at the time wished to learn more. Among the new books, the most influential was the first English translation of a manuscript originally written decades earlier by an educated and widely traveled Moor named al-Hasan ibn Muhammad ibn Ahmad al-Wazzan al-Fasi.

Al-Hasan's remarkable life coincided with a number of dramatic events in world history that he witnessed and recorded. He was born in the Islamic city of Granada, Spain, just as Columbus was setting forth on his first voyage west. Leaving Andalusia with the Muslim diaspora, al-Hasan's family resettled in Morocco in North Africa about A.D. 1500. The son of a prominent family, al-Hasan, according to biographer Pekka Masonen, grew up to become an ambassador for a Moroccan king:

> In Fez, young al-Hasan ibn Muhammad received a sound education at the Islamic university of al-Qarawiyyin. Thereafter, he entered the service of the Wattasid Sultan Muhammad II al-Burtuqali ("the Portuguese," 1504–26). He carried out several commercial and diplomatic missions on behalf of his sovereign, but his true motive for travelling seems to have been wanderlust and personal curiosity.

His journeys in the royal service took him to Timbuktu, Constantinople, and Mecca; and, in 1517, al-Hasan sailed on a diplomatic mission to Egypt, arriving in January just in time to witness the Turkish Ottomans overthrow the Egyptian Mamluks at the battle of al-Raydaniyya. Though his subsequent descriptions of Africa would become the literary standard in Europe for three centuries, al-Hasan of Morocco actually never explored farther into Africa than Egypt and Sudan—only a small fraction of the world's second largest continent. He knew almost nothing of that vast region south of the Sahara that would play a dramatic role in the shift of global power from the ancient eastern Mediterranean, to less advanced western European countries on the coast of the Atlantic Ocean. Only while in Egypt did al-Hasan learn of the imminent threat to the Muslim-Genoese-Venetian monopoly of the rich Far East trade, posed by the near miraculous arrival in the Indian Ocean of western European "infidels" who had just circumnavigated the entire continent of Africa for the first time. These Westerners had started out many decades earlier in search of a mythical Christian African kingdom.

❖

LONG BEFORE THE birth of Jesus there had flourished in East Africa the magnificent city-state of Aksum. Ideally situated to control the long flow of trade passing from Asia and East Africa through the Red Sea to the Mediterranean, Aksum and her sister-cities Adulis and Matara became great cosmopolitan centers in the ancient world. By Roman times, the wealth and influence of Aksum was envied throughout the Mediterranean, and its people, the Ethiopians, were widely famed for piety, justice, hospitality, and a long, unbroken tradition of literature.

In the fourth century A.D., the shipwrecked missionary Frumentius of Tyre evangelized Ethiopia under King Ezana, who established the world's first Christian state. In the first centuries after Christ, Africa produced Christianity's first intellectuals—Clement of Alexandria, Origen, and Augustine. This period, however, was relatively brief. In 711, conquering warriors of a new and rapidly growing faith swept across North Africa and even onto the Iberian Peninsula of western Europe. The Christian rulers of Ethiopia had been tolerant of all religions, including Judaism and Buddhism. Because Christian Ethiopians had offered refuge to persecuted Muslims, the Prophet Muhammad, according to Islamic tradition, had instructed Muslim armies to leave Ethiopia in peace. And so, as Muslim horsemen raced west and north, Aksum of Ethiopia remained isolated in East Africa—its ancient golden churches and priceless libraries untouched.

Seven centuries later, persistent tales of an immortal Christian king named Prester John linked with fabulous stories of the long-lost Christian kingdom of Ethiopia were to fire the imagination and zeal of the Portuguese crusader Prince Henry. After expelling the Muslims from Portugal early in the fifteenth century, when Spain was still struggling to evict its own Muslim population, the Portuguese quickly sought to press its momentum by piercing the Muslim blockade on the spice wealth of the Far East. Seeking to enlist the mythical Prester John as an ally against the monopoly, Henry set out to learn if there really existed in Africa "any Christian princes, in whom the charity and the love of Christ were so ingrained so that they would aid him against those enemies of the faith."

Born in 1394 as the third son of King João I of Portugal, and Philippa, daughter of the English Prince John of Gaunt, Henry was a scientist as well as a Crusader. Retreating to the extreme southwestern tip of Portugal and the towering ledge overlooking the narrow entrance to the Mediterranean at the edge of the known world, he set up something new in Europe—a research and development center for maritime discovery that utilized the latest instruments and ideas. At the time, few in the Mediterranean world imagined that India could be reached by sailing around Africa. To initiate the quest for Prester John, and subsequently introduce Portugal's golden age of discovery, Henry began launching dozens of ships on short voyages south down the uncharted western coast of Africa in an expedition that would take many decades.

Fearing they were approaching the abode of the dead should they venture too far out into the unknown ocean, Henry's sailors tentatively hugged the coasts of Mauritania, Cape Verde, and Senegal at the westernmost bulge of Africa, and at every new landing the Portuguese inquired about Prester John. Each time, they returned home with disappointing tidings, but they also returned with new charts, extending their knowledge of the Atlantic.

Henry did not set out to enslave Africans, but eventually the Portuguese bankers financing the royal expedition complained of seeing no profit after two decades of costly exploration. On the coast of Guinea in 1444, one of Prince Henry's ships for the first time raided a town and captured several men, women, and children. Gomes Eannes de Zurara, a contemporary chronicler, reported the disturbing scene:

> Mothers would clasp their infants in their arms, and throw themselves on the ground to cover them with their bodies, disregarding any injury to their own persons, so that they could prevent their children from being separated from them.

Trade names of locations reveal the sources of wealth that the Portuguese would eventually realize along the edge of upper West Africa—the Pepper Coast, the Ivory Coast, the Gold Coast, and the Slave Coast. So, when in 1460 Prince Henry the Navigator died, the national quest to find Prester John did not go to the tomb with him. Portuguese ships continued inching southward down the west coast of Africa and returning with riches.

While still exploring after another two decades, the Portuguese observed that where the world was thought to end in deserts and reefs, the barren coast of West Africa abruptly revealed a land of lush tropical rainforests teeming with strange creatures and plants. A few weeks later, the Portuguese became the first Europeans of record to cross the equator and enter the South Atlantic. And then, on August 28, 1482, a decade before Columbus sailed into the Americas, the Portuguese explorer Diogo Cão became the first European to reach the mouth of the great Congo (Zaire) River, six degrees south of the equator. Here he found unexpected evidence of an impressive advanced civilization; Africans unknown to the Mediterranean world yet refining gold, silver, copper, and iron and clothed in fine garments, who told him they were subjects of a great faraway king named Nzinga a Nkuwu. This was the Kongo Empire, one of several sophisticated states within greater Angola, a country then as large as Portugal, France, and Germany combined.

The timing of Cão's visit, ten years before the discovery of America, would be crucial to western Europe's attempt to colonize the latter. "Without slavery not only would the price of sugar have risen," wrote the French philosopher Montesquieu, "without slavery the nations of Europe would never have achieved so quickly the political and economic supremacy, which they have held for the last five hundred years." More Africans, one out of every four, would come to America from Angola, including Kongo, than from any other comparable region in Africa, making Angola the "Black England" of America. Less than two centuries after Portugal's discovery of the Congo River in 1482, young Jamestown's earliest African population would be overwhelmingly

Angolan, as would be the black populations of Dutch New York, the Spanish West Indies, Mexico, Columbia, and Brazil.

❀

UPON CAPTAIN CÃO's return to Europe, news of the discovery of a rich new land stunned the Mediterranean world. Portugal's King João II, "greedily awaiting material details about the empire of the *manikongo* [king]," ordered him to go back at once. On the second voyage to the Congo River the following year, Cão realized that, if anything, he had underreported the size and sophistication of this civilization. The "lost" kingdoms of Angola had a monetary system and governed through multilayered political bureaucracies that levied taxes and tolls to support colorful royal courts, a civil service, road maintenance, and large armies. He observed that the inhabitants of Angola were not Muslim and wondered if this was indeed the Ethiopian country of Prester John. Precolonial Angolans retained a faint memory of a sea to the north that was the destiny of the Nile, for they informed General Fernandez de Enciso in 1518 that the Congo River began eastward in the heart of Africa "in high mountains, from which another great stream flows in an opposite direction." Beyond that, the people of Angola had no knowledge of the Mediterranean world.

At close examination, however, there are unexpected cultural similarities between Europeans and Africans south of the Sahara that appear commonly rooted in early Near East traditions. Angolans never ventured into the Atlantic Ocean on their western border. They believed Kalunga (the Atlantic Ocean) was the threshold to an "Other" world where time runs counter to that of this world, where day is night. Aside from mining *nzimbu* (cowrie) shells on the coast for their currency, out of reverence Angolans generally shunned the Atlantic; indeed, their kings, once enthroned, were forbidden to gaze upon the sea ever again.

This awe of the Atlantic was of the same origin as that of Prince Henry's superstitious Mediterranean sailors, and further back, of the ancient Egyptians, for the people the Portuguese found in Angola were not indigenous. They were the Bantu, relatively recent newcomers who had originated long ago in the area east of the Sahara, likely around Uganda along the Nile where once they had been in contact with the larger Mediterranean world. Far-ranging colonizers, the Bantu of the Sahel grasslands on the edge of the Sahara had set out to discover new regions when their populations exceeded the limits of the land to feed them, as described in almost forgotten oral "boasting songs:"

> *On our departure from Kongo*
> there were nine caravans under nine chiefs with their staff of office.
> We brought with us the basket containing the relics of our ancestors,
> which are used in the installation of chiefs.
> *We brought the grass rings for the chiefs' roof-tops.*
> The paths we traveled were safe.
> The villages we built were peaceful.
> We kept all together.
> *We were careful not to separate.*

Dominating greater Angola when Diogo Cão arrived were three nations—Bakongo, Mbundu, and Ovimbundu—part of the western branch of the massive Bantu migrations that had begun surging south and west around A.D. 1000. Unlike the earlier Khoisan hunter-gatherers of Central Africa, the Bantu were an advanced, permanently settled farming and herding people who forged iron tools and weapons, and who lived in the same towns year-round. Their kindred, the Eastern Bantu, built the stone towers and temples of Great Zimbabwe that were ignorantly or maliciously attributed by late Arab and European colonizers to the Queen of Sheba, or to the Egyptians or Phoenicians of ancient times.

Each of the three Bantu nations within greater Angola contained several kingdoms. The most powerful were Kongo, Ndongo, Loango, and Matamba. Each state, according to African historian John Thornton, possessed "jurisdiction, income raising, military, and legislative functions that claimed comprehensive loyalty and service within its boundaries." Westerners later gave this region the infamous reputation of the "deepest darkest heart of Africa," when in fact it was one of the greatest civilizations ever achieved independent of Mediterranean technology and influence. The Jesuit father Francisco de Gouveia admiringly described Ndongo's capital city, Kabasa, as being surrounded by a heavily populated countryside dotted with a thick complex of neatly spaced towns. The town of Angoleme, near Massangano on the Kwanza River, was as large then as the major Portuguese city of Evora, with "five to six thousand thatched dwellings that probably housed twenty to thirty thousand people." So densely populated was the area that when fire destroyed Angoleme in 1564, one hundred thousand Bantu were displaced.

Markets in the Mbundu kingdom of Ndongo included a wide array of goods from outside the nation. They traded in copper, ivory, and cotton "from as far away as Kongo," notes Thornton, and "attended regular markets in their own district and regional markets to obtain what they did not produce—iron and steel from favored regions in an area famous for its steel production or salt from the region south of the Kwanza."

Precolonial Bantu law, both secular and religious, was complex and, as in Europe and Asia, murderers and thieves were severely punished, as were the irreligious. Elders were greatly respected and children were cherished. Cannibalism was abhorred and never existed in Bantu culture. Wisdom and art were esteemed highly, and Bantu proverbs in the form of Anansi tales later passed to the West and down through the generations as the "Brer" Fox and Rabbit folk stories of Uncle Remus. Angolans wove silklike textiles and, skilled musicians, invented a variety of musical instruments, including a stringed, boxlike device that crossed the Atlantic and became the American banjo.

The successful and generally peaceful spread of Bantu culture stemmed in great part from their ability to manufacture iron several centuries before arriving on the western Atlantic coast. Mbundu kingdoms gave their kings the title of *ngola* (iron blacksmith), from which comes the name of the country, "Angola." Angolans, like other Central African Bantu, hunted and fought with bows and arrows, but their favored weapons in war were iron swords and battle-axes. In ancient times, the Bantu had produced carbonized steel before Europeans, and they made the basic iron tools of European and Asian agriculture long before the first Europeans arrived on their coast. With their iron axes and iron hoes, these precolonial Bantu felled trees, cleared land, and broke the earth to plant a variety of crops unknown to Europeans. Dense agriculture produced by iron tools gave the Bantu permanence, and with that permanence they evolved sophisticated state, religious, and military institutions.

Like their Eastern Bantu cousins, the Mbundu nation and the people of the kingdom of Ndongo in particular, raised cattle herds along with goats, chickens, and guinea fowl. During their migrations from East Africa centuries earlier, the Bantu, to feed their cattle, had pioneered the cultivation of a variety of grains that mature well in the hot dry climate of the Sahel. Simultaneously, they became the world's foremost cattlemen; a particular Bantu custom was for a bridegroom to give cattle to the bride's family. The Bantu barter of cattle would continue in Jamestown and, as will be seen, opened to many Africans a way to escape slavery.

Nzinga a Nkuwu, the manikongo of Kongo, received the Portuguese graciously, opened trade, and, shortly thereafter, converted voluntarily and was named by the pope Dom João da Silva ("King John of the Wood"). One hundred years before the first English settlement was built in America, missionaries arrived in Angola from Italy, Portugal, and Spain to build churches and baptize thousands of converts.

❦

KING JOÃO II OF Portugal, not persuaded that Cão had discovered the Christian kingdom of Prester John, in 1487 decided to launch two expeditions, one by land and one by sea, to reach East Africa. For the overland mission, he chose Pero da Covilha, a young, married diplomat with children, to go east unaccompanied, disguised as a Muslim. For the sea voyage, he appointed the explorer Bartholomeu Dias to take a naval fleet from Lisbon and continue exploring south down the west coast of Africa.

One year later, on February 3, 1488, Dias became the first European to round the southern tip of Africa—a voyage much farther over the Atlantic than that of Columbus three years later. However, on the verge of becoming the first navigator ever to pioneer the sea route from the Atlantic to the Indian Ocean and reap the wealth of the India trade, Dias, to his disappointment, was forced by his superstitious crew to turn back. In the crowd that met him at the Lisbon docks was a still unknown Christopher Columbus, who wrote in his copy of French Cardinal Pierre d'Ailly's *Imago mundi*:

> [Dias] announced to the King that he had sailed as far as the Cape of Good Hope, and showed him a chart of the voyage. I was present at court that day.

As a result of Dias's discovery, Columbus immediately left Lisbon and carried to Spain his proposal to reach India by sailing west. Meanwhile, Pero da Covilha, making an amazingly long, circuitous trek alone, accomplished what Dias and his ships could not. Reaching the Indian Ocean in 1493, he entered Ethiopia on foot. Though he was warmly welcomed by the Christian king of Ethiopia, writes historian Daniel J. Boorstin, Covilha was made a palace prisoner, unable to return to Portugal and his family to reap the honors for his successful expedition:

> In this Realm of Prester John, actually ruled by Alexander "Lion of the Tribe of Judah, and King of Kings," he became a Portuguese Marco Polo, so useful at court that the King would not let him leave. Convinced that he would never return home, Covilha married an Ethiopian wife who bore him several children.

Covilha eventually sent a letter back to the king of Portugal, describing his long journey to Mecca, India, Ormuz in the Persian Sea, and Madagascar in the Indian Ocean. He affirmed that the Portuguese would be on the right track if they continued sailing around Africa, assuring the king of Portugal that his fleet could easily penetrate into these Eastern seas and come to make the coast of Calicut, for there was sea everywhere.

The previous year Columbus, having persuaded the king and queen of Spain to finance him, had made his first visit to what would later be named America. His discovery caused a controversy that delayed by a decade Portugal's plan to reach the Indian Ocean by sailing around Africa. In March 1493, King João II, upon learning of Columbus's discovery of islands in the New World, proclaimed them to be the property of Portugal, the foremost European sea power in the Atlantic. Tensions between Portugal and Spain mounted but war was averted at the last moment when the pope arbitrated the Treaty of Tordesillas in 1494. This treaty fixed a famous, though then obscure, vertical line about sixty degrees west, giving to Spain all of the Americas with the exception of Brazil, which, along with the eastward route around Africa, went to Portugal.

Manuel I succeeded João in 1495 and resumed Portugal's interrupted quest to reach India and the rich spice markets. The man that King Manuel chose to take the Portuguese into the Indian Ocean was Vasco da Gama, who, like Covilha, was a skilled diplomat rather than a rough soldier like those Spain would send to the Americas. Building a fleet of four ships, da Gama departed Lisbon in July 1497. Rounding Africa's southern cape, he continued north up the East African coast to Mozambique, where he found a hostile Muslim port. Crossing the Arabia Sea, da Gama finally reached Calicut, India, in May 1498. There he met two Moors from Tunis who could speak Castilian and Genoese. Astounded to see Christian ships in the Indian Ocean, the first words from the stunned Moors to da Gama, according to one of the explorer's crew, was a curse:

"May the Devil take thee! What brought you thither?" . . . he told them that we came in search of Christians and spices. They said: "Why does not the King of Castile, the King of France, or the Signoria of Venice send hither?" . . . [Da Gama] returned to the ships, accompanied by one of the Moors, who was no sooner on board, than he said these words: "A lucky venture, a lucky venture! Plenty of rubies, plenty of emeralds! You owe great thanks to God, for having brought you to a country holding such riches!" We were greatly astonished to his talk for we never expected to hear our language spoken so far away from Portugal.

Having journeyed for a century, the Portuguese now moved quickly. To overturn the Muslim monopoly with India, the Molluccas, Siam, and China, they destroyed the Muslim fleet and seized Ormuz to control access to the Persian Gulf in 1510. By the time of al-Hasan's visit to Egypt, the Portuguese navy was poised to enter the Red Sea and strike like a dagger into the heart of Islam. In Egypt, al-Hasan heard rumors that the Portuguese were making an alliance with the Christian king of Ethiopia, reputedly a descendant of the ancient dynasty of King Solomon of Jerusalem and Makeda, the Queen of Sheba. After many centuries, Ethiopia, situated at the gateway between the Red Sea and the Indian Ocean, was once again the key to the East.

Western Europe's arrival in the Indian Ocean, however, would be tragic for Christian Ethiopia. Though the Portuguese dominated the sea, Muslims held the land. Aided by Turks and Arabs who furnished soldiers and firearms, and heedless of Muhammad's instruction, a furious Somali Muslim warlord named Ahmed Gran, son of an Ethiopian Christian priest and a Somali prostitute, invaded Ethiopia in the 1520s, defeating a powerful army of spearmen, beheading Ethiopian priests, sacking and burning towns, and stripping the ancient churches and irreplaceable libraries of their golden panels and treasured jewel-encrusted ceremonial objects of antiquity. Sir Richard Burton wrote:

Aided by a violent famine which prostrated what had escaped the spear, [Gran] perpetrated every manner of atrocity, captured and burned Aksum, destroyed the princes of the royal blood on the mountain of Amba Gesha and slew in A.D. 1540, David, third of his name and last emperor of Ethiopia.

In this crisis, Ethiopia appealed to the pope; in response, the new king of Portugal, João III, sent a large navy led by Vasco da Gama's sons. Landing at Massawa with four hundred musketeers, they marched to confront Ahmed Gran's army of ten thousand infantry and a large cavalry. In a pitched battle, the Somali general was killed by a Portuguese musket, but not before he had reduced the glory of ancient Aksum to ashes. Today Ethiopia, now hedged on the east by Somalia and Eritrea, remains cut off from the Red Sea that she had ruled from before the time of Christ—as a result of Ahmed Gran's invasion five centuries ago.

❖

IN 1518, WHILE returning from his voyage to Egypt, al-Hasan's ship was captured near Crete by the Spanish corsair Don Pietro Bovilla. Recognizing the Moroccan ambassador as a person of importance, Bovilla, brother of the bishop of Salamanca, determined that al-Hasan might be useful to the pope and delivered him from the customary fate of life as a galley slave. That year al-Hasan was presented to Pope Leo X (Giovanni de' Medici). This pope, who rose to the office through family connections, lived more like a Renaissance prince than a priest and reveled in luxury and the arts:

> Leo X is a pope for whom the historians have harsh words. He is usually depicted a "gilded butterfly"; a person whose sole interest in life was pleasure and luxurious life—love of music, drama, fine arts, literature, learning, and hunting.

At the beginning of the sixteenth century, as western Europeans were beginning to dominate the Indian Ocean, Muslims were invading Christian lands circling the eastern Mediterranean. Alarmed by his shrinking sphere of influence, Pope Leo prized the much-traveled courtier al-Hasan as a rare source of military intelligence on the enemy, and he gave the Moor a large salary to prevent him from attempting escape. Al-Hasan ibn Muhammad converted and was baptized with the

Christian name Giovanni Leone (John Leo), after the pope. However, he is best known as Leo Africanus for his 1526 manuscript *Descrizione dell' Africa* (Description of Africa), about his travels in North Africa.

During the years of his Christian "captivity," the Moor traveled about Europe and immersed himself in the life of an Italian gentleman of privilege under the patronage of a line of popes. His portrait was painted by the artist Sebastiano Luciani of Venice. Though before his death Leo Africanus was to return to North Africa and his Muslim faith, in Europe his description of Africa, that is, of the Muslim-occupied northern parts of Africa, was frequently reprinted as *the* authoritative last word on that continent. In 1600, in London, the English courtier John Pory translated into English an Italian copy of *Descrizione dell' Africa* that he titled *A Geographical Historie of Africa, written in Arabicke and Italian by John Leo, a More* [*sic*]. Pory's translation was read by William Shakespeare who immortalized al-Hasan as the title character for his 1604 play, *Othello, The Moor of Venice*—though the poet's tragic treatment of the African's life was fictional.

John Pory's English translation also served Shakespeare's fellow poet Ben Jonson as an important source for King James's blockbuster *Masque of Blackness*. Pory, a talented writer who had squandered his early promise on the bottle, would a few years later make history as the first Speaker of the first representative legislature of English North America—the Virginia House of Burgesses. In that office, in 1619 he would participate in a conspiracy that would bring the first Africans to an English colony in America, and give an ironic twist to Jonson's storyline of Africans coming to the British Empire.

Meanwhile, in London, *Masque of Blackness* was receiving mixed reviews.

· 2 ·

Jagas

MANY IN THE elite London audience that night in 1605 were enthralled by the exotic pomp and pageantry of *Masque of Blackness*. Some critics, however, were harder to please. In his scathing review, Sir Dudley Carleton, who, in 1619 would receive a critical piece of evidence in the real-life drama involving the transport of Africans, wrote to a friend:

> At night we had the Queen's Maske in the Banqueting House . . . Their apparel was rich, but too light and courtesan-like for such great ones. Instead of vizzards, their faces, and arms up to the elbows, were painted black, which was disguise sufficient, for they were hard to be known . . . you cannot imagine a more ugly sight, than a troop of lean-cheek'd Moors.

To another friend, John Chamberlain, Carleton also criticized how Queen Anne and her black-faced ladies left the stage and entered the audience to choose dance partners:

> He [the Spanish ambassador] took out the Queen, and forgot not to kiss her hand, though there was danger it [the black paint] would have left a mark on his lips . . . Their black faces and hands, which were painted

and bare up the elbows, was a very loathsome sight and I am sorry that strangers should see our court so strangely disguised.

Of more substance than the queen's appearance in the play to others were James's troubling allegories of divine right to rule, the proposed British superstate, and peaceful coexistence with Catholic Spain. James's 1604 treaty was universally unpopular even though both England and Spain were weary of war. First, English nobles and merchants were making quite a good living as privateers carrying out random lightning raids on Spanish ships and ports in Spain and America. Second, treaty or no treaty, the English and Spanish still hated and cursed each other as "limbs of Antichrist." Contemporary historian Arthur Wilson claimed the Jesuits had convinced superstitious Spaniards that when the English left Catholicism during the reign of Henry VIII:

> They were transformed into strange horrid shapes, with head and tails like beasts and monsters. So easy it is for those Jugglers [the Jesuits], when they have once bound up the Conscience, to tie up the Understanding also.

Then there was James's demand for the divine right to rule with absolute power by decree. The English House of Commons strongly opposed absolute monarchy and held rulers accountable to English law. In response to James's attempt to fuse the island kingdoms into one superstate, Parliament also refused to sanction any federal government unless Scotland adopted English law. Having first proposed the union of England and Scotland to Parliament in 1604, James addressed the House of Commons again in 1608, expressing his frustration that its members were resisting his will:

> This I speak, because of the long time which hath been spent about the Treaty of the Union. For myself, I protest unto you all, when I first propounded the Union, I then thought there could have been no more question of it, than of your declaration and acknowledgment of my right unto this Crown, and that as two Twins, they would have grown up together. . . . But

now finding many crossings, long disputations, strange questions, and nothing done, I must needs think it proceeds either of mistaking of the errand, or else from some jealousy of me the Propounder, that you so add delay unto delay, searching out as it were the very bowels of Curiosity.

Parliament also resisted the coined term "Britain" because, as the ancient Roman name for England, it suggested subservience to the Church of Rome. The House of Commons would not concede to identifying the English as Britons until the 1700s, nearly a century later.

When it came to financing his quest for an empire with extended colonies, James quickly learned that Parliament, not he, controlled taxes, the largest revenue generator. The first English colony in America would be financed, not by the English Crown or by the government, but by a joint stock company of English investors, "adventurers," chartered by the king. Selling such monopolies was one of the few ways James found he could raise money, for the House of Commons viewed James's schemes and spending habits as wasteful and extravagant: the stupendous bill he sent them for *Masque of Blackness* became one sorely contentious case in point. When James threatened that "it is sedition in Subjects to dispute what a King may do in the height of his power," the House of Commons aggressively fought back and challenged even the royal monopolies.

Struggling for supremacy on a shoestring budget, James, not backing down, became more adamant in his demand to rule unopposed, lecturing Parliament that monarchs, like gods:

> have power to exalt low things, and abase high things, and make of their subjects like men at the Chess; A pawn to take a Bishop or a Knight, and to cry up, or down any of their subjects, as they do their money.

The conflict ran deeper than the politics of the moment. James claimed, *"Rex est lex loquens"* ("what the king speaks is the law"). Having previously established and defended hard-won rights over difficult centuries, the representative-composed English Parliament was unwilling as a matter of principle that English law should be abrogated by any king's caprice. Though James, a highly principled individual, would likely have made a just and wise dictator, as dictators go, the issue was precedent. If popular contemporary plays—*Philaster* (1609), *The Maid's Tragedy* (1610), and *A King and No King* (1611)—are any indication, the English public at large seems to have sided with Parliament against James on the issue of divine right.

Controversial also in England was James's attempt to wed his son Charles to the Spanish princess Maria. King Philip III demanded that Charles become Catholic as a precondition to marriage, meaning a future Catholic king for England. English nobles had received vast properties belonging to the Catholic Church when the monasteries were dissolved by Henry VIII, and a Catholic king would strip them of this property. Furthermore, England's underclasses remembered the human bonfires of Protestant preachers tied to the stake during "Bloody" Mary Tudor's Catholic reign and recoiled at the prospect of another Catholic monarch. Class distinctions aside, Protestants were especially wary of James because his wife Anne had already jolted the English by converting to Catholicism when he became king of England in 1603.

But James stubbornly pursued the Spanish marriage regardless of public opinion. Spain had been fabulously enriched by its American ventures and James, eager to impress the world and irresponsibly addicted to extravagance, wanted a bride for his son who would bring a great dowry. Philip III of Spain exploited his desire for the marriage, and the Spanish ambassador Count Gondomar would gain such influence over James that he even sent the Spaniard to interrupt and dismiss the English Parliament after the House of Commons voted to oppose the proposed union. Complained James to Count Gondomar:

> I am surprised that my ancestors should ever have permitted such an institution as the House of Commons to have come into existence. I am a stranger, and found it here when I arrived, so that I am obliged to put up with what I cannot get rid of.

The mood between the absolutist Stuarts, and the republican House of Commons in particular, would grow steadily worse.

❖

THE CLASH BETWEEN James and Parliament over his proposed superstate was similar to the political schism that had begun to trouble Angola, "Black England," in the fifteenth century. Angola's precolonial oral history has survived in written form because, as John Thornton points out, it was collected in the sixteenth century by Angolans who were educated in Europe: "Unlike leaders in so many other parts of Africa, West Central African elites left a substantial written record of their own."

The prevailing Western theory holds that, after the arrival of Europeans in 1482, the kingdoms of Angola and other Central African countries began lusting for European goods and culture and were subsequently destroyed by the Atlantic slave trade. As seen, however, the sophisticated Bantu were not Stone Age primitives. They had developed advanced governments, permanent agriculture, and domesticated cattle and were producing cloth, iron, and copper, and trading afar before 1482.

In fact, traditions recorded by literate sixteenth-century Angolans point to an unrelated development as the cause of Angola's decline. Upon arriving in West Central Africa from the east between A.D. 1000 and 1100, the Bantu nations settling Angola had established numerous independent ministates, each made up of one capital with a dozen or so surrounding villages containing, on average, five thousand subjects each. In A.D. 1375, Nimi a Nzima, ruler of the small kingdom of Mpemba Kasi in the Kwilu Valley, north of the Congo River in modern-day Democratic Republic of Congo, made an alliance with a neighboring king, Nsaku Lau, ruler of Mbata, to assure the continuance of their dynasties.

Nzima's heir was Lukeni lua Nimi. Upon becoming king, Lukeni led a combined army south across the Congo River into Angola around 1400 to attack the kingdom of Mwene Kabunga in revenge for an insult made by a ferryman against his mother. The history of Kongo begins with Lukeni lua Nimi. As the first manikongo (derived from *mwene*, meaning "blacksmith," of Kongo), he founded a city on a mountain in his newly won territory and named it Mbanza Kongo. Through mostly peaceful alliances he then formed and headed a federation of neighboring kingdoms: Soya, Vungu, Kakongo, Ngoyo, and Mpangu were voluntary provinces, while Nsundi and Mbamba were conquered. In this federation, two aristocracies existed, as in England. In the case of Kongo, the manikongo's extended family was the upper aristocracy, whereas the families of former kings who had voluntarily stepped down a rung to become federation governors under the manikongo were the lower aristocracy. This lower provincial nobility retained numerous independent rights under Lukeni, including the right to choose their own governors, collect their own revenues, and raise their own armies. Under this system, the manikongo was dependent to a large extent on the loyalty of his federation partners.

Following Lukeni's death, two of his nephews ruled consecutively until his son, Nkuwu a Lukeni, came of age and was made king. Nkuwu's heir was Manikongo Nzinga a Nkuwu, who was king in 1482 when the first Europeans under Diogo Cão visited the Congo River.

The voluntary, independent nature of the Kongo federation, however, had begun to change *before* the Europeans came in 1482. In the fifteenth century, as the city and suburbs of Mbanza Kongo reached a population of one hundred thousand (of Kongo's overall population of half a million), the manikongos, with a huge local army at their command, became more powerful than the other provinces in the Kongolese federation. With this power, manikongos at Mbanza Kongo, like King James of England, began promoting centralization of power—an empire or superstate. They began insisting on decree rule and demanded the right to collect revenue throughout the federation, as well as the right to approve or reject officials appointed by the surrounding provinces.

This centralization of power at Mbanza Kongo provoked resistance in the provinces, particularly among the ministates that had been added by force. The nobles of these provinces protested centralization by evoking the memories of the early founder Lukeni lua Nimi and his original free federation of states. To counter these protests and to promote centralization, new manikongos revised the story of the origins of Mbanza Kongo. To discredit the old federation concept, they discredited its founder, alleging that Lukeni had perpetrated a particularly odious crime: stabbing to death his pregnant mother before crossing the Congo River as a fugitive.

The subsequent rise of the fifteenth-century Kongolese superstate sparked similar expansion programs in such rival Angolan kingdoms as Ndongo, Loango, Matamba, Benguela, Songo, Mbwila, Libolo, Masinga, and Malemba, which also began adding, by force or by alliance, smaller neighboring states. Like Kongo, they, too, reduced defeated kings to the role of district governors while retaining their former political apparatus as district governments. And, as with the new empire of Kongo, these superstates also provoked resentment and rebellion in outlying districts whose rights were reduced. Therefore, when Europeans first visited in 1482, Angola was already embroiled in an ongoing and thoroughly African political debate over divisive issues of expansion and centralization *versus* regional autonomy. Also, when the Portuguese arrived, rivalry among Angola's superstates was intensely fierce, and competing rulers were keen to pursue military and trade alliances to further each his own political agenda.

To this end, Mvemba a Nzinga, the son and heir of Nzinga Nkuwu of Kongo, voluntarily embraced the Portuguese as trade partners in 1510 and, like his father, he, too, became a Christian. The pope bestowed the title "King of Ethiopia" on the baptized manikongo and, taking "Alfonso" as his Christian name, Mvemba a Nzinga renamed his capital city Mbanza Kongo "São Salvador" in honor of the Savior. He encouraged mission building throughout his provinces and, a century later, thanks to this, many Angolans would arrive in Jamestown with a Christian background that greatly aided their assimilation into the English colony.

Manikongo Alfonso I shrewdly gathered from the Portuguese a wealth of knowledge about the wider world of religion, commerce, politics, and technology. One of the first monarchs in the world to own two European printing presses, invented forty years earlier,

Alfonso frequently communicated through letters with the pope in Rome and the king of Portugal on matters of state, trade, and religion. He also established a foreign diplomatic corps of skilled representatives, including West Africans and "New Christian" Jews, to attend to his affairs in Rome and Lisbon; and he sent many promising young Kongolese men to be educated in the finest universities of southern Europe. Some married into the European elite and some returned to Angola to serve in his court. His son Enrique became the first black bishop of the Catholic Church.

Though willing to trade, convert, and assimilate to a point, the Bantu iron kings of Angola steadfastly refused to surrender their individual autonomy to Portugal. While acknowledging the spiritual authority of Rome, they refused to be colonized or subjected by European monarchs, and their kingdoms were too powerful to be conquered by European armies without African allies: Kongo, for one, could field ten thousand soldiers with iron weapons. Nor could the manikongos be seduced with cheap European trinkets, bright cloth, and rum. Administrators of large states, they had an intelligent grasp of trade issues and were wise to the nuances of international diplomacy. As early as 1514, Manikongo Alfonso, quick to see through shady deals, complained to the king of Portugal of fraud practiced by the former Portuguese governor at São Tomé, alleging:

> He sold our goods at the lowest price possible. With the money he bought an untrained slave from Goa and another. He sent us them in one of the first ships, saying they were the trained carpenters. At the same time he sent us some blue cloth all gnawed by rats. All this we have been able to endure because of the love of our Jesus Christ.

Alfonso and successive manikongos were also careful not to legitimize their thrones on European military power. Portuguese kings, eager to please those they could not conquer, sent ships and cannons to intimidate the African rulers' enemies to earn their respective favor. Manuel I of Portugal, for example, instructed his royal envoy Gonçalo Rodrigues in 1509 to serve the king of Kongo however he deemed, and to accept whatever payment offered: "from captives that the said Manicomgo makes in this war or in whatever service God gives you."

As the manikongos continued to use Portuguese services to extend and centralize their superkingdoms and put down subsequent rebellions, they frequently chose to pay Europeans with Jaga prisoners taken in battle. Jagas deemed "rebels" by the manikongos, were Angolans in outlying districts who opposed absolute rule, centralized power, and loss of autonomy to African rulers of the superstate. (The first Africans who would arrive in colonial America beginning in 1619 came fully aware of the concepts of independence and autonomy later embraced by American colonialists, for thousands of early African Americans frequently were ex-Jaga rebels who had been captured by Angolan super kings and sold for export to America. Christian dissidents from Europe and Jagas from Africa, who frequently were also Christian, were both exiled to America with little choice.)

Europeans certainly affected the latter stage of independent Angola's collapse externally, sometimes as pawns and sometimes as exploiters. However, African resistance to African superstates—not European materialism, European armies, greed, cultural corruption, or slavery— initially sparked the destructive civil wars pitting Angolan kings against Angolan princes that would weaken the country in the sixteenth and seventeenth centuries, and open the way to European colonization.

❖

IN 1560, IN a preview of what was to come later, the relationship between Kongo and Portugal tilted momentarily in Portugal's favor when a manikongo named Álvaro I, facing a powerful Jaga rebellion in some of his recently added provinces, called up the Portuguese army to save him. The king of Portugal sent General Francisco de Gouveia Sottomaior and six hundred soldiers to his aid. The victory, however, was high for Álvaro who, in return for the military support, was forced to sign formal papers "in which the King of Kongo confesses to be his [the king of Portugal's] vassal." From that time and until he could extricate himself from his debt, the manikongo in his letters to Lisbon addressed the king of Portugal not as previously as "my brother," but as "my lord and brother."

In 1571, Portugal sent a new ambassador to exploit the opportunity presented by Kongo's capitulation: Paulo Dias de Novais, the grandson of Bartholomeu Dias whose discovery of the southern Cape of Africa seven decades earlier had been quickly eclipsed by Vasco da Gama's voyage into the Indian Ocean. The arrival of Novais would signal a momentous change in Portuguese policy regarding Angola. No longer content with merely trading with the iron kingdoms and baptizing African converts, the ambitious King Sebastião intended to conquer and colonize all of Angola and, if possible, all of Central Africa.

Motivating the new Portuguese attitude was the quest for gold. The slave export trade, though lucrative, was not filling the royal treasury in Lisbon: The taxing authority that the Portuguese government set up to regulate trade with Angola was weak and inefficient, and European traders found ways to bypass it. Disaffected Portuguese slave merchants on the island of São Tomé off the Gabon coast were becoming wealthy, but not the kings of Portugal. Sebastião hoped to emulate Spanish successes in the Americas and either find gold and silver in Angola or use the country as a springboard into the interior of Central Africa, where he might find gold and silver.

However, there was an impediment to Portuguese imperial ambitions in Angola. The Church was reaping a fantastic harvest in conversions throughout the country, and therefore Rome opposed any military adventures that would unsettle Angola. By the middle of the sixteenth century, several large Kongolese districts in northern Angola had become predominantly Christian and were loyal to the Church. Sebastião turned to his councilors to find a loophole and, in 1572, falsely claiming he was acting with the authority of the pope, he commissioned Novais to "subject and conquer the kingdom of Angola"—a commission that would indirectly affect the future English colony of Virginia. If Novais succeeded, Sebastião would reward him with a territory the size of a kingdom: a hereditary grant of thirty-five leagues on the coast of Angola "and as far inland as he can go." Unlike grants issued by earlier

Portuguese kings and contrary to the Church's direction, nothing in King Sebastião's commission to Novais recognized the rights of independent African states in his way.

Upon taking office, one of Governor Novais's first official acts was to grant formal recognition to the Mbundu kingdom of Ndongo, whose king, the ngola, had requested missionaries and formal ties with Portugal. Secretly, Novais intended to use the treaty as an opportunity to subjugate Ndongo and place a Portuguese colony in its Cambambe district where there was rumored to be silver. The Ndongo-Portuguese treaty, however, immediately caught the attention of Manikongo Álvaro I of Kongo who, among his titles, claimed to be "king of the Ambundos"— the Mbundu nation—which included the kingdom of Ndongo. Because Kongo had become a vassal of Portugal, the manikongo could not appeal to the pope the loss of Ndongo. So, to undermine the Portuguese-Ndongo alliance, Álvaro sent agents to work on the ngola.

On the island of São Tomé, Portuguese merchants, many of them New Christians who had fled the Inquisition and intermarried with Africans to create a Portuguese-African mestizo society, along with other Portuguese of the untitled gentry who resented the heavy levies imposed on them by Portugal, actually supported Kongolese independence from Portugal and preferred the manikongo as their king. On behalf of Álvaro, Portuguese emissaries from São Tomé hastened to the Ndongo capital city of Kabasa to persuade Kiluanji kia Ndambi that Governor Novais secretly wanted more than to simply baptize his people and open trade. In particular, one Portuguese merchant who was "much trusted" by the ngola informed him that Lisbon coveted the rich silver mines of Cambambe.

The ngola was persuaded by these Portuguese agents and, during a joint expedition with Novais to put down Jagas in 1579, a company of Ndongo soldiers suddenly turned on their new Portuguese allies, inflicting heavy casualties and sacking their baggage train. Novais and a remnant of his army—originally seven hundred soldiers—managed to escape to the castle at Nzele in the kingdom of Kongo.

Plotting revenge against the ngola, Governor Novais then reinforced his reduced land force with the army of the Kongolese Duke of Mbamba and pulled together a naval fleet that included a caravel, two *galeotes*, and several gunships. In September 1580, he led his new allied infantry with the fleet up the Kwanza River and into Ndongo territory. The ngola's troops responded—and decimated the combined Portuguese-Kongolese army. Governor Novais survived only because the manikongo at the last moment sent a large Kongolese relief force to his rescue.

Novais was now in a much weaker position than before. Not only was Ndongo still unconquered, but the manikongo had repaid his debt by saving the Portuguese army from total destruction . . . and Kongo was again free of Portuguese control.

After much deliberation, Governor Novais determined that Ndongo's vulnerability might be that which had briefly delivered Kongo to Portugal. Lately, following the Kongolese model, increasingly ambitious ngolas had one after the other enforced a new central bureaucracy at the city of Kabasa to bring all of Ndongo's provinces under their absolute control. This was, to repeat, a purely African political development that originated before European contact. Lesser aristocrats known as *makotas*, who ruled the older royal districts within Ndongo, resented losing power in the bureaucratic realignment. Furthermore, Ndongo had aggressively added to the kingdom several ministates it reduced to mere local districts, governed by *sobas*, who had once been kings. These sobas sometimes incited Jaga rebellions to throw off the yoke of Ndongo and recover their former autonomy.

The resulting civil tension presented Governor Novais an opportunity to conquer Ndongo and open all of Central Africa to Portuguese exploitation. He made a pitch to Ndongo's outlying provinces, promising them restoration of their previous independence. Sobas who ruled over Ilamba and Kisama accepted the offer, and suddenly the ngola faced a sizable internal rebellion. Novais's third army pushed up the Kwanza River in 1586 in yet another invasion. Deep in Ndongo country, the Portuguese governor built Fort Massangano with the Kwanza River as his lifeline to supplies on the coast. Outraged by the insolent intrusion, the ngola launched raids to dislodge the fort. However, situated on the river within range of the Portuguese fleet's guns and heavily defended by both European and African soldiers, Fort Massangano withstood Ndongo's assaults. Intent on conquest and riches, Novais then continued up the Kwanza to its junction with the Lukala River and there at Cambambe, where he hoped to find the ngola's silver mines, he built a second fort. Sensing the momentum, more sobas defected to Governor Novais, who eventually fielded an impressive army of ten thousand seasoned soldiers—Portuguese, Christian Kongolese, and Ndongo Jagas—combined.

Then disaster struck. On May 9, 1589, Governor Novais became ill from the tropical climate and died, and all of his efforts to restore the lost glory of Bartholomeu Dias faded in the mists of the Lukala valley. He was succeeded by Luis Serrão, who decided to immediately launch the massive allied army from Cambambe straight into the Ndongo heartland and take the capital city of Kabasa. But while the Portuguese were assembling the invasion, Quiloange Angola, the new ngola, quickly made an alliance with the queen of the powerful kingdom of Matamba to the east. Matamba had also previously requested Christian missionaries and diplomatic relations with Portugal but, like the ngola of Ndongo, she, too, eventually came to suspect that Lisbon meant to seize Angola.

As Governor Serrão's huge, well-equipped, allied army began marching east along the Lukala River, the loyalist Ndongo-Matamba forces moved west from the mountains of the Malange plateau to stop them. The date of the decisive battle of the Lukala was December 20, 1589. Gazing up at the highlands, Governor Serrão was stunned by the discipline of the Ndongo-Matamba host approaching him. Armed with battle-axes and swords of tested Bantu iron, and arrayed in the traditional Bantu two-horned formation, Quiloange Angola's main force of three large squadrons, with an additional great number of troops forming a seemingly endless crescent-shaped line, then descended upon a ten-thousand-strong European-led army of cannons, muskets, horses, armor, bombards, and rebel allies. Serrão's black and white companies shattered and, overwhelmed on all sides, his cavalry and musketeers fell back while desperately fighting to survive complete destruction.

Typically in pitched battles, the Bantu fought until one side retreated. But Central Africa had never before engaged in a clash of this magnitude. Even so, Quiloange adapted more ably than did Governor Serrão. Surrounded on three sides with the river at their backs, Serrão's soldiers—European and African—lost their nerve, dropped their guns, and fled by the thousands from the iron axes of the advancing Mbundu. Loyalist Ndongo troops pursued the panicked enemy down the Lukala River, overrunning Cambambe, slaying them and taking captives along the way. Ships and cannons covering the Portuguese retreat failed to halt the rout, and the Portuguese governor barely escaped to Fort Massangano after three weeks on the run.

❧

ON THAT MEMORABLE day on the Lukala River in the season of Kutanu, the Mbundu kingdom of Ndongo tested its iron against a great modern invasion of supposed superior military technology. Tens of thousands collided—nations against nations, kingdoms against kingdoms. It was the first epic battle ever fought south of the Sahara, and Ndongo's decisive victory stalled Portugal's attempted conquest of Central Africa for the next three decades. Despite internal defections, an African superstate had thoroughly and convincingly routed a European one.

After this disastrous defeat, the rebel Jagas deserted the Portuguese and returned to Ngola Quiloange Angola. The Portuguese colonial ambition was back where it had started nearly a century earlier, almost knee deep in the Atlantic Ocean. Along the Lukala River, the people of Ndongo celebrated. Witnessing this, the king of Kongo in northern Angola seized the initiative and, wary of becoming Portugal's vassal ever again, pressed the pope to appoint a Catholic bishop independent of Portugal. Manikongo Álvaro III also gained control over the Angolan Church's finances and acquired from Rome the right to promote civil officials loyal to him rather than to Portugal. Kongo essentially broke away from Angola, forcing the Portuguese to search for a new African ally to help achieve its colonial objectives against mighty Ndongo. Portugal's ambitions in Africa were further slowed when, beginning in 1580, it lost its autonomy to Spain for what would be almost half a century.

Then another obstacle appeared on the horizon in the 1590s. Protestant Dutch and English merchants arrived and began trading around the mouth of the Congo River. The manikongos, now aware of Portugal's new policy of conquest and colonization, desired distance from the Portuguese and were quick to take advantage of opportunities presented by the Protestant newcomers, opening trade with them, to Portugal's dismay. The corsairs of William of Orange's Dutch Sea Beggars, and the privateering English Sea Dogs of Queen Elizabeth I, had established fierce reputations as aggressive anti-Catholic pirates since Francis Drake had rounded the globe three decades earlier. These Protestant buccaneers had become as troublesome to Spain and Portugal in the Atlantic as had Muslim pirates in the Mediterranean. One summer rampage by a Drake or a Raleigh through gold-rich Spanish settlements in the Americas could send the entire economies of Spain and Portugal, and by extension Italy and all of Europe, plummeting.

Self-consciously trailing the older established empires of Spain and Portugal in power, lands, wealth, and global influence as the seventeenth century dawned, the northern Protestant kingdoms of western Europe were about to embark on superstate schemes of their own in America, Africa, and Asia. And pitted in this struggle of empires were two competing nobles enmeshed in a deadly game of intrigue. The victor's prize would be a ship of Angolan captives of war heading for America.

· 3 ·

A Game at Chess

THE SON OF a Spanish governor of Granada and the Canary Islands, Count Gondomar was disarming, urbane, and well read—a superb choice by King Philip III for the ambassadorship to the English court of King James, who preferred intellectual courtiers conversant in Latin and French to the swaggering English swashbucklers violently vying for his favors. Gondomar would serve two terms as Philip's ambassador to England: the first from 1613 to 1618, when enraged Londoners attacked his house and forced him from England, and then from 1620 to 1622, at which time he attempted to recover a stolen shipment of enslaved Africans.

Through flattery and a common interest in literature, Gondomar built a special rapport with James Stuart, which, along with the lure of the Spanish marriage proposal and his insight into the complicated personality of the king of England, placed the Spanish party in high standing at court. Both of James's parents had died violently: His mother, Mary, Queen of Scots, along with her lover, was widely suspected in his father's assassination when James was an infant, and the king of France had teased young James that he was born a bastard. His mother was eventually beheaded by Elizabeth for alleged complicity in a plot to return the throne to a Catholic monarch. Since infancy, James, who always wore protective padding under his shirt, had been targeted in numerous Catholic assassination plots, including one in which he had stood in stark terror mere inches from an assassin's naked blade. Perhaps because of the many attempts on his life, James preferred connivance or "kingcraft" to violence when it came to getting his way. Though dutifully married and father of several children by Anne, James was fond of handsome men, lavishing on his favorites immense sums of money as well as titles and estates that he could not afford, prompting Londoners to smirk at the time, "*Rex fuit Elizabeth: nunc est regina Jacobus*" ("Elizabeth was king: now James is queen").

James was a royal slob who never bathed and who wore his shirts until they disintegrated on his body. He preferred to spend his time hunting and running the kingdom from outside of London, detesting the decorous ceremonial show that the English then, as now, sought of their monarchs. His open disdain for this English peculiarity especially catered to by his predecessor Elizabeth I, as much as any other grievance, caused his subjects to detest their king. The sentiment was mutual, as Nicolo Molin, the Venetian ambassador to James's court reported to the Doge of Venice:

> King James does not caress the people nor make them that good cheer the late Queen did, whereby she won their loves. This king manifests no taste for them but rather contempt and dislike. The result is he is despised and almost hated. In fact his Majesty is more inclined to live retired with eight or ten of his favorites than openly, than is the custom of the country and the desire of the people.

By nature incompatible with the English image of a monarch, James I was, except for a small ring of friends, an alien in his own kingdom and became even more so in the second half of his reign. This alienation offered Spain an opportunity.

Ambassador Gondomar, a much better chess player than James, commiserated with the British king over his troubles with Parliament, and their close friendship was deeply resented by the English aristocracy who held a special hatred for the Spaniard and used Gondomar's delicate intestinal condition to mock him as a stereotypical windy Spanish braggadocio. But Gondomar's craftiness was not underestimated, and he was blamed for nearly all of James's unpopular decrees. In a satirical political play about the proposed marriage between Prince Charles I of England and the Spanish princess, entitled *A Game at Chess*, the brilliant English playwright Thomas Middletown based his leading antagonist, the cunning Black Knight, on Count Gondomar. The play was presented ten times in 1624 to sellout crowds at the Globe Theatre before the Spanish ambassador complained and the king's Privy Council suppressed it and arrested Middleton.

Though hissed by the English as the personification of the sinister Mediterranean villain, Count Gondomar as James's chief councilor (which is essentially what the Spaniard became during his terms in England) deserves the credit for the success of England's peace with Spain at a critical moment in the birth of the British Empire and English North America. He was not, however, motivated by humanitarianism. His monarch, Philip III, desired peace with England because English privateers could not be restrained any other way from looting the Spanish Empire's vessels. The count had also served Spain as a military officer, actively repelling English and Dutch privateering fleets three times when Elizabeth still ruled England. A tough, fierce nationalist and militant Catholic sectarian, Gondomar could be vengeful and was, as in the case of the privateer Sir Walter Raleigh, not inclined to leniency when his enemy was within his grasp. Dangling the Spanish marriage proposal before James, Gondomar controlled the throne of England.

❋

AMONG THOSE MOST apprehensive about the direction in which King James seemed to be taking the country were the English Puritans, who strongly opposed anything that hinted of conciliation with Rome. A growing force to be reckoned with in Parliament, the Puritan movement was then actively engaged in stripping the Anglican Church of "papist" trappings. James's open courting of Catholics was as outrageous to them as his commissioned *Masque of Blackness.*

English Puritans opposed theatricals of all kinds because London playhouses were then dens of drunkenness, violence, robbery, and vice, frequented by prostitutes who openly engaged their trade during intermission, or, if the play was a flop, even before. It is therefore ironic that an actor who drank and frolicked would become the greatest Puritan champion of the day. Making his debut in *Masque of Blackness* in 1605, along with his young wife, was nineteen-year-old Robert Rich II, the teenage son of Baron Robert and Lady Penelope Rich, who had since divorced. Young Rich would again appear in blackface in Ben Jonson's play *Masque of Beauty* in 1608, which, as a delayed sequel to *Masque of Blackness*, again featured the "daughters of Niger." Portraying African torchbearers, Robert Rich and his comrades were, according to drama historian Ronald Bayne, "chosen out of the best and most ingenious youth of the Kingdom, noble and others." At the end of a masque, the actors would customarily step forward and remove their disguises to reveal themselves to the surprised applause of their aristocrat peers, but in *Masque of Blackness* this was impossible because their disguises were painted on. This fit the young man who would one day masquerade as one of King James's favorites while secretly pillaging Spanish ships in violation of James's treaty.

In the beginning there was little to suggest that Robert Rich II would amount to much more than a spoiled playboy. His immensely wealthy father owned England's largest private fleet, and the elder Rich's success gave young Rich leisure to engage in hunting, sailing, tilting (a jousting sport on horseback), the theatre, poetry, and the decadent pursuits of the privileged upper class. He attended Cambridge before becoming an undergraduate of Emmanuel College in 1603 and there deservedly gained a notorious reputation for womanizing, dueling, and drinking, none of the habits generally associated with the Puritans of whom he would one day become leader. But, as his contemporary, Arthur Wilson, had observed, young Rich was also an ardent patriot with a sober side:

Though [Rich] had all those excellent endowments of body and fortune that give splendour to a glorious court, yet he used it but as his recreation; for his spirit aimed at more public adventures, planting colonies in the western world rather than himself in the King's favour.

From the Devereaux family on his mother's side, Robert inherited his dark looks, courtly connections, and appreciation of fine art. From his father's side, he had inherited incredible wealth; and, from both, a double portion of audacity. Rich's father, who had gained his fortune as a privateer during the reign of Elizabeth, was an early investor in the Virginia Company of London's colony of Jamestown. His son followed in his steps, overseeing the colony's affairs from England through such agents as his kinsman Sir Nathaniel Rich and his business manager, Maurice Thomson. Lord Delaware, Shakespeare's patron Lord Southampton, and young Rich, who in 1619 was to become the second Earl of Warwick, were the three most socially prominent investors in the Jamestown venture in the first two decades of the colony's life.

Though through his mother's connections Rich was a favorite in James's inner court, he began to champion Puritan radicals and religious and political dissidents, to the king's displeasure. The puzzle of the young rake's peculiar affinity for Puritans has never been explained satisfactorily by the great number of worthy English scholars and historians of the past three centuries who have noted it. Rich was described by his own kinsman, the Duke of Manchester, as "a Puritan sailor of very unpuritanical manners." Part of the explanation for his mysterious relationship, as an aristocrat, with the republican-minded Puritans likely lies in his necessary close contact with them. Many of the lords and wealthy gentry who were most prominent in financing the earliest American colonial ventures were Puritans, and their working partnerships with him may explain his sympathies for them as well as his protection of the persecuted religious dissidents who frequently peopled their colonies.

But business relationships alone do not completely explain why Rich would take such an extraordinary leadership role as a republican in the English Civil War a few decades later. For Rich, the basis of his ideological opposition to the absolutism of King James—who highly favored the Rich family, made him a lord, and promoted his brother Henry to the prestigious position of captain of the royal guard and later to the earldom of Holland—was the English aristocracy's lingering resentment against King Henry VIII for his cruel treatment of his noble-born wives while attempting to obtain a male heir for the continuance of the Tudor dynasty. Robert Rich's grandmother was Lettice Knollys, a cousin of the unfortunate Anne Boleyn beheaded by her husband Henry. This displeasure with the peccadilloes of royalty among certain members of the English aristocracy who were also frequently the aristocrats financing American colonies, bred in them a liberal tolerance for rebels and republicanism. Calvinist Puritans, as a logical conclusion of their doctrine of the individual's direct relationship with, and responsibility to, God, insisted that civil and ecclesiastical rulers must be subject to law. Robert Rich, the "very unpuritanical" Puritan, was thus a political Puritan rather than a religious Puritan. King James intensely disliked Puritans and would hound them throughout his reign. Puritans, warned James, wanted *parity*, not *purity*. In a letter to Anglican archbishop William Laud who was the king's henchman in persecuting religious dissenters, Lord Conway described the later roles of Robert and his brother Henry Rich:

> The Earl of Warwick [Robert Rich] is the temporal head of the Puritans, and the Earl of Holland [Henry Rich] is their spiritual; or rather the one is their visible and the other their invisible head.

Robert Rich, as an English Jaga, would earn the firm confidence of Puritans and dissenters such as the Pilgrim Separatists, some of whom he hid from the king on his own estate at Leighs Priory in Essex. Commenting on Rich's significant role leading up to the English Civil War, Lord Clarendon portrayed the second Earl of Warwick as

> a man of a pleasant and companionable wit and conversation; of an unusual jollity; and such a license in his words and in his actions, that a

man of less virtue could not be found out; so that one might reasonably have believed that a man so qualified would not have been able to have contributed much to the overthrow of a nation and a kingdom. But with all these faults, he had great authority and credit with the people, who, in the beginning of the troubles did all the mischief; and by opening his doors and making his house the rendezvous of all the silenced ministers, in the time when there was authority to silence them, and by being present with them at their devotions and making himself merry with them . . . he became the head of that party and got the style of a godly man.

Rich was aware of Gondomar's thinly veiled attempt to return England to the Catholic fold and to limit English ventures in the Americas, given by papal decree to Spain at the Treaty of Tordesillas. As a Protestant and a patriot, he regarded Spain as England's most dangerous foreign enemy and, exploiting King James's ambition to colonize abroad, would seek a base in America from which to attack Spain without the king's knowledge. According to historian Wesley Craven, to Rich:

The spoiling of Spanish commerce was a legitimate, honorable, and patriotic part of his large commercial interests. He considered the use of colonies as a base for such activities a reasonable privilege belonging to one who had invested heavily in their establishment, and partly for this reason he regarded the more southern colonies as of the greatest value. He attempted to divert the Puritan migration to the Caribbean area, and led in the work of the Providence Island Company, its settlement off the Mosquito Coast becoming in the 1630s the most famous pirates' base in the West Indies, and he undertook single handed the settlement of Trinidad and Tobago. When at the outbreak of the civil war in 1642, Parliament commissioned him lord high admiral, his fame as an enemy of Spain had become so great that his preparations of the royal fleet were viewed with sincere alarm by the Spanish ambassador for fear that his real intent might be some attack on Spanish America. In fact, he did in that year send another fleet of his own with 1100 men who for three years scoured the West Indies for plunder, attacked and held for ransom important towns, and even captured and held for a year the colony of Jamaica.

All of this would come later in Rich's career. The very first evidence of his future conflict with the Stuarts began to emerge in 1612 in his involvement with the struggling new colony of Jamestown, Virginia.

❖

ROBERT RICH WAS only twenty-six when, in looking after his Virginia interests, in September 1612 he dispatched a man-of-war to supply the then five-year-old Jamestown settlement. The one-hundred-ton *Treasurer* would play a major role in the survival of the young colony before, seven years later, directly causing the dissolution of the Virginia Company. On the 1612 voyage, the vessel carried sixty-two settlers and a commission from the shareholders of the Virginia Company of London to expel "foreign intruders." The great charters of Virginia and Northern Virginia (later known as New England) at the time stretched almost the entire length of the eastern seaboard of North America, thus placing Jamestown in fierce competition with the French in Canada, the Dutch at New Amsterdam (later New York), and the Spanish in Florida. Although leased to the Virginia Company of London, the *Treasurer* was co-owned by young Robert Rich and his cousin Thomas West, Lord Delaware, who was governor for life of Virginia though he preferred to live in England.

In command of this warship of fourteen cannons and sixty musketeers was another of Rich's cousins, Samuel Argall. Seeking his fortune and a knighthood, the bold Argall as captain of the *Treasurer* would in three years destroy French settlements in Canada, force loyalty from the Dutch at New York, attack Spanish ships, and discover a shorter northern course between England and America that would increase Jamestown's profitability. However, the *Treasurer*'s first expedition after arriving in Jamestown was to sail up the Nansemond River to intimidate Algonquian natives and steal their corn.

The weroance (king) of the Algonquian Pamunkey peoples, Powhatan—unlike Álfonso I in Angola a century earlier—resented Europeans and, regarding the Jamestown settlers as a potential commercial, political, and military threat, did not embrace the religion they brought. Powhatan had inherited a kingdom to which he had recently added, through military conquest, a number of lesser Algonquian kingdoms, to form a small empire that he had not yet fully secured when the English first arrived in 1606. Powhatan desired English beads, axes, and guns, but he was more concerned that the Europeans would aid his conquered enemies around Chesapeake. Therefore, he soon determined to chase away the white interlopers even as they built Fort James in his domain in 1607. Beginning in 1609, Powhatan besieged Jamestown with a constant blockade; by the time Captain Argall and the *Treasurer* appeared in 1612, the disillusioned colonists were ready to pack up and return to England en masse. It was the period at Jamestown known as the "Starving Time" during which an alarming number of English settlers died from arrows, hunger, disease, and Spanish sabotage, leaving only a few dozen survivors. The timely arrival of Rich's warship not only allowed them to hang on, but also let them take the offensive.

Argall ended Powhatan's siege by committing a famous kidnapping: After returning from the Nansemond raid, he took the *Treasurer* up the Rappahannock River to acquire more corn. It was on this voyage, in January 1613, that he learned from Weroance Japazaws of the Patowomacks that a daughter of Powhatan's was visiting nearby. Young Pocahontas was familiar to the English of Jamestown from visits she had made to the settlement before Captain John Smith departed for England after being injured in a gunpowder explosion, but she had ceased coming when her father gave her in marriage to an Algonquian, "Captain" Kocoum, in another part of his empire.

Realizing the prize at hand, Captain Argall bribed Japazaws with a copper kettle to entice Pocahontas to tour Rich's *Treasurer*. The scheme worked and, once she was onboard, Argall locked Pocahontas in the ship's cabin, informing her that she was his hostage for the "ransoming of so many Englishmen as were prisoners of Powhatan." He took her back to the colony on the *Treasurer* and placed her in the custody of Deputy Governor Thomas Dale. With the daughter of their chief enemy as prisoner, the English settlers of Jamestown demanded a treaty. Powhatan relented and attacks on the fort ceased, though a lasting peace was never established. In the following months of her captivity, Pocahontas converted to Christianity, took the name Rebecca, and married one of the English settlers in Jamestown. He was the recently widowed John Rolfe, lately of Bermuda.

Rolfe's tobacco had not yet turned the colony around, and Jamestown was costing its investors more money than it was making. At that point in time, Jamestown's future looked bleak. The company had sent John Smith and his men to Chesapeake Bay in 1606 to find gold and a river route to the South Sea. Neither was discovered, and investors began searching for a profitable reason to stay—sassafras, lumber, furs—anything that could be traded abroad. In London, some of the colony's shareholders were beginning to default on their financial pledges.

In 1616, the Virginia Company financed a voyage to bring John Rolfe and Pocahontas, with their young son Thomas, plus a dozen other Algonquian natives, to England to convince the public that whites and natives were getting along and to promote the colony as a solid investment. In truth, relations between Jamestown and Powhatan were barely tolerable. The Pocahontas tour was a propaganda blitz to obscure bad news coming from the colony, to encourage investors to stay on board, and to persuade reluctant Englishmen to migrate to Jamestown.

They sailed on the *Treasurer.* The trip was a great success. During her captivity, Pocahontas had been instructed in religion by educated ministers in Jamestown as well as in courtly manners by certain dissolute sons of nobility exiled to Virginia and, not at all the stereotypical native nature child as portrayed today, she was eager to learn. Her poised Europeanized conduct as "Lady Rebecca," along with her Christian conversation, was presented as proof that natives could be "civilized," and she created a sensation in London that far exceeded the company's expectations. Introduced to King James at court by Lord Delaware,

Pocahontas attended, among other diversions, two winter masques with the king and played cards with Queen Anne.

From what would later unfold, it is clear now that in England in the summer of 1616, Robert Rich met with Argall and Rolfe to concoct a scheme to turn the colony of Jamestown into a pirate base from which to secretly launch the man-of-war *Treasurer* against Spanish and Portuguese merchant ships in the West Indies in the outlawed tradition of grand old Elizabethan privateers. Discretion was required, for at that time King James was in sensitive negotiations with the king of Spain to have Prince Charles I marry Philip III's daughter Maria. To give the *Treasurer* a thin coat of legitimacy in this highly illegal undertaking, Rich had secretly bribed Scarnifissi, an agent of the Catholic Duke of Savoy in Italy, to provide him with a letters of marque permitting him to attack Spanish ships. Savoy at that time was engaged in a war against Spain and was frantically seeking money to purchase arms. To get around the Stuart treaty with Spain, many English ex-privateers surreptitiously acquired such marques, or privateering licenses, from foreign princes engaged in wars against Spain.

The English were addicted to piracy more than were any other European nation except the Dutch, because England had so little to trade. Asia and India had no need for wool, which was the one thing the Britons had in abundance. England actually set out to find a northwest passage with the hope that it would lead to markets for its wool in colder countries. Piracy was tempting in a dirt-poor island nation with a surplus, thanks to Elizabeth, of big guns and fast ships. Moreover, English privateers of the Elizabethan era regarded raids on Spanish and Portuguese ships and settlements not only as personally profitable but as their civic and religious duty on behalf of God, their Protestant religion, and their country. One of the first unpopular acts of James upon becoming king in 1603 was to lock up the dangerous privateer Sir Walter Raleigh in the Tower of London on a weak accusation of treason. Raleigh, a national hero in England, was also a friend and employee of the Rich family, and this association would eventually threaten Robert Rich's pirate plans for Jamestown.

By outlawing privateering against Spain, James's 1604 peace treaty motivated English lords and merchants previously engaged as pirates to seek other means of gaining wealth. Hence the chartering, mere months after the fragile cessation of hostilities between the two leading Catholic and Protestant countries, of what would prove to be the first successful English colony in America—Jamestown. Robert Rich led all Englishmen both in investing in new American colonies and in creating global trading companies, even while he also continued to secretly mastermind unlawful anti-Spanish pirate raids. Three years before becoming the second Earl of Warwick, young Rich, in the tradition of his father and grandfather, by 1616 had already put together a superb organization of merchants, politicians, accountants, financiers, spies, propagandists, pamphleteers, explorers, musketeers, sailors, mercenaries, and pilots that he employed in legitimate ventures as well as schemes that violated the Spanish treaty. All this he was doing under the king's nose while keeping his head safely attached to his shoulders. As the English historian Samuel Rawson Gardiner noted:

> If there was one thing upon which King James prided himself, it was his hatred of piracy. . . . Yet Rich coolly and deliberately did what was far worse than anything perpetrated by Raleigh under the strongest possible temptation.

Rich's success was due in part to the multilayered network of agents he organized around him, something Sir Raleigh never rivaled. But Rich kept his head because of the great affection of the king and queen for his mother, Lady Penelope, who had boldly supported them in the Essex affair at the risk of her own life.

While Rich, Rolfe, and Argall plotted piracy in the summer of 1616, King James, ignoring the protests of Spain, released Walter Raleigh from the Tower of London after twelve years, to pursue a phantom: While in prison, the aging privateer had convinced James's son Prince Henry that he could find the Spaniards' long-sought fabled city of El Dorado—and its valuable gold mines—in the South American region of Guiana (now part of Venezuela). Raleigh, with Rich's help, was gathering the expedition in 1616 while Pocahontas and John Rolfe were in England.

During a business visit to London, Captain John Smith, who managed a short reunion with Pocahontas, learned of the El Dorado expedition. According to Smith, Raleigh, before returning from Guiana on a previous unsuccessful voyage to find the golden city in 1597 (during Elizabeth's reign), had left behind his trusty servant Francis Sparrow,

> who wandering up and down those Countries some fourteen or fifteen years, unexpectedly returned [to England]: I have heard him say he was led blinded into this City by Indians.

Captain Smith, who had come to London to propose planting a new colony north of Virginia, derided Raleigh's venture to Guiana, noting that the Spaniards themselves had launched more than twenty expeditions into the Amazon forests to find El Dorado, without success. King James, however, urgently needed money and Captain Smith's sensible but lackluster plan to monopolize codfish could not compete with Raleigh's dazzling assurances of a city of gold. This was one of the rare times when even the Spanish ambassador Gondomar could not sway the king. Parliament's refusal to raise taxes had placed James on a miserly budget and, burdened with mounting bills, he was in a mood to gamble that Sir Raleigh could find El Dorado and eliminate the entire royal debt in one voyage. James let Raleigh sail though he sternly warned him to leave Spain's Guiana settlements in peace.

As one of Raleigh's key investors and also a political leader of the Puritan movement, Robert Rich was keenly interested in the expedition to Guiana, though not for the phantom city of gold. Trees, not El Dorado, attracted Rich to the venture: The Amazon forests of Guiana were said to flourish with logwood timber from which was extracted valuable red dye for wool cloth. Robert Rich believed Guiana could be profitably settled with English Separatists—specifically, the Pilgrim clothmakers who had fled to Holland to avoid King James's persecution.

Though heavily involved in Raleigh's Guiana venture, Rich did not drop his buccaneering plans for Virginia. He characteristically kept many irons in the fire. After plotting the Jamestown piracy scheme with Argall and Rolfe, he used his considerable influence with the Virginia Company in the autumn of 1616 to request the shareholders appoint his two friends to the highest administrative offices in Jamestown. Rich wanted the company to name Argall deputy governor of Virginia, and Rolfe to be made the colony's secretary-recorder. Both positions were critical to the piracy scheme. Ships could not dock at Jamestown without the governor's permission, and the colony's secretary-recorder was responsible for logging all ships arriving and departing, as well as recording their cargo. Unless he controlled these two key offices, Rich could not run his pirate ships, with their stolen Spanish booty, in and out of Jamestown in secret. The Virginia Company, ecstatic over the wild mania that Pocahontas's appearance had created in London, gladly approved Rich's motions at the Michaelmas meeting of 1616, promoting respectively the man who had kidnapped her and the man who had married her, to the offices Rich requested. At the time, the other company shareholders had no clue of Rich's piracy scheme and certainly would not have gone along with it for fear that King James would dissolve their charter for North America.

By March 1617, newly appointed Deputy Governor Argall, along with Secretary John Rolfe and his wife Pocahontas, was ready to leave London for Virginia on the ship *George*. But on the day of departure, Pocahontas died suddenly and mysteriously at the London docks at Gravesend. Wind and tide would not wait, and John Rolfe quickly buried his wife in the nearest churchyard before returning to the *George* hours later for the voyage to Virginia. On the way he dropped off their ailing child, Thomas, with Walter Raleigh's cousin, Sir Lewis Stukely, in old Plymouth, on the Devonshire coast. Sir Raleigh and his fleet left Devon for Guiana that same month.

Six weeks later, the new deputy governor and secretary-recorder for the Virginia colony stepped off the *George* in Jamestown to take office. While the *George* had been preparing to leave England in March, Lord Rich had placed a new captain, Daniel Elfrith, in charge of his corsair

Treasurer. Elfrith outfitted the ship for war and arrived in Jamestown soon after the *George.* Governor Argall immediately put Lord Rich's covert piracy scheme in action. Announcing publicly that he was sending the *Treasurer* to Cape Cod to catch fish for the colony, Argall instead manned the ship with a crew of experienced musketeers trained for sea service, provisioned her, and sent her off to raid Spanish targets in the West Indies. Later that year, Governor Argall warned curious settlers to stay away from the *Treasurer* when she returned to Jamestown after plundering the Spanish, posting a public edict: "None to go aboard ye Ship now at James Town without ye Governor's leave."

Meanwhile in the Caribbean, Robert Rich's other venture was in trouble. Sir Raleigh's fleet, after several weeks' prowling along the South American coastline, had reluctantly concluded what John Smith already knew: there was no El Dorado in Guiana. As Raleigh considered his next move, dreading to report to King James that the expensive expedition was a bust, one of the fleet's captains, against Raleigh's orders, attacked a small, meaningless Spanish town, Saint Thomas, in South America. Raleigh's son was killed in the action, and the English were repulsed. In London, upon receiving preliminary news of the attack against Saint Thomas, the opportunistic Count Gondomar sought an audience with King James, according to the contemporary historian James Howell, claiming that he only had one word to say to him:

> The King wondered what could be delivered in one word, whereupon, when he came before him, he said only, "Pirates! pirates! pirates!" and so departed.

In the summer of 1618, Raleigh's luckless Guiana fleet returned home and into a storm of official condemnation. Hoping to at least salvage the Spanish marriage proposal, King James, at Gondomar's insistence, again clapped Raleigh in the Tower of London and demanded the death penalty for him. Meanwhile, Count Gondomar's spies had heard rumors that Rich's corsair *Treasurer* was now performing raids out of Jamestown. Suspicious of the young nobleman and emboldened by his success in getting Raleigh's death sentence, the Spanish ambassador began to seek evidence to implicate his wealthy patron, Robert Rich.

But Spain's black knight would find the young Puritan chieftain a more formidable opponent than Raleigh. Even as Sir Raleigh faced the ax for piracy in 1618 and Gondomar was closing in, Rich coolly prepared the *Treasurer* for a second pirate raid from London to Jamestown and onward to the Spanish West Indies. This time, her stolen prize would be determined by a terrible battle being fought far away in Angola. An actor who played a "blackamoor" coming to the British Empire in 1605, Rich in real life was about to become instrumental in bringing the first Africans to Britain's first American colony in 1619, as the king of the English pirates.

· 4 ·

Into the Realm
of Kalunga

A S THE *TREASURER* set sail from Jamestown, an empty
Spanish slaver was heading for the Portuguese colony at
Angola. Portugal at the time was under Spanish control and was entertaining less defined schemes of conquering Central Africa than those
proposed by the now-deceased King Sebastião, as Spain, past its prime,
focused on defending its own far-flung empire against encroachment
from fledgling English and Dutch trading companies trying to wedge
into its markets.

Lisbon had its own domestic problems to worry about. Spain had
introduced the terrible Inquisition into formerly tolerant Portugal in
the 1590s, and suddenly, like the Protestant dissidents facing Anglican
wrath in England, Portuguese Jews, who had been extremely valuable
in the rise to prominence of that Catholic country, were forced to go
into exile or become "New Christians" to escape persecution. Many
Jews fled to faraway colonies in Angola, Columbia, and Brazil, or to
other countries. Later, as the Inquisition spread beyond Portugal to its
colonies, Portuguese merchants in Angola, who were "denounced to
the Inquisition for being secret Jews," moved their base of operations
from Mpinda, at the mouth of the Congo River, to about 150 miles
south down the Atlantic coast to Luanda, near the mouth of the Kwanza

River. They flourished, and a few years later Lisbon also relocated the colonial government from Mpinda to Luanda to reap export duties on the African captives those merchants were now transporting along trade routes south of Kongo. Luanda was the mining location for Central Africa's nzimbu shells, Angola's currency, which Portugal therefore now controlled.

By moving to Luanda, the Portuguese colonial government was also much closer to the Mbundu nation and less than one hundred miles east of the border of the foremost Mbundu kingdom of Ndongo, suddenly the most powerful African state poised between Portugal and its long-standing ambition to colonize all of Central Africa.

Shortly after the Portuguese moved to Luanda, there rose to rule Ndongo the last great Mbundu iron king before the coming of the legendary Nzinga Mbandi. He was her father, Mbandi Ngola Kiluanji. Seeking a military alliance with the Portuguese at Luanda to expand his kingdom over neighboring ministates, Kiluanji in 1616 requested the return of Catholic missionaries and expressed his desire to trade. He also permitted the Portuguese to rebuild Fort Massangano on the Kwanza River three decades after the decisive battle at the Lukala River. The Portuguese missionaries who had left Ndongo in 1589 returned and resumed their work, and the most popular Christian names taken by Kimbundu-speaking converts became Antonio, Francisco, João, Maria, and Isabel. Ndongo's powerful armies still kept Portuguese colonial ambitions bottled, and for a time the governors from Lisbon were content to trade with the ngola as equal partners.

But as in neighboring Kongo in the 1570s, the kingdom of Ndongo in 1616 suffered an internal crisis that had nothing to do with European colonialism. According to Mbundu tradition, civil war broke out because Ngola Kiluanji allowed brothers of his favorite wife to go unpunished for several crimes that had offended the lesser makota nobility. Those abuses further aggravated the simmering resentment that Ndongo's lesser aristocracy held against the ngolas, for stripping them of power in the process of centralizing the government at the royal capital of Kabasa. Hard pressed by a large Jaga rebellion, Kiluanji, like a previous king of neighboring Kongo, responded by calling on the Portuguese governor at Luanda for soldiers and heavy artillery. But before the Portuguese arrived, a number of Kiluanji's rebellious sobas, led by Kavulo ka Kabasa, lured the king into an ambush on the Lukala River in early 1617 and beheaded him.

As civil war descended upon Ndongo, the kingdom faced another peril when, in 1617, there appeared in northern Angola an ominous menace known as the Imbangala—African mercenaries with whom Portuguese government officials quickly allied themselves. This unholy partnership exposes the deterioration of state affairs in Portugal during its loss of sovereignty to Spain from the latter end of the sixteenth century to about the middle of the seventeenth century. Among other ill-advised policies at this time, Spanish-controlled Portugal allowed its governors in Angola to profit directly from duties on slave exports. This gave avaricious short-term governors, with no qualms against devastating colonial Angola, the incentive to violate government-set slave export quotas. The demand for labor abroad, particularly on thriving Caribbean sugar plantations, required more slaves than Lisbon allowed to be exported from Angola during peacetime. Typically, Europeans purchased slaves from Africans who traditionally made slaves of other Africans who were either criminals or Jaga rebels. However, Angola's many kingdoms were fairly stable at the beginning of the seventeenth century and therefore the availability of Jaga prisoners of war was not meeting the labor demands of Spanish and Portuguese enterprises abroad. In addition, the kingdom most aggressively engaged in suppressing Jaga rebellions was Kongo, in Northern Angola; but fearing loss of autonomy as Portugal continued to attempt to colonize Angola, Kongo was reluctant to export slaves through Portuguese-controlled Luanda. It was while mulling over how to increase the supply of slaves for export, that certain Portuguese merchants and government officials at Luanda first encountered the notorious blood cult of the Imbangala.

Who the Imbangala were and how they came to be in Angola is debated. Andrew Battel, of Lord Robert Rich's hometown of Leighs, Essex, was a captured English seaman forced to serve the Portuguese in Benguela around 1599 to 1602. He believed the Imbangala were not originally Bantu, and that Sierra Leone was their true homeland. Described variously as the Jagas, or the Ingas, and sometimes confused with those reactionary independence movements, the Imbangala in fact were foreign mercenaries who were able to enter Angola *because* of the unrest caused by local Jaga civil rebellions. Distinct from the Jagas but sometimes allied with them, the Imbangala were not an ethnic people but a rootless rampaging class of renegade marauders organized into several loosely associated companies led by independent African commanders not bound to any higher authority or even to each other. When Imbe Kalandula, a page of another Imbangala named Elembe, left to form his own army, Elembe's soldiers deserted to Kalandula. Battel reported that "by great troops they run to him and follow his camp in hope of spoil."

The sole ambition of the Imbangala was to take spoil, and not, as in the case of the Jagas, to win civil rights. The Imbangala built no towns but roamed in large bands while subsisting by pillaging settled law-abiding Bantu districts. Battel stayed with Kalandula's band for a year and a half, and said of their tactics that

> they do reap their enemies corn, and take their cattle. For they will not sow, nor plant, nor bring up any cattle, more than they take by wars.

The Imbangala lived in military camps called *quilombos*, into which they ritually initiated young males of fighting age for battle, and taught them capoeira, a form of martial arts. The Imbangala had women in their camps but cruelly buried all newborn babies alive so that the marauders would not be slowed down. Battel observed that they instead kept their numbers strong by recruiting the adolescent sons of their enemy victims. These recruits were made to wear a distinctive collar until they became proficient at war and killed someone, at which time they became full-fledged Imbangala soldiers.

According to their victims, though Imbangala descendants today dispute this, they cultivated their dark reputation by deliberately embracing evil.

A Capuchin priest, Cavazzi da Montecuccolo of Italy, who lived in a region of Angola that the mercenaries occupied for a decade, reported that, to enhance their reputations as witches and as a show of bravado to terrify their Bantu victims, the Imbangala ate people. This cannibalism was a deliberate ritualistic act to create fear in their enemies, rather than the raiders' preferred diet. Their religion was the worship of particularly violent and reprehensible ancestor spirits who, according to John Thornton, differed greatly from the moral ancestor spirits who preserved law and peace, such as were traditionally worshipped by the Bantu: "These moral deities were so terrified by the Imbangala that, when they came, the deities jumped in local rivers to hide and only around 1668 did they decide to venture out again, as the Imbangala were becoming more settled and moral."

There is no doubt that, in the seventeenth-century, just the word "Imbangala" alarmed even the great, mortal manikongo of Angola.

The mercenaries' military strategy was crude but terrifyingly effective. Customarily, a large Imbangala raiding force numbering around sixteen thousand soldiers would enter an inhabited region about harvest time and make a large encampment. Their presence forced the Bantu to either fight them or withdraw from their fields and let the invaders take the harvest and cut down the palm trees to collect the sap for palm wine. So great was the Imbangala thirst for palm wine that, before 1602, the targets they chose for attack often depended on the number of palm trees in the region. After devastating the kingdom of Benguela in less than half a year, the Imbangala invaded another district simply because "they wanted palm trees." The Imbangala not only consumed the land, they also depopulated entire districts for decades. When after many weeks the strength of the Bantu inhabitants was sapped, the Imbangala would launch a major assault on their fortifications and capture and eat whoever they found there. Horrified by the Imbangala reputation as witches and cannibals, and vulnerable to the harvest time sieges, the settled Bantu of Angola fell village after village, district after district, to the chilling stranglehold of these merciless marauders.

At first, in the 1590s, Portuguese merchants had simply followed the meandering Imbangala bands while trading guns in exchange for the

Bantu they captured. These traders soon took a more active role and even helped the Imbangala cross the Kuvo River to attack kingdoms in central Angola. One such invasion was conducted by Kalandula, who led one of the largest Imbangala bands in the early seventeenth century. Composed of twelve companies, his army terrorized and wasted the entire realm, selling the survivors to Portuguese traders who shipped three slave voyages of Benguela prisoners during Imbangala depredations. Following that profitable campaign, the merchants persuaded Imbangala companies to cross into Portuguese territory north of the Kwanza River to raid other districts, including Bantu Christian regions loyal to Rome.

Then, Portuguese governors Manuel Cerveira Pereira in 1616 and Antonio Gonçalves Pita in 1617 legitimized the Imbangala by hiring them to join the *guerra preta* (Portugal's black army in colonial Angola) so that they could direct their gruesome raids for their personal profit. Luanda-sanctioned Imbangala raiders armed with European guns were particularly devastating. Dispatched by a Portuguese governor to the kingdom of Kisama to "save the souls of the idolaters there," the Imbangala did not simply conquer: they emptied the country of all inhabitants and sold them to the same governor who had sent them. Such raids were in violation of Rome's policy of peaceful conversion, but Lisbon under Spanish control did little to stop them. As Imbangala invasions increased revenue by slave export duties through Luanda, the raids also depopulated the country and ravaged the land, which drew protests not only from priests but also from baptized African rulers and Portuguese settlers observing the nightmare creeping across Angola. Manikongo Álvaro II in 1617 complained to Pope Paul V about Portuguese governors who sent Imbangala companies to invade the lands of baptized Kongolese subjects:

[The Portuguese officials in Angola] commit numerous unjust acts, making alliance with a nation of extremely barbarous men [Imbangala] who live on human flesh. May Your Holiness deign to find a remedy for this. I beg him to accord me his immediate protection.

By the time the manikongo's complaints reached Rome, the corrupt Portuguese officials who had hired the Imbangala were packing their bags to retire wealthy.

When Lisbon sent Luis Mendes de Vasconcelos to govern the Portuguese colony at Luanda in late 1617, the Catholic bishop of Kongo hoped that reform would follow. Unlike some previous short-term governors, Vasconcelos came to stay. Upon arriving in Angola, he at first found the Imbangala mercenaries repugnant and dismissed them from the guerra preta, denouncing them as those "who sustain themselves on human flesh and are enemies of all living things and thieves of the land where they enter."

The high-minded governor even demanded that any of his predecessors who had used the Imbangala be put to death and their property confiscated. The challenges of his mission in Africa soon reversed his decision. Vasconcelos had ambitiously promised Lisbon to march from coastal Luanda across Central Africa to the new Portuguese colony in Mozambique in East Africa, thereby establishing a land route over the continent from the Atlantic to the Indian Ocean to circumvent the perilous sea voyage around the southern Cape of Africa. Governor Vasconcelos expected the king of Portugal to reward him handsomely for colonizing Africa; and he especially coveted the promised hereditary title of "Viceroy of Ethiopia," along with revenues from slave export duties and the rights to bestow knighthood and appoint church officials in Africa if he succeeded.

Though initially promised one thousand additional Portuguese infantrymen and two hundred cavalrymen for his mission, Vasconcelos discovered in Luanda that Lisbon expected him to muster an army in Africa. The first enemy that Vasconcelos would face in crossing Central Africa was Ndongo. Even though this Mbundu kingdom in 1618 was still suffering civil war following the assassination of Ngola Kiluanji one year earlier, the terrible lesson taught to the Portuguese by Ndongo at the Lukala River in 1589 was not lost on Vasconcelos. Ndongo was a powerful state, and the governor, without the support of the manikongo, would need a powerful and dependable ally to conquer it. Against his conscience and to the dismay of the bishop of Kongo, he reluctantly recalled the Imbangala. In stunning abuse of the Christian rite, Vasconcelos, in an unsuccessful attempt to appease the bishop, had two of the Imbangala generals who had ravaged the kingdom of Kisama, baptized João Kaza ka Ngola and João Kasanje. Their bands were joined by a third Imbangala company led by one Captain Donga. The Portuguese governor was now prepared to use Imbangala terror on a scale grander than had all of his predecessors at Luanda.

❖

At four thousand feet, the tropical Malange highlands in north-central Angola are cool and enchanting. Misty waterfalls splash over huge oblong rocks and dance through supple hills down to the fertile valleys of the Lukala. Belying the serene beauty, the heart of Mbundu country has seen much bloodshed in the past four hundred years and today it is littered with still-active cold war–era landmines, making it one of the most tragic places in the world, even in peacetime. However, no single battle up to modern times was as terrible as that spawned by the Portuguese invasion of 1618/1619.

For weeks, the mountain kingdom of Ndongo received reports of massive thundering black and red clouds of ships, musketeers, cannons, and cavalry moving up the Kwanza River from Luanda on the edge of the dreaded Atlantic realm of Kalunga. At the royal capital of Kabasa, between the Lutete and Lukala rivers, sat a worried new king. He was Mbande, son of Ngola Kiluanji and half brother of Princess Anna Nzinga, and in the summer of 1618 he had only reigned a few months while fending off rival contenders for his father's throne. As Vasconcelos approached, the young ngola's patrols who were shadowing the invaders relayed grim news, via talking drums, that the large army was turning neither to the right nor the left. It was headed straight for Ndongo's royal city. Then came the worst news of all. Marching with the Portuguese were the Imbangala.

Because Rome had not approved an invasion of Ndongo, Governor Vasconcelos first had to provoke an incident. To do this he moved the presidio of Hango eastward down the Lukala River to Ambaca, deep inside Ndongo and less than fifty miles from the ngola's court at Kabasa. This was a blatant trespass, and the local ruler, Kaita ka Balanga, a soba loyal to Mbande, immediately attacked the stockade, the response that Vasconcelos sought. Claiming he was forced to take punitive measures against aggression instigated by the new ngola, Vasconcelos brought his allied army up the Kwanza River without waiting for approval from Lisbon or Rome.

After decades of misfires, the timing was ripe. When Vasconcelos came to Ambaca, Mbande had not yet regained the loyalty of his rebel lords and he would have to meet the invading army with less than half of Ndongo's military force. Nevertheless, the Portuguese governor quickly discovered why Ndongo had remained independent for more than a century after the Portuguese first came to Angola. Unlike previous governors who gained power through their court connections, Vasconcelos was a veteran officer who had won distinction during the wars of the Counter-Reformation in Christian Europe. A hero of action in Flanders, he had authored a book on European military tactics. But arraying his musketeer forces in tight formations based on the European model was not the way to campaign across Central Africa. Like overly ambitious governors before him, Vasconcelos was initially humiliated when soba Kaita ka Balanga inflicted heavy losses on his Portuguese elite in August 1618. In desperate straits, the governor wisely bowed to African experience and called up his three Imbangala companies to break Balanga's siege on the presidio. At almost the same spot where the Portuguese had fled before Ndongo and Matamba thirty years before, the Imbangala companies, armed with European guns, clashed with Balanga's line of iron swords and battle-axes in the second-greatest Central African battle, next only to the battle of the Lukala in 1589. After intense fighting, Balanga's company, surrounded and outgunned, fell back, and the Imbangala seized the Lukala River crossing. Governor Vasconcelos's army emerged from the siege at Ambaca and began ferrying men, muskets, cannons, and horses across the Lukala, forty miles from Kabasa.

Throughout the mountain kingdom, iron *ngongo* bells clanged the call to arms as men shouted *"Ita! Ita!"* ("War! War!"). Though the majority of rebel sobas, with their professional armies, had not yet sworn allegiance to Ngola Mbande, even at reduced strength Ndongo fielded an impressive force. Several hundred fighters quickly mustered as local commanders activated civilian militia companies. The kingdom of lion-hunting Bantu cattle herders—husbands, fathers, and sons—seized their curved axes, swords, and bows and followed captains into battle. Mbande's military commander dispatched supply trains ahead to the front line. Women marched forward to cook for the soldiers and tend the wounded. The very old and the very young were sent to safety in the hills. For all of their modern weaponry, the Europeans coming up the Lukala were not the enemy that alarmed Ndongo. The ngola feared the Imbangala companies experienced in African tactics and carrying European guns that were massing in front of the Portuguese lines.

At the second clash, Ndongo's civilian militias took the initial brunt of the brutal Imbangala assault, and for hours they held the line. But they lacked the discipline of Ndongo's absent professional armies and, in the heat of battle, they wilted and fell back. Imbangala hordes raced through the gaps and began spreading out into the countryside—burning, plundering, butchering, consuming, and binding. Over the following days, Ndongo resistance strengthened in places but their collapsed ranks had exposed many villages to indescribable atrocities. In the shifting tide of battle, royal Kabasa, a city of thousands, was left momentarily undefended, and Imbangala soldiers fought against Balanga's force street by street before being repulsed. Meanwhile, the rest of the royal district suffered terribly.

With the Imbangala present, the Portuguese infantry and cavalry would be inconsequential in the battle and, except for his heavy artillery, Vasconcelos found the best use of his white soldiers to be in escorting long coffles of traumatized, hollow-eyed prisoners of both sexes and all ages westward down the Lukala, then down the Kwanza to Luanda on the Atlantic coast.

Then, the ongoing rape of Ndongo suddenly ceased. The rainy season had begun and rain disables a musket fuse. So in late September 1618, Vasconcelos's first assault paused and temporarily retreated back across the Lukala. Not acclimated to the interior, the governor and many Portuguese soldiers became ill and withdrew to Hango. Vasconcelos left his teenage son in charge of the Imbangala at Ambaca.

Kabasa was momentarily spared from destruction, but unlike the ngola who met the Portuguese at the Lukala thirty years earlier, Mbande did not take advantage of the lull. He made no alliances with other kingdoms, nor did he make concessions to his rebel sobas; he did not retreat to a more strategic location, or appeal to the bishop of Kongo. When the rains stopped in January 1619, the impatient Imbangala again surged forth and royal Kabasa made her last desperate stand.

The Mbundu believed that time in this world is opposite to that in the spiritual realm: midday here is midnight in the land of ghosts. In February 1619, the kingdoms of the living and the dead merged as fire consuming the thatched houses of the great city of Kabasa mixed with the smoke of Imbangala muskets and Portuguese cannons ripping away the remnants of the civilian militias, to obscure the sun and turn noonday into darkness. Defiantly, Kaita ka Balanga refused to retreat and, pierced by Imbangala musket balls, he died defending the broken palisades of Kabasa. The Imbangala poured into the city and an exultant Portuguese soldier described Ngola Mbande at this moment as fleeing his capital, abandoning his mother and his royal wives "in our power, who with many prisoners and slaves were carried away as captives." The long rule of Ndongo's independent ironsmith kings at Kabasa ended in fire and black smoke.

The Portuguese victory was due both to Ndongo's own crippling civil war and to the Imbangala: "As Vasconcelos had Imbangalas the wars were without any danger but with discredit to the Portuguese." Such was the opinion at the time of Manuel Bautista Soares, bishop of Kongo, who recognized that Vasconcelos's defeat at Ambaca revealed the Portuguese general to be incompetent in waging war in Africa. Condemning the invasion of Ndongo in a letter to the king of Portugal, Bishop Soares blasted Vasconcelos's deal with the devil:

In place of leaving off with the [Imbangala] he embraced them, and he has gone to war with them . . . killing with them and capturing innumerable innocent people, not only against the law of God, but also against the expressed regulations of Your Majesty.

Thousands of unburied bodies polluted the rivers in the battle's aftermath. Vogado Sotomaior, then *ouvidor geral de Angola*, Portugal's chief justice of Angola, received reports from the battlefield that Kabasa had been "sacked in such a way that many thousand souls were captured, eaten, and killed." He reported that, in Imbangala fashion, all "the palm trees were cut down so that the area was effectively barren of them." So great was the devastation in their wake that, when the Portuguese returned the following year, the army "met no resistance in any part of the back country, those provinces having become destitute of inhabitants."

Some estimate that Vasconcelos's campaign eventually captured as many as forty thousand prisoners over three years' time. "Although many people had been killed or enslaved," says Thornton, "others simply fled the region—either hiding in the hills or the bush or following the king to his new headquarters on the Kindonga Islands in the Kwanza River." In the fiscal year 1619 alone, Portuguese and Spanish shipping documents recorded that thirty-six ships arrived in Luanda to transport fifteen thousand Angolan prisoners, mostly from the capture of Kabasa, to various ports around the Atlantic.

Ndongo was a kingdom nearly the size of Portugal; the fury of the Imbangala was concentrated on the royal district, a narrow corridor thirty miles wide and fifty miles deep between the Lukala and Lutete rivers. The Imbangala even enslaved four thousand African Christian porters in charge of Vasconcelos's supply train. Prisoners winding westward along the Kwanza River were men, women, and children with both Christian and non-Christian names that would shortly be counted in the first Virginia census; Antonio, Maria, Jiro, Francisco, and Margarida. Never in the history of the Atlantic slave trade would so many Africans from so small an area be taken in so short a time, greatly influencing the identity of the first African-American generation born at Jamestown a few months later, and culturally binding them fast together in a strange, new land.

❖

THE DISTANCE BETWEEN Kabasa in the highlands and Luanda on the western coast was over 150 miles. The forced exodus lasted from September 1618, the beginning of the Portuguese invasion, through April 1619. The exodus on average claimed 20 percent mortality. Adults—commoners and nobility alike—were bound about the neck with a large, forked tree branch and marched together in coffles. Young children were thrown into sacks to be toted to market. As Kabasa's survivors came down from the highlands to the ocean, to them the border of the Other World, they could see cavernous slave ships gathering on the coast to carry them west into the kingdom of spirits.

Entering Luanda, they were imprisoned within *quintalões* (slave enclosures), and stripped and branded with glowing irons on the sides of their bodies, with symbols identifying Angola as their port of origin. In this condition, many of the prisoners waited exposed for weeks and months as word carried across the Atlantic that large shipments of slaves could now be acquired at Luanda. During this time, scores of additional captives arrived daily from continuing Imbangala rampages into neighboring Christian Kongolese districts. Though soldiers and fierce dogs guarded the prisoners, Portuguese records reveal that the quintalões were so overcrowded with the thousands enslaved in Vasconcelos's campaign that hundreds of Ndongo captives left unattended simply walked away from Luanda. Their growing numbers along the Angolan coast in the following months created such a nuisance that the Portuguese governor sent repeated expeditions against them.

For the first time, supply outpaced demand, though not for long. Two months after Kabasa fell, Captain Manuel Mendes de Acuna, of the frigate *San Juan Bautista*, arrived among a swarm of Spanish slavers eager to export the human harvest. Acuna was a licensed trader from Seville who carried his employer's contract to export slaves.

To regulate the trade, Spain awarded general contractors exclusive contracts (*asientos*) to ship slaves to specific ports. These contractors were called *asentistas*. Lisbon banker Antonio Ferdandes Delvas, a New Christian who, despite his wealth, lived in fear of the Catholic Inquisition that had spread to his native country, had won an asiento contract to supply two ports in the Americas with slaves for the years 1615 to 1622. Each asentista was given a quota of Africans to be exported and, for his bid of 115,000 ducats annually, Delvas was allowed to ship between 3,500 and 5,000 Africans a year from Luanda, Angola to Cartagena, Columbia, and Vera Cruz, Mexico.

Delvas, who did not sail, had hired Captain Acuna and others to actually deliver Angolan captives to these two ports. A veteran of the Atlantic triangular trade, Acuna learned when he entered the port of Luanda in May 1619 that, on this voyage, he would not have to sail two hundred miles up the winding Congo River to the Maleba Pool to haggle over a handful of sickly captives in the humid inland *feira* slave markets of the back country. In his negotiations with Governor Vasconcelos, Acuna found the rates very reasonable and, around the middle of May 1619, began loading the first of 350 Bantu prisoners, or "pieces," males and females of all ages, onto the *Bautista*. The Bantu captives were mostly from the invasion of Ndongo, though among them may have been some Christian Bakongo prisoners captured in the civil war between Manikongo Álvaro III and the Duke of Nsundi, as well as some of Vasconcelos's Christian porters who had been seized by the Imbangala in the confusion of war. Upon reaching the ship's capacity of 350 prisoners, Captain Acuna slipped the *Bautista*'s mooring and departed from Angola under deceptively clear skies in late May 1619.

The *Bautista*, or "Baptist," was a prophetically named ship. For the Angolans onboard, her voyage to America that summer would be an especially harrowing baptism of travail, storm, and fire rarely experienced in the long and tragic history of the slave trade. There is no record in their own words expressing their great dread during that voyage, but among Angolans shipped on Portuguese and Spanish ships from Luanda in that same century were others who described the despair they shared with those buried alive in the *Bautista*. In the dark hold of the slave ship, writes Thornton, they revealed to each other their "chilling fear of being killed, eaten by white cannibals, crushed to make oil, or ground to make gunpowder that drove some of the human cargo on the ship to jump into the sea." Jose Monzolo, an Angolan nobleman who was enslaved and shipped to a Portuguese colony in South America, told priests in 1659 that the prisoners feared the Spanish slavers would kill them to "make the flags for the ships from their remains, for when they were red it was from the blood of the Moors, and desperately fearing this many threw themselves in the sea on the voyage." African prisoner Ottobah Cugoano stated that during a voyage to Grenada, the captives determined that death was preferable to whatever lay ahead: "a plan was concerted amongst us, that we might burn and blow up the ship, and to perish all together in the flames."

From this ordeal a brotherhood was born in the bowels of the slave ship. Since slaves traveling together had frequently been purchased together in quantity to work on large plantations or in mines, fellow voyagers who came over together on a particular vessel often remained close friends for life, united by a common ordeal. Africans on French vessels called themselves *bâtiments*, meaning "ships." Mbundu people, such as the Ndongo who came on Portuguese and Spanish slavers, identified themselves with a Kimbundu word for the ghostly beings who inhabited the Atlantic realm of Kalungu. The word was *malungu* and, for those Mbundu prisoners who survived the middle passage, it came to signify "comrades who came over the sea from the same homeland in the same ship." It is the earliest word to mean "African American."

White cannibals were fears of the imagination, but other killers—smallpox and dysentery—were real. African prisoner Venture Smith described his passage to Barbados in the same century, a voyage that despite a deadly outbreak of smallpox on board was considered reasonably successful. Upon arriving he testified that "there were found out of the two hundred and sixty that sailed from Africa, not more than two hundred alive."

Of the two thousand prisoners shipped on six slavers from Luanda to Mexico in 1619 under Delvas's asiento contract, only 1,161 Africans—

little more than half—were delivered alive. This was exceptionally high as compared to the 20 percent mortality typically expected.

As for the *Bautista*, at the end of June, one month into the voyage, Captain Acuna recorded that he "had many sick aboard, and many had already died." Before the frigate crossed the Atlantic and reached the West Indies a few weeks later, more than one hundred Africans on the *Bautista* had died of sickness. And Vera Cruz, her intended destination, was still nearly one thousand miles away.

Fearing the entire shipment would be dead before reaching Mexico, Captain Acuna paused briefly in the Caribbean for medicine and supplies that he paid for with twenty-four "slave boys he was forced to sell in Jamaica where he had to refresh." Of the original 350 Angolans who crossed on the *Bautista* in the summer of 1619, only 147 would finish the voyage to Vera Cruz in August. However, not all of the slaver's losses were due to sickness. Leaving Jamaica in early July, the slave ship had entered the Gulf of Mexico between Cuba and the tip of the Yucatán Peninsula when, on Saint Swithin's Day, July 15, and less than five hundred miles from Vera Cruz, Captain Acuna, while gazing at a massive band of low, ominous clouds coming in from Africa, first noticed that the *Bautista* was being stalked.

· 5 ·

Alias,
the "Dutchman"

IN CUBA, THEY still tell the legend of El Mulato (literally, "the mulatto"), the pirate born of a Spanish conquistador and a beautiful African slave, and who ran away from home at age thirteen to hide in the mangrove orchards on the Isle of the Pines, where he was captured by the greatest of the English privateers, Sir Francis Drake. Drake, upon observing the young man's vehemence against Spaniards, adopted him and took him to England where he reared him in the Puritan faith and gave him the surname "Grillo," meaning "cricket." Also called "Lucifer de los Mares" (Lucifer of the Seas), Diego Grillo, born the illegitimate son of Captain Domingo Galván Romero and an African woman on his Cuban plantation in 1558, grew to adulthood in England. With Drake's support during the reign of Elizabeth I, El Mulato went to sea in command of his own Puritan corsair, the *Spirit*, to ravage Catholic fleets around Cuba, and his name reached even the king of Spain. He frequently sailed in consort with Dutch Huguenot Sea Beggar captain Cornelio Jol, alias "Captain Wooden Leg" or "Peg-leg." Two decades later, Admiral Jol would mastermind the Dutch West India Company's capture of Luanda from the Portuguese.

Grillo's homeport was Devon, in the south of England, and there he knew two English Puritan privateers of equal notoriety—Daniel Elfrith, who sailed for Lord Robert Rich, and John Colyn Jope. Captain Jope, the so-called Dutch mystery man in John Rolfe's famous letter, and called "Flemish" in a letter that John Pory wrote to Sir Dudley Carleton, in fact came from Merifield in Stoke Climsland Hundred, near the Cornwall-Devon border of England, where he was a neighbor of Sir Francis Drake and Sir Walter Raleigh. Although the Jopes were of French-Belgium origin and John Colyn Jope sailed with Dutch papers, as was customary for English privateers during the reign of James I, his ancestors had come to England with William the Conqueror and he was an English subject, a Cornish man, and neither Flemish nor Dutch. Through his wife, Mary Glanvill, Jope was the brother-in-law of the powerful Sir John Glanvill, a noted jurist and a Member of Parliament, who lived nearby at Kilworthy in Tavistock. Sir Glanvill would organize the fleet for King Charles's attack against Cadiz, Spain, in 1625. Jope's high-powered connection may partly explain why Rolfe and Pory did not release Jope's full name in the international scandal that was about to explode.

A Calvinist minister, in 1619 thirty-nine-year-old Reverend Jope commanded the 140-ton *White Lion* sailing out of Plymouth, England, and Flushing, in the Netherlands. In discussing the first Africans to arrive in America, schoolbooks today refer to this vessel as "anonymous," though in fact the *White Lion* was a famous English warship. She was one of the corsairs in Francis Drake's fleet when he rampaged through the Spanish West Indies in 1585 and captured Cartagena. This seemingly cursed ship, then under Captain James Erisey, was responsible for Ralph Lane and his soldiers' evacuation of Roanoke in 1586, when she slipped an anchor during a storm shortly before the arrival of Sir Raleigh's one hundred English men, women, and children who, left unaided by Lane's departure, soon disappeared from the face of the earth. The *White Lion* also served as Lord Admiral Charles Howard's second ship against the Spanish Armada attack in 1588.

Early in 1619, about the time that Kabasa was being besieged by Portuguese governor Vasconcelos and the Imbangala, Captain Jope, with a crew of eighty men, set sail in the *White Lion* for the West Indies with a letters of marque from the Protestant Dutch Prince Maurice, son of William of Orange, authorizing him to take Spanish and Portuguese prizes. It was about that same time that Deputy Governor Samuel Argall and Secretary John Rolfe of Jamestown, Virginia, dispatched Daniel Elfrith and the *Treasurer* on her second raid of the West Indies on the orders of Lord Robert Rich, now the second Earl of Warwick. However, the *Treasurer*'s letters of marque were no longer valid, due to the peace treaty its sponsor, the Duke of Savoy, and King Philip III of Spain made before the warship left England for Virginia in 1618. Letters of marque supposedly distinguished a privateer from a pirate, but as English ambassador Sir Thomas Roe complained after another of Rich's ships attacked the junk of the Grand Moghul's mother in 1615, English ships carrying foreign marques were then viewed as little more than a "common pretence for Pirates." When the *Treasurer* went to the West Indies for her second raid in 1619, she had lost even her pretence and was now a full-fledged pirate vessel. Her noble owner and crew alike were in danger of being beheaded in the Tower of London like Sir Raleigh or hanged in the dockside gibbet if King James caught their ship plundering.

Prowling the West Indies separately in the summer of 1619, both Jope and Elfrith heard the widespread rumor that Captain Grillo, El Mulato, was planning to ambush a fleet of six Spanish treasure ships that gathered in their haven in the Bay of Nuevitas before setting out to Spain. Eager to join in the plunder, the two men, on opposite ends of the West Indies, both raced to Cuba to join him. They arrived too late. El Mulato had by then attacked the Spanish treasure fleet and, according to rumor, had already set sail to retire fabulously wealthy. Disappointed, Elfrith and Jope agreed to sail the *Treasurer* and the *White Lion* in tandem to hunt for prey. It was a natural consort. Both were Cornish and both, like Lord Rich for whom Elfrith worked, were fervent anti-Catholic Puritans. In late June, the hungry and armed *White Lion* and the *Treasurer* sailed from Cuba together to patrol the Windward Passage at the mouth of the Gulf of Mexico in hope of spotting a straggling Spanish gold ship bound for Europe.

After a few weeks, in the middle of July, they instead sighted the *San Juan Bautista* on the last leg of her long voyage from Luanda to

Mexico and, not knowing what cargo she carried, the pirates gave chase. The *White Lion* and the *Treasurer* were sleek men-of-war streamlined to outrace fat frigates, and they overtook the *Bautista* in the Gulf of Mexico's Bay of Campeche, a few hundred miles east of Vera Cruz. Trapped against the coast, the Spanish slave ship put up a fierce fight and damaged the *Treasurer* significantly. Outgunned by the two warships, however, the Spanish vessel took a ferocious pounding herself, and Captain Acuna was eventually forced to surrender his splintered ship and row himself and his crew ashore at Campeche while the pirates helped themselves to the prize. Jope, followed by Elfrith, boarded the smoking vessel and discovered, upon opening the cargo hatch that instead of Spanish gold, she carried African survivors from Vasconcelos's terrible assault on Kabasa five months earlier. Figuring ship capacity, food, water, and the distance to Jamestown, Jope and Elfrith selected sixty or so of the healthiest Bantu men, women, and children and transferred them to their vessels—about thirty or so for the *White Lion* and the same number for the *Treasurer*.

After the two English corsairs departed, the *Bautista* captain and his crew rowed back to the Spanish hulk to reclaim the remaining 147 African prisoners and to survey the damage. Captain Acuna determined the ship was no longer seaworthy and ordered his crew to row the surviving Africans to land. In the Spanish port in the Bay of Campeche, he hired another frigate, the *Santa Ana* commanded by Rodrigo Escobar, and transferred the Africans to her for the final few hundred miles to Mexico. The troubled voyage in which Captain Acuna had lost more than half of his three hundred Angolan captives would finally end in Vera Cruz at the latter end of August, about the same time that the *White Lion* and the *Treasurer* would appear in Chesapeake Bay off the Virginia coast.

❖

UNLIKE FRIGATES SUCH as the *Bautista* that contained up to four hundred passengers, corsairs did not have large cargo space for extra passengers. Because they were designed to subdue ships, they carried a much larger crew than did merchant vessels, and therefore they had to cram aboard more water and food in addition to gunpowder, cannon shot, muskets, and assorted war gear. Due to early Spanish occupation, there were few ports in the West Indies in the early seventeenth century in which English ships could resupply without fear of attack from the Spanish navy or Catholic pirates. The *Treasurer* had been at sea since the winter of 1618/19, and it was now summer and she was short of food and water. From later accounts it also clear that she had been substantially damaged in the fight with the *Bautista* and was likely taking water during the voyage to Jamestown.

Also extremely short of supplies was the *White Lion*. Captain Jope, it is known, at the time contemplated the unthinkable—casting some of the captured Angolans into the sea. The acting governor of Bermuda, Miles Kendall, reported that Jope on his return from attacking the slave ship, was forbidden by the governor

> to come into any of the said harbors. [Jope then] gave him notice that he had fourteen Negroes aboard which he should be forced to cast over board for want of victuals.

Kendall relented and, according to his statement, received fourteen of the *White Lion*'s African prisoners in payment for the food supplies.

The *White Lion*, followed four days later by the *Treasurer*, appeared in Chesapeake Bay in late August with Africans to trade. Relief, however, was brief. As details of their exploit against the Spanish slave ship spread over the Atlantic, a storm slowly began to build. For, as it happened, Captain Manuel Mendes de Acuna of the *Bautista* was a cousin by blood and by marriage to Diego Sarmiento de Acuna, otherwise known as Count Gondomar—the Spanish ambassador to King James' court who, just one year earlier, had persuaded James to behead Sir Walter Raleigh for piracy against Spain and who was now pursuing evidence against Lord Rich and the first English American colony of Jamestown for operating as a pirate base. The horrendous ordeal for the sixty-odd Bantu men, women, and children who had survived the bloody fall of

Kabasa, the deadly march to Luanda, and then the plagued voyage of the *Bautista*, only to be stolen by English pirates in a fierce sea battle, had not ended. Powerful men in England, Spain, and Virginia were about to enter a struggle over the purloined Africans that would eventually dissolve the Virginia Company's monopoly on North America. The first Africans arrived in English-speaking America in late August 1619, sixteen months before the Pilgrim *Mayflower* reached America. But, would they remain?

PART II

The Founders Land at Jamestown

ACCORDING TO THE Traditional account of the 1619 arrival of the first Africans, one day around the "latter end of August" an anonymous "Dutch man o war" under the command of a certain "Captain Jope" mysteriously appeared in Chesapeake Bay and traded "twenty and odd" Africans who came from who knows where, to the English settlers of Jamestown, Virginia. This detail-challenged official version is based on the vague and deliberately misleading accounts of two eyewitnesses, John Rolfe and John Pory, who were soon after accused by the king's Privy Council, as well as by the Virginia Company of London, of lying about what really happened that day to protect their patron, Lord Rich. The motive for obscuring the real story is obvious. King James, months earlier, had beheaded Rich's partner, Sir Walter Raleigh, for piracy.

Rolfe's and Pory's versions of that unknown day in the "latter end of August" were part of a deliberate cover-up of what came to be the most important incident early in English colonization that would determine the future shape and character of colonial America. If not for the scandal over this small group of stolen Africans, there would be no Maryland, no North Carolina, no Delaware, no Rhode Island, no Pennsylvania, no Maine, no Connecticut, no Massachusetts, and no Plymouth Colony.

There would have been no Catholic colonies, or Dissenter colonies, or Reform colonies. What is today the United States could very well have become a southern Canada, if not for the Black Mayflower voyages of 1619.

The conspiracy that erased that day from popular history still haunts Jamestown after four centuries.

As chapter 6 unfolds, Robert Rich's scheme is unmasked and the Virginia Company collapses. Then in chapter 7, the wily Count Gondomar discovers the missing Africans in Jamestown and moves to destroy the colony and recover what he regards as his property.

· 6 ·

Unmasked

TO UNDERSTAND WHY the combined voyages of the Black Mayflower was *the* decisive event in the development of thirteen original colonies, the investigation begins some months *before* the *White Lion* and the *Treasurer* joined forces to capture the *San Juan Bautista*.

London was abuzz with gossip as early as 1618 that Robert Rich's corsair was "roving on ye Spanish dominions in the West Indies," using Jamestown as her supply base. Nervously aware of King James's great hatred of pirates and of the jar that held Sir Walter Raleigh's severed head, a majority of stockholders in the Virginia Company of London opted to recall Rich's agents—Samuel Argall and John Rolfe—as deputy governor and secretary-recorder of colonial Virginia. In an earlier attempt, the company had ordered Virginia's absentee governor-for-life Thomas West, the Lord Delaware, to go to Jamestown and bring Argall back to London to answer questions. As part owner of the *Treasurer* with Rich and therefore implicated in that vessel's piracy, Lord West reluctantly set sail from England in his ship *Neptune* in 1618. But, before arriving in Virginia, he and dozens of his servants mysteriously perished at sea.

William Camden, chronicler in King James's court, recorded at the time that Lord West had died "not without suspicion of poison." It happened that Captain Daniel Elfrith and the *Treasurer* had encountered the *Neptune* at sea as Lord West was sailing to Jamestown. It was rumored in London that someone from the *Treasurer* assassinated West to prevent him from ousting Argall and Rolfe from Virginia. The widowed Lady Delaware publicly suspected that Lord Robert Rich was behind her husband's death, a death she described as "notorious" in complaints she later made against Rich, Argall, and Rolfe. Lady Delaware was probably steered by Rich's enemies in the Virginia Company to accuse him and his agents of the dark deed.

Though he was not responsible, Rich benefited from West's death, for the Virginia Company of London now hesitated in recalling Argall and Rolfe out of fear of alienating one of the only two prestigious lords remaining in the company. Investors hoped Lord Rich would get the message and cease using Jamestown as a pirate base. He did not, for when crewmembers of Lord West's trouble-plagued *Neptune* returned to London later in 1618, they reported to the company that they had witnessed something suspicious at the time that the *Treasurer* pulled alongside the stricken ship to offer assistance.

At his departure from England earlier in 1618, just before meeting the *Neptune*, Captain Daniel Elfrith of the *Treasurer* had sworn by oath to government officials at Gravesend that he intended to sail his vessel to Jamestown and from there go on a fishing voyage to Cape Cod. This cover story was necessary because King James's police patrolled London's docks to inspect English ships for evidence of privateering. Elfrith persuaded Gravesend officials, likely through a bribe, that the *Treasurer* would be engaged in legitimate trade when she left England. A few weeks later when it came alongside Lord West's stricken ship at sea, Captain Edward Brewster of the *Neptune* observed that

> the *Treasurer* was not provided for a fishing voyage nor had salt, hooks, lines, fishermen, or men skilled in fishing at the tyme she was set forth from the port of London, nor other things that were fitting for a fishing voyage.

Upon clearing the Port of London, the *Treasurer*'s crew had carelessly thrown off the camouflage of fishing tackle to reveal, as Brewster reported:

> powder, shot, wastclothes, ordinance, streamers, flags and other furniture fit for a man of war . . . laden aboard her by the means, knowledge, or direction of Captain Argall.

The *Neptune*'s startling news that the *Treasurer* was heavily armed for war alerted Virginia Company stockholders that Lord Rich was still using Jamestown as a base of operations for illegal raids on the Spanish West Indies. The company had good cause for alarm. The paper trail linking it to the rogue *Treasurer* was as troubling as the timing of the news. The corsair was owned by two prominent members of the company and was leased to the company to be "wholly employed in trade and other services, for relieving the colony."

It was also well-known that Lord Rich had supplied sailors and arms to Sir Raleigh for the Guiana expedition. Furthermore, King James's Spanish friend, the influential Gondomar, was said to be investigating Robert Rich over the *Treasurer*'s 1616 adventure in the West Indies. Most Virginia Company stockholders were concerned that should King James regard the company as complicit with the Earl of Warwick in the *Treasurer*'s piracies, he might revoke the Virginia charter and dissolve the firm. Therefore, when the returning *Neptune* crew alerted the company that Rich's pirates were preparing to launch yet another raid on the Spanish West Indies, the shareholders determined to finally go through with recalling Argall and Rolfe and face the fallout of accusing Rich, one of its most prominent investors, of piracy.

Sir Edwin Sandys, a Member of Parliament, was appointed president of the Virginia Company at this time and it fell to him to run the pirates out of Jamestown. Sandys controlled the majority of stockholder votes, and the company appointed his friend and loyal ally Sir George Yeardley the new governor of Virginia with orders to sail to Jamestown to replace Argall and question him about stolen booty that "it is reported he hath gotten together to the Colony's prejudice." Argall was also to be investigated for seizing company assets in the colony, including Lord Delaware's trade goods from the *Neptune*.

As soon as Yeardley replaced Argall, Lord Rich reacted quickly to save both his protégé and the loot that was stashed in his storehouse at Jamestown. Delaying Yeardley's departure from England for a few days, Rich in the early spring of 1619 secretly launched a small fast ship, the *Eleanor*, to speed to Virginia. The *Eleanor* crossed the Atlantic just in time. Ten days before Sir Yeardley sailed into Chesapeake Bay to arrest Argall, "there arrived a little Pinnace privately from England about Easter for Captain Argall, who taking order for his affaires, within four or five days returned in her." Sir Yeardley was forced to send word to London that, upon docking at Jamestown, he found "Argall . . . gone with his riches." More ominous, the *Treasurer* was also missing.

About five weeks after fleeing Jamestown, Samuel Argall arrived in Plymouth, England, in Rich's pinnace (a light sailing ship) with the booty he had amassed at Jamestown. Coincidentally, two agents representing the English Pilgrim Separatist exiles in Leyden, Holland, were in London at the time seeking a patent from the Virginia Company to allow the Pilgrims to settle in Jamestown. On May 8, 1619, Robert Cushman reported bad news in a letter to the congregation in Holland. The Pilgrims' request was tabled indefinitely by the company because of a great uproar among the stockholders over an unrelated matter. Cushman described the cause of that trouble:

> Captain Argall is come home this week (he upon notice of the intent of the Counsel, came away before Sir George Yeardley came there, and so there is no small dissention) . . . it seemeth he came away secretly.

After coming ashore at Devon, Argall packed up the loot and sent it to Lord Rich and then went to London to confront the company. President Sandys called a special session to ask Lord Rich and the ousted Argall the burning questions of the hour—where was the *Treasurer* at that moment and what was she doing? (At this time the *Treasurer* and the *White Lion* in fact had just joined in consort off Cuba and were a few weeks away from the fateful meeting with the *Bautista* in the Bay of Campeche). During that meeting in London, neither Argall nor Rich divulged the *Treasurer*'s location nor the purpose of her voyage. Instead, Lord Rich's friends within the company raised their voices against the Sandys faction, and rash accusations and countercharges of "treason" flew from both sides. Such recriminations were lethal to the reputation and morale of the investment firm. Leaks about the clamorous rift between these high lords and knights of England spread to waterfront taverns to the great manor halls. The prestigious stockholders of the Virginia Company were described as so fractious "that Guelfs and Ghibellines were not more animated one against another."

The first sword was drawn during the next Virginia Company shareholders' meeting a few weeks later at the Earl of Southampton's palatial estate in a fashionable London riverside suburb. The prominent Southampton was a leading voice with Sir Sandys in calling for reforming Jamestown. The business meeting at Southampton's estate was an important gathering—England's ranking lords and financiers came to lay the foundation of empire—but the troubling *Treasurer* affair again dominated the meeting. Voices grew louder until one of Sandys's supporters, Captain Edward Brewster, one of the survivors from the *Neptune*'s poisoned crew a year earlier, suddenly rose, brandishing his sword to challenge Samuel Argall to fight. Confronted in Southampton's home, Argall, who was up for a knighthood and did not want to be arrested for dueling, coolly declined the invitation with, according to eyewitnesses, "as fair terms as he could." But Captain Brewster, "not being satisfied did swear that he would revenge himself upon Samuel Argall with his sword."

A few days later on a public street, Captain Brewster pulled his blade again and blocked Argall, who was coming down the steps of the Sheriff's Court in the Guildhall of London. Having just paid a sizable bond on a warrant sworn against him by Sandys's allies, Argall was now in the mood to accept Brewster's challenge and drew "his sword to defend himself." Argall proved the better swordsman and, according to eyewitnesses, "made two or three most dangerous thrusts against the body of Brewster but he did not or could not pierce his body." Those who witnessed the duel suspected that Captain Brewster was wearing armor beneath his clothing, very much in violation of the dueling code. The outcome after a fatal blow from Brewster would have been the deliberate murder of Samuel Argall. Quickly realizing his vulnerability, Argall closed with Brewster and "took his sword from him which he did give to a Constable."

In May, June, and July 1619, as the Rich and Sandys factions glared at each other across the table while waiting for the *Treasurer* to surface somewhere in the Atlantic, the Pilgrim application to settle in Jamestown was tabled. John Cushman wrote to the Separatist congregation in Holland that

> the Virginia Counsel was now so disturbed with factions and quarrels amongst themselves, as no business could well go forward . . . ever since we came up no business could by them be dispatched.

Time was running out for the Pilgrims. English Puritans and Separatists were strongly influenced by Calvinist doctrine that required the separation of Church and State, and they strongly opposed England's monarchs holding the dual office of head of the Anglican Church. Anglican archbishop William Laud, with King James's approval, had sent agents into Holland seeking to arrest outspoken Separatist leaders in exile and extradite them to England to be tortured, tried, imprisoned, or executed. The Pilgrims' hope of escaping to Guiana had faded, following the Raleigh debacle and the king's withdrawal of Rich's Amazon charter in 1619. Both Lord Rich and Sir Sandys were sympathetic to the plight of the Leyden Separatists, and, if not for their squabble over the *Treasurer* affair, the Pilgrims would no doubt have received a patent from the Virginia Company, and history would be ignorant of Plymouth Rock. But because of the company's schism that summer, the Pilgrims were forced to stand by in Holland. Their future, though they did not know it at the time, rested on two ships about to attack a Spanish frigate loaded with enslaved Africans captured at the fall of Kabasa.

❖

MEANWHILE IN JAMESTOWN that same summer, Governor Yeardley and a few settlers loyal to Sandys kept London updated almost weekly on the latest rumors about the *Treasurer*'s movements at sea. Sir Yeardley and cape merchant Abraham Piersey wrote Edwin Sandys that the *Treasurer* was expected to return any day from "seeking Pillage in the West Indies of the King of Spain's Subjects," and they claimed to have evidence that her raid was indeed sanctioned "by direction from my Lord of Warwick." Anxious that Sir Yeardley press the investigation, Sir Sandys sent him a letter stressing the point:

> We cannot but in particular commend you carefully upon the proceedings of the *Treasurer* set out by Capt. Argall . . . we pray you therefore according to our former instructions that nothing be neglected in that business.

Then the president of the Virginia Company made a fantastic blunder. He broke the law. In mid-June, the *White Lion* and the *Treasurer* joined in consort off Cuba to take Spanish prizes. On June 21, three weeks *before* the pirate attack on the *Bautista*, Sandys, without the consent of the full company, sent a letter ordering Governor Yeardley to

> give diligent order that the ship [*Treasurer*] be seized upon immediately upon her return [to Jamestown], and examination taken of her course and proceeding that Justice may be done to all parties as the case shall require.

At the time he issued the secret order that Rich's corsair "be seized upon," Sandys had only a suspicion that the *Treasurer* was about to commit piracy. Yet he instructed Yeardley to confiscate a fellow Englishman's private property without prior complaint filed by the offended party (in this case, Spain). Sandys's order was a blatant violation of due process and had been given despite the fact that he was the Member of Parliament leading the fight to subject King James to law. To most Englishmen, this unlawful order was worse than Rich's piracy. Sandys gambled that the *Treasurer* would return with Spanish contraband, as in fact she would—in the form of the *Bautista*'s Africans. But without a formal complaint first being filed by a victim, which was impossible because no crime had yet been committed, he violated Lord Rich's rights, and any future action that the company contemplated against Rich in court was now compromised.

The blundering did not end. In Jamestown, Sir Yeardley revealed the secret order to seize the *Treasurer* to a few top officials, including, amazingly, to John Rolfe. Perhaps Yeardley was distracted. The summer of 1619 was a giddy time for the young colony: another event momentarily eclipsed the ongoing *Treasurer* controversy. With approval from Parliament and the Company, in July Jamestown elected its first assembly to govern its affairs, the first representative institution in America.

At the end of August, one month later, completely unaware of the growing turmoil their piracy had provoked on both sides of the Atlantic, the *White Lion* and the *Treasurer* arrived in Chesapeake Bay with, between them, the sixty African men, women, and children from the *Bautista*.

Captain John Colyn Jope and the *White Lion* were the first to land. Kecoughton, also known then as Point Comfort (now Old Point Comfort), was a small colonial outpost built on the shore of Chesapeake Bay between the mouths of the James and York rivers to prevent hostile ships from reaching Jamestown forty miles upriver. All arriving vessels were required to stop first at Point Comfort and send upriver for the governor's permission to proceed on to Jamestown. John Rolfe and John Pory, two men implicated with Lord Rich and Samuel Argall, left the only accounts of what happened that day and what they wrote must be reviewed critically.

As the colony's outgoing recorder, Rolfe was still obligated to send shipping reports for the fiscal year 1619 to his enemy Sir Sandys, the company president in London. The widower of Pocahontas stated in the carefully edited report filed in January 1620, that

> at the latter end of August 1619 a Dutch man of war of the burden of a 160 tons arrived at Point Comfort. The Commander's name Capt. Jope, his Pilot for the West Indies one Mr. Marmaduke, an Englishman. They met with the *Treasurer* in the West Indies, and determined to hold consort ship hitherward, but in their passage lost one the other . . . [Jope] brought not anything but 20 and odd Negroes, which the Governor [George Yeardley] and Cape Merchant [Abraham Piersey] bought for victuals (whereof he was in great need as he pretended) at the best and easiest rate they could.

Rolfe recorded that the *White Lion* (he purposefully did not identify the ship by name) traded about two dozen Africans she had seized from a Spanish prize, to Yeardley and Piersey, new officers loyal to Edwin Sandys. Rolfe implied that Jope was allowed to trade at Jamestown only because the colony had compassion: Jope, said he, pleaded that he had to refresh in Virginia or starve "as he pretended." (Captain Jope probably threatened to throw the Africans overboard at Jamestown, as he had threatened when Captain Miles Kendall refused to let him anchor at Bermuda.) Rolfe also pointed out that

> [Jope] had a large and ample Commission from his Excellency [the Dutch Prince Maurice of Nassau] to range and to take purchase in the West Indies.

However, Rolfe did not write in his report to Sandys that Lord Rich's *Treasurer* also carried Africans when she arrived in Virginia four days behind the *White Lion*, and he omitted it for good reason. As noted, the *Treasurer*'s marque had expired months earlier when the Duke of Savoy made peace with Spain, and thus her participation with the *White Lion* in the attack on the Spanish *Bautista* was an illegal act of piracy.

Carrying a valid letters of marque, however, the *White Lion* was duly licensed by a foreign prince to take Spanish prizes and there was therefore less controversy about her participation in the *Bautista*'s capture. This was a key defense point that arose in later accusations leveled against Rich and Argall in London. Lord Rich and his agents would claim that Captain Elfrith legally purchased the Africans from the *White Lion* only *after* Captain Jope alone took them from the *Bautista*. Rich would further claim that the *Treasurer* was not involved at all in the attack on the Spanish slave vessel. But Lord Rich's version did not explain why the *Treasurer* returned from her West Indies voyage so damaged that she was like as "not to put to sea ever again." Or why Captain Acuna of the *Bautista* stated to Spanish authorities in August that, on "the voyage inbound, he was robbed at sea off the Coast of Campeche by English corsairs." His testimony of "corsairs" in plural implicated the *Treasurer* as taking part in the attack along with the *White Lion*.

In describing the arrival in Chesapeake Bay of the *Treasurer* behind the *White Lion*, Rolfe was in the very least derelict in not identifying her cargo, and his letter only noted that Lord Rich's ship did not stay long in the colony because, for some reason he did not explain, no one would trade with her

> three or four days [after the *White Lion*] the *Treasurer* arrived. At [Elfrith's] arrival he sent word presently to the Governor to know his pleasure, who wrote to him and did request myself, Leiftenante [William] Pierce and Mr. Ewens [William Evans] to go down to him, to desire him to come up to James City. But before we got down he had set sail and was gone out of the [Chesapeake] Bay. The occasion hereof happened by the unfriendly dealing of the inhabitants of Kecnoughton [Point Comfort], for he was in great want of victuals, wherewith they would not relieve him nor his company upon any terms.

As Rolfe described, the *Treasurer* mysteriously departed Virginia after spending just a few hours in the bay. But Rolfe also neglected to mention in the letter to Sandys that he, Rolfe, had actually helped the ship escape before Yeardley could seize her.

Upon bringing the *Treasurer* into Point Comfort that day, Captain Elfrith had sent word to the governor in Jamestown forty miles upriver to know his pleasure. He expected that governor to be his employer, Samuel Argall, who in fact had fled Jamestown a few months earlier to avoid being arrested by Yeardley. Alerted to Elfrith's confusion and mindful of Sandys's directive to seize the ship, Governor Yeardley quickly appointed a delegation of friendly faces—John Rolfe, lieutenant William Pierce, and merchant planter William Evans—to go down to Point Comfort to lure the *Treasurer* up the James River to Jamestown, where he would be waiting with the colonial militia to seize the pirates and their booty. Rolfe claimed that while he and his two companions were rowing down the James River to Point Comfort, Captain Elfrith took the *Treasurer* out to sea and fled the colony; and that he, Rolfe, then returned to Jamestown and informed Yeardley that the corsair had disappeared before he got to Point Comfort.

Rolfe's version was not what actually happened. Though Argall was gone, his influence at Jamestown was still strong, and Yeardley could not have made a more unwise choice of men to entice the *Treasurer* to come up to Jamestown. In the same letter in which Rolfe described the arrival of the two ships to Virginia Company president Edwin Sandys, Rolfe himself acknowledged that he was implicated in wrongdoing with Argall and, furthermore, he defended the ousted governor to Sandys:

Withall in conclusion [I] cannot choose but reveal unto you the sorrow I conceive to hear of the many accusations heaped upon Captain Argall with whom my reputation hath been unjustly jointed, but I am persuaded he will answer well for himself. Here have also been diverse depositions taken and sent home by the *Diana*, I will tax no man therein: but when it shall come to farther trial, I assure you that you shall find many dishonest and faithless men to Captain Argall, who have received much kindness at his hands and to his face will contradict, and be ashamed of much, which in his absence they have intimated against him. Lastly, I speak on my own experience for these 11 years, I never amongst so few, have seen so many falsehearted, envious and malicious people (yea amongst some who march in the better rank) nor shall you ever hear of any the justest Governor here, who shall live free, from their scandal and shameless exclamations, if way be given to their report.

Rolfe was not the only person closely linked to Argall in the small party that Yeardley sent to Point Comfort to greet the *Treasurer*. William Pierce had been appointed by then governor Samuel Argall to command the colony's militia in 1617. Furthermore, following the death of Pocahontas, John Rolfe had married Pierce's daughter. Also appointed by Argall in 1617 was Captain William Tucker, who commanded the Jamestown port of entry at Point Comfort. Tucker was the brother-in-law of Maurice Thomson, who just happened to be Lord Rich's business manager. Argall, while governor, had placed these men in vital positions to abet the comings and goings of the *Treasurer*. Now, though fled, he still had friends in high office at Jamestown. Governor Yeardley had removed none of these men after arriving in Jamestown and in fact had sent them to coax the *Treasurer* into his trap. Small wonder the vessel escaped.

There is more evidence of a conspiracy to help the corsair flee. A few of the *Treasurer*'s share of stolen Africans at that time mysteriously appeared on Jamestown plantations owned by Argall's agents. One of the group that Yeardley dispatched to meet the ship at Point Comfort was William Evans, who was soon afterward found in possession of a young Angolan man named "John." Rolfe's new father-in-law also obtained an African: The 1625 Virginia census shows that a black woman named Angelo, or Angola, listed that year in Pierce's household in Jamestown, had arrived in Virginia "on the *Treasurer*." Since the vessel was reported sunk in a nearby creek in February 1620, the timing requires that Angelo entered the household of Pierce as one of the prisoners taken from the *Bautista* by the *Treasurer* and delivered to Jamestown in August.

In addition, an old inventory of Captain William Tucker's household at Point Comfort in 1625 reveals the presence of an African man and woman named Antonio and Isabell, and their young son William. It might be presumed that Antonio and Isabell were part of the "20 and odd" Africans that the captain of the *White Lion* sold to Yeardley and Piersey in 1619. However, the men purchased these Africans not to sell to other planters, but to work on their own plantations further up the James River, as their probated wills reveal. The presence in the colony of Angelo, William, Isabell, and John indicates that Tucker, Pierce, Rolfe, and Evans—men friendly to Lord Rich and Samuel Argall—all met Daniel Elfrith at Point Comfort on that controversial day in late August, *before* Elfrith took the *Treasurer* out to sea a few hours later.

There was another conspirator. John Pory had arrived in Jamestown with Sir Yeardley in June as the colony's new secretary, to take over duties formerly held by John Rolfe. Pory, a one-time Member of Parliament and the translator of Leo Africanus's *Description of Africa* that influenced Jonson's *Masque of Blackness*, was to make history the following month as the first elected Speaker of Virginia's House of Burgesses. But unknown to the company at the time it sent him to replace Rolfe, and revealed only when secret letters were misdirected, John Pory, like Rolfe, was a secret agent for Lord Rich. Pory's letter describing the arrival in Jamestown of the *White Lion* and the *Treasurer* was also deliberately written to protect Lord Rich, but Pory took a different tack than did Rolfe. He completely omitted any reference to pirated Africans. According to Pory, in his letter to Sir Dudley Carleton at The Hague that September, the occasion of Jope's arrival in Jamestown

> was an accidental consortship in the West Indies with the *Treasurer*, an English man of war also, licensed by a commission from the Duke of Savoy to take Spaniards as lawful prize.

Pory, like Rolfe, avoided identifying the *White Lion* by name and made absolutely no mention of Africans or stolen Spanish booty when recording the arrivals of the *White Lion* and the *Treasurer*, though it was his job as secretary-recorder to do so. Pory also claimed that the *Treasurer*'s Savoy marque was still valid when it was not.

Pory accidentally revealed that the *White Lion*, though a ship licensed in Flushing (Vlissingen, the Netherlands), was not Dutch but was indeed an English ship, when he described her as an "English man of war *also*" [italics added].

John Pory was aware of the growing firestorm in the London Company and in King James's court over the *Treasurer*'s pirate voyages to the West Indies. He was aware because the company had appointed him, with Yeardley, to reform the colony and identify pirates. While Pory did not deny that the *Treasurer* was raiding the West Indies in 1619, he blamed Samuel Argall to shield the true mastermind, Lord Rich, who he depicted as merely the innocent bewildered owner of the corsair:

> Hither she [the *Treasurer*] came to Captain Argall then governor of this colony, being part owner of her. He more for love of gain the root of all evil than for any true love he bore to this Plantation [Jamestown] victualed and manned her anew and sent her with the same Commission [the invalid Savoy marque] to range the Indies.

When Pory was caught exchanging damning letters with his secret benefactor Rich, he smoothly explained to the enraged Sandys:

> [If Lord Rich] be offended in ought, it will be in respect of his more than ordinary affection towards Captain Argall, whose faults Sir George Yeardley was bound by commission, and for the saving of his own reputation also, to discover. Yeardley, I think, would not rob Captain Argall of [Lord Rich's] love, for he hath in him to deserve much, nor would he have his lordship to have spent so much love upon any man in vain.

Lord Rich, wrote Pory, was to be faulted only for trying to reform the wayward Argall and "only doth wish that Captain Argall being rich, a Bachelour and devoid of charge, would not so excessively intend his own thrift." In fact, everything Argall did, he did on Rich's orders. Historian Alexander Brown concluded that the letters written by Rolfe and

Pory describing the 1619 arrival of the Africans "were evidently written more for the purpose of concealing the facts than of revealing them."

After being alerted by Rolfe, Pierce, Evans, and Tucker of his pending arrest, Captain Elfrith immediately took the *Treasurer* and her remaining two dozen Africans out to sea and fled for Bermuda and its English colony, where Lord Rich owned a tobacco plantation. The Bermuda colony was chartered to the Bermuda (or Somers Island) Company of London, mostly made up of Virginia Company investors. Interim Bermuda governor Miles Kendall, who was loyal to the Sandys faction, seized the *Treasurer* and confiscated her Africans when she arrived in September 1619. A few weeks later, Nathaniel Butler, a man loyal to Lord Rich, arrived as the new Bermuda governor and promptly confiscated the Africans from Kendall on behalf of Rich. The company then took the questionable stance that the *Treasurer*'s Africans, stolen or not, were rightfully the joint property of all of its investors and started a nasty struggle with Rich over their ownership.

To make matters worse for Rich, Captain Nathaniel Powell captured one of the *Treasurer*'s officers at Jamestown and took him to Governor Yeardley, who wrung from him a confession that the ship had robbed a Spanish vessel by Lord Rich's direction. Yeardley passed on this news to Edwin Sandys in London. To distance the company from the *Treasurer*'s involvement in the *Bautista* African piracy, Sandys took this information to the king's Privy Council. Lord Rich and his pirate accomplices were caught by surprise, according to historian Wesley Craven:

> Sandys assembled the council, without in this case giving previous notification to Warwick, made public the contents of Yeardley's letter, and declared it to be their duty in his opinion to notify the privy council. This notification was given on February 25, 1620, when Sandys appeared before the lords of the [privy] council and disavowed any connection of the company with the *Treasurer*. He also produced a letter to show that the Spanish agent in London [Gondomar would not return to England until a few weeks later] had received full satisfaction as to the company's

part in the affair. This involved no little danger to Warwick, for not only did it threaten "suddenly ere he was aware a confiscation of his ship and goods," but it involved also a personal danger of no small consequence.

The Earl of Southampton had just sought to reconcile Rich and Sandys by getting Rich to agree to abandon Jamestown as a pirate base if Sandys agreed to keep his name out of the investigation. But now Sandys had violated this agreement that he and Rich had just solemnized by oath in a church. His revelation to the king's Privy Council of testimony illegally forced from one of the *Treasurer*'s crewmen and implicating Rich, doubly incensed the Earl of Warwick and persuaded him that Sandys intended to see him executed on the gallows for the act of piracy. Sandys had even notified the Spanish agent who was standing in for the absent Count Gondomar. Astounded at being betrayed by a countryman and mindful of the fate of Sir Raleigh, Lord Rich upon learning of Sandys's testimony, prayed

> God deliver me from the clemency of the Spaniard and from them that would inform for him, especially without warning.

Lord Rich protested that Sandys's public revelations about the *Bautista*-African affair left him, not only

> in the mercy of our own king, but [he] must have been brought under the clutches of the king of Spain which perhaps would not have been removed till he had crushed him to pieces.

The last hope of reconciliation betrayed, the Virginia Company of London spiraled to destruction. The feud surfaced in court from 1622 to 1623, when Lady Delaware and the first Duke of Buckingham filed lawsuits against Argall seeking to recover financial losses. Buckingham, George Villiers, was King James's favorite. He had invested in the trade goods that were sent over to Virginia with Lord Delaware on the 1618 voyage of the *Neptune*. Buckingham and Lady Delaware maintained that they incurred losses because Argall, while governor of Virginia, had forced some of the *Neptune*'s crew to serve aboard the *Treasurer* on the voyage that seized the *Bautista*'s Africans in July 1619. They also accused Argall of selling off the *Neptune*'s trade goods after Lord Delaware's death, and pocketing the proceeds.

Parliament was then engaged against King James in the opening duel between republicanism and absolutism that would continue to vex England for the next few decades. Referring to the *Bautista* piracy and the subsequent company squabble over the ownership of pirated Africans, King James lashed out against Edwin Sandys and the House of Commons by declaring the Virginia Company to be a seminary to a seditious parliament. Ordered by James to investigate the dissension within the company, the Privy Council eventually issued its report:

> [It] is notoriously known how they with Captain Argoll [*sic*] and other friends, partly peradventure through discontent for being removed from their places, but principally through fear, (their accounts, depredations, piracies and misgovernment being now questioned before the Counsel and in the Company's Courts), perpetually disturbed and disgraced by several ways, both to his Majesty and to the world, all the present proceedings of the Company, to the great disheartening of the Company here, and no small disadvantage of the Colony.

His enemies' campaign to destroy him even provoked Lord Rich to challenge Sandys's ally Lord Cavendish to a duel. England at this time had only recently embraced this lesser-praised innovation of the Renaissance dubbed the "duel of honor," or the "private affair of honor." The affair of honor drew immediate condemnation from King James when, in 1609, two of his favorites, the Scotsman Sir James Stewart and the Englishman Sir George Wharton, had a falling-out and butchered each other on the field at Isington in the first widely reported English duel of honor between gentlemen. Grieved by the senseless loss of his two friends, King James had them both buried in the same grave at Isington and then issued the "Proclamation against Private Challenges and

Combats," in which he banned dueling as "a vein that bleeds both incessantly and inwardly." James's hatred of dueling was why Argall, who was about to be knighted by the king, had been reluctant to cross swords with Brewster earlier. The king had ordered Attorney General Francis Bacon to vigorously prosecute duelists regardless of their social rank and further campaigned against dueling by requiring that all royal portraits show him holding a walking cane instead of the obligatory rapier then in vogue in portraits of the English nobility. Nevertheless, dueling continued unofficially in England and, after the revelation of the *Bautista* affair, King James's officers had to scramble to prevent a rash of confrontations involving Lord Robert Rich and Captain Samuel Argall against their enemies in the Virginia Company of London.

Lord Rich, an accomplished swordsman, was more willing than was the cautious Argall to call out their enemies. To elude the king's officers, in July 1623 Rich proposed to Lord Cavendish that they cross the Channel and fight each other in Ghent. Upon learning this, King James ordered Rich and Cavendish to remain in England under house arrest. Cavendish complied but Rich, bent on revenge for the loss of his ship and the collapse of his piracy scheme, disobeyed and crossed the Channel to keep the appointment, disguised as a common fishmonger, with the king's officers in hot pursuit. Several days later, a member of the Privy Council wrote a letter to Lord Rich's distraught wife informing her of her husband's detainment in Ghent and his pending return under house arrest.

After being taken back to London and eventually released on his oath that he would not pursue the skewering of Cavendish, Lord Rich set about using his political influence to bring down those in the Virginia Company whom he believed were plotting to send him to the scaffold over the *Bautista* affair. He presented a petition to King James that contained "many scandalous suggestions as well against the whole [Virginia] Company, as some special Members thereof." King James investigated Lord Rich's complaints and, already bitterly angry at Edwin Sandys for his parliamentary opposition to royal monopolies and the Spanish marriage, ordered the anti-Rich leaders of the company to be placed under house arrest for defaming Rich. In response, Sir Sandys and Lord Cavendish presented a counterpetition to King James, again alleging that

Rich had sent the *Treasurer* to attack the *Bautista*, resulting in the theft of Spain's Africans. Perhaps foolishly expecting King James's gratitude, Sir Sandys was stunned when James ordered his Privy Council to seize the Virginia Company's books for a general audit.

King James used as an excuse to get the firm's records, an "anonymous" pamphlet then circulating in London. After Rich's agent, Nathaniel Butler, arrived as governor of Bermuda in late 1619 and got into a fight with investors over the legal ownership of the *Treasurer*'s Africans, the firm accused him of setting up Bermuda as a pirate base for Lord Rich, just as Argall had done previously in Jamestown. In addition, Count Gondomar, upon returning to England in March 1620, had persuaded King James to launch an investigation of Lord Rich to recover those same Africans as Spanish property stolen from his cousin's ship. Just before a commission arrived in Bermuda in 1622 to interrogate Butler and seize the Africans in question, Lord Rich, as he had done in rescuing Argall from arrest at Jamestown in 1619, sent a fast ship to Bermuda to save Butler. To evade the Privy Council inquiry, Nathaniel Butler cooled his heels in Virginia and there penned an anonymous article entitled "The Unmasked Face of Our Colony in Virginia," which blasted Sandys and the London-based company for mishandling Jamestown's administration.

King James was delighted with Butler's article. By 1622 he had determined to take over the Jamestown colony personally, and Butler's much publicized pamphlet gave the king a legal reason to assign the Privy Council to seize the London firm's records. In doing so, King James had found an opportunity to solve a problem of his own making: his emptying of the royal purse on frivolities. Raleigh's golden city had evaporated, and the king was the poorer for investing in it. Plays like *Masque of Blackness*, along with banquets, games, hunting parties, and tilting tournaments, were expensive and, having sold every monopoly he controlled, James was plagued with mounting bills because the unsympathetic Parliament refused to raise taxes to bail him out. William Camden had recorded in his diary as early as February 1619 that the "King commands his Privy Councilors to deliberate how to raise money to clear his debts." By dissolving the Virginia Company and taking over Jamestown and its lucrative tobacco trade, the king would not only improve his private finances but also strike a vengeful blow at the investors, such as Edwin Sandys, who were his leading critics in Parliament. The business's bitter internal feud gave him a valid reason to do so.

After the king's lawyers audited the firm's finances in view of Nathaniel Butler's charges, the bad news was announced to the gathered investors of the Virginia Company in London on May 7, 1623. Lord Cavendish was required to stand and read before the investors the reasons that King James gave for dissolving the company. James accused the company of harboring pirates and, above all, cited the *Treasurer*'s involvement in stealing Africans from the Spanish slaver in 1619:

> Neither could this depredation of that colony [Virginia] content but a ship called the *Treasurer* set forth by the said Earl of Warwick and sent to Virginia on an old Commission of hostility from the Duke of Savoy against the Spaniards procured by some means and put into the hands of the said Captain, the said *Treasurer* being manned with the ablest men of the Colony and new victualed from thence, was set out on Roving on ye Spanish Dominions in the West Indies, where after sundry Acts of Hostility committed and some purchase gotten she returned to Virginia at the end of ten months or thereabouts. But finding Capt. Argall, the setter of her out, departed from thence, she withdrew herself instantly from the new Governor's power and went to ye Somer Islands [Bermuda] then discharging her booty, *in which were a certain number of Negroes.*

Sandys and Cavendish appealed to Parliament to overturn the dissolution of the Virginia Company, but on April 28, 1624, King James firmly informed the House of Commons that the affairs of Virginia were now the Crown's concern and no longer within Parliament's jurisdiction:

> Whereas we have taken notice that some of the Virginia Company have presented a Petition to our House of Commons, and doubting it might occasion the repetition and renewing of those Discords, and Contentions, which have been amongst them and which by our great care, and the Directions of our Counsel are in a good way to be composed, We

do signify to our House of Commons, that we hold it very unfit for the Parliament to trouble themselves with those matters, which can produce nothing, but a further increase in schisms and faction and disturb the happy and peaceable proceeding of the Parliament which we hope your cares (as hitherto they have done) shall concur with ours to bring to a good issue. As for these businesses of Virginia, and the Bermudas, ourself have taken them to heart, and will make it our own work to settle the quiet and welfare of those Plantations, and will be ready to do anything that may be for the real benefit and advancement of them.

With this, the Virginia Company of London was dissolved, and its monopoly to settle North America, broken. The Atlantic coast was opened for colonization, at the discretion of the kings of England, to a broad range of interests, faiths, and commercial ventures under the British flag as a result of an act of piracy that delivered a handful of Bantu Angolan men, women, and children to Jamestown in the summer of 1619. According to historian Wesley Craven, the colony of Virginia, originally a merchant venture, was forcibly made a royal colony by order of King James because of:

the dispute with Sandys over the famous ship, the *Treasurer* . . . Yeardley immediately gave order for his seizure, but the captain was able to make his escape and sailed for Bermuda. Shortly after the *Treasurer* arrived there "so weather beaten and torn as never like to put to sea again," and *with a cargo of negroes*. [Italics added.] . . . From this breach grew a feeling more bitter than that arising from any other of the famous quarrels, and it was of greater importance in the final disruption of the company.

Thus, at a critical moment in the birth of English colonialism, the king's response to a little-known, long-ago scandal over the theft and legal ownership of a small group of enslaved Africans from Angola determined the future of America.

However, the struggle for possession of those Africans did not end with the dissolution of the Virginia Company. A riding accident and an injured child forced Gondomar out of England and spared Lord Rich from sharing Raleigh's fate. In March 1620, Count Gondomar returned with vengeance to destroy Jamestown and reclaim the Africans of the *Bautista*.

The Black Knight's
Last Pawn

KING JAMES, THOUGH personally irresponsible with money, had early perceived that the old English Channel and Mediterranean markets, once the backbone of Europe's economies, had suddenly shrunk in importance relative to the New World. "New World" meant, not just the Americas, but also Asia and Africa linked through increasing travel and discovery to western Europe. For small poor countries like England, Scotland, and Wales to compete in the emerging new world order then dominated by the powerful Spanish Empire, they would have to pool resources and find a way to coexist with Spain and other European rivals.

Not just global politics but domestic pressures also required England to change. Just four years before *Masque of Blackness* invited Africans to come to "Britannia," the aged Elizabeth I, in one of her final popular acts, ordered all "blackamoors" expelled from England because, as she said, "there are already here too many." In fact, there were hardly any Africans in London, and the few dozens who were there had been brought against their will. With a native-born population increasing like hares, England—and indeed all of Europe—teemed with idle white peasants. Elizabeth scapegoated Africans for causing crime, inflation, and unemployment, to mask her inability to solve England's staggering economic and social problems. The unavoidable fact was that the city of London's white population in 1596 had increased 400 percent from the previous century to a booming quarter of a million people.

England's currency system was also outmoded. The realm's smallest coin, one single, tiny, silver halfpenny, purchased a round of ale for everyone in a crowded tavern. Crime increased with unemployment, and the first generation of the emerging seventeenth-century industrial age overwhelmed punitive responses held over from the medieval era. London had eighteen overcrowded prisons at the time, a prison for every crime. Each prison, according to Geffray Mynshull in 1618, was a self-contained hellhole of misery, "a place that hath more diseases predominant in it than the Pest house in the Plague time, and it stinks more than the Lord Mayor's dog-house or a Paris garden in August."

Public punishment was the first London stage. In the surge to witness a public hanging at Tyburn, a mob of frenzied Londoners crushed to death more innocents in a moment than the condemned criminal had murdered in a lifetime. The heads of notorious seditionists were lopped off in the Tower of London and morbidly displayed in the middle of London Bridge as a warning. At Bedlam, paying spectators gathered every day to mock and mimic the gyrations of insane inmates. At Bridewell, where prostitutes were incarcerated, a balustrade had to be enlarged to hold back the prurient crowds who came to leer as impoverished women were flogged half-naked upon entering the prison.

Overcrowded London was breeding callousness, crime, subversion, and cynicism as thickly as plague rats bred lice. In response, with a meaningless gesture, Queen Elizabeth contracted with a German slave trader named Caspar Van Senden to round up London's few dozen Africans and ship them off in exchange for English prisoners captured by Moroccan pirates in North Africa. Then, in 1601, the queen made her second futile attempt to relieve London by deporting its few remaining Africans.

Within two years of the last African expulsion, Elizabeth died and James became king. *Masque of Blackness* and James's vision of a greater Britain premiered the same year that the merchant firm of Colthurst,

Dapper, and Wheatley commissioned the building of the bark christened the *Susan Constant*. A few months later, the flagship *Susan Constant*, with two other vessels, delivered Captain John Smith and about one hundred Englishmen to the shore of Chesapeake Bay. *Masque of Blackness* officially signaled the end of isolationist England, symbolized by Elizabeth's virginity. Two years after the Scotsman became king, Smith and his men were hewing logs to build England's first permanent American settlement, fittingly named James' Town. Following the scandal over the *Bautista* affair, other colonies under the guidance of James and his Stuart heirs would follow—Plymouth and the New England charter in 1620, Maryland in 1633, Rhode Island and Connecticut in 1636—and before the century-long Stuart dynasty finally ended, twelve of the original thirteen colonies would be established and the new British flag, combining English and Scottish symbols, firmly planted on both sides of the Atlantic. By the end of the seventeenth century, "Britannia" would be an emerging first-class global power, and Ben Jonson's description of the Stuart "radiance" in the prophetic *Masque of Blackness* would seem justified.

❖

BUT IN THE beginning, in 1607, few Europeans were willing to migrate to Jamestown, and twelve years later the struggling colony still desperately needed inexpensive laborers. Upon arriving in Jamestown in late August 1619, Captain John Colyn Jope of the *White Lion* found planters who wanted workers but could not afford them. His crew starving, Jope settled on trading some two dozen Africans to Governor George Yeardley and cape merchant Abraham Piersey for a chest of Indian maize.

Yeardley and Piersey undoubtedly knew that the *White Lion* had stolen the Africans from the same Spanish slaver that the *Treasurer* had also raided. King James did not recognize the right of English sailors to privateer under alien marques, invalid or not, and he would have considered Jope as much of a pirate as Elfrith. But frontier Virginia was not England, and the neglected settlers of Jamestown, like those of Bermuda, frequently ignored London laws and trafficked with pirates who often brought them better merchandise than the shoddy trash sold to them at extremely high prices by company investors who had a monopoly to trade with the colony. Even such reformers as Yeardley and Piersey overlooked the questionable circumstances of Jope's arrival in Jamestown, because they wanted his Africans as laborers to plant tobacco and make them rich.

Governor Yeardley sent five women and three men of the *White Lion* Africans upriver from Jamestown to work on an uncultivated piece of wilderness optimistically called a "plantation," which he named Flowerdew after his wife, the former Temperance Flowerdew. That the women outnumbered the men was not unusual, for it was well known by slavers that Bantu women were the farmers in precolonial Angola, and that Bantu men made crafts and tended cattle. Two years later, Flowerdew had become the first successful plantation in Virginia, boasting the colony's first windmill and some barns.

The status of the first Africans in Jamestown, whether they were held as indentured servants like Englishmen or as slaves, has been long debated. Typically, white indentured servants remained in bondage for only three to seven years before being freed. Sir Yeardley's will, proved February 14, 1628, stated:

> To wife Temperance . . . as touching and concerning all the rest of my whole estate consisting of goods, debts, servants, *negars* [italics added], cattle, or any other thing or things, commodities or profits whatsoever to me belong or appertaining either here in this country of Virginia, in England or elsewhere, together with my plantation of one thousand acres of land at Stanly in Warwick River, my will and desire is that the same be all and every part and parcel thereof sold to the best advantage for tobacco and the same to be transported as soon as may be, either this year of the next, as my said wife shall find occasion, into England, and there to be sold or turned into money.

Therefore, he had retained the Africans two years after indentured servants customarily would have been released, indicating he regarded them as chattel slaves. Yeardley's widow and children did not follow his order to sell the Africans. Skilled workers were hard to come by in Jamestown. Most white laborers who had been spirited away from England and dumped in the colony were urbanites, convicted deer poachers and other criminals, or orphaned children. So when the governor's son, Argoll Yeardley, settled in Upper New Norfolk in Nansemond County, Virginia, in 1637, he had with him two of the original *White Lion* Africans, a man and a woman with first names only, Andulu and Maria. By their names it appears the man was a non-Christian and the woman a Christian who had been converted by Catholic priests in Angola before capture. "Ndulu," from which the name "Andulu" is derived, was the name of a kingdom adjacent to Ndongo that was also attacked by Imbangala and Portuguese invaders under Governor Mendes de Vasconcelos. Maria, on the other hand, was likely an Ndongo or Kongolese subject captured and delivered to Luanda and then placed on the *Bautista.*

In 1653, Argoll Yeardley sold two young African girls named Doll and Denise to two planters—his father-in-law John Custis, and John Michael. These children, respectively ten and twelve years of age, were daughters of Andulu and Maria and represent the second generation of the *White Lion* Africans. This sale is further evidence that the Yeardley family held the original Africans as slaves rather than as indentured servants.

An incident that occurred in 1624 implies that at least some early white Virginians were uncomfortable with slavery. Jamestown planters in the seventeenth century customarily provided their indentured servants with food and drink, accompanied by music and dancing, for celebration of holidays and the end of harvest. But in 1623 to 1624, Governor Yeardley did not allow this practice at Flowerdew despite the fact that his laborers had increased his fortunes from almost nothing to make him the wealthiest man in the colony. According to John Pory, who sailed to Jamestown with him in 1619, Yeardley "brought only his sword with him" when he arrived; eyewitness John Rolfe, also in 1619, noted that both Yeardley and Piersey traded corn to get the *White Lion* Africans at "the easiest rate they could." Yet four years later, Yeardley owned one thousand acres under cultivation, and the finest house in Jamestown, all appraised at the considerable sum of £6,000 sterling.

Two white neighbors, John Radish and Robert Fytts, considered Governor Yeardley's ban against celebrating the harvest at Flowerdew an undue hardship on the Africans. At an "unseasonable time of the night," Radish invited the Bantu men and women, along with the white servants at Flowerdew, to come to his house "and there gave them entertainment and made them drink." Rum, music, and dancing continued late into the night until Yeardley's servants became so "disordered in drink" that they were "not able to go home." When Yeardley complained, the Jamestown Court fined Fytts and sentenced Radish to be placed "neck and heels" in the public stocks.

Yeardley held only half of the Africans delivered to Virginia by the *White Lion*. The remaining dozen or so Angolans were acquired by Abraham Piersey who, though he was the cape merchant, did not trade them to other planters but rather put them to work on his lands, including Flowerdew Plantation, which he bought when Yeardley decided to sell out in 1624. Piersey's plantation, called Piersey's Hundred, which spanned one thousand acres, included Flowerdew's windmill and several tobacco storage buildings and warehouses. Piersey also obtained more than two thousand acres at Weyanoke and fifteen hundred acres on the Appomattox River, near the present site of William and Mary College.

An incident in Jamestown in 1626, when Piersey brought charges against a white settler named Richard Crocker for allegedly slandering him, shows the severity of life for Virginia's underclass. Piersey, a prosperous member of the legislature, as well as the cape merchant, had a monopoly to trade goods in the colony and he charged staggering prices. Crocker, a small farmer, was overheard grumbling about the cost of nails to a fellow farmer. The court found Crocker guilty of slandering Piersey and fined him three hundred pounds of tobacco. Thinking it a clever punishment, the judges, with a ruling typical of medieval times, also required Crocker to be nailed through his ears to the Jamestown pillory. Life under Piersey's management could no doubt be unpleasant for the Bantu prisoners, though their master was selfishly compelled to see that they were physically healthy as long as they worked and that medicine did not exceed the cost of purchasing a replacement worker.

By toil and sweat, the Angolans cleared Piersey's land and then remained to raise his crops and his cattle after his white servants served their indenture contracts and left to begin their own farms. It was not coincidental that the two plantations on which the Bantu worked were the first two successful financial ventures the English enjoyed in America. The colony's plantations produced high-density crops and cattle almost exclusively (Angolans had excelled in producing both, long before the Portuguese arrived in 1482). The great success of Flowerdew and Piersey's Hundred encouraged Jamestown during a rough time in the colony's history—a period that included a terrible massacre in 1622 that killed hundreds of English settlers, and the dissolution of the company in 1624. In the midst of these troubles, the colony could point to Flowerdew and Piersey's Hundred as evidence that England should not abandon North America to invest wholly in Asia, as indeed it nearly did. Had they been free and allowed equal opportunity to build their own plantations, these Bantu, with their knowledge of iron, agriculture, and cattle, would have rivaled white planters in Virginia, as in fact some of the free blacks of their generation proved.

Piersey's will shows he held *White Lion* Africans until his death in 1627, implying that he, like Yeardley, also regarded his black laborers as permanent slaves and not as indentured servants who would have been released earlier. It is worth considering how these Africans in particular came to be regarded as private property, as slaves, since slavery was not widely practiced within England. A possible clue appears in the records in 1623, just prior to the dissolution of the Virginia Company, when Lord Cavendish stated the company's position that the *Bautista* Africans "belonged as Shares to ye Mariners." This indicates that the firm regarded their human booty as the jointly shared property of all of its investors, and not the private property of Yeardley and Piersey. However, after the business was dissolved and its joint assets were liquidated, divided up, or sold for debts in 1624, Yeardley and Piersey kept the *White Lion* Africans as their private share of the company's assets.

When Piersey died, his extensive estate was valued at nearly £500. In his will he charged his wife to "make sale of all the estate as aforesaid to the profit it can be sold for." As the enslaved Africans were part of the estate, Piersey intended for his family to sell them off and return to England. However, Piersey's widow still retained the Ndongo men and women he had purchased from Captain Jope in 1619, when she remarried a Virginian named Samuel Mathews, a Puritan who had previously offered testimony favorable to Lord Rich and Samuel Argall in the *Bautista* scandal. A penniless, indentured servant upon arriving in Virginia, Mathews, like Yeardley and Piersey, would become wealthy through the labor and skills of the captured Bantu.

Built at the convergence of the Warwick and the James rivers, Mathews Manor, or Denbigh Plantation as it is also known, has recently been fully restored, including the African living quarters, and both it and Flowerdew have a tangible connection to the historically important first Africans of the *White Lion*. At Denbigh, the Angolans that Samuel Mathews acquired through marriage to Piersey's widow were key participants in a unique experiment to reform Jamestown's economy, which fluctuated from harvest to harvest. Jamestown produced very little in addition to tobacco to stabilize the colony in drought or when tobacco prices fell on the world market. Advisors in England were pushing Virginians to diversify. Coming from the iron kingdoms of Angola, the first Africans were already familiar with market diversification, having produced steel, textiles, leather, vegetables, fruit, wheat, and livestock. Before his death, Abraham Piersey had experimented with diversification: for example, his Angolan farmers had planted "wheat in August, September, October, November, December and reaped good Crops again in May, June, July, August." After acquiring Piersey's Bantu workers, Mathews set out to continue and expand Piersey's short-lived experiment. John Ferrar, an investor with the old Virginia Company of London, visited Mathews at Denbigh and was enthused that this planter was successfully branching out beyond tobacco. Ferrar wrote in 1649 that Mathews hath a fine house, and all things answerable to it; he sows yearly store of hemp and flax, and causes it to be spun; he keeps weavers, and hath a tanning house, causes leather to be dressed, hath eight shoemakers employed in their trade, *hath forty Negro servants, brings them up to be traders in his house.* [Italics added.]

In 1649, Mathews's forty African workers were composed of the surviving *White Lion* Bantu plus their children who had been born in Jamestown. Ferrar describes the Denbigh Africans as not only engaged in planting, herding, weaving, tanning, and cobbling, but also serving as the principal traders selling plantation products to supply international ships leaving Jamestown for the long Atlantic voyage back to Europe. The Bantu had in one generation mastered European currency and rate of exchange as well as the *roanoke* shell currency of the Algonquian.

All three slaveholders, Yeardley, Piersey, and Mathews, also had white indentured servants and, through them, obtained headrights that added extra land to their holdings. But these white servants left after a few years to start their own farms. The unpaid Bantu remained long after the English servants disappeared and were more important to the success of the three leading plantations in Jamestown. Their contribution was more than stoop labor. In the absence of gold and silver in Virginia, settlers achieved wealth principally through agriculture. Native skills that set the Mbundu men and women apart from urban Londoners who knew little about farming and from Algonquian natives who knew absolutely nothing about domesticating animals made them highly prized, skilled laborers.

If the first Africans were amazed or intimidated upon arriving in Jamestown in 1619, it was most likely their reaction to the primitive condition of the colony and not to English technology or culture. From day one, Jamestown's location on a sluggish stretch of the James River posed vexing problems. The water carried disease, and from 1609 to 1612 Tidewater Virginia entered a cyclical drought. Hundreds died at Jamestown in those three years, more from sickness and starvation than from Algonquian arrows. The neglected festering condition of Jamestown, made more miserable by England's use of it as a penal colony, served as a vivid metaphor in such propaganda pamphlets as "Leah and Rachel, or The Two Fruitful Sisters," distributed in 1656, which advertised Jamestown as

> an unhealthy place, a nest of rogues, abandoned women, dissolute and rookery persons; a place of intolerable labor, bad usage and hard diet. . . . There were jails supplied, youth seduced, infamous women drilled in.

The overburdened streets of London were scraped of thousands of English men, women, and children, mostly poor, who were shoveled into the insatiable engine of torment that was Jamestown and still, a decade after it was born, the colony could not grow. Four out of five settlers died prematurely. Forty years was considered a long life. Death came from sickness, climate, hunger, sabotage, native attacks, and inexperience. The English public was well aware of the rate of failure, and the Virginia Company was forced to drop its commercial, religious, and patriotic requirements, in favor of interviewing any disgruntled group anywhere in Europe and Asia, who might even remotely be willing to go to North America. The company would have "transplanted the Grand Lama of Tibet with all his prayer wheels, and did actually nibble at the Chief Rabbi."

Into this tiny profane death-haunted European outpost perched on the edge of the American continent, surrounded by thousands of hostile neighbors, were thrown Africans taken from a large, sophisticated, orderly Angolan society. As the *White Lion* glided up to the Jamestown dock, the Ndongo men, women, and children on her deck must have been startled by a sight they had never seen—a skeleton of a village half devoured by wilderness. When these first Africans came, there was no assurance that the small settlement with its handful of stick huts was going to last another day. Yet, once they mastered its two social barriers—the English language (barely standardized even in England) and Protestant customs—the Bantu were as prepared as anyone to participate fully in American colonial life. Whites were not strangers to them. In the century that followed the arrival of the Portuguese in 1482, thousands of Angolans had converted and been drafted into the Portuguese guerra preta and had fought with guns and armor. Many Angolans were familiar with European technology long before the *Bautista* slave ship had left Luanda in 1619.

When the Black Mayflower arrived, primitive Jamestown was a mostly male-occupied stockade with no history, no culture, and no civic pride. It was notoriously reported that during "the starving time" not long before they landed, some English settlers were driven by hunger to dig up buried human corpses in Jamestown and eat them. The Bantu would have abhorred such reports as typical of their barbaric Imbangala enemy. Under this neglected state of affairs, it would be unrealistic to view African contributions as minimal merely because of their small number. They were among the few present in the colony who were accustomed to both urban and rural living. It was through their labor that Denbigh and Flowerdew became model plantations with great halls, at a time when most Jamestown residents lived in huts. Due to the Africans' skills, Denbigh Plantation developed into a port town in its own right, with ships of many nations riding at anchor not far from Mathews's front door. Ferrar, in 1649, depicted Denbigh as the ideal plantation, at which the Mbundu were good at making things grow from the earth, at increasing herds and flocks, and at barter:

> Mathews yearly sows abundance of Wheat, Barley, &c. The Wheat he selleth at four shillings the bushel; kills store of Beeves, and sells them to victual the ships when they come thither: hath abundance of Kine, a brave Dairy, Swine great store, and Poultry . . . and in a word, keeps a good house, lives bravely, and is a true lover of Virginia.

As with Europeans and Asians, the early proximity of the Bantu peoples to their domesticated livestock also increased their immunity to diseases borne by animals. The Bantu therefore did not wither away after coming in contact with Europeans, unlike enslaved natives of

North America who had not domesticated animals and who therefore had no physical immunity to European diseases. Still, the future of the Bantu of the *White Lion,* like that of English settlers, was tenuous in Tidewater Virginia and became even more uncertain when, in addition to everyday hardship, the long shadow of an old pursuer unexpectedly caught up with them.

❖

USING ANY MEANS short of open war, Gondomar's secret mission was to get the English out of the Americas and, failing that, to limit them to as few American settlements as possible. For most of Gondomar's time as ambassador to England, the second greatest threat to Spain's interest in the Americas was the colony of Jamestown, which also served as a haven for the greatest threat, English pirates. According to John Ferrar, who had been Edwin Sandys's associate in the Virginia Company's front office, Ambassador Gondomar, through his spies, was able even to infiltrate the most private closed-door meetings of the Virginia Company of London and then use this inside intelligence through his intimacy with King James, to contribute to the firm's downfall in 1624. Ferrar charged that

> Gondomar exerted double diligence, procuring, by Spanish gold, spies, who informed him of everything that was done at these meetings; and, what added greatly to his influence, the Spanish party at court, carried every thing with a high hand.

Gondomar personally tried to recover the Acuna family's stolen cargo of Africans from Jamestown even as he carried out Spain's agenda to destroy the colony. He was greatly aided in that endeavor by the blundering president of the Virginia Company of London. Hoping to clear the company of suspicion of complicity in the *Treasurer* affair, Sir Edwin Sandys had appeared before the king's Privy Council on February 25, 1620, and revealed Governor Yeardley's findings regarding the *Bautista* piracy and the *Treasurer*'s involvement. Sandys literally gave King James and Gondomar the names of Lord Rich, Samuel Argall, John Rolfe, and the ships involved in the piracy of the Africans—Africans whom Gondomar considered to be personal property stolen from his family.

The timing of Sandys's testimony to the Privy Council in 1620 killed Lord Rich's recently chartered Guiana colony that was to replace the old Raleigh scheme in South America. At that moment Captain Roger North, brother of Lord North, was sailing to Guiana under Rich's commission with 120 men to establish a Puritan settlement. Gondomar, who returned from exile to London that March, exploited Sandys's intelligence about the attack on the *Bautista* slave ship to convince King James that Rich meant to use Guiana as a secret war base to pillage Spanish ships and towns in the West Indies. Once again, the king, for fear of jeopardizing the Spanish treaty as well as the Spanish marriage proposal, heeded the ambassador and quickly recalled Captain North to London on suspicion of treason. On May 7, James also commanded Lord Rich to deliver up his commission for Guiana.

A week later, on May 15, Rich's cousin, Samuel Argall, who to perform a social function was appointed to attend the Spanish ambassador, was abruptly confronted by Gondomar with damning details of the *Treasurer*'s seizure of the *Bautista* and the theft of the latter family's Angolan slaves. Gondomar also accused Rich and Argall of having previously conspired with Sir Walter Raleigh to seize Spanish settlements in Guiana. Betrayed and compromised by Sandys, Lord Rich was enraged when he delivered up the Guiana commission to the king on May 23. At the Extraordinary Court of the Virginia Company that same day, Sandys, under fire from investors who were suddenly sympathetic to Rich, was compelled to deny that he had ever discussed the *Bautista* matter *directly* with the Spanish ambassador. According to the minutes of that meeting:

> [Edwin Sandys] desired that before they proceed into other business he might speak a few words for the clearing and justifying himself for whereas it is divulged that he should incense the Spanish Ambassador against Capt. Argall, as also against the Lord North and Capt. North

his brother he vowed and protested that he never did see the Spanish Ambassador but in the streets nor never sent or received any message to or from him, neither letter or any other writings.

Made aware at last of the identity of the English corsairs that had captured the *Bautista* Africans, and buoyed by his recent success in having Sir Raleigh beheaded, Gondomar attempted to persuade King James of a conspiracy linking Raleigh's Guiana escapade and the capture of the *Bautista*, and in June also launched an inquiry in court against Lord Rich to expose his involvement in the taking of the *Bautista* Africans. Subpoenaed by the Spanish ambassador, one of the *Treasurer*'s sailors, Richard Stafford of Staplehurst, Kent, testified that the *Treasurer* and a "Dutch ship" were involved in stealing Africans from a Spanish frigate in the West Indies at the exact time the *Bautista* was captured. Also called by Gondomar, the sailor Reinhold Booth, of Surrey, admitted that the *Treasurer* was in consort with the *White Lion*, which he identified by name, at the taking of the Spanish frigate.

The Spanish ambassador was never quite able to bring enough evidence to stir King James to act against the son of Lady Penelope Devereaux Rich, and the case dragged on until he retired from office and returned to Spain. However, Gondomar was not done with his mission to recover his family's stolen slaves. Having failed to persuade James to force Lord Rich to return the *Treasurer*'s share of the *Bautista* Angolans, he next attempted to recover the balance of the pirated Africans delivered to Jamestown by her consort, the *White Lion*. Many of those Bantu by that time were at Samuel Mathews's Denbigh Plantation. Samuel Mathews had been a close friend of Samuel Argall and would now have to pay a price for that association.

Count Gondomar's quest regarding the Africans dovetailed with his endeavor to destroy colonial Jamestown. Having survived the bitter early years before 1625, and with the gradually improving profitability of Virginia tobacco due to tariff protections and royal colony status in the late 1620s, planters around Jamestown were beginning to look for more land. The necessity of using the Atlantic and its coastal rivers to transport tobacco from American plantations to markets in Europe meant that the most convenient directions for English Virginia to grow were north and south, keeping close to the coast, in settlements up the rivers they discovered. Despite the lucrative potential in an expanded fur trade and the lure of gold, there was at that time no great rush by the English to explore west into the interior to the Piedmont and beyond to the Appalachian Mountains. Tobacco was king, and the tobacco economy developed along the American coast, not west to the highlands. Because of climate and geography, the most sensible direction for Virginia to expand was southward, into the region later named the Carolinas. But Gondomar successfully lobbied King James against colonizing the southern territory, though the Carolina region was within the old Virginia charter, by arguing that if Virginians spread south, their inevitable clash with the Spanish in Florida would provoke war between Spain and England.

Frustrated, the Jamestown legislature then determined to extend the colony northward. Proposing to "win the forests of Virginia," two Jamestown planters with large holdings, Samuel Mathews and William Claiborne, received from the Privy Council of King Charles I (James's son and successor), authority to begin exploring the region now known as Maryland (then also within the old Virginia charter). Claiborne built a fort on Kent Island and soon had a flourishing trade in furs. Mathews won fishing rights in addition to fur trading privileges around Chesapeake Bay, to which ventures he set some of his *White Lion* Bantu servants.

About this time there arrived in Jamestown Lord George Calvert, first Baron of Baltimore, who had held a high position in King James's court before becoming a Catholic through the proselytizing of Count Gondomar. Calvert's conversion came at the height of expectations for a marriage between Prince Charles and the Spanish princess Maria, a time when persecuted English Catholics had cause to hope that their condition was about to improve. However, despite Gondomar's fair promises, the prospect for the royal marriage eventually died. The Scottish Stuarts had high regard for Calvert, but English intolerance against Catholics forced him to offer his resignation to the king after the collapse of the Spanish marriage affair.

Departing England, Lord Calvert set sail for the Americas hoping to build a haven for oppressed English Catholics. Upon arriving at Jamestown, he applied to the House of Burgesses to settle in Virginia. Suspicious of the Catholic baron's close ties to Count Gondomar, the Virginians required him to take an oath to the Church of England, which he refused to do. Determined to establish a new Catholic colony, Baron Baltimore began exploring the coast immediately north of Jamestown and soon found suitable anchorage. By law, however, the land was still subject to the old Virginia Charter. So, Calvert returned to England and requested from Charles I a patent to establish a Catholic colony in the lands now named Maryland. Because his father had in 1624 dissolved the Virginia Company over the *Bautista* incident, King Charles was free to grant Calvert his colony. Maryland, North and South Carolina, Delaware, Pennsylvania, Rhode Island, New York, and New Jersey would all be carved from Virginia's original grant. Virginians, it turned out, had paid dearly for the stolen Africans.

Mathews and Claiborne, in particular, were outraged when King Charles began slicing greater Virginia apart. Forbidden to extend their plantations to the south because of the Spanish ambassador's manipulations, they were now cut off from spreading north by a new Catholic colony established by a protégé of Gondomar. Believing themselves stalemated by Spain's cunning Black Knight, they protested to King Charles but were unsuccessful in their attempts to influence his decisions.

Then Count Gondomar advanced yet another pawn in his campaign to destroy Jamestown and recover "his" Africans. In the wake of the dissolution of the London company and his father's takeover of Jamestown as a royal colony in 1624, King Charles named John Harvey as the first royal governor of Virginia after the death of George Yeardley. Having begun his career as a minor English civil servant, Harvey had advanced rapidly with the help of Gondomar's pervasive influence over the Stuarts and soon proved a capable tool against the colony. During his life and later, Governor Harvey would be reviled by Virginians as one of the worst of a bad lot to come from London with the power of the king's seal. English government appointees to royal colonies in America had a great deal in common with the typical inefficient, vainglorious, or corrupt Portuguese officials appointed over the colony of Angola. They were usually lifelong civil servants. The historian Herbert L. Osgood observed that, traditionally, appointments:

> under the English government throughout our colonial period were secured largely through privilege, influence, and favoritism. Merit, impersonally considered, played some part, but in a large proportion of cases it was subordinate. These considerations go far to explain the inferior character of many colonial appointments. They were part and parcel of the British civil service and exhibit its defects.

Many of the royal officers sent to the colonies came from the English Navy and therefore they ruled with that institution's infamous tyrannical heavy-handedness:

> In many cases military and naval officers of inferior rank, or persons who had held lower positions at court or were relatives of some influential nobleman were selected to be governors. In too many cases they lacked the proper experience, or were narrow and selfish in their aims. They too often came for gain rather than service. Sometimes they followed in civil life the methods of the camp or the quarter-deck. Again, while laboring zealously to uphold the legal rights of the crown, they often failed to win the loyalty of the colonists by the pursuit of measures which were clearly for their benefit. . . . Of the less acceptable class among them, John Harvey appointed by King Charles I to governor of Virginia was an example. Previous to his appointment as governor in 1628, Harvey had served in the English navy.

Harvey's personal relationship with Gondomar suddenly put the future of the Bantu at Denbigh Plantation in question. John Ferrar recalled that, as part of the commission appointed by King James to find evidence of the Virginia Company's mishandling of the colony in 1623, Harvey had been instrumental in the Spanish scheme to have the Virginia Company's patent "most unjustly taken away"—a feat that Spain accomplished "by Gondomar's procurement . . . and the Spanish Faction and his Gold prevailed then to destroy Virginia." From London, Ferrar also reminded Virginians that John Harvey had been appointed governor of the colony by "Gondomar's procuring, sent thither [to Virginia] at the Dissolving of the Company to ruin the Poor plantation." This was not the first allegation that Harvey had been bribed by a foreign power to betray England. Ferrar, who described the new governor as "a great Braggadocio" and "a vain headed man always and a Fantasticke fit for any impression of gain," recounted an incident in Venice when the Englishman John Lakes, suspecting Harvey of being in the hire of the Persians, challenged Harvey with verse to a sword duel:

> Then said Lakes, "I make your Epitaph: for then you must be killed— Here lies Captayne Har: that came from far to serve the Persian in his War: And was he not worse than a Turk that all Christendom Could not set a work?"

After Governor Harvey arrived to take up his office at Jamestown, the Virginia assembly of legislators soon had cause to heed Ferrar's warning. Treating farmers as he would a rough crew of sailors, Harvey displayed an arrogant style of management made more intolerable by his physically abusive treatment of those who opposed his policies. The friction that grew between Governor Harvey and the Virginia Assembly echoed the ongoing test of wills between King Charles I, who was continuing his father's policy of absolute rule, and the English Parliament, which was stubbornly resisting. To bypass the budgeted appropriations established by the Virginia Assembly, Harvey levied and personally pocketed fees and fines, without the Virginia council's approval:

> Virginians were put off by the offensive manners and arbitrary conduct of Gov. John Harvey. He is charged with multiplying fines and levying

excessive fees, and even with appropriating money which belonged in the treasury of the province. Already fees had been to an extent regulated by law in Virginia, though this had not been done in the case of those which went directly to the governor. There is no doubt that Harvey was arrogant and even brutal in conduct, and that at times he tried to play the petty tyrant. He admitted having assaulted one of the members of the council.

Furthermore, Harvey was accused of protecting the claims of Gondomar's protégé Lord Baltimore in Maryland against those of the very colony he governed.

A bitter personal animosity also sprang up between Governor Harvey and Samuel Mathews over the Angolans that Mathews had acquired by marrying Piersey's widow, and over Mathews's Maryland rights. In 1635, Mathews challenged the king's governor on the floor of the Jamestown Assembly, and that incident led to what is known in American history as "the thrusting out of Governor Harvey"—the first time that an American colony rebelled against an officer of the king of England.

The incident began when sisters Mary and Elizabeth Piersey accused Mathews of altering the estate of Piersey's Hundred, or Flowerdew as Mary renamed it, following the death of her father. After marrying Piersey's widow, the stepmother of Elizabeth and Mary, Samuel Mathews had taken the Bantu men and women from Flowerdew and moved them to Denbigh plantation and, in addition, claimed much of the land of the original Flowerdew Plantation. Mary and Elizabeth went to court to have the Africans and their father's plantation returned to them. Once the colony's two brightest success stories, Flowerdew and Denbigh faced off in a bitter war.

Mary Piersey had married a merchant named Thomas Hill. Elizabeth Piersey married Jamestown merchant Richard Stephens. Elizabeth Piersey Stephens turned to John Harvey for help, and an attraction developed between the pretty twenty-year-old married woman and the new governor. When Captain Stephens died around 1632, the young widow Stephens married Governor Harvey at once. Harvey then tried to force Mathews to turn over the Angolans. Eventually, Samuel Mathews relinquished his claim on Flowerdew plantation but refused to give up the Africans. All the grievances of the Virginians over what they considered the infringements of Catholic Maryland and Harvey's despotism exploded when, in April 1635, Representative Mathews rose in the Virginia Assembly to denounce the governor's arbitrary rule. His appeal to his fellow Virginians, who until then had uneasily endured Harvey's abuses, won immediate popular support. When Governor Harvey ordered the Virginians against their wishes to trade their precious cattle to the Catholics of Maryland, Samuel Mathews, who had a growing herd under the care of his Ndongo hands at Denbigh Plantation, dashed his hat to the ground and stamped it cursing, "A pox on Maryland!" His fellow Virginians rallied behind him and declared that they would rather be clubbed in the head than sell cattle to Marylanders.

At this time, the Virginia Assembly was held in Governor Harvey's house in Jamestown, having moved from the choir of the Jamestown church before the Yeardley administration. However, members of the legislature one night met secretly to discuss options against Harvey's administration. Informed of the private council, the next morning Governor Harvey promptly arrested three plotters and, when they inquired about the charges against them, informed them that they would know at the gallows. At the next meeting of the assembly, Harvey, intending to send a warning to the growing opposition, demanded the three men be tried under martial law, which carried the probable penalty of death. The councilors informed the governor that the men must receive a civil trial.

> Harvey then became very angry, and after sitting down and bidding the councilors be seated, put to them the question, "What do you think they deserve that have gone about to persuade the people from their obedience to his Majesty's substitute?" An immediate answer was required. The first individual to whom the question was directly put was George Menefie. He replied sarcastically that he was only a young lawyer and dared not "upon the sudden" deliver his opinion. William Ferrar and Captain Mathews then objected to the proceeding of the governor as strange and unprec-

edented. Mathews compared it to the accusation by Richard III against Lord Hastings before the council. After this the rest of the councilors found their voices and opposed the governor's course. "Then followed many bitter languages from Harvey until the sitting ended."

This, in 1635, was the first open colonial rebellion against a representative of an English monarch. Governor Harvey would later complain directly to King Charles that Samuel Mathews was "the prime actor in the late Mutiny in Virginia." At the next session, the situation became even more tense as Mathews physically restrained Harvey to sit and be silent when the governor became violent after learning that the colony was circulating a petition against him:

> The governor, rising in a rage, struck Menefie on the shoulder, exclaiming, "I arrest you for suspicion of Treason to his Majesty." Captain Utie, who stood near, said, "And we the like to you, sir." "Whereupon I," writes Mathews, "seeing him [Governor Harvey] in a rage, took him in my arms and said, 'Sir, there is no harm intended against you, save only to acquaint you with the grievances of the Inhabitants, and to that end I desire you to sit down in your chair.'"

Then Mathews and the assembly informed Harvey that he was to be shipped back to England immediately to answer charges presented by the Virginia colony:

> In the midst of these occurrences, on a signal from Dr. Pott, the governor's house, where the council was sitting, was surrounded by armed men. The three men whom Harvey had arrested were now released. The governor found his protests of no avail. So imminent seemed the danger of personal injury to him that a guard was appointed. The council also took possession of his commission and instructions. The burgesses of the late assembly were called together by the insurgents. When the burgesses met, they approved the doings of the council, and recorded the fact that Sir John Harvey was thrust out of his government.

The Virginians drew up the charges and dispatched two assemblymen to accompany Harvey to England to present them to King Charles. However, immediately upon arriving in England, Harvey had the two messengers, Doctor Francis Pott and Thomas Harwood, arrested. With the two Virginians in prison, John Harvey proceeded to London just before Christmas to present his case alone before the Privy Council, with the king present. Aware that many of his republican enemies in Parliament had business interests in Jamestown and believing the colony had directly challenged his authority, Charles I insisted that Harvey return to Jamestown if only for a single day.

Harvey sailed back to Virginia with an order from the king commanding Samuel Mathews and four of the leading insurgents to come to London at once and face the infamous Star Chamber, the secret English court with far-reaching powers to investigate and prosecute threats to domestic security. Forced to comply with the summons, the five Virginians sailed to London, where they would be held answering the charges for two years.

During the time that Mathews was detained in England, the Harveys plotted to bring additional charges against him: While Mathews was facing the Star Chamber, the widow of Jamestown planter Captain William Holmes, apparently on information supplied her by the Harveys, filed civil action in London alleging that, in 1627, Mathews's African servants burned down one of Abraham Piersey's barns in which was stored tobacco owed to Holmes. Governor Harvey sent his agent, along with his wife's sister, to sack the absent Mathew's Denbigh Plantation and seize the Bantu that Mathews had not sent afield to trade:

> Mr. Kemp, the secretary, with the said Hill's wife and others entered Mathews' house; broke open the door of several Chambers, and also of his trunks and Chests, and all his writings, carried away part of his goods and eight of his Negroes and Servants.

In an orgy of vengeance, the governor also rounded up the leading legislators who had thrust him out of office and jailed them under threat of a martial court. For his opposition to Harvey, the Reverend Anthony Panton, minister of York Parish, was stripped of his property and parochial tithes, and banished from Jamestown under threat of death if he returned. This would lead to the undoing of Harvey and his cronies: Rev. Panton sailed to London and presented his case, with ample evidence of Harvey's graft and tyranny. At this time, England had had about enough of the Stuarts. On the eve of all-out civil war in England, Charles I, realizing that he would only fuel the growing opposition against him in Parliament if he stood by such a corrupt administrator, finally agreed to make Harvey step down as governor of Jamestown.

Samuel Mathews was at last free to leave England. Upon his return to Jamestown and Denbigh, he found his great hall broken up and plundered by the looting Harveys. His fields were untended, his cattle had strayed, and above all, the Angolan men and women were gone. Questioning witnesses, Samuel Mathews located the Africans at Flowerdew plantation in the custody of former governor John Harvey. Count Gondomar meanwhile had died and Harvey, unable to transport the slaves to the Acuna family in Spain, was working them at Flowerdew. Without the crafty Spanish ambassador alive to oppose him, Samuel Mathews successfully went to court and had the Africans returned to Denbigh.

The death of Count Gondomar and the dismissal of John Harvey as governor assured that Jamestown was to be the destiny of the Bantu transported there by the *White Lion*. For the next thirty years, the founders of African America traveled different roads in search of the same prize—freedom. For some, their achievements of equality and even success were to rival those of English neighbors in Virginia. For others, the dream never materialized.

PART III

THE FOUNDERS
SEEK FREEDOM

THOUGH THE BANTU of Angola certainly resisted getting on the frigate to sail to America as slaves, the fact is that they were descendants of a great nation of colonizers who had started from the faraway Nile a thousand years ago to successfully cross the continent of Africa. Bantu songs tell how they carried the relics of their important chiefs with them as they moved west, tending them with respect in hopes of receiving blessings. This reverence, according to them, was the reason for their successful colonization of the world's second largest continent. In the words of the old Angolan proverb, "Where your ancestors do not live, you cannot build your house."

In 1619, these voyagers borne westward across the Other world on the Black Mayflower now live at Jamestown, in the New World. A virgin continent stretches west before them, as once did Africa. They are beginning anew on the James River as their forebears did on the Nile and later on the Congo. With a rich colonizing history behind them, they are prepared for the challenge. From a faceless collective identification as "twenty and odd Negars," and from the near anonymity of such first names as Antonio, Mary, and Francisco in the Virginia census of 1625, these ghostlike founders of African America rapidly materialize as flesh and blood in colonial records. By the 1640s, they face social situations that are becoming more and more complex. Many of the first Bantu generation at Jamestown, as in Dutch New York, acquire surnames, freedom, and property within three brief decades. John, who becomes John Graweere, takes a position as an officer in the Jamestown administration. The husband and wife Antonio and Maria, who become Anthony and Mary Johnson, build themselves a successful tobacco plantation by exploiting English law. Margaret, as Margaret Cornish, enters a forbidden affair with the white son of a Virginia legislator. Soon after landing at Jamestown, they and their fellow travelers have quickly surfaced in various documents as individuals and personalities. They appear as people coping with the same universal problems faced by all people, and so from that time an African American social history is visible and accessible.

Immediately after arriving at Jamestown and being assigned to area plantations, the thoughts of the first Africans turn to freedom—freedom to pursue their own ambitions and prosperity, freedom of religion, and freedom to choose their own government. Individual stories of such forced immigrants as John Pedro, Mary and Anthony Johnson, Antonio Longo, and others reveal how the ongoing struggle between Lord Robert Rich and his Puritan friends against the absolutist Stuarts, pressured Virginians to free some Africans during the long anticipated eruption of the English Civil War. Other Africans, like John Graweere, Benjamin Doll, and Emanuel Rodriges, will borrow from their Angolan culture to purchase their freedom, and the freedom of their comrades and, in the process, lay the foundation of the Underground Railroad while at the same time creating one of America's great industries. Others, like Philip Mongon and Domingo Mathews, will use their cunning to gain freedom. The men and women of the first African generation of Jamestown will form an extended community—born in the slave ships—that will survive two centuries of slavery and spread as the western frontier expands.

The chapters in part 3 tell the individual stories of the founding fathers and mothers of African America at Jamestown, and their quest to win and hold freedom.

· 8 ·

The First Martyr

ONE OF THE Africans taken from the *Bautista* slave ship by the corsair of Lord Robert Rich in 1619 would, after winning freedom, choose to take up arms against the Puritan earl and fight under the Catholic banner. Born in Angola in 1593, John Pedro, the baptized son of Bantu Christians, was taken prisoner of war at the age of twenty-five when the Imbangala forces under Governor Vasconcelos overran the Ndongo army of soba Kaita ka Balanga in 1619. Forced to march over one hundred miles with thousands of his countrymen to the port of Luanda, John Pedro was there branded, sold, and placed on the *San Juan Bautista* in May 1619. Along with 349 others, he endured the ordeal of the maiden middle passage across the Atlantic before the frigate was attacked in the Bay of Campeche in July by the pirates of the *White Lion* and the *Treasurer*. John Pedro was among those Africans taken as prize by the latter.

The fugitive *Treasurer*, as described previously, arrived in Virginia four days behind the *White Lion* but had to flee to avoid Governor George Yeardley's attempt to seize her. She appeared in the islands of Bermuda a few weeks later and put in at Saint George's Town. It was then September. Like Yeardley in Virginia, acting Bermuda Governor

Miles Kendall, a man also loyal to Edwin Sandys, suspected that the *Treasurer* had been involved in piracy and ordered Captain Daniel Elfrith to turn over the ship. Short on food and water, and with his crew on the point of mutiny, Elfrith reluctantly surrendered his damaged vessel at Saint George's. Governor Kendall and a company of musketeers forcibly removed the Bantu captives and locked them in a longhouse. However, Captain Elfrith managed to conceal the ship's documents, papers that would have proved the *Treasurer*'s involvement in the *Bautista* piracy, and he told Governor Kendall that he had purchased the Africans from a "Dutch" ship.

John Pedro and his fellow countrymen did not remain imprisoned for long. The always-resilient Lord Rich had persuaded the investors of the Bermuda Company to appoint his agent, Nathaniel Butler, as the new governor. Butler landed at Saint George's to replace Miles Kendall in October 1619. He immediately unlocked the longhouse and assigned John Pedro and the two dozen or so other *Treasurer* Africans to work on both his and Lord Rich's plantations at Bermuda. Butler also seized an additional fourteen Africans that Kendall had recently acquired from the *White Lion*, claiming that Kendall had "stolen" them. These he set to work on the company's general lands.

Governor Butler was aware of the piracy scandal brewing over the *Bautista* slaver, and the need to be discreet. Butler wrote Lord Rich in October 1620 that he would keep the African men and women hidden away in Bermuda and then "I will (silently) deliver them over to Your Lordship . . . after one year." But the trouble did not die down after a year. By the spring of 1621, both Rich and Butler learned that their enemies in the Virginia Company were claiming that, because Lord Rich was a member of the Virginia Company as well as the Bermuda Company, the Africans that the *Treasurer* had taken from the Spanish slaver in 1619 were legally the joint stock of all of the investors in those companies. This would make the case of the *Bautista* Africans doubly divisive. Not only did his enemies in the two firms accuse Rich of stealing Africans from the Spaniards, they also accused him of stealing the same Africans from *them*. Rich responded by protesting that he had not stolen the Africans from anyone, that he had purchased them at his own expense from the *White Lion* and that they were his property alone.

At this same time, King James, at Gondomar's urging, had commissioned his Privy Council to investigate details of the stolen Africans at Bermuda. Parallel with that investigation, the Virginia and Bermuda companies set up a special commission to sail to Bermuda to study the threat that the growing number of anti-Spanish pirates gathering there posed to Virginia should Spain retaliate against the colony. Bermuda, said company stockholders, was a vital security interest to Virginia:

> this being a business which mainly concerned Virginia, for so long as the same Islands shall be in safety it is probable that none will attempt to surprise Virginia, but now as the case standeth the Somer [Bermuda] Islands is much frequented with men of war and pirates, with whom the inhabitants there are grown in great liking, by reason of the commodities they bring unto them, insomuch that by a letter from one of their Ministers directed to Sir Thomas Smith and read in open Court the robbing of the Spanyards (as being limbs of Antichrist) is greatly commended: And ye ship called the *Treasurer* after her robbing of the Spaniard belonging to Captain Argall, is there entertained and divers men of Warr set out to the same end are there refreshed, one Kerbie also a professed Pyrate as is reported doth haunt those Islands insomuch as if there be not a strict Course taken herein it will be made an other Argier [Algiers].

As scrutiny from several areas focused on Bermuda in the African piracy furor, another drama involvng Spain and England unfolded in those islands. Rock-rimmed Bermuda's location in the stormy North Atlantic makes it one of the world's most infamous sites for shipwrecks, as Shakespeare first dramatized a decade earlier. Early in 1621, a large three-hundred-ton Spanish treasure frigate named the *San Antonio* was driven by a tempest onto the reefs of Bermuda and began to sink.

Governor Butler organized a rescue operation and saved a sizable cache of gold ingots, jewels, and choice Spanish tobacco, along with dozens of Spanish passengers. It was perhaps not out of compassion that Butler rescued the drowning Spaniards: England and Spain regularly ransomed each other's castaways, particularly those of the aristocracy, and wealthy gentry.

Informed by Rich's spies in England that officers of the king's Privy Council were about to sail to Bermuda to seize all the Africans and arrest him for receiving stolen contraband and entertaining pirates, Nathaniel Butler quickly sought to conceal the evidence. As he had promised Lord Rich one year earlier, Governor Butler in 1621 placed some of the Africans, including John Pedro, Maria, and Antonio, along with the Spanish survivors of the *San Antonio* wreck, onboard the ship *James*, bound for England. Five weeks later, the *James* arrived at the port of Southampton and John Pedro, Maria, and Antonio were taken to the Earl of Warwick's great manor at Leighs [or "Leez"] Priory in Felsted, Essex.

Lord Rich owned extensive farmlands and pastures in addition to his foreign tobacco plantations, tanning factories, iron mines, and fleet of ships constantly coming and going. At Leighs Priory, a multitude of servants planted acres of wheat and tended the earl's cattle, goats, and sheep. The English nobility lived more extravagantly than did the Spanish and Portuguese, and the worldly Puritan Lord Rich held court as if he were a ngola in Angola. Like Ndongo princes entering the old royal city of Kabasa, courtiers and agents streamed to the great hall of Leighs Priory, seeking the English lord's favor and trade. From the four corners of the globe also came Rich's captains and merchants of sassafras, wool, glass, iron, tobacco, wine, logwood, silk, sugar, hemp, flax, fish, and fur, as well as his far-ranging pirates bearing stolen plunder.

John Pedro was probably unhappy at Leighs Priory, however. The Angolan, a devout Catholic as will be seen, would have found himself in a den of anti-Catholic activism at Felsted. Symbolically, Rich's Tudor mansion stood on the grounds of a twelfth-century Augustinian priory seized in the great dissolution of the monasteries in 1539. By the

seventeenth century, Leighs Priory was a hotbed of anti-Catholic con-
spiracies hatched by the Puritans, the most extreme anti-Catholic Protestant sect. Committed to his faith, John Pedro was likely pressured to
convert at Leighs Priory, yet he persisted in the Catholic religion of his
parents who had been baptized by Jesuit and Dominican missionaries
in Angola long before the Portuguese invasion of Ndongo. John Pedro
also refused to anglicize his Latin surname. His countryman Antonio,
on the other hand, converted from Catholicism to become a Protestant
and eventually adopted the English spelling of his name Anthony,
just as his future wife, Maria, became Mary. Although they anglicized
their Portuguese names, they did not, however, abandon their Angolan
identity. In America, Anthony and Mary Johnson would name their
plantation Angola in memory of their home country.

Hounded by the Virginia Company, as well as by Count Gondomar
and the king's Privy Council—all seeking evidence of the *Treasurer*'s
participation in the *Bautista* piracy—Lord Rich determined that neither
John Pedro nor Antonio could remain in England. In 1621, Rich put
Antonio on the ship *James* bound for Bennett's Welcome—a Virginia
plantation at Warrosquoke (also known as Warwick's Squeak) owned
by Edward Bennett, a wealthy Puritan and Rich's friend.

For John Pedro, however, a very different adventure unfolded.

❖

THE HIGHEST-RANKING PURITAN of England, Lord Robert Rich's crucial role in the founding of New England in 1620 has been strangely
ignored. Before his great falling-out with Edwin Sandys in the summer
of 1619, Rich became acquainted with a London merchant named
Thomas Weston through the Virginia Company of London. The members of the London Ironmongers Company, a kind of guild or union, had
pooled their money to invest in the Jamestown venture and attended
the Virginia Company's meetings in London. Weston, an ironmonger
who operated secretly as an illegal arms dealer, was eager to enter the
African triangular trade and at the company's business meetings he
frequently buttonholed Lord Rich, who was the owner of England's

largest private fleet. In 1618, King James had given Rich a commission to trade Africans from Guinea in West Africa, though there is no evidence that Warwick's Guinea Company ever actually trafficked in Africans. Unlike the Hawkins family of the Elizabethan era, the nationalist Earl of Warwick disliked dealing with Spanish and French colonies, and it is improbable, given his notoriety as an anti-Catholic privateer, that Lord Rich's ships would have been welcome in their ports. Furthermore, in 1618, though they desperately needed manpower, the struggling planters of the colonies of Jamestown and Bermuda could not afford to purchase large annual shipments of Africans necessary to make Warwick's Guinea Company profitable.

The Guinea Company in fact served Rich as a front for piracy. Though Rich was never active in the triangular trade, Weston had begun early to visualize a system similar to the Atlantic triangular trade but involving England, Virginia, and Holland. Through his agent Edward Pickering, Weston had made a contract to sell cloth trade goods manufactured by English religious dissidents who had fled King James's persecution and were living as refugees in Holland. In the course of time, Weston had been made aware that these pilgrims (in the sense of their being religious journey-takers)—and this is the group we now think of as Pilgrims—desperately wanted to leave Leyden, which was within King James's reach. The Dutch government had offered to take the Pilgrims to Dutch New York but Weston urged the Pilgrims to instead settle in Jamestown under the charter of the Virginia Company of London. Plans were drawn up with the Virginia Company's blessings but hit a snag when Weston was arrested in 1619 for evading customs. Weston was frequently in trouble with authorities; the Pilgrims found him unreliable and sought other options. Those were few. Fractured by the court cases surrounding the *Bautista*, the Virginia Company was hemorrhaging internally, which made the proposed Pilgrim move to Jamestown uncertain. Furthermore, through Edwin Sandys's indiscretion and Count Gondomar's manipulations, Lord Rich's scheme for Guiana fell through in early 1620, ending the Pilgrims' plan to settle in South America.

Then in the gloom of disappointment, a glimmer of hope. Angry that the Virginia Company of London had ordered the seizure of the *Treasurer* and revealed the theft of Africans from the *Bautista*, Lord Rich in early 1620 left the firm and, with Buckingham and other investors, proposed a northern charter that would rival that of his enemies in the Virginia Company. It would be called the Council of New England. King James, eager to divide the Parliament opposition concentrated in the Virginia Company, further reasoned that Rich's New England venture, unlike his proposed Guiana scheme, would be sufficiently far enough away from the temptation of rich Spanish targets in the West Indies, and he approved the New England charter. Lord Rich's grant overlapped Virginia's monopoly of North America and initiated the cultural, political, and religious schism of North and South in what would many years later become the United States. The controversy that led to the Pilgrims' founding of Plymouth and the opening of New England was caused by the 1619 *Bautista* scandal, making the first imported Africans indirectly responsible for creating the diverse personality of America.

Learning that Rich's New England venture was in the works, Thomas Weston raced across the Channel to Leyden in 1620 to convince the Pilgrims to settle on the new charter. In his memoirs, Rich's business partner Sir Ferdinand Georges, wrote that it was necessary

> that means might be used to draw unto those their enterprises, some of those families that had retired themselves into Holland for scruple of conscience, giving them such freedom and liberty as might stand with their liking.

The involvement in the New England venture of the prominent Puritan Lord Rich helped the Separatists' decision. Pilgrim leader William Bradford wrote that the congregation at Leyden

> heard both from Mr. Weston and others that sundry Honorable Lords had obtained a large grant from ye king for ye more northerly parts of that country, derived out of ye Virginia patents, and wholly secluded from their

Government, and to be called by another name, viz. New England unto which Mr. Weston and the chief [of the congregation] began to incline.

The Pilgrims sailed for America on the *Mayflower* in September 1620. Lord Rich took his seat as an executive officer of the New England Council on November 3, 1620, one month before the Pilgrims arrived in what is today Massachusetts and founded the new colony of Plymouth. However, they had not obtained a patent to settle on the New England charter and at the time, were squatters.

Thomas Weston, the agent who had urged the Pilgrims to go to New England, ran into difficulty once more. In March 1621, before setting up his trade scheme with the Plymouth colony, he was caught selling cannons to the Turks, the same Muslim pirates who were attacking English ships. King James seized his assets and, a year later, Weston, facing trial for treason, fled England to set up yet another venture called the Wessagussett colony (at present day Weymouth near Boston) also on the New England charter. Meanwhile, the Pilgrims, who had settled in America without permission, acquired a patent from Lord Rich and the New England Council through London clothmaker John Pierce and an association of "merchant adventurers" in June 1621.

Having avenged himself against the Virginia Company for the African *Bautista* affair and the confiscation of the corsair *Treasurer*, Lord Rich, in support of the settlements being built on his lands, commissioned Captain Thomas Jones to take the *Discovery* to New England to fish and trade with Plymouth and Weston's new colony.

Thomas Jones was once thought to be the captain of the *Mayflower* on the historic voyage to Cape Cod in 1620, though more recent evidence proves that the Jones of the *Mayflower* was in fact Christopher Jones, of no known relation to Thomas. However, Thomas Jones did sail to Plymouth very early as a captain in the fleet of Lord Robert Rich. Though engaged in legitimate business, Captain Jones, like Daniel Elfrith, from time to time seized a few ships, Muslim and Indian as well as Catholic, while sailing for Lord Rich. In 1617, Thomas Jones almost destroyed England's trade relations with India when, while sailing the corsair *Lion* for Rich, he fired on a rich junk in the Indian Ocean that belonged to the Great Moghul's mother. Captured by Captain Martin Pring, the pirate Jones was sent back to England as a prisoner aboard the ship *Bull* to face charges. This did not end his career. Rich bailed him out of prison and immediately put him in command of a new ship to continue both legal and illegal ventures at sea. Jones, with the Irish pirate John Powell on a ship called the *Black Bess* sailing under a Dutch marque, seized a Spanish frigate voyaging from Angola to the West Indies in 1625 and delivered to Jamestown the ship and an African from that prize—a black man named Brass. Brass had been captured in the ongoing war that Portugal, and its Imbangala allies were fighting against the new ngola of Ndongo, the Catholic warrior queen, Anna Nzinga.

Commanding Lord Rich's ship *Discovery* in November 1621, Thomas Jones was one of the most knowledgeable navigators to sail the world's oceans in the early seventeenth century, when voyages to Malaga, Madagascar, Iceland, Guinea, Angola, India, Jamestown, Guiana, and Newfoundland were still epic undertakings. To get him away from Gondomar's reach, Rich also placed John Pedro on the *Discovery*. In late 1621, bound for America and the Pilgrim settlement called Plymouth founded ten months earlier on Rich's New England charter, John Pedro was setting out to make history as the first black man and the first Catholic to live in the Pilgrim colony.

After an unexplained and suspicious delay in the West Indies, Captain Thomas Jones brought the *Discovery* into Cape Cod in August 1622 in consort with Thomas Weston's ship, the *Sparrow*. According to the starving Pilgrims of the Plymouth colony, the *Discovery* arrived just in time:

> In the end of August came other two ships into our harbor, the one (as I take it) was called the *Discovery*, Captain Jones having the command thereof, the other was that ship of Mr. Weston's called the *Sparrow*, which had now made her voyage of fish, and was consorted with the other, being both bound for Virginia . . . of Captain Jones we furnished our selves of such provisions as we most needed, and he could best spare, who as he used us kindly, so made us pay largely for the things we had.

And had not the Almighty, in his All-ordering Providence, directed him to us, it would have gone worse with us, than ever it had been, or after was: for, as we had now but small store of corn for the year following: so for want of supply, we were worn out of all manner of trucking stuff, not having any means left to help our selves by trade; but, through God's good mercy towards us, he had wherewith, and did supply our wants on that kind competently.

To settle Wessagussett, Thomas Weston had hired fifty to sixty London sailors who arrived in Plymouth on two ships, the *Charity* and the *Swan*, about the beginning of July 1622. The Pilgrims soon discovered that Weston, in his haste to flee England, had hired the riffraff of the London waterfront, whose true natures were soon revealed:

These we received into our town, affording them whatsoever courtesy our poor condition could afford. There the *Charity*, being the bigger ship, left them, having many passengers which she was to land in Virginia. In the mean time, the body of them refreshed themselves at Plymouth, whilst some most fit sought out a place for them. That little store of corn we had, was exceedingly wasted by the unjust and dishonest walking of these strangers, who though they would sometimes seem to help us in our labor about our corn, yet spared not day and night to steal the same, it being then eatable, and pleasant to taste, though green and unprofitable. And though they received much kindness, set light both by it and us; not sparing to requite the love we showed them, with secret backbiting, reviling, etc. the chief of them being forestalled and made against us, before they came, as after appeared: Nevertheless for their master's sake, who formerly had deserved well from us. We continued to do them whatsoever good or furtherance we could, attributing these things to the want of conscience and discretion, expecting each day, when God in his providence would disburden us of them, sorrowing that their over-seers were not of more ability and fitness for their places and much fearing what would be the issue of such raw and unconscionable beginnings.

Apart from this gang of London thieves, Weston's commander, Captain Phineas Pratt of the *Sparrow*, obtained from Captain Jones three of the *Discovery*'s crew to help build Weston's new settlement. One of those three was John Pedro. Disgusted by their conduct, he and his two white companions shared the Pilgrims' low regard for the Londoners of the *Charity*. Pedro observed them devour the Pilgrims' small store of food and spitefully mock them after their bellies were full and the fields empty. Much of the trouble was due to the absence of the hapless Weston, who had gotten shipwrecked further up the coast. By the winter of 1622/23, his neglected colony was starving, reduced to living on nuts, clams, and oysters, and during this time the first execution in New England, that of a starving thief from among Weston's troublesome Londoners, was carried out. The Londoners also stole from the local native inhabitants. Edward Winslow at the time expressed the shame felt by the Pilgrims:

> What great offense hath been given by many profane men, who being but seeming Christians, have made Christ and Christianity stink in the nostrils of the poor infidels, and so laid a stumbling block before them: but woe be to them by whom such offenses come.

The Pilgrims' friend, King Massasoit of the Wampanoag warned that another king, Wituwamat, was organizing to attack Wessagussett as well as Plymouth because of the Londoners' conduct. Captain Miles Standish marched out to parlay with Wituwamat and his ally, Pecksnot. At this meeting, Standish was persuaded that Wituwamat was resolved to rid the land of all the English and therefore, faced with preserving relations with local natives or saving his countrymen, Standish treacherously poisoned the cornmeal at the parlay and then slew Wituwamat and his warriors. Realizing the lasting enmity his actions had stirred among the natives and mindful of the source of the trouble, Standish then strongly advised the settlers of Wessagussett to abandon the colony and return to London. John Pedro was still welcome at Plymouth and remained, but the Londoners were not and they were sent back to England on the *Charity*, leaving the *Swan* behind. Safely at home in England, they began spreading tales damaging to the New England venture, provoking the Pilgrim Edward Winslow to describe them as that

> disorderly colony that are dispersed, and most of them returned, to the great prejudice and damage of him [Weston] that set them forth; who as they were a stain to old England that bred them, in respect of their lives and manners amongst the Indians: so it is to be feared, will be no less to New England in their vile and clamorous reports, because she would not foster them in their desired idle courses.

Winslow, however, commended some of the failed colony, such as John Pedro, who were not of the London crew hired by Weston:

> I would not be understood to think there were no well deserving persons amongst them: for of mine knowledge it was a grief to some that they were so yoked.

During his time in Plymouth, John Pedro marched with Miles Standish to explore Massachusetts. Onboard the *Sparrow*, he fished along the New England coast. He met the famous Tisquantum, known more famously as Squanto. He was there during Plymouth's own terrible "starving time" and shared hardships with the Pilgrims. He joined the Pilgrims in cutting trees for pales (pickets) to ring the tiny Plymouth settlement in defense against hostile attack. After the disruptive Londoners returned to England, Pedro and the two Englishmen from Rich's ship *Discovery* lived in Plymouth for several months, but the New England colony was not to be his home. Given the Pilgrims' evangelistic urge, there is little reason to believe that the Catholic John Pedro in Plymouth, as at Leighs Priory, was not once more targeted for Protestant conversion. Once again, he refused.

He would remain in Plymouth for about a year and a half. Lord Rich and the New England Council had appointed Francis West, of Jamestown, to the position of admiral of New England, with the responsibility of guarding Plymouth and other ventures north of Virginia from French, Dutch, and Spanish interlopers. Admiral West was the brother of Thomas West, Lord Rich's old business partner Lord Delaware, who died in 1618 while sailing to Jamestown to relieve Samuel Argall as governor. Captain West sent word to the Plymouth colony that Rich's surviving *Discovery* crew members were to be sent to Virginia aboard the *Swan* and, in 1623, John Pedro at the age of thirty landed at the colony of Jamestown.

The untitled and frequently landless younger sons of the English aristocracy traditionally found careers in the military, and so it was that Francis West appeared in the early history of Jamestown as both soldier and planter. Lord Delaware and his brother Francis were Rich's first cousins on the side of his mother, Lady Penelope Devereaux Rich. Lord Delaware before his death was with Lord Rich a co-owner of the *Treasurer*. Whether Rich, and later Francis West, originally regarded John Pedro as a temporary or permanent servant is not clear, since the unfinished contracts of indentured servants could be inherited, bought, traded, and turned over for debt.

The 1625 Jamestown census identified "John Pedro, a *Neger* aged 30" in the muster of Captain Francis West at his plantation in Elizabeth City on the Hampton River but revealed little else than that he had arrived two years earlier on the *Swan* with a white servant of Lord Rich named Benjamin Owin, also originally from the ship *Discovery*. At his plantation in Elizabeth City, Captain West listed his wife and child and six servants, including John Pedro, in that census. The West inventory included two barrels of corn, fourteen goats, and four kids. His plantation was not poor but certainly not wealthy. The inventory goes on to reveal Francis West's real importance to the colony—10 muskets, 3 pistols, 6 swords, 416 pounds of powder, and 10 pounds of lead. Captain West commanded Fort Algernon, guarding river access to the Jamestown plantations in the interior. He was in charge of the local militia in addition to serving as admiral of New England and was also the local representative to the Virginia House of Burgesses in Jamestown. Upon the death of

George Yeardley, West also briefly served as governor of Jamestown, until John Harvey was appointed.

It would be decades before Jamestown forbade Africans from carrying guns. John Pedro, listed in West's muster, served as a soldier at Fort Algernon. Since West, as both a Virginia captain and the New England admiral, seems to have paid more attention to military and civic duties than to raising tobacco, it is also probable that Pedro accompanied him on various military expeditions both at sea and on land.

Whether John Pedro was regarded as a slave, an indentured servant, or a professional soldier by Captain West, he was a free man by the early 1650s when he was clearing land for his own plantation and purchasing servants, white and black, to extend his holdings through headrights. Land records show him progressing from Isle of Wight County to adjoining Surry County and to Lancaster County as newer shires were carved from older counties. John Pedro's patent for land in the Lancaster, later Middlesex, area of Virginia places him on the Dragon Run Swamp just before he mysteriously disappeared from colonial records in 1653. Before this time he had reunited with fellow Angolans who had crossed the Atlantic with him on the *Bautista*, including John Graweere in Surry County, and Anthony and Mary Johnson at Bennett's Welcome, which was next door to West's plantation. He also became reacquainted with Antonio and Isabel, living with their young son, William, at Captain William Tucker's farm at Elizabeth City. They were all Angolan Christians like himself. In 1648, there were three hundred Africans in Jamestown among the fifteen thousand European settlers; and by then the first malungu communities of Angolan Christian freemen, many of whom had arrived via the Black Mayflower, were beginning to pop up in half a dozen places in Tidewater Virginia.

But in addition to his community, John Pedro had another loyalty—to his faith. His business dealings as a freeman show him involved with an emigrant from the English country gentry named William Eltonhead who was a Catholic and a friend of Lord Calvert, Baron of Baltimore. The Eltonheads had an enslaved Angolan man named Francisco, who would later become the freedman Francis Payne. By this time John Pedro had married a woman, yet to be identified, and they had at least one child, Matthew, who married into the Mayo family and from whom many descendants survive in Virginia to this day, though the Pedro surname has now been anglicized in a variety of forms.

❖

THE EXPLANATION FOR John Pedro's abrupt disappearance after 1653 can be found in the sweeping events that descended upon Jamestown and Maryland as a result of the long anticipated civil war between Parliament and the Stuart monarchy in England. That turbulent time may also explain why Pedro, John Graweere, Francis Payne, and Anthony and Mary Johnson became the earliest freed blacks in Jamestown and, with other Angolans then living in Dutch New York, also the earliest free black property owners in all of North America.

The tension between the English Parliament and the Stuart monarchy had begun with the 1605 premiere of *Masque of Blackness* in the reign of James I and expanded into a national drama during the reign of his son. Though Parliament and King Charles I tussled over many policies, the final debate that led to the English Civil War was, as every English school child knows, the controversy generated when Charles broke with tradition and levied England's landlocked shires for ship-money in 1634, to enable him to go to war with the French and the Dutch. According to the unanimous verdict of English-born historians, the two Englishmen most responsible for fomenting public opposition to the king's ship-money levy that subsequently led to civil war were John Hampden and his friend, the Puritan noble and pirate Lord Robert Rich, second Earl of Warwick.

Parliament responded to King Charles's ship-money levy by announcing that it and not the king was the final authority to decide if the interests of England were served by going to war with the French and the Dutch. Several shires refused to pay the levy, and notably Lord Rich's county of Essex was the most delinquent in collecting the king's fees. English peasants were faced with selling their livestock, their livelihood, to pay the levy, and Lord Rich respectfully but firmly informed the king that he would not be collecting any ship-money for his Highness because, as he said,

> His tenants were old men and had been accustomed to the mild government of Queen Elizabeth and King James. They could not bring themselves to consent, at the end of their lives to so notable a prejudice to the liberties of the kingdom nor were they willing voluntarily to deprive their posterity of those benefits which they had themselves inherited from the ancestors as a sacred deposit, though they were ready one and all to sacrifice life and goods for his Majesty.

Provoked by the national coolness to his levy scheme, King Charles focused his bitterest wrath upon Lord Rich, who was arrested and his mansion at Leighs Priory searched for evidence of conspiracy to commit treason. Although he never personally hated the Stuarts and as an aristocrat never supported abolishing the monarchy, Rich remained steadfast to his Calvinist-influenced convictions concerning personal accountability. Most of the English aristocracy would support Charles in the coming civil war, but a few lords, notably the Puritan colonial investors Rich, Brooke, Pym, and Say and Sele, supported Parliament.

In March 1642, sensing the inevitable, to check King Charles the House of Commons ordered Lord Northumberland to hand over his commission as lord high admiral to Rich, who was not only one of the most prominent Calvinist rebels but, by common consent, also England's last remaining spiritual heir to the dashing Elizabethan privateering heroes Hawkins, Drake, Cavendish, Essex, Mountjoy, and Raleigh. King Charles quickly countered the move and ordered that the fleet be turned over instead to the royalist Sir John Pennington. Northumberland acquiesced to Parliament and surrendered his commission to Lord Rich. It was Parliament's single best move on the eve of civil war.

In June, Charles called upon Rich to resign as high admiral. Days later, Parliament stubbornly reaffirmed the commission to the Earl of Warwick. On July 3, Lord Rich while aboard the ship *James*, the same ship by which he had sent the Angolan Anthony Johnson to Jamestown in 1621, wrote a letter to the king appealing the order to surrender his commission: "I shall humbly beg of your Majesty I may not be divided between two commands." In response, Charles accused him of "High Treason" and raised his standard at Nottingham on August 22, 1642, thus forcing the issue. The first English Civil War had started.

In the American colonies, settlers still considered themselves to be loyal Englishmen and aligned typically along the sides that divided England. Catholics and most Anglicans sided with their sovereign, whereas Puritans and Dissenters in Jamestown supported Parliament. In the same year that the war started, Charles appointed as governor of Jamestown William Berkeley, a staunch royalist firmly committed to the king's cause who would keep the colony loyal to the throne throughout the civil war in England. One of Governor Berkeley's first measures was to enact a strict conformity law requiring obedience to the king and the Church of England. Jamestown had been settled originally by a good many Puritans, contrary to the later myth of the colony's alleged Cavalier origin that was created by royalist planters, such as Robert Beverly, in the early eighteenth century. Unwilling to conform to Berkeley's order, many of these Jamestown Puritans, Lord Rich's friends, were forced out of Virginia and resettled along the Severn River (near Annapolis) in Lord Baltimore's Catholic colony, which had a tolerance clause. Maryland now contained the volatile ingredients for its own civil war.

The first group of Catholics had actually arrived in English North America in 1619. They were, of course, the thirty-odd black Christians among the sixty Angolans that the *White Lion* and the *Treasurer* stole from the Spanish slaver *Bautista*—John Pedro, John Graweere, Margaret Cornish, Isabell and Antonio Tucker, Maria and Antonio Johnson, and others. However, scholars, arguing against strong evidence to the contrary, disallow this recognition, claiming *all* Africans were forcibly baptized before leaving Angola, and that the Africans specifically delivered to Jamestown in 1619 had been "seasoned" in the West Indies on Spanish plantations before being brought to Jamestown—a claim refuted by Captain Acuna's statement that his ship was captured *after* leaving Angola for Mexico and also by the Delvas contract under which the *Bautista* was sailing.

Catholic missionaries had been active in Angola an entire century before 1619 and had won thousands of voluntary converts among the Bakongo and Mbundu nations. Antonio, Maria, John Pedro, Francisco, and Margarida were voluntary Christians and the children of black Christians in Angola from the eastern provinces of Ndongo and Kongo; they had already taken their Christian names while in Africa. They had not been forcibly baptized by a Catholic bishop just hours before boarding the slave ship departing from Luanda. Imbangala mercenaries had raided Christian and non-Christian Bantu provinces alike and mingled the captives together before trading them to the Portuguese for export to America. Those Angolans who were indeed forcibly baptized, such as Jiro, Congo, Cossongo, and Pallassa, in fact did not remember their new names upon arriving in Jamestown and continued to be called by their African names. As John Thornton states, Antonio, Francisco, Maria, and other Africans with Portuguese Christian names would have been familiar with the Catholic catechism long before they left Angola and arrived in Jamestown:

> Such a rudimentary instruction was probably oriented to the syncretic practice of the Angolan church, which followed patterns, already a century old, from the Kongo church that had originally fertilized it. Thus, early 17th century Spanish Jesuits, conducting an investigation of the state of knowledge of the Christian religion among newly arrived slaves [in Brazil], found that, for all the problems they noted, the Angolan slaves seem to have adequate understanding of the faith by the time they arrived. . . . In 1621, the [Portuguese] campaigns went deep into Kongo, and thousands were captured at the battle of Mbumbi at the very end of the year. These would all have been Christian, indeed, probably third or fourth generation Christian. Since they took the Christian names voluntarily, they would make these names known to their new masters in Virginia. People with a Spanish/Portuguese last name that is also a first name like John Francisco or John Pedro (on the 1625 [Virginia] census) are following an Angolan naming pattern. The source of the Iberian names, in our opinion, is

not the forced baptism given by the Portuguese in Luanda. In our opinion, whatever names people might have received in those circumstances would probably have been either forgotten or rejected when circumstances changed. Rather we think these names were taken voluntarily in Africa long before their owners were enslaved when the people were baptized.

But until better scholarship is acknowledged, the recognition for the first group of Catholics to arrive in English America is assumed by Europeans who landed in Maryland on the ship *Ark and the Dove* in 1634, fifteen years later, on Lord Baltimore's charter. Jesuit Andrew White recorded at that time the following:

25 March, 1634 we celebrated Mass for the first time in the island [St. Clement's]. This had never been done before in this part of the world.

That voyage of the *Ark and the Dove* from Southampton, England, carried 20 Catholic gentlemen of adventure and about 250 assorted craftsmen, mostly Protestant. Lord Baltimore had died, and the proprietorship of Maryland passed to his son Cecelius Calvert, who placed his brother Leonard Calvert as governor in the colony.

Among the articles governing Catholic Maryland was Calvert's admonition to

preserve peace and unity amongst all the passengers and to suffer no scandal or offence, whereby just complaint may be made by them in Virginia or in England . . . and to treat the Protestants with as much mildness and favor as justice will require.

This admirable directive was necessitated more by political reality than religious tolerance. England was a Protestant country, and the Calverts could only hope to maintain their Maryland charter by avoiding confrontation with Protestants. Maryland was not a democracy; Lord Baltimore ruled the colony as a palatinate or viceroyalty, and as such his direct rule was subject only to King Charles. Maryland at that time included lands that would become eventually Delaware and the southern portion of Pennsylvania. Because of political pressure from England, Lord Baltimore did in fact allow a fair degree of tolerance, and early Protestant Puritan reformers as well as Quakers, Baptists, and other Separatists would indeed find religious freedom in Maryland.

Virginians led by William Claiborne and Samuel Mathews for a long time continued to challenge Baltimore's charter, and a number of heavy skirmishes broke out until Captain Cornwaleys at last managed to put down Virginia's military adventures. Then came 1642 and the outbreak of civil war in England. Stripped of their Virginia property by royalist Governor Berkeley in 1642, the Jamestown Puritans, after fleeing to Maryland, informed their foremost protector in England of their plight. He was, of course, Parliament's newly named lord high admiral, Robert Rich, Earl of Warwick. Meanwhile, late in 1642, there arrived on the coast of Maryland a ship commanded by Captain Richard Ingle who, depending on which source is consulted, was either a republican patriot of Parliament . . . or a pirate. Captain Ingle made some rude remarks about the king and was promptly imprisoned on a charge of treason by loyal Marylanders. The alleged buccaneer escaped and fled back to England, where Lord High Admiral Rich supplied him with letters of marque from Parliament. Lord Rich was Lady Baltimore's cousin, but politics trumped family. Captain Ingle soon returned with a large warship suitably named the *Reformation* and rallied the disinherited Virginia Puritans exiled in Maryland. Aided by an armed company supplied by William Claiborne and Samuel Mathews of Denbigh Plantation, and perhaps including some of the Denbigh Africans, Captain Ingle put the colony's pro-Catholic governor to flight and took control of Maryland, ransacking the royalist settlers.

In England, meanwhile, the war was turning against King Charles. As admiral of the naval fleet, Lord Rich bottled up the ports of Denmark to prevent the king of that country, Charles's uncle, from coming to his rescue. He did likewise to Holland and France. The sea was the key to

England's land battles. If the armadas of Spain had succeeded during the reign of Elizabeth in putting an army on the ground in England, the English today would likely be speaking Spanish. With support from the sea choked off, King Charles's army was defeated at Marston Moor in 1644 and again at Naseby the following year. Lord Baltimore correctly judged the tide of war and, to hold on to his colony in the coming Puritan Commonwealth, he named as governor a Protestant, William Stone, of Virginia. It was a timely appointment for, in 1648, the army of Parliament and the Puritan Roundheads captured King Charles. Making further concessions to Parliament, Lord Baltimore allowed the Maryland assembly to pass in 1649 the Act Concerning Religion, which granted tolerance to all Christian sects that acknowledged the Holy Trinity and refrained from slandering Mary and the Apostles.

Back in England, King Charles was tried before a high court of peers that included Lord Rich. The irascible Rich, who had dangerously stood in defense of the Puritans against the Stuarts, now dangerously rose in defense of the Stuarts. He opposed the Puritans whom he had brought to power and voted against executing the king. But unfortunately for Charles, Robert Rich was once again in the minority. The High Court pronounced that England's monarch, as

a tyrant, traitor, murderer, and public enemy to the good people of this nation, shall be put to death by the severing of his head from his body.

On January 30, 1649, Charles Stuart I was brought before the public and beheaded at Whitehall Palace, where four decades earlier a young Robert Rich had performed before a happier royal family in blackface in *Masque of Blackness*.

Even after Charles's execution, Jamestown under Governor Berkeley remained loyal to the Stuarts. Berkeley even sent an officer to Charles II in Holland to swear loyalty and to personally extend to the orphaned heir of Charles I a place of refuge in Jamestown. Charles II declined and remained in Holland, but he recommissioned Berkeley as governor of the colony. At this time several royalist families fled England for Jamestown, and among them were the ancestors of some later well-known American founding fathers who, in 1776, would reconsider their former devotion to the king of England and their former distaste for republicanism.

In response to the colony's obstinate loyalty to the Stuarts in exile, the English Parliament cut off trade with Jamestown and sent a commission of officers with a fleet of warships to the colony to present terms. Four commissioners landed at Point Comfort and proceeded to Jamestown. The terms they offered the rebellious assemblymen were fair but firm. The velvet hammer was Parliament's proclamation that all servants and slaves in Jamestown who would join in support of Parliament should be set free. These laborers, mostly young, strong, and male, presented a significant military threat to the royalist Virginia landowners they outnumbered. It is possible that, during the 1640s, Virginians on both sides of the English Civil War granted freedom to some enslaved Africans to encourage their loyalty in those tense years. This decade recorded the first significant number of free people of color in the colony, and the earliest land acquisitions by free Africans. The 1640s also saw a dramatic rise in enslaved Africans fleeing plantation bondage.

Wary of a potential land army of freed African and English servants, and staring at a fleet of trained cannons off Point Comfort, the royalist Virginia Assembly at Jamestown blinked. Governor Berkeley resigned and Richard Bennett, nephew and heir of the Puritan Edward Bennett of Bennett's Welcome (the same Bennett who freed Antonio and Maria from slavery), was made governor. Jamestown was now subject to the Puritan Parliament. This brief respite from monarchy would not come again until the American Revolution.

The commissioners of Parliament then left Jamestown and sailed immediately to Maryland to offer the same terms to the Catholic royalists and they, too, forsook the Stuart cause and surrendered to the English Commonwealth, but only on condition that Maryland remain the proprietorship of the Catholic Lord Baltimore. The representatives of Parliament assented.

As peace seemed at hand, once again Virginia in 1649 pressed its old claim against the Catholic colony that had been given what it considered to be its northern lands. Though the king of England had stripped the Virginia Company of its greater charter in 1624 and essentially claimed North America for himself, that king was now dead and his heirs no longer in power. It was a contentious question at a critical time in American history: Whom did England now consider the legal holders of North America? The Roundheads, under the victorious Cromwell, were not anxious to answer the question. Their hold on power in England was tenuous, and they did not want to inflame further tension until they solidified their position. The Lord Protector's response therefore was a weak affirmation of the status quo—a continuance of the Stuart recognition of an independent Catholic Maryland as long as religious tolerance was observed.

The Virginians, however, ignored Cromwell's decision in favor of Maryland and instead heeded the timidity of his response. With assistance from the now reconciled Virginia Puritans living on the Severn, they prepared to attack St. Mary's and seize the government from Lord Baltimore's servants. Two of the Parliament commissioners in 1649 had been Richard Bennett and William Claiborne—men with old scores to settle against the Catholics of Maryland. In 1652, under pretense that their commissions from Parliament were still valid, they ordered Lord Baltimore's appointee, Maryland's Governor William Stone, to resign his office. Confronted with a sizable Puritan army, Stone stepped down, and the Puritans took over Maryland. One of the first acts of the new Puritan administration was to rescind Maryland's tolerant Act Concerning Religion, passed in 1649. Maryland Catholics were looted of their property and harassed, and the Jesuits went into hiding as vengeful Virginians railed against "popery, prelacy, and licentiousness of opinion." In response, Lord Protector Oliver Cromwell fired off an order in 1653, rebuking Jamestown and instructing his fellow Puritans "to forebear disturbing the Lord Baltimore, or his officers, or the People in Maryland." A few weeks later, Lord Baltimore sent a letter chastising Governor Stone for cowardice and ordering him to reclaim the government at St. Mary's. Now events quickly propelled Protestants and Catholics toward America's first sectarian war. Stone raised up the yellow and black standard of Lord Baltimore, and two hundred Catholics from Jamestown and Maryland gathered to support him.

Among the Catholic men equipped with musket and sword in 1654 was African American landowner John Pedro.

The Protestants had confiscated Maryland land records and were holding them in the home of Richard Preston in Providence (presently Annapolis). When Stone sailed his Catholic army up the Severn River to Providence in the heart of Puritan Maryland and arrested Preston, the Protestants of Virginia and Maryland responded by raising militia companies and seizing the man-of-war *Golden Lyon* lying at anchor in Chesapeake Bay. The two sides clashed on March 24, 1655, at the Battle of the Severn River near Horn Point. After a savage bombardment of cannon fire from the *Golden Lyon*, the Providence army prevailed against St. Mary's and killed nearly fifty of the two hundred Catholic soldiers.

After Stone surrendered, the Protestants released the majority of surviving Catholic soldiers after they swore to post bond, but a dozen Catholic leaders, including the wounded Governor Stone, William Eltonhead, and John Pedro were hurried in front of a drumhead court martial before Cromwell could interfere from England. The Virginians sentenced Stone and the other Catholic leaders to death but then pardoned them in response to the intercession of their wives and daughters.

However, there would be no pardon for four of the Catholic soldiers. Why these four were singled out from the many Catholics taken prisoners by the Protestants is not immediately clear. One of the four sentenced to be shot was William Eltonhead, a wealthy Catholic transplant from Lancashire, England, and close friend of Lord Calvert. Standing next to Eltonhead before the firing squad was his friend, the free Angolan American John Pedro. Muskets flashed and these four men fell dead, the first religious martyrs in colonial America. It is possible that Anthony Johnson, Antonio Longo, Philip Mongon, Benjamin Doll, and John Graweere, all now freedmen, were among the Protestant soldiers of Virginia who witnessed the executions.

John Pedro's sacrifice was not in vain, for the battle of the Severn was not a lost cause. The Catholic Calverts returned to govern Maryland in 1658, and the Toleration Act was reaffirmed. Two years later Charles II, son of the executed Stuart king, was restored to the throne of England, and he returned William Berkeley to govern Virginia, overturning the Puritan planter party headed by Bennett, Claiborne, and Mathews.

In the first generation of Jamestown, few individuals black or white could match the adventures of John Pedro. Before the age of thirty, he visited the ports of Jamaica, Mexico, Bermuda, and England; and in America he lived in Plymouth, Jamestown, and Maryland and knew the first families of these colonies. But the greatness of John Pedro was not that he was the first African to visit faraway places. He was notably a man of conscience and conviction. He was free and a highly respected sixty-year-old soldier at his execution.

· 9 ·

Two Save the Colony

A N ALGONQUIAN SURPRISE attack on Jamestown in 1622 claimed the lives of hundreds of settlers and nearly wiped out the colony. The massacre would have been much worse but for the intervention of a baptized Algonquian named Chanco, who warned his English employer the night before the assault:

> Such was (God be thanked for it) the good fruit of an Indian converted to Christianity; for though three hundred more of ours died by many of these Pagan infidels, yet Thousands of ours were saved by the means of one of them alone which was made a Christian.

In 1650, two young, baptized Angolan men would have a chance to reprise Chanco's role and prevent another massacre. What they knew could also help them escape slavery.

❋

IN THE SPRING of 1617, a false dawn of security and cautious optimism had pervaded the small settlement of Jamestown. The drought that had caused the "starving time" was over, and John Rolfe's improved Spanish Varina tobacco was starting to bring in a little cash. Native attacks had tapered off following the abduction of the Algonquian ruler's daughter, and at that time Pocahontas and Rolfe were away on a successful tour of England to drum up interest in the Virginia venture. It was a premature spring but few at Jamestown heeded the ominous signs.

Captain George Yeardley was interim governor in early 1617, and he, reflecting reformer Edwin Sandys's social integration philosophy, allowed settlers to trade European firearms to natives. Settlers were also setting up their own trading deals with various native kings and employing native servants. The Algonquian were freely coming and going from Jamestown. Spanish spies reported back to King Philip III that the English of Virginia had determined to intermarry with the native population to create a Christian mestizo, or Creole, society in which both English men and women were permitted to marry natives.

This optimistic portrait of Jamestown, population around one thousand, depended much on the inclusion of one particular native woman and her child. Then newly appointed Deputy Governor Samuel Argall and Secretary John Rolfe returned to Jamestown on the *George* in May 1617 with tidings that Pocahontas had suddenly died in London. Her ailing son had been left behind in England.

This should have been alarming news but many did not seem to realize its significance. Samuel Argall understood. The man who had abducted Pocahontas had never been deceived by the settlers' fragile peace with her father, Wahunsenacaw, who on the throne was known as Powhatan, the name of his kingdom. As absolute ruler of fifteen to fifty thousand subjects, Weroance Powhatan *was* the State—the most powerful single individual in all of North America in the early seventeenth century. Not merely a leading member of a native league of nations, Powhatan by conquest had made himself the hated dictator over an uneasy realm of subjugated kings in Chesapeake, and he was wary of new developments within his lands. As long as the English traded exclusively through him, he tolerated them and Jamestown. As long as they turned their guns on his enemies and aided his conquests, he fed them. However, the English from the beginning sought to bypass Powhatan to trade directly with the lesser kings scattered around

Chesapeake Bay, both within and without the weroance's empire. This would cost them dearly.

Argall knew that Powhatan deeply resented having his absolute authority undermined. Anglos, Angolans, and Algonquian—the names are similar and, in each of their native homelands, people were independently grappling with different facets of absolutism, royal monopolies, and nontraditional government. Powhatan was highly intelligent, perceptive, ambitious, and, like all absolute rulers, casually brutal when crossed. He had not forged his Pamunkey empire in the Algonquian tradition of his royal predecessors. He had begun restructuring Algonquian government before Captain John Smith and the *Susan Constant* arrived in Chesapeake Bay in 1607. Some theorists contend Powhatan's new expansionist and centralization policies were influenced by contact with earlier Spaniards who had settled in Chesapeake many years earlier, and some even claim that Powhatan and his half brother Opechancanough had Spanish blood. It is likely, however, that Powhatan was not part-Spanish and that the political transition ongoing when John Smith arrived in 1606 was in fact the absolute ruler's response to increasing encroachment from the north and the west by foreign Iroquoian-speaking people. Upon becoming weroance through matrilineal succession in the 1590s, according to custom, Powhatan had inherited the Pamunkey kingdom. But quite untraditionally, he then expanded his realm through ruthless conquest of neighboring Algonquian kingdoms. Subsequently, he also attempted to overturn the Algonquian accession custom by installing his own sons and daughters as kings and queens over subjugated Algonquian kingdoms to ensure loyalty and to build a royal dynasty. Some did not submit to Powhatan, such as the Chesapian Indians to his east, among whom Raleigh's "lost" settlers had taken refuge. In response, in 1606 Powhatan wiped out the Chesapians in a genocidal campaign of extinction.

Like the manikongos and ngolas of Central Africa, Powhatan understood the difference between trading partnerships and colonization. He refused to consider a relationship in which English governors would be his superiors and, knowing full well that acceptance represented the surrender of his autonomy, would not bow when Christopher Newport attempted to place upon his head a copper crown sent to him by King James.

Though brutal while putting down rebellion, Powhatan was no more aggressive than Samuel Argall, who had bombarded Algonquian villages for refusing to trade maize during the "starving time." Later on, some settlers charged that colonial administrators were too harsh when retaliating against native attacks, but others argued that Powhatan was contemptuous of them because they were not brutal enough. There was never a question as to which side of the debate had Argall's support. He believed that terror was the colony's best weapon against the much larger native population and, despite the false peace that had followed the abduction of Pocahontas, never doubted which course Powhatan would take against the English when he saw the opportunity. Powhatan and Argall were absolutely the wrong men to carry out the vision of English–Native American ethnic and social integration promoted by some contemporary English statesmen. Tragedy lay ahead for Jamestown and for the Algonquian, and from that tragedy grew a powerful distrust that poisoned European and Native American relations across the continent in the following centuries.

After he took office in 1617, Governor Argall's official letters to the home office in London were glowingly optimistic because he needed Virginia Company investors to have confidence in his administration. But privately, he disagreed with the firm's social integration experiments and believed that the English and the Algonquian were becoming too familiar, that Jamestown had failed, in his words, "to keep in fear the inconstant Savages." On the day that he returned to Jamestown as governor, Argall had been shocked to find that acting governor George Yeardley had trained and enlisted Algonquian warriors as musketeers for the militia company charged with protecting the governor:

In May he arrived at Jamestown, where he was kindly entertained by Captain Yeardley and his Company in a martial order, whose right hand file was led by an Indian.

Furthermore, before Argall arrived to govern in 1617, Captain Yeardley, confident that Pocahontas's abduction had brought lasting peace, had allowed the town's defensive walls to rot:

> Yea, the very Courts of Guard built by Sir Thomas Dale, was ready to fall, and the Palizados not sufficient to keep out hogs.

With Pocahontas dead and her young son, Thomas, in England, there was now no one with the authority of royal Native American lineage to protect Jamestown from Powhatan and his superior forces. Captain John Smith's *General History of Virginia*, published in England in 1624, was largely based on information supplied to him by John Rolfe and revealed what Governor Argall would not tell the company in London:

> In Jamestown he [Argall] found but five or six houses, the Church down, the Palizados broken, the bridge in pieces, the well of fresh water spoiled; the store-house they used for the Church the market-place, and streets, and all other spare places planted with tobacco; the Savages as frequent in their houses as themselves, whereby they were become expert in our arms, and had a great many in their custody and possession; the Colony dispersed all about, planting Tobacco.

After surveying the colony's vulnerability to attack, Governor Argall,

> not liking those proceedings, altered them agreeable to his own mind, taking the best order he could for repairing those defects which did exceedingly trouble us; we were constrained every year to build and repair our old Cottages, which were always a decaying in all places of the Country.

In May 1618, Governor Argall also posted an edict that redrew the sharp lines separating the English and the Algonquian—rules that had existed under Governor Sir Thomas Dale before Yeardley had become

the interim administrator. The penalty for disobeying Argall's orders
was sometimes death:

Proclamations:
> Against private trucking with Savages & pulling down pallisadoes.
> Against teaching Indians to shoot with guns on pain of death to learner
> and teacher.
> Against teaching Indians how to hunt deer or hogs without the Gov-
> ernor's leave.
> To go armed to Church & to work.
> No man to shoot but in defense of himself against enemies till a new
> supply of ammunition comes on pain of a year's Slavery.
> No trade with ye perfidious Savages nor familiarity lest they discover
> our weakness.

But these strict rules remained in effect only as long as Argall
remained governor. In 1619, as Argall fled the *Bautista* scandal, newly
knighted Sir George Yeardley returned to Jamestown not as acting governor but as the appointed governor. He resumed his policies of social
and ethnic integration, and again the Algonquian were welcomed at
Jamestown and in the homes of settlers.

Encouraged by the late Pocahontas's high-profile conversion, and
envious of Spain's colonization of Mexico, the English adopted Spain's
policies toward natives, failing to consider the differences between
the Algonquian and Aztec farmers. To achieve the idealized blended
society in Jamestown, the Virginia Company proposed to take native
boys and girls from their homes and educate them to European ways,
including Christianity and European-style agriculture, at a special college. Algonquian fathers traditionally taught their sons to hunt and
fight. Women were the farmers and raised their daughters to produce
and prepare food. In the eyes of the Algonquian, the English were proposing to feminize Algonquian boys. What the English planned to do
with their children appalled and alienated even friendly native kings
who intensely hated Powhatan of the Pamunkey.

Their loathing of the proposed college worked to Powhatan's advantage. Immediately upon learning of Pocahontas's death in London, her father began plotting a massive assault on the English settlement and its outlying plantations. Powhatan's scheme was cleverly designed not only to kill as many Jamestown settlers in one sudden sweep as possible but to limit the severity of English reprisals afterward. Powhatan set the date of the attack to occur after his subjects' seasonal harvest had been gathered, allowing the Algonquian to put by supplies and be far away from Jamestown when the expected counterattack came. For Powhatan's plan to work against the devastating firepower of English muskets, Algonquian soldiers had to cross the battle line covertly to infiltrate the enemy in large numbers and surprise them. Powhatan determined the date would be the Christian Good Friday holiday feast to which settlers traditionally welcomed natives into their homes. His ingenuity would help create the lasting stereotype in European minds of all natives as being treacherous.

Though Powhatan died in April 1618 before initiating his plan, his sibling Opechancanough, who was not his legal heir by Algonquian tradition, assumed leadership over the empire through strength of personality. He also resumed his brother's plot to strike the *tassantassas* (strangers), as the Algonquian regarded the English interlopers in Virginia. Opechancanough secured his claim as Powhatan's successor in three years and then he prepared to attack. Obedient to their new leader's orders, hundreds of Algonquian soldiers held the secret even as they mingled in Jamestown. Settlers unwittingly loaned their boats to natives who rowed up and down the rivers notifying other villages of the impending attack. Governor Yeardley was clueless.

At eight o'clock on Good Friday morning, March 1622, Algonquian men were sitting down to breakfast at the settlers' tables when, at a general signal, they all suddenly rose and began slaughtering their hosts. Algonquian military strikes traditionally spared women and children to adopt, enslave, or marry, but this particular attack falls under the description of a massacre—an attempted genocide like that waged by Powhatan against the Chesapians in 1606. Entire settler families—men, women, and children—were indiscriminately shot with English muskets, clubbed to death, and mutilated. For 140 miles along the James River, Algonquian raiders attacked every plantation, as well as Jamestown itself. The assaults were so well coordinated and sudden that few discerned the weapon that brought them to destruction. Of the English population, 347 out of 1,200 were killed in a single day. According to Samuel Purchas:

> Master John Berkeley, Captain Nathaniel Powell and his wife, and Captain Maycocke—all gentlemen of birth, virtue, and industry, and of the Council there, suffered under this their cruelty and treason.

Of the Africans who had been pirated three years earlier from the *Bautista*, who were working on some of the plantations attacked, none were reported slain though many white servants who worked alongside them in the fields perished that day. The Africans frequently traded with local natives as representatives of the Jamestown settlers. This close contact with natives may partly explain why they survived the massacre unscathed. However, it also true that many Native Americans, such as the Creek people, regarded black-skinned people with awe as being spirit beings—ghosts.

Antonio (Anthony Johnson) survived at Bennett's Welcome, although fifty-three whites were killed there. Next door, Lawne's plantation was wiped out, as well as Basse's plantation, yet Antonio, Francisco, Margaret, and other *Treasurer* Africans at Warrosquoke lived. The *White Lion* Angolans at Flowerdew and at Weyanoke were untouched in the assault that claimed twenty-seven lives at those plantations. At Piersey's plantation four English servants were killed but Africans were spared. Angela, along with another black woman and a black child, also lived through the attack on Jamestown.

In shock, survivors at eighty scattered farms fled for Jamestown, hoping to find ships to take them to safety in the bay. Governor Yeardley, who had assured settlers that they could safely place their plantations wide apart, now had to sail down the James River picking up the wounded and fleeing. South of the James River, all plantations were abandoned along a twenty-mile stretch to Hog Island. To relieve the colony, the governor sent out desperate calls for assistance, but aid from England was at least two months away by the speediest ships. As the smoke died and victims were buried, Yeardley, at last heeding the examples of former governors Dale and Argall, imposed rigid new laws against integration and built new forts. Bearing the brunt of the blame, he also took a militia company into the field to push the Nansemond natives out of the plantations they had taken over.

All able-bodied men including Africans, free and slave, were expected to defend the colony from native attack before Virginia banned slaves from carrying arms in 1639. Because only about six hundred Englishmen of fighting age were left alive in the colony to defend against upward of five thousand hostile Algonquian, there is little doubt that the settlers summoned the *Bautista*'s adult male Bantu to help the Jamestown militia against the Algonquian in the following months. Antonio (Tucker), John Pedro, Philip Mongon, Tony Longo, and others were listed in seventeenth-century Virginia musters. Most of them would have been experienced Ndongo soldiers who had been captured in Angola while fighting the Imbangala and Portuguese in 1619, or Kongolese Jaga militants who had been taken prisoner in the Nsundi rebellion against the manikongo at the same time and loaded onto the *Bautista* with the Ndongo.

Captain William Tucker had been the commander of Point Comfort in 1619. Before the *Treasurer* fled Jamestown for Bermuda, Tucker acquired from her the two Angolans named Antonio and Isabel. In Jamestown about the time of the massacre, this husband and wife became parents of the first ethnically African child born in English-speaking North America. They named him William Tucker, after the captain of Point Comfort and baptized him into the Anglican faith at Jamestown sometime before 1624. Following the massacre of 1622, Captain Tucker, as leader of the Point Comfort militia that would have included that child's father, Antonio Tucker, along with Doctor John Pott, met with representatives of the Algonquian on May 22, 1623, on the pretense of making peace. As many feigned speeches were going on during this meeting, Doctor Pott poisoned the wine as planned. Captain Tucker and his men then fell upon the natives, slaying two hundred Algonquian soldiers and several important leaders. Weroance Opechancanough managed to escape but eventually signed a treaty that barred his subjects from crossing the river into Jamestown proper. Attacks and reprisals ceased, and in the following years Jamestown relaxed its guard again. But in 1644, Opechancanough took advantage of the colony's distraction over the English Civil War and launched a second surprise assault on Jamestown that claimed five hundred English lives in a single day. In retaliation, royalist Governor William Berkeley sent out a company of militia and captured the king. Not long after, Opechancanough was shot in the back by a soldier guarding him. Native plots and attacks, however, did not end with his death.

❈

CAPTAIN WILLIAM HAWLEY, an English Puritan adventurer, had previously served as the deputy governor of Barbados, when he arrived in Jamestown on the eve of the English Civil War in 1641 to build a plantation in Northampton County. Among the Virginia headrights Hawley claimed in 1646 were Philip Mongon, Domingo Mathews, and another African named Tony (Antonio), who were all living in the colony before that year. Headrights were frequently recycled from county to county and it is impossible to say when exactly these three Africans had arrived in Virginia. Instead of coming with Hawley, they were possibly among the original *White Lion* Bantu or were born to a *White Lion* African couple at Samuel Mathews's Denbigh Plantation, as Domingo's surname indicates. As the cases of William Tucker and another black Virginian, Sebastian Cane, demonstrate, Africans sometimes took the surnames of English employers and slaveholders. Their Latin first names—Felipe, Domingo, and Antonio—may indicate that the parents of the three Africans had been Catholics in Angola who were brought across the ocean in 1619, or that they themselves arrived that year on the *White Lion* as children.

Hawley was prominent in political circles but he was also often broke, and his creditors included William Stone, later governor of Maryland. To cover his debts, Captain Hawley frequently loaned Philip Mongon and Domingo (Mingo) Mathews to his creditors, including neighboring tobacco planter John Foster, who was to have their labor for four years. Foster, however, had trouble getting Mongon and Mathews to work, for in 1648 he stated that

> the Negros which he had of Capt. William Hawley were very stubborn and would not follow his business . . . he feared that he should be undone by them.

He complained that the two Africans worked at their leisure and suspected that they were planning to run away. This was during the English Civil War, when Jamestown planters feared that their servants would rise up for one side or the other, and it is probable that Mathews and Mongon were inspired to escape slavery when they learned other planters set their English and African servants free. The two men essentially staged a sitdown strike, to force Foster to the bargaining table. Foster appealed to Hawley who, in 1649, wrote out an agreement stating that if they agreed to work four years for Foster, the slaves would be "free men, and labor for themselves."

But in 1650, before the four years were up, the two Angolans discovered a plot that would hasten their freedom. Hawley's plantation was near a number of Gingaskin villages and among his servants was a local native. The Gingaskin were allied with much-feared Native Americans called the Nanticoke, and both peoples were being elbowed out of their traditional lands by encroaching English settlers who were pressuring them to retire to a reservation. The terms were unreasonable. The 1,500-acre reservation that the settlers promised the Gingaskin was reduced to only 650 acres by the time the title was conveyed. Resistance was certain. The Nanticoke were not Algonquian but were related to the powerful Iroquois to the north, and they were reputed by other native peoples to be great magicians, according to the eighteenth-century Moravian missionary John Heckewelder, who knew the Nanticoke:

> They are said to have been the inventors of a poisonous substance by which they could destroy a whole settlement of people, and they are accused of being skilled in the arts of witchcraft. It is certain they are dreaded on this account. I have known Indians who firmly believed that they had people among them who could, if they pleased, destroy a whole army by merely blowing their breath toward them. Those of the Lenape and other tribes who pretend to witchcraft say that they learned the science from the Nanticoke.

Captain John Smith had made early contact with the Nanticoke in 1608 and described their strongly defended towns:

> They conducted us to their pallizadoed town, mantled with the barks of trees, with scaffolds like mounts, breasted about with breasts very formally.

In their contact with the Gingaskin and Nanticoke in Northampton County, Philip Mongon and Mingo Mathews learned that the natives intended to poison the wells of the English and then massacre them. After the two Africans relayed the news to the settlers and the massacre was foiled, the grateful Virginians granted them freedom in 1650.

One year later, Mongon married a Jamestown widow named Martha Merris, an Englishwoman, leased some land, and became a planter. It is not known if they had children. Within a decade, Martha died and Philip remarried an African woman named Mary, and they had a son, Philip Mongon II. Like any other English freeman, Philip Mongon was a member of the militia, owned two muskets, wore armor, and carried a sword at his side.

Seventeenth-century Virginia markets were little different from the markets of Angola, where local produce, iron, slaves, and cattle were traded for European pots and pans, axes, and bright cloth. The currency in Angola, nzimbu shells, was similar to Algonquian and other barter currencies in which the English also traded from Asia to America as late as the early nineteenth century. As Algonquian currency, roanoke, or *rawrenoke*, were shells strung on rawhide strings. In the role of frontier trader, Mongon once negotiated the ransom of an Englishman taken captive by Assateague natives; for this, the captive, Browne Herrick, rewarded him with half a ton of tobacco.

Beginning with his refusal to work as a slave, there is nothing in the record of Philip Mongon's life in the colony to suggest that he, though a minority, felt intimidated by the white majority at Jamestown. There is however documentation to suggest that he expected to exercise all the rights enjoyed by free white Englishmen while also violating some of the minor laws frequently violated by them. He had a temper when provoked and was not afraid to reveal it even to the highest English authorites. When brought to court in May 1660, according to genealogist Paul Heinegg, the black freedman "was acquitted of stealing hogs but was fined one hundred pounds of tobacco for throwing some hogs' ears on the table where the justices were sitting."

In another court case in 1685, Mongon apologetically admitted that he had

> rashly and indiscreetly also unadvisedly by my wonted most hasty humour most notoriously abused and defamed my most loving friends and neighbors John Duparkes and Robert Jarvis, and endeavored maliciously to defame the same persons.

Apart from having coleased three hundred acres of land on Mattawaman Creek with Peter Duparkes, possibly a kinsmen of the insulted John Duparkes, it is not known what sparked the venting of Mongon's "hasty humour," though the men were probably drinking at the time.

Another similar occasion shows he continued to socialize with local white farmers as the colonies began passing tougher restrictions against Africans. In the autumn of 1687, a group of neighbors gathered at Mongon's home with his wife and son, for a harvest celebration that included music, dancing, and the drinking of rum. A wealthy white planter couple named Cowdrey were Mongon's guests, with another white farmer, George Corbin, two tenant workers named Booker and Baker, and their wives. Indeed, all of the guests at Mongon's house that day were white. For some reason, "after much drinking and carousing," Booker drew the ire of the other celebrants, and blows began to fall. In the melee, Mongon produced his gun. Describing the incident, Booker's wife Ann later related in court that the guests

> did drink to a great height until at last all the said persons fell upon my said husband and did most cruelly beat him, my husband crying, "for god sake spare my life."
>
> Corbin replied, "thou short arse devil, I will kill you immediately, for a man is no more to me to kill in my humour then a mouse."
>
> Old Mongon after many bad words asked his son for the sword, who answered he could not tell but would immediately strike his heels as high as his head which he immediately did. The said old Mongon fetched out his gun and said "it please god I will kill some body immediately for I must do it," upon which I ran away and the said Mongon's son followed me and gave me several kicks upon which the said Corbin said "an old bitch, kick her to death."
>
> And this examinant further saith that she heard William Cowdrey and William Baker say [to Mongon] "kill him kill him, what you stay so long about him that we may go to drinking again." They made a fire to burn [Booker] and did fling him in the fire and burn some part of him but he was hauled out again by my self and the old Negro.

The fine for those, including Mongon, who assaulted Booker and his wife was five hundred pounds of tobacco each. Skin color was apparently not an issue in the trial.

Another minor run-in with the law occurred after Mongon loaned his musket to a Gingaskin named Charles who he had hired to hunt game for him. The black man who had won his freedom by revealing a native conspiracy should have been sensitive to the settlers' fear of armed

Indians. While in the field, the armed Gingaskin met a white man and severely beat him. Facing a fine of twenty pounds of tobacco for every day the victim was unable to work, Mongon quickly apologized in court and avoided the penalty.

In 1663, the community became aware that Mongon was having an extramarital affair with Margery Tyer, a free, single English woman. After she gave birth to a mixed child, the court threatened to give her twenty lashes of the whip for refusing to name the father. She relented, and her penalty for "the filthy sin of fornication" was reduced to ten lashes, though the justices promised she would be whipped again if her relationship with Mongon continued. Mongon was not whipped but was ordered to turn over five hundred pounds of tobacco for the offense of adultery and also required to post a bond for the care of his illegitimate offspring, to "save the parish harmless from the said child." This was a typical punishment for anyone in the colony, regardless of the ethnicity of the partners, who engaged in extramarital sex, and implies no special enmity against the black man.

Mongon's son married a free black woman also named Mary, and both Philip Mongon I and Philip Mongon II patented land in Accomack County, Virginia, near the plantation of a prominent Virginian, John Custis, with whom they transacted business from time to time. In addition to socializing with whites, the Mongons also interacted with fellow Angolans. The younger Mongon became the guardian of the children of another free black man named William Harman who died prematurely. The Mongons also mixed with the free black Carter family of Northampton County. There was a small but identifiable Angolan malungu community, on Savage's Neck near Savage's Creek, where these black families lived, and neighboring whites and Gingaskin natives were part of that community.

Though Philip Mongon saved Virginia from a terrible massacre, a vital service for which the colony rewarded him with freedom, the colonial administrators were sometimes at odds with his views on liberty. In 1645, while still a slave, ironically, he had been whipped for providing refuge to a white servant who ran away from an abusive master. Still, he paid his debts and performed his public service to Virginia when called, and his descendants followed his example. His grandson married the black woman Dinah Harman. One of the children of Dinah and Philip Mongon III was Esther Mongon, who married Henry Stephens. Three descendants of the black Stephens-Mongon family of Northampton County volunteered to fight in the American Revolution. Isaac Stephens of Northampton County served as a soldier, while Simon Stephens and his brother Stephen Stephens of Accomack County served aboard the ship *Accomac*. In return for their patriotic service, the young U.S. government paid their survivors with bounty land.

As a freedman, Philip Mongon had used his unique Bantu skills with cattle to support his family in early Virginia. In addition to the three hundred acres at Mattawaman Creek, he started another plantation of 250 acres on Pocomoke Creek near the Maryland border and raised livestock along with a highly prized light bay mare, in addition to growing tobacco. Exhibiting his Bantu background, Mongon the elder was a skilled butcher and prepared several cattle, lambs, and hogs for the funeral of a wealthy Jamestown planter for which he was handsomely paid. He recorded all of his livestock at court and, though he was illiterate, preserved Northampton County records contain his mark in Kimbundu fashion—a drawn bow and arrow.

Like Mongon, another Bantu man of early Jamestown would use his peoples' cattleman skills to pioneer a major American industry and at the same time introduce a way for hundreds of Africans to escape slavery before the door of freedom banged shut near the end of the seventeenth century.

That the Child
Shall Be Free

JOHN ROLFE CAREFULLY chose the two men who were to accompany him when he went down to Point Comfort to greet the *Treasurer* in late August 1619. He had to select companions who would not reveal that he intended to alert the pirates, with their stolen Africans, to flee Virginia. The first man Rolfe chose was his new father-in-law, Lieutenant William Pierce. The second was his close friend and neighbor at the Tappahannah settlement across the river from Jamestown. William Evans was an English merchant who had come to Virginia to build a plantation, and now he rowed downriver with Rolfe, hoping the *Treasurer* was bringing laborers he could hire. For each worker whose ship fare he paid, he could collect one headright from the Virginia Company. Each headright was a grant of fifty acres.

A few days after greeting the ship, which carried only Africans for trade, Evans patented four hundred acres, claiming eight headrights. In 1625, six years after the brief meeting with the *Treasurer* at Point Comfort, land documents reveal that he had an African named John Graweere working on his thousand-acre plantation, which suggests that Graweere arrived in 1619 either on the *Treasurer* or on the *White Lion*, since no other ship brought a large group of Africans before that time.

Evans owned the largest plantation at Tappahannah (now in Surry County), south of the James River. Other planters who owned land in the prime neighborhood were a who's who of early Jamestown, including Rolfe, Pierce, George Sandys, future Governor Samuel Mathews, and Captain Ralph Hamor. The Evans estate was known as College Plantation. The land, originally donated to the colony by the East India Company, was to be the site of the college for native children, before that plan was canceled by the massacre of 1622. Evans chose to live in England but traveled frequently between London and Jamestown, and he appointed an overseer to take care of the plantation in his absence. At one time, twenty and more servants labored at College Plantation, and John Graweere was not the only African. Michael and Katherine, two African teenagers, arrived there by 1628, eventually married, had children, and took the surname Blizzard following a famous Virginia hurricane.

Adjoining Evans's land was the plantation of a Jamestown legislator named Robert Shepherd who had among his servants an enslaved black woman named Margaret Cornish. She, too, was one of the *Bautista* Africans and was noted in the Jamestown census of 1625 simply as "Margaret." About 1635, John Graweere and Margaret Cornish had a son who was considered a slave of Robert Shepherd, like his mother. The legal status of an African child at this time in Jamestown was determined by the condition of the mother, not the father. If the mother was a slave, the child was a slave regardless of the legal status of the father.

At this time, before it was outlawed in 1705, some Jamestown slaveholders allowed Africans to raise cattle and crops of their own to purchase their freedom. This practice, identified also in precolonial Africa, was akin to an ancient Roman custom that permitted slaves to accumulate property to eventually acquire their liberty. The Siete Partidas laws, later adopted by Spain and Portugal, were an ancient acknowledgment that slavery was not a natural condition for mankind. This custom played to Ndongo skills. John Graweere, with Evans's consent, raised cattle, chickens, and hogs to purchase freedom for

himself as well as his enslaved wife and son, as recorded in the Jamestown General Court:

> John Graweere being a negro servant unto William Evans was permit-
> ted by his said master to keep hogs and make the best benefit thereof to
> himself provided that the said Evans might have half the increase which
> was accordingly rendered unto him by the said negro and the other half
> reserved for his own benefit.

But Graweere's plans for the future did not unfold as he hoped.
After bearing his son in 1635, Margaret entered into what would be
a long relationship with a young white gentleman who lived near the
Shepherd plantation.

The Sweets owned a plantation on the Blackwater River and were
a wealthy and influential family with a legislator in the Jamestown
Assembly. The affair was revealed when Margaret bore an obviously ethnically-mixed child. The infant came to the attention of
the Jamestown court and a subsequent inquiry revealed the father
to be Robert Sweet. In the early years of Jamestown, sex between
masters and indentured Englishwomen or African servant women
was strictly forbidden and publicly punished, as was any sexual
relationship outside of marriage, regardless of color. Not until more
than a century later did the social restrictions of the Anglican Church
against extramarital sex diminish and the sexual abuse of enslaved
African women increase, when, after the American Revolution and
the beginning of the separation of Church and State, the Church
of England lost power in America, and the number of children by
master-slave rape rose dramatically. Before the year 1800, according
to genealogist Paul Heinegg, of the nearly four hundred early black
Tidewater families he researched who became free, only three individuals descended from the union of a slaveholder and a slave. On
the Eastern Shore of Virginia, historian Douglas Deal found only
one such case. Observers in the nineteenth century *assumed* mulattos in the South were the offspring of white slaveholders and slaves.

However, before the Nat Turner Rebellion, many mixed children were the offspring of free blacks and whites, the most common cases being children born of free black fathers and white mothers who were married, legally or not.

When the Sweet-Cornish affair came to light, Robert and Margaret were charged with fornication, tried, and convicted on October 17, 1640:

> Whereas Robert Sweet hath begotten with child a Negro woman servant belonging unto Lt. Sheppard, the court hath therefore ordered that the said Negro woman shall be whipped at the whipping post and the said Sweet shall tomorrow in the forenoon do public penance for his offence at James City church in the time of divine service according to the laws of England in that case provided.

English custom required that the offenders come publicly to church dressed only in white, holding a white stick as a sign of humility and repentance. Robert Sweet appeared before the congregation of the Jamestown church on Sunday, clad in a white sheet, according to Bishop Meade's history of early Virginia. The sentence of thirty lashes given to Margaret Cornish was also prescribed to white women found guilty of adultery or fornication with white men, and to white men convicted of sex with unmarried black women. The fact that Cornish was sentenced to be whipped and Sweet was not may have less to do with color than with their class status. She was a servant, and he a gentleman and the son of a Jamestown assemblyman. First offenders could avoid the whip and even the gallows by a custom known as "benefit of clergy." That is, if they could recite a single verse from the Bible they were spared the punishment. The most commonly recited verse was Psalms 51:1. However, the benefit of clergy was frequently not used because most people, except for the clergy, were illiterate.

Devastated by the affair, John Graweere immediately went to court for custody of his child from its mother. Five months after his wife's trial, on March 31, 1641, he sold livestock to buy his son's freedom and then, significantly, recorded it in court:

[That] the said Negro did for his said child purchase its freedom of Lieut. Sheppard, the court hath therefore ordered that the child shall be free from the said William Evans or his assigns.

For John Graweere and Margaret Cornish, there was no reconciliation; he did not purchase her freedom with that of their son. Graweere's declaration in seeking his child's freedom was pointed: Margaret had broken the laws of the Church, and Graweere informed the Jamestown court that he wanted to remove his child from her custody as well as from slavery on the Shepherd plantation because

he desired his child should be made a Christian and be taught and exercised in the church of England.

Whatever Robert Sweet and Margaret Cornish may have confessed in court and in church, the pair was not repentant and continued their relationship despite the colony's strong disapproval. Margaret Cornish named Robert Sweet's first son Robert Cornish. She bore another child out of wedlock in 1642 and named him William Sweet. In 1645, she bore yet another son by Sweet whom she named Anthony Cornish. Margaret also bore Sweet a daughter whose freedom was purchased by another Angolan American family.

The Angolan who adopted the mixed daughter was Emanuel Driggus (Rodriges), a servant of planter Francis Pott who, when he moved across the bay to the Eastern Shore, brought Driggus and a number of other blacks with him. Driggus, stirred by a common Angolan kinship, adopted this illegitimate child when Margaret Cornish faced further censure. Margaret spent most of her life in slavery until, motivated more by the cost of caring for her than by humanitarian reasons, Robert Shepherd freed her in her old age as she became less useful to the family. In 1670, she moved to Lawns Creek Parish, where the General Court of Virginia exempted her from taxes because of her age.

After purchasing the freedom of his son, John Graweere moved to Lancaster County, Virginia, around 1647, where he reunited with his

Early Angolan markets included merchandise from several kingdoms. Because of their extensive and lively trade, Angolans were well prepared for the market economy of Colonial America and frequently traded as agents of Jamestown planters, or for themselves when freed. From an 1891 German chromolithograph. *New York Public Library*

This mid-seventeenth-century Italian watercolor by Catholic missionary Antonio Cavazzi pictures the legendary first king of Ndongo forging iron. Angolans were making iron long before the first Europeans arrived in 1482, and the Ndongo word *ngola*, meaning "iron blacksmith," became the name of the country, Angola. The metal-manufacturing skills of the Angolans would be valuable in Colonial America. *University of Virginia Library*

This early eighteenth-century watercolor by Catholic missionary Bernardino Ignazio shows African clerics and a robed soba (local chief) kneeling before the altar in a village mass in Angola. The popularity of the Angolan Church, established about 1510, resulting in thousands of voluntary conversions in the sixteenth and seventeenth centuries, questions the theory of universally forced baptisms among early Africans arriving in America. It also explains the smooth transition of some of the first Angolans into English Jamestown society after they were freed from slavery. *University of Virginia Library*

Alvaro, king of Kongo, receives Protestant Dutch envoys to counter Portuguese attempts to colonize Angola in 1589. Already expanding their super states when the first Europeans arrived in 1482, the kings of Angola continued trading captured Jaga insurgents to the Dutch, as they had previously to the Portuguese. This engraving was made in 1689 by Dutch artist Olfert Dapper. *New York Public Library*

Illustration of a Bantu slave coffle from an engraving that accompanied the account of David Livingstone's 1865 expedition to Central Africa. This scene is reminiscent of the forced march of Ndongo captives to the Angolan coast after Portuguese and Imbangala armies destroyed the royal city of Kabasa in 1619. *University of Virginia Library*

Inigo Jones's 1604 sketch of an African queen, one of the characters in Ben Jonson's 1605 play, *Masque of Blackness*, in which King James I welcomes Africans to the new British Empire. *Arts Council of Britain*

Mid seventeenth-century engraving from a portrait by the Flemish master Anthony Van Dyck (circa 1620), of young Lord Robert Rich, 2nd Earl of Warwick, about the time that he sent the corsair *Treasurer* to the West Indies to attack Spanish ships in response to Spanish Count Gondomar's influence on James I of England. *New York Public Library*

Engraving by Johann Theodore de Bry (1618) from the 1617 illustration by Georg Keller, shows Captain Samuel Argall of Lord Rich's corsair *Treasurer* (pictured on the right) abducting Pocahontas in 1613. Six years later the same ship consorted with another corsair, the *White Lion*, to seize the first Jamestown Africans from the Spanish slave ship *Bautista*. The one-hundred–ton *Treasurer* is not drawn to scale. *University of Virginia Library*

An illustration of the first "twenty and odd" Africans landing at Jamestown in 1619. This depiction was created in 1917 by famed American illustrator Howard Pyle, who was noted for his attention to historic detail. The 140-to-160–ton corsair *White Lion* is in the background. Her consort, Lord Rich's ship *Treasurer*, arrived 3–4 days later carrying more Africans from the plundered *Bautista*. *New York Public Library*

Engravings, such as this one, of Sir Walter Raleigh's 1618 execution for piracy against the Spanish in America, circulated in anonymous seventeenth-century pamphlets. Raleigh's beheading, upon the demand of James I of England and Spanish Ambassador Gondomar, prompted agents of Lord Robert Rich to cover up details about the Africans that his ship *Treasurer* stole from the Spanish slave ship *Bautista*. *University of Virginia Library*

Engraved cover of the anonymous 1624 English booklet *Vox Populi*, lampooning Spanish ambassador Count Gondomar and his delicate digestive condition (see his "throne" and carriage). The English despised the Spaniard because of his strong influence over King James and vilified him in plays and pamphlets. After demanding the execution of Sir Walter Raleigh, Count Gondomar pursued the prosecution of the corsairs *White Lion* and *Treasurer* for the piracy of the first Jamestown Africans from his family's slave ship, *San Juan Bautista*. *British Library*

Tobacco shipping label from the seventeenth century shows Africans in Virginia waiting as a ship comes in to transport harvested tobacco to Europe. The Angolans' iron-age agricultural skills contributed greatly to the survival of Jamestown – the first English speaking American colony. *Georgetown Preparatory Academy*

This mid-seventeenth-century Italian watercolor by Catholic missionary Antonio Cavazzi, who knew Ngola Anna Nzinga, shows her armed with a bow and wearing a Christian crown. The baptized ruler of Ndongo, Anna Nzinga made war against Portuguese colonizers as well as African rivals. She lived at the same time as the charter generation of Black America, many of whom came from her kingdom. *University of Virginia Library*

Print depicting a fleet from the victorious English Parliament in 1652 demanding the surrender of royalist Jamestown and the freeing of all servants and slaves who promise to support Parliament in the English Civil War. Free Africans first began acquiring land around Jamestown about this time. *New York Public Library*

Another engraving by Father Cavazzi depicts Anna Nzinga using a subject as a throne when meeting the Portuguese governor at Luanda, Angola. The legendary incident occurred about 1620. *University of Virginia Library*

A slave auction in Dutch New York in 1643 is depicted in this 1895 illustration by Howard Pyle. The Dutch West India Company forced the Portuguese out of Luanda, Angola, between 1635 and 1648, and during this time Jamestown planters sailed to Dutch New York to acquire Angolans as slaves for Virginia. *University of Virginia Library*

The burning of Jamestown in 1676 at the climax of Bacon's Rebellion is pictured in Howard Pyle's 1901 illustration. Promised freedom, many enslaved Africans joined Nathaniel Bacon's populist army and were the last to surrender to British forces. *New York Public Library*

An 1840 woodcut from *A History of the Amistad Captives* shows slaves packed tightly together in the crowded cargo hatch of a slave ship. As slave laws were codified, fewer Africans found access to liberty in Colonial America. In 1691, the Virginia legislature forbade freeing slaves unless the slaveholder transported them out of the colony. At the codification of slave laws in 1705, the legislature outlawed the custom of letting African slaves raise crops and cattle to purchase their freedom. Finally, in 1723, Virginia forbade the freeing of any African from slavery unless the slave performed some service to the colony such as reporting a planned slave rebellion. *New Haven Colony Historical Society*

old companion from the *Bautista*, John Pedro. Those were turbulent times, and their reunion was perhaps strained due to their religious differences. During this period, England was engaged in its civil war and the American colonies were becoming a battleground between Puritans, Anglicans, and Catholics. As indicated in colonial records, at the time Graweere purchased his son's freedom in Surry County, he had converted to the Protestant Anglican Church, whereas John Pedro was about to give his life for the Catholic cause.

In those days, every town and county seat had in its square, a church, and a whipping post, along with a pillory and bilboes, or stocks. Punishment was severe in Jamestown, and colonial courts sentenced offenders to be branded, whipped, pilloried, or maimed by piercing. English spectators in Jamestown, as in London, gathered and lustily hurled abuse and garbage as criminals were punished in the town square. In Lancaster County, freedman Graweere rose to become an officer of the Virginia Court during the Puritan-led Bennett administration, and one of his duties was to punish white lawbreakers at the public whipping post. Those brought before John Graweere were white men and white women, both free and indentured. His position as an officer of the court indicates that Graweere (sometimes then written Grasheare or Grasher) was well respected in Jamestown. Even otherwise upstanding members in the community from time to time violated laws, such as by indulging in drunkenness, fornication, adultery, cursing, loitering, skipping church, or gossiping, all of for which they were publicly punished, as amply recorded in Jamestown court records. There is no court record that John Graweere was ever implicated in the smallest offense that would have jeopardized his position. Whether he remarried is not documented, though it is likely that he did.

As for his son by Margaret Cornish, some researchers indicate he may have been an early free black planter named Mihill Gowen, who was born about 1635. Gowen flourished and was the ancestor of the very large free Gowen, or Goins, family now spread throughout the country. One of his descendants was elected to the Mississippi legislature in the nineteenth century. Many of his descendants fought as patriots in the

American Revolution and one, John "Buck" Gowen, rose to the rank of major in that war and eventually became a general. On November 7, 1775, the English governor general of Virginia, John, Earl of Dunmore, issued a proclamation in King George III's name that offered freedom to Africans willing to fight for the British against American rebels. Some responded, but Judge William Bryan observed that many free blacks enlisted as patriots in the cause of American independence:

> In the times of our Revolutionary War free Negroes and mulattos mustered in the ranks with white men. . . . That class of persons were equally liable to draft—and frequently volunteered in the public Service.

There is no record that Robert Sweet ever spent a halfpenny toward freeing Margaret Cornish or raising their children. However, the offspring of the couple increased greatly and survive today with the surnames Cornish and Sweet, or, as it is sometimes spelled, Sweat. Several of the mixed Sweets enlisted in colonial companies fighting the Cherokee, and a number of them also fought as patriots in the American Revolution. Some married into the Pamunkey tribe of Powhatan's and were listed as "Indians." Immediately following the Revolution, the Sweets were among the earliest English-speaking Americans, black or white, to cross the Mississippi River into the West. Some of the free Sweets of color became wealthy and were listed in government records as white or mulatto. Other Sweet descendants were classified as black, and one served as the test case in an important higher-education civil rights lawsuit in the twentieth century, the first case in which a person of color was admitted to a white Southern university.

Emanuel (Manuel) Driggus, the man who adopted the mixed daughter of Margaret Cornish and Robert Sweet, was also identified under the Portuguese name of "Emanuel Rodriges" indicating his Angolan origin. One of his companions, Bashaw Fernando, also had a Latin name, and his presence on the Francis Pott plantation suggests both of them were acquired from Angola together. Pott was a close friend of Samuel Mathews and was also involved in the thrusting out of Governor

Harvey in Jamestown. It is therefore likely that Driggus and Fernando were born to the "20 and odd" *White Lion* Africans. If so, they were captured at the time the Portuguese invaded Ndongo. As a Bantu from Angola, Driggus, like his countryman John Graweere, was skilled with cattle, and he used this to the advantage of his community. He was still enslaved on Pott's plantation in Magotha Bay in 1645 when the Englishman gave him a cow and a calf to start his own herd.

Driggus married his first wife, a slave named Frances, before Pott traded him and Bashaw Fernando to a planter named Stephen Charlton. To make sure that the black family would not be cheated, the planters, at his request, affirmed Driggus's private livestock in court. On December 30, 1652, Francis Pott and Stephen Charlton acknowledged, "Ye said cattle, etc. are ye proper goods of the said Negroes." Manuel Driggus traded some of his livestock that year to purchase the freedom of his adopted daughter Jane (Sweet-Cornish) from Pott, and four years later he also gave a black heifer to a young slave on a nearby plantation, adding to the evidence of an extended malungu kinship in the early Angolan American community at Jamestown.

A few months later the county court of Northampton, representing the interests of planters plagued by employee theft, halted the practice of buying property from all servants, black or white. But Driggus was quick to respond and had the court record his family's legal ownership of hogs, cattle, and chickens

> that were now in their possession the which they have lawfully gotten, and purchased in their service formerly under the said Capt. Pott, and since augmented and increased under the service of Capt. Stephen Charlton. These are the proper goods of the above said Negroes and they may freely dispose of them either in their lifetime or at their death.

Manuel Driggus would eventually claim ten children and of those, three were adopted and another five were by his first wife Frances (Francesca). While Driggus was able to use his cattle to purchase the freedom of his adopted daughter Jane and aid in purchasing the freedom of two other children on the Nathaniel Littleton plantation, he was not always able to ransom his own children from slavery. In December 1657, his former master, Francis Pott, sold his oldest natural daughter Ann to a white planter named Pannell to have and to hold the same with all her increase forever. When Pott died, his widow remarried William Kendall who apparently disapproved of slavery and, within a year, he began to release the Africans that his new wife had brought to the marriage. He freed Manuel Driggus about the same time he freed Bashaw Fernando.

As a free man, the African-American Emanuel Driggus, whose Portuguese name means "God is with us," continued to give calves and heifers to purchase the freedom of black slave children not his own. In doing so he changed the lives of hundreds of their descendants for centuries. Both Driggus and another black Angolan Christian freedman, Francis (Francisco) Payne, were men highly regarded by their white neighbors. When an English sailor named George Williams fell sick in Jamestown far from home, Driggus befriended and nursed him. In his will in 1667, Williams bequeathed

> to Manuel Driggus, Negro, for his care and trouble in tending me in my sickness, my wages due me for Eleven Month's service on the Ship *Louis Increase* of Bristol.

After his wife Frances died, Manuel Driggus married an Englishwoman, Elizabeth, in 1661. To ensure that he would not desert his new wife, he gave her a three-year-old gray mare, along with ownership of its future increase. At that time, mares were valuable in Jamestown. Because of the scarcity in the colony of women, black or white, Elizabeth would have been courted by a number of white Virginians. However, Driggus's careful cattle investments won him the bride, and she bore him two more children.

Of his later descendants, his grandson Azaricum Driggus became a wealthy planter. Another descendant was Captain Winslow Driggers, who led a militia company of raiders, white planters, protesting British taxes in the Carolinas on the eve of the American Revolution, until he was captured and hung by British loyalists. Another Driggus descendant was the famous Captain Gideon Gibson, who also led white farmers in raids on British officials who were seizing their livestock for taxes. Gibson was praised as a patriot and an orator on the floor of the Carolina Assembly House, and several illustrious political families of the eighteenth and nineteenth centuries were related to him. The surname Gibson is common among the malungu communities (known today as Melungeons) of Virginia, Tennessee, North Carolina, and Kentucky.

Relationships that went beyond the front gate were strong among the malungu families of early Jamestown. These ties would withstand universal hostility in the South over two centuries of slavery. Jamestown Africans shared a responsibility to their descendants and to countrymen who were in the same degraded condition. They helped one another by drawing from their Bantu culture. Their skill with cattle was why the king of Kongo had sought to break the tentative alliance between Portugal and the ngola of Ndongo in the sixteenth century. Ndongo was famed for raising cattle and grain, and Manikongo Álvaro stood to lose his monopoly of the kingdom's resources if the Portuguese established direct contact with the ngola at Kabasa. When these Mbundu people were captured and sent across the sea to Brazil, Mexico, Dutch New York, Jamestown, and Maryland, they introduced their advanced Bantu cattle culture into these colonies and, unheralded, became the first cattle experts in North America. Around Chesapeake, according to historian Philip D. Morgan,

> there were more cattle in the all-black or mixed-race quarters than in those composed solely of whites. . . . In 1697, for instance, at an all-black quarter in Charles County, one old black man and two elderly black women, together with four children, managed a herd of fifty cattle and forty-eight hogs.

Many traditions and terms of Kimbundu-speaking Ndongo later appeared in the American West, of all places. Their word *kraal*, for cattle enclosure, became "corral." *Dogie* was a Bantu word that in Angola meant "small calf." It was not the Spanish word *vaquero* but the Kimbundu word *bukra* that became *buckaroo*, meaning "cowboy."

Spanish vaqueros are heralded for teaching the cattle culture to American cowboys in the Southwest and were indeed superb at working herds on horses they acquired from the Moors of North Africa. However, it has been unrecognized that Bantu who were sent to Central and South America from Angola first taught the vaqueros about tending cattle on the open range. And the Western cattle culture that developed in North America owes as much if not more to the Mbundu Angolans of Jamestown as to Spaniards. William Ashworth was born free in 1793 in South Carolina, and through him a direct lineage can be established from the Bantu people captured in Angola and taken to Jamestown, whose descendants later moved into the American West, not as slave cowboys but as free black cattle barons. In 1673, the Jamestown planter Edmund Lister transported his Angolan "cattle hunters" to South Carolina just as that colony was opening up. By 1708, their skill with cattle greatly impressed South Carolinians, who numbered them and other black herders at around one thousand experienced range hands. Immediately following the American Revolution, Ashworth moved his cattle from the Peedee River into Louisiana. His sons crossed the river into the Texas frontier before the fall of the Alamo and before any other English-speaking white cattleman. These freeborn Bantu cattle barons built up the first large non-Spanish cattle herds without requiring an education from vaqueros because, in colonial America east of the Appalachians, their fathers had developed a unique North American cattle culture. They pioneered the use of saltlicks to control cattle movement without fences. Bantu Americans also bred a dog that can take down a bull by tenaciously fastening on its nose—the leopard dog—and they first plaited bull whips to control cattle in the dense undergrowth east of the Mississippi, before taking up the Spanish lariat on the open Western Plains. Sadly overlooked for centuries, the origin of the North America cattle culture begins at Jamestown with the arrival of Black Mayflower Bantu cattlemen like John Graweere, Manuel Driggus, and others pirated from the Spanish frigate *Bautista*.

One of the most striking features of the free founders of African America at Jamestown is how their descendants stuck together long after moving west. Children of the first families of seventeenth-century Virginia—the Gowens, Drigguses, Deals, Johnsons, Carters, Harmans, Sweets, Cumbos, and many more—can be found establishing communities together two centuries later far away from Jamestown. The genealogy of just a few families illustrates the pioneering spirit of the nation of Bantu colonizers who, after migrating west across Africa long ago, and being forced into slave ships in Angola, began colonizing America almost as soon as they touched land.

Ties That Bind

I N THE FIRST Jamestown generation, African-born Benjamin Doll rose from slavery to own a three-hundred-acre plantation in Surry County, Virginia. To acquire his land via headrights, Doll purchased the passage to Virginia of six English servants who were then indentured to him. Following the example of John Graweere, he earned the money to purchase indentured servants by raising horses, cattle, goats, poultry, and crops while still in bondage. A rarity among white as well as black Virginians at the time, Doll was also literate, perhaps the first African American in Jamestown to read and write English. A white widow in Surry County, Judah Hide, authorized him to act as her attorney in 1659.

The Dolls are one of several of Jamestown's black families who can be documented over many generations as migrating west from the Tidewater colony. Doll married a black woman whose name has not yet been found, and they had at least one son named John, born about 1648. John Doll acquired about two hundred acres in Isle of Wight County and married a black woman with the Angolan-Portuguese name of Isabell. Through them, the Doll family survives today under various spellings such as Daule, Doyal, Dial, Dale, and Deal. They are typical of the early Angolan malungu families who retained ties to original black families long after they came to America and settled at Jamestown. James Doyal descended from John and Isabell Doll, and, in 1768, he and his wife Elizabeth moved from Tidewater, Virginia, to Bladen County, North Carolina, and bought land. His neighbors there included the Angolan Cumbo and Johnson families, also descended from the first generation of Jamestown Africans several decades earlier. James and Elizabeth (Hill) Doyal had at least three children. Eldest son Tapley Dial, born before 1776, moved to Opelousas, Louisiana, after the American Revolution and became the head of a family that listed several free people of color. Tapley Dial married Sarah Johnson in 1816, a descendant of Antonio Johnson, one of the original Africans who was sent by Lord Robert Rich to the Jamestown plantation of Edward Bennett in 1621.

Tapley's brother was Peter Dial, who was head of a Robeson County, North Carolina, household of six free blacks in 1800 and later, of ten "free colored" in 1820. In the Carolinas, the anomalous free *malungu* communities were known by various names such as Brass Ankles and Lumbees. In Appalachian Virginia, Tennessee, and Kentucky, they were identified as "Melungeons" and "Ramps." In Ohio they were called "Carmel Indians," and in Louisiana they were frequently called "Red-bones." The surnames, however, were the same, and whatever regional names they were called, they were people of color who descended from old Angolan American *malungu* families that included those brought to Jamestown before the Pilgrims established New England in 1620. They lived free during times of slavery in land-owning communities scattered throughout the South and held their lands by force of arms as well as by cunning.

In addition to sons, James and Elizabeth Doyal also had a daughter, Keziah, who married the free black James Ashworth of South Carolina. This couple of color moved to Orange, Texas, to pioneer Bantu cattle ranching before any white cattleman. Another descendant of John and Isabell Doll was William Dales of Brunswick County, Virginia. He and his wife Sarah were parents of Mary Dole, born in 1767, who married the free black man Andrew Jeffires of Greensville County, Virginia. Their many children married free people of color and also established free communities in North Carolina.

❖

THE AFRICAN CUMBO family first appeared in Jamestown documents in September 1644, and they, too, survived and traveled far from the colony over many generations. That year, the Virginia House of Burgesses ruled Manuel Cambow was a *Christian* servant and ordered that he was to serve as other Christians in indenture. He was freed in September 1665 and, two years later, was granted fifty acres in James City County, near the free black Mihill Gowen, son of John Graweere and Margaret Cornish. In the papers that recorded the land patent, Cambow was described as a Negro. Several clues indicate that Manuel Cambow was a Bantu from Angola. First, Cambow (possibly derived from Kambol, a royal name of Ndongo) was an African with a Christian Portuguese name who appeared in Jamestown between 1619 and 1650, when West India Company records show that virtually all of the three hundred or so Africans in Jamestown were being brought to the colony by Protestant pirates raiding Portuguese and Spanish slave ships sailing from Luanda, Angola. Second, a few generations later, to escape laws restricting the rights of black Americans, Manuel Cambow's descendants were telling census takers that they were Portuguese. Third, his descendants merged quickly and easily into the Angolan malungu communities in Jamestown and married into the free families of Collinses, Driggers, Gowens, Hammonds, and Matthews.

Manuel Cambow had only one son, but he had many grandchildren. Among them was Richard Cumbo II, who was born free in Virginia about 1715. Richard was a tobacco planter, and in the course of his lifetime he appeared in court. On one such occasion in February 1741, a servant had run away from a nearby plantation. The Charles City County sheriff demanded that Cumbo help him catch the runaway. Cumbo, whose son would be a patriot soldier in the American Revolution, refused and was fined twenty shillings. Following a number of slave revolts led by free blacks, the situation for descendants of the first Jamestown generation became extremely difficult in the Tidewater colony; in January 1744, Richard Cumbo's brother William sued a white man named Hubbard Williams for trespass, assault, and battery in Charles City County. William Cumbo shortly thereafter left Virginia and moved to Cumberland County, North Carolina. His fortunes improved on the new frontier, and by 1761 he had acquired about two hundred acres in Granville County, where a large free community of color developed.

In May 1742, Charles City County officials presented another of Richard's brothers, Paul, to the jury for not going to church. The previous year, in June 1741, Richard had faced the same charge. Ironic as it is that people of color were once forced to attend white churches that would be off limits to them after the Civil War, there might be more here than is mentioned in the records. In the eighteenth century, before the American Revolution, refusal to attend the state-approved Anglican Church frequently indicated religious dissent by non-Conformists such as Baptists, Quakers, and others. About this time, numerous people of color, including several members of the Cumbo clans, began moving en masse to the Carolinas. Several factors were responsible for the move to the central Carolina and The Piedmont Virginia frontiers in the mid-eighteenth century: new land, resentment of legal restrictions in Tidewater Virginia such as a law forbidding people of color from owning guns, and religious dissent. By the end of the eighteenth century, as popular religious revivals swept white America, many people of color were joining New Light denominations, such as the Baptists. This may have been in large part because the Anglican Church of Virginia and the Catholic Church of Maryland had submitted to colonial laws forbidding pastors and priests from blessing mixed marriages. The "blood quantum" enforced in colonial law, in addition to outlawing black and white marriage, forbade people of a certain percentage of African ancestry from marrying other people of color with more or less African ancestry. For example, in some places before the Revolution the Church could not marry a person of two-thirds African ancestry to a person of one-third African ancestry, because the latter was considered legally white. Until the strict "one drop" rule of Jim Crow was enacted in the twentieth century, the states adopted less rigid colonial blood quantums after the American Revolution and differed in defining who was white and who was a person of color:

> In Tennessee, state law limited the term [persons of color] to those whose parent or grand-parent was a full-blooded Indian or Negro (i.e., descent to the third degree). North Carolina's law extended it to "all Negroes, Indians, and mulattos . . . to the fourth generation, inclusive" (i.e., individuals with one-eighth-degree Negro or Indian ancestry).

Breakaway New Light Protestant churches, especially those on the frontier, ignored restrictions based on the blood quantum and blessed all marriages. Free blacks regarded the state Church, whether in Anglican Virginia or Catholic Maryland, as part of the colonial establishment perpetuating race laws against people of color and resisted as best they could. Free blacks and mulattos could avoid the blood quantum complication by passing as Portuguese, Turks, or Moors and generally married people of mixed ancestry like themselves who had also descended from African families of Jamestown, free before 1705. They moved west and became founders of free malungu communities far beyond Tidewater Virginia.

In July 1790, Molly Cumbo married James Matthews, a mixed freeman, in Halifax County, Virginia. Yet another free person of color, David Gowing (Gowen), was surety for the marriage. Cumbo, Matthews, and Gowen are all descendants of Jamestown Angolans of the early seventeenth century. Molly's sister Sarah married Ezekial Matthews of the same free family in Halifax County on April 23, 1793. Another free person of color, Allen Going (Gowen), was the bondsman. Thomas Cumbo married Charlotte Collins, another free person of color, and Turner Cumbo, who later moved west, married Rebecca Cannady (Kennedy) of Charles City County, Virginia. Turner's son, Walker Cumbo, received a Christmas present of "a cow and two calves" from a black grandfather, James Cannady, still living in James City County.

In the middle of the eighteenth century, the region of present day Bladen County, North Carolina, near the border of South Carolina, saw a growing concentration of free malungu communities leaving James-town. In frontier areas of North Carolina, elected officials were some-times lenient in ethnic designation enforcement, in an effort to help their constituents avoid race laws. In 1786, Cannon Cumbo headed a free household of eight white males, four white females, and one "Black." He later acquired one hundred acres in Bladen County and two hundred acres in nearby Robeson County and associated with other free people of color, including Horation Hammon to whom he sold land. He was also a neighbor to the famous free black pre-Revolution hero, Gideon Gibson. Although Cannon Cumbo was recognized as white in Bladen County in 1786, when he moved to Robeson County four years later he and his family were recorded as free people of color. The Cumbos fought the legal restrictions of the complicated blood quantum laws and came to be regarded as Portuguese by their white neighbors in Robeson; later, they were known as Lumbee Indians. Cannon Cumbo Jr. married Tabitha Newsom, daughter of Moses Newsom, about 1785. One freeborn son of the Newsom family was a leader in the Nat Turner Rebellion in 1830.

Some descendants of the original first-generation Bantu Americans remained in the Tidewater counties and did not migrate. Many descen-dants of the old Angolan Manuel Cambow served as patriot soldiers from Virginia during the American Revolution. Daniel Cumbo, born about 1760, was a patriot from Charles City County. Surviving the war, Daniel and his family were described as free persons of color in James City County in 1813. Michael Cumbo was another free patriot from Charles City County who fought for American independence alongside Daniel Cumbo, John Cumbo, and Peter Cumbo. Described as mulatto in James City County in 1782, Stephen Cumbo also fought the British during the Revolution.

For their services in the American Revolution, the new federal gov-ernment awarded each of these soldiers with a few hundred acres of frontier wilderness. Not only did this bonus land sustain the black descendants of the African founders, it was an incentive for them to move west of the Appalachian Mountains and away from the harsh race laws of "settled" America that would have restricted their population and left them landless eventually.

Buried alive in such ships as the *Bautista*, the *White Lion*, the *Treasurer*, and the *Fortune*, and transplanted in Jamestown before 1650, the free black community took root and branched off in all directions. By the 1730s, descendants were moving into Maryland, Delaware, and North Carolina. By the 1790s, they were clearing land in Kentucky, Tennessee, South Carolina, and Georgia. And by 1810, they had reached Ohio, Mississippi, Louisiana, and Texas. By the eve of the Civil War, they would be scattered in clustered communities across half of the United States, still carrying the surnames of their ancestors from early Jamestown: Cumbo, Driggers, Johnson, Mathews, Harman, Sweet, Gowen, Tucker, Gibson, and more. They stubbornly held on to freedom for generations through the worst of slavery, and they survived and flourished. Their character and their identity came from their Jamestown ancestors, and just these several families among the many reveal the stubborn independence, inherent ingenuity, and strong sense of community that served their descendants well.

Making Hay

THE FIRST POPULAR Americanism in the English language originated with a Jamestown man who was both a pirate and a Puritan. Typical of his odd blend of larceny and piety, in an edict issued in 1617, Governor Samuel Argall ordered Jamestown farmers to "make hay while the sun shines, however it may fare with the generality." A black Jamestown man named Antonio Longo certainly followed that advice, if sometimes to a fault in the opinion of some of his white neighbors. The Longo family story again challenges the stereotype of early Africans in colonial America. Blacks in fact swaggered with the same rashly confident step of white America, for the spirit of the era did not indwell only a certain color. The earliest black Virginians rebelled, dreamed big, filed lawsuits, and fought exploitation. Some became more successful than many of their English peers.

Tony Longo was a first-generation Bantu-American founder who first surfaced in colonial records on the Nathaniel Littleton plantation in Northampton County, Virginia, in the 1630s. The surname "Longo" may have derived from the Angolan kingdom of Longo, or Loango, that became a Christian state along with neighboring Kongo early in the sixteenth century. After obtaining his freedom, Longo married an Englishwoman named Hannah in 1652 and the couple had a son, James.

In the course of time, Tony Longo acquired 250 acres and cleared it for farmland and cattle.

Like his English neighbors, Longo occasionally challenged authority, as he did when the white man John Neene interrupted him in his cornfield during harvest in 1655 and attempted to serve a warrant for him to appear in court. Longo had testimony that Neene needed in a lawsuit against another man but, hard at work to get his corn to market first, the black farmer ignored the white planter and refused to accompany him to the home of Judge Peter Walker. John Neene left and shortly returned to the Longo farm with Judge Walker only to catch an earful as Longo retorted to his demands in the presence of the judge, "What shall I go to Mr. Walker's for? Go about your business you idle rascal." When Neene waved the warrant in his face, the black man replied, "Shet of your warrant, have I nothing to do but go to Mr. Walker, go about your business you idle rascal." Neene testified that Longo's wife Hannah then chimed in with her husband and berated him

> with such noise that I could hardly hear my own words. When I had done reading the warrant [Tony Longo] stroke at me, and gave me some blows.

Neene sued Longo, and the court handed down the most severe sentence it could for his offense against the authority of the court. Longo was given thirty lashes on two consecutive days. Not many years later, Jamestown would outlaw the testimony of Africans in such lawsuits.

Tony and Hannah Longo had three children before she died sometime before 1669. Tobacco prices fell and Longo, like many distressed white farmers at the time, appealed for relief to Governor William Berkeley. The magistrate relieved him from paying taxes but as was the custom in granting such relief, bound his son and two daughters out as laborers until they reached the age of twenty-four. The two girls were indentured to a white planter to be brought up in "housewifery, spinning, knitting and such like," while his son was indentured to Edmund Scarborough to be trained as a shoemaker. Alone and advanced in years,

Longo grieved over the absence of his children and soon petitioned the court for their return. The judges partially relented and allowed one daughter to come home to care for him. Furthermore, the heirs of Edmund Scarborough released James early from his court-imposed indenture, so that he served only four years of the eight-year term.

As a free man, James Longo acquired two hundred acres near Nandua Creek in Accomack County four years later. Working as a farmer and a part-time carpenter, James increased his livestock and was in good standing with local white planters. But from time to time the rebellious streak in the father resurfaced in the son, and James Longo was once arrested for responding contemptuously to a warrant to appear in court. In another case, after Jamestown passed a law forbidding blacks and whites from marrying, James Longo was forced to post a bond for being the father of a child by his common-law English wife, Isabel Hutton. However, the mixed couple defied the court and remained together, and the following year she was again called to court and testified under oath that James Longo, "negro or mulatto," was the father of the second child she was then carrying. Refusing to acknowledge the marriage, the magistrates convicted "Isabel Hutton who lives at James Longoes of having a Bastard Child by a Mulatto." The same court ordered that Longo be arrested for treating in a contemptuous manner an officer it sent to him with a warrant. James would leave seventy acres of land to each of his three children, and the rest of his estate to his English common-law wife.

Like the father, the son also resented others interfering in his business affairs. The Longos were hardworking settlers with no record of the typical and frequent colonial offenses of drinking, fornicating, or gaming. James Longo was, however, frequently embroiled in conflicts over work and property. He was accused of planting crops on a day of fasting, and of working on Christmas. Another time, he was called before the court for building a barrier across an unofficial road that ran by his house. Longo considered the informal footpath to be an unlawful trespass across his land. Ordered by the court to remove the roadblock, he complied but then rebuilt it after someone pilfered his corn.

After repeated altercations over the barrier, the court lost patience and ordered him imprisoned after first spending an hour in the stocks. Only then did the fence stay down.

Another incident occurred between Longo and a young Englishman who owed a day's labor to the free black farmer in exchange for a loan. Ignoring his responsibility, the young man, Richard Sholster, was taking a pleasant horseback ride with the daughter of John Washbourne, an officer of the court, to go cherry picking. Unfortunately the path they traveled, the aforementioned disputed thoroughfare, ran by the house of James Longo, who concluded that the obviously healthy young Sholster was shirking his debt. Sholster later testified that Longo

> came running and leaped over the fence furiously and took up a corn stock in his hand and lay hold of your deponent's horse's bridle and fell a calling this deponent rogue and rascal and several of the scurrilous words over and over again threatening to beat me and asked me why I did not come to pay him a day's work. I civilly answered that in expectation of a season to plant in I did not come. Presently after he laid his hands upon my shoulder in a violent manner and furiously pulled me off the horse to the ground, the force of which fall hurt my head and shoulder and caused great pain upon the same, and the girl that sat behind me on the said horse did vehemently cry out being frightened at his actions.

This assault on a white man cost Longo the relatively small fine of one hundred pounds of tobacco, probably because the judges sympathized with those attempting to retrieve loans from deadbeats. Longo then sued Sholster in court over the unpaid debt.

The Longos were involved in more than their own personal interests and actively participated in the larger African malungu community at Jamestown. On a nearby farm owned by George Hack, the enslaved Angolan George Francis (Francisco) fathered a child by a young English maidservant named Dorothy Bestick. Longo, who had been legally declared a bastard in court, sympathized with the couple. Typically, such an illegitimate child would be bound out as a servant for up to twenty years, but Longo and a white neighbor named Jane Fitzgerald stepped forward to pay the maid's fine for fornication and agreed to serve as godparents to the mixed child, assuring the court that it would not become a burden to the county if Dorothy was allowed to keep it.

When James Longo died at the age of seventy he was wealthier than some of his white peers, with a two-hundred-acre plantation, several head of livestock, and frontier rarities such as a mirror and a Bible that he left to son James and daughters Mary and Elizabeth. But prosperity for the Longo family in Virginia began to decline after his death. His children, facing growing ethnic alienation like many other free blacks after nearly a century of sacrifice and backbreaking work, sold off the family estate and moved to Maryland and Delaware for fresher opportunities around 1730. Longo family history reveals another early custom of seventeenth century Virginia that would change in time as Americans became more color conscious: colonial authorities fined James Longo in 1685 for failing to attend a muster of the local militia.

❀

WHEREAS TONY AND James Longo were confrontational and tended to be contemptuous of legal machinery when they believed they were being wronged, their contemporary, the affable, fun-loving William Harman, mingled easily with Jamestown society—black and white—and was less openly defiant, though finding more creative ways to buck the colonial system that was becoming increasingly racist.

William Harman, of the first African-American generation of Jamestown, spent his early years being traded or inherited from planter to planter until he landed on the plantation of William Kendall about the middle of the seventeenth century. This young Bantu, like John Graweere, Emanuel Driggus, Benjamin Doll, and Manuel Cambow, was a skilled cattleman and while enslaved built up a herd of cattle along with horses and hogs that would be the key to his freedom. When Kendall offered Africans on his plantation the opportunity to purchase their freedom for five thousand pounds of tobacco "clear of ground leaves or trash," Harman sold off some of his cattle to buy tobacco; in

1666, he was a free man. That year, he also gave a mare colt to a free black woman named Jane Gussall as a jointure for marriage. Jane, the twenty-two-year old daughter of Margaret Cornish and Robert Sweet, had been adopted by Manuel Driggus. Before marrying Harman she had been left a widow by the death of her first husband. Jane was a second-generation descendant of the *Bautista* Africans.

William and Jane Harman settled on King's Creek in Northampton County, joining a small but growing malungu community. Times were prosperous on King's Creek, and the Harmans eventually had a half dozen children. Angolans and Englishmen had left homelands in the Old World that were centuries old, steeped in customs, with complex social and religious systems: village life in Angola had been as culturally rich as the country life of squires in England. Each also had their colorful bustling cities, but Virginia in the seventeenth century was drab and boring, with little in the way of a social life. Jamestown, the largest town in the colony, was about the size of a remote rural Ndongo village tucked away in the mountains far from the big cities of Mbanza Congo, Angoleme, and Kabasa. Jamestown's frontier life was full of toil and sorrow, and Virginians therefore relished the religious holidays and harvest times when they could come together with their neighbors. As a free black man, William Harman is described by historian Douglas Deal as "a gregarious, personable man" who "befriended slaves, other free blacks, and whites, both poor and moderately well off," and his home was a popular meeting place for whites and blacks in the neighborhood.

When guests could not come to the party at his house, Harman brought the party to them. Harman's neighbor, a Dutch planter named John Michael, had denied his six black servants the traditional Yule celebration and so he became suspicious of the cheer being spread on his plantation during the Christmas holidays of 1672. Harman, according to Deal, came to the Michael plantation three times between Christmas and the New Year, once on the pretence of seeking his lost mare, and each time that he appeared, drinking and shooting among the slaves started again. Michael suspected Harman was somehow breaking into his liquor cache but could never prove it. Hearsay testimony alleged that Harman told the three men and three women to "have a great care they were not discovered how they came by their drink." Michael's overseer later stated that Harman had cautioned the slaves "not to drink so much on Sundays for fear they should be discovered." Suspected but never charged, Harman soon after moved his family a short distance away from King's Creek to Cherrystone Creek.

His new neighbors included the free black families of John Francisco and Francisco Payne. Again, these were malungu people who came directly from Angola with Latin Christian names. There, as at King's Creek, Harman quickly became the center of social activity in the neighborhood. Several neighbors came to help with his wheat harvest in the summer of 1683 as was customary, and among them were a half dozen white men and women, some of whom were wealthy planters. That evening, as they enjoyed a pipe around Harman's fireplace after a hard day's labor, a spat broke out between a white man and a white woman who were brother and sister. The widow Frances Waterson had taken up with Captain Nathaniel Walker in an arrangement questioned by her brother, Captain Nathaniel Wilkins. The Englishman Matthew Somers, testified that he:

being by the fire lighting my pipe did hear Nathaniel Wilkins ask the widow Waterson when she was married to Capt. Walker. She replied, what was that to him or to that effect. Then the said Wilkins told her he was ashamed that they lived so like rogue and whore together and bid she go and play the whore with him again in the straw.

Reproached so by her brother, Mrs. Waterson

was in a terrible rage and bid her brother [after calling him] a cuckold, "go home about your business & mind the whore" his wife.

Such intimate social interaction in a black family's home indicates that everyday white Virginians were slow to comply with segregation laws enacted by the Virginia legislature and did not always agree with

the increasingly hostile attitudes of the relative few planter elite dominating the Jamestown legislature near the end of the seventeenth century. At the time, class was still a more important distinction than race
although the latter was rising in importance. Harman's black neighbor
Francis Payne died and his widow Amy, who was English, remarried a
physically abusive Englishman named William Gray. Often drunk, Gray
would soon go to prison for beating her. In dispensing of her dead black
husband's property, Amy had given his gun to the free black William
Harman but the loutish Gray beat her for it and angrily retrieved the
gun, and the case went to court. The white judges ruled that the musket
rightfully belonged to Harman even though the House of Burgesses in
Jamestown had outlawed guns in the hands of blacks in 1640. The law
applied to slaves but not to free blacks, when the incident occurred in
1675. Free blacks would remain armed until Virginia passed legislation
in 1738 forbidding them from owning firearms, whereupon many free
black farmers moved to North Carolina. In 1672, Harman was still able
to testify on behalf of a fellow Angolan, when a white man alleged that
Harman's neighbor John Francisco had not made good on a promised
cattle trade. Twenty years later the testimony of free blacks would not
be admitted into court.

Having been purchased from slavery as a child by her adoptive
father, Jane (Sweet-Cornish) Driggus Gussal, before marrying William
Harman, was raped as a teenager by an indentured Irishman beneath
her class, and she had borne a daughter. Jane refused to keep the child
and her sister-in-law raised it. Her first marriage to Gussall lasted just a
few months until his death. She and Harman had a happy marriage for
about a decade before she died. Among the children she had by William
Harman were Francis, Manuel, and William Harman II.

Their eldest daughter Francis Harman was at one time hired as a
servant to Colonel John Custis, whose son was the stepfather of Martha Custis, wife of the first American president, George Washington.
The Custises were Jamestown's leading planters and while in the Custis mansion, Francis Harman was privy to family secrets. Apparently
Francis shared her father's gregarious nature for she revealed around

town that Mrs. Tabitha Custis had affairs with two prominent white men, Robert Pitt and Joseph Webb, and she also told the wife of the blacksmith that Colonel Custis, during a domestic shouting match, had called his wife a "papist bitch." Whether Francis Harman "defamed and scandalized" Tabitha Custis "by gross and approbrious language altogether false and untrue," as the court later ruled, is questionable, given Tabitha's reputation. But Harman was a black servant woman, though not a slave, and the Custises were one of the most socially prominent white families of Virginia. She received thirty-five lashes for being indiscreet about the Custis household. Hers, according to Deal, was the severest punishment of the kind given to any woman in Jamestown to that time.

Nevertheless, free descendants of William and Jane Harman later fought as patriots in the American Revolution under General George Washington.

The Harmans and Longos were among the free blacks who achieved modest success and lived more or less comfortably in early Jamestown. Other free blacks became quite prosperous and acquired white servants and maids as well as black slaves. But as will be seen, yet other free black Americans remembered blacks still in bondage.

· 13 ·

The Shirt

THE JAMESTOWN ASSEMBLY in 1669 debated the legality of prosecuting a slaveholder for premeditated murder if a slave died while being punished. The legislature decided that because the slave was the slaveholder's property it was unthinkable that the slaveholder would maliciously kill the slave:

> Whereas the only law in force for the punishment of refractory servants resisting their master, mistress, or overseer cannot be inflicted upon Negroes, nor the obstinacy of many of them be suppressed by other than violent means, be it enacted and declared by this Grand Assembly if any slave resists his master (or other by his master's order correcting him) and by the extremity of the correction should chance to die, that his death shall not be accounted a felony, but the master (or that other person appointed by the master to punish him) be acquitted from molestation, since it cannot be presumed that premeditated malice (which alone makes murder a felony) should induce any man to destroy his own estate.

The brutal fact is that, for most of the seventeenth century, all colonial servants, black and white, were abused more or less equally under this reasoning, and those who ran away had hell to pay. Planters were mostly free to run their plantations as petty tyrants. The prudent slaveholder was inclined to keep the laborer in peak working condition but only as far as his purse allowed. If a servant was injured or became ill, the plantation owner weighed the cost of purchasing a replacement against the high fees that doctors charged.

Servants complained of being beaten while in their sickbed by masters who thought they were shirking their duties. Black and white, male and female, young and old, suffered the same whip and club, sometimes unto death. In colonial Jamestown there are accounts of black and white servants fleeing such abuse and running away from the plantation together. However as the decades passed and indentured whites began to escape the underclass, the runaways were mostly black.

Free blacks frequently were found to encourage and assist runaway servants and, in September 1672, wealthy Surry County planters complained that blacks, free and enslaved alike, exploited idleness on Saturday and Sunday, to meet and discuss insurrection and trade in stolen goods. Their concerns prompted a ruling that African servants could not own linen cloth, and must wear only coarse blue clothing to distinguish them in case they ran away, much like the clothing of convicted criminals in the penal system today:

Whereas information hath been given to this Court that the too Careless and inconsiderable Liberty given to Negroes, not only in being permitted to meet together upon Saturdays & Sundays, whereby they win opportunity to consult of unlawful projects and combinations to the danger & damage of the neighbors, as well as to their Masters, and Also that the apparel commonly worn by Negroes doth as well Heighten their foolish pride as induce them to steal fine Linen and other ornaments, for the prevention whereof it is hereby ordered and published to the Inhabitants of this county that the Act of Assembly for prevention of servants going abroad be put in due execution and from hence forth No Negro shall be allowed to wear any white linen, but shall wear blue shirts and shifts that they may be hereby discovered if they steal or wear other linen, and if the Master of any Negro shall pretend that blue is not to be had for men and women Negroes for their shifts and shirts, caps or neckclothes, then he shall supply that want in course Lockerham or canvas, and this to be duly observed until a by law be made to confirm the same.

To aid escape, enslaved Africans needed clothing that would not give them away.

Blacks of the first Jamestown generation that had been set free, like the Carters, for example, naturally sympathized with slaves who came later in the seventeenth century at a time when the colony, due to rising costs, began restricting the release of Africans from lifelong labor. Descendants of the Carter family became some of the most successful and prosperous free persons of color in later years and survive today.

Their ancestors first appeared in Jamestown on the Nathaniel Littleton plantation in the early seventeenth century. During the 1640s, Paul and Hannah Carter had six children; Elizabeth, Edward, Paul, Mary, Thomas, and James. Paul Carter died on the Littleton plantation, but his wife Hannah was set free and given freedom dues in 1665 by Francis Pigot, who inherited the Littleton servants. Freedom dues were paid to indentured servants who had served out their contracts. Hannah, however, served longer than the typical indentured servant, and Pigot probably released her so that he would not have to care for her in her old age. Two blacks, Francis Payne and Emanuel Driggus, gave the colony assurances that they would provide for Hannah and see that she did not become a welfare case and she was invited to live in the home of another black man, Bashaw Fernando. Therefore, three Angolans with Portuguese Christian names saw to the welfare of a fellow Angolan in the first-generation malungu community. Either alone or in association with other blacks, as well as with sympathetic whites, the free blacks of Jamestown used various means to help their enslaved countrymen as well as those in extreme poverty. They put up cattle to purchase their freedom, aided the elderly and infirmed, adopted fatherless children, provided for widows and for single women and their illegitimate mixed children, all in addition to taking care of their immediate families under social and economic circumstances that would have been burdensome to them as a minority. Yet they remained racially tolerant of whites and natives with whom they sometimes intermarried, socialized, and transacted business. With the emerging Quaker movement, the black Jamestown community of the seventeenth century also laid the foundation of the Underground Railroad that helped Africans escape slavery through a complex system of clandestine allies.

The road to freedom was not easy for the children of Paul and Hannah Carter. Thomas Carter and his wife Ellenor had two, with another on the way. The will of Francis Pigot demanded as the price of freedom that they first produce ten thousand pounds of tobacco for his heirs, and a further stipulation required them to leave the county upon their release. But Pigot's sons ignored these severe conditions and, two years after their father's death, they simply freed Thomas and Ellenor from all obligations. Thomas Carter became a tobacco farmer but, as was also the custom in the free English underclass during hard times, he apprenticed three of his children to a white friend on the condition that they receive freedom dues at the end of their indenture. He also required the neighbor to teach his children to read.

Thomas Carter's namesake son Thomas II and his wife Elizabeth were charged with aiding fugitive slaves in a Jamestown underground network operated by free blacks and sympathetic whites. A black man named Caesar, who was enslaved to Jamestown plantation owner John Armistead, stole a bolt of white linen and some cloth tape to have a shirt made. He asked his wife Nell, who was enslaved on another plantation, to make the shirt, telling her he was going to run away. She pleaded with him to return to the Armistead plantation but, determined to escape, Caesar asked his wife's cousin Great Tom, "not to let her want for anything for that he was going away and would be no more a servant." Caesar then made his way to the home of the free black Carter family, and Thomas Carter gave the fugitive shelter and food, knowing it was against the law. Caesar then slipped onto the nearby Robins plantation where two servants, Toby and Little Tom hid him. Another African named Conjur, who served on a neighboring farm, also fed him secretly and, in exchange for some berries Caesar picked, a white farmer named Robert Forster gave him a gourd filled with corn flour. After this, a white widow, Alice Cormack, took him into her house and fed him. He in return supplied her and her family with wild game and the Widow Cormack made him a shirt from the bolt of linen, warning her children to "say nothing of Caesar's coming there." After a few months however, Armistead's posse tracked Caesar down and he was captured, tried, and hung. Thomas Carter and Alice Cormack were convicted of harboring a fugitive slave. For aiding Caesar, according to Deal, the English widow was whipped with twenty-five lashes and imprisoned for a month, and the free black Thomas Carter received twenty-nine lashes and an hour in the pillory.

Some of Carter's descendants continued to shelter runaways many years later. The *North Carolina Gazette* carried an advertisement on November 14, 1778, accusing Abel Carter of harboring a black man who ran away:

> Negro fellow named Stuart. Tis supposed he is harbored about Smith River by one Abel Carter, a free Negro, as he has been seen there several times.

One of Abel Carter's sons was John Carter, a patriot who fought in the American Revolution in battles at West Point and Kings Ferry in Captain Quinn's Tenth Regiment.

❖

SEBASTIAN CANE WAS another first-generation African of Jamestown involved in aiding runaway blacks. Like John Pedro, Cane had a Portuguese name indicating his origin in Angola. "Sebastian" was the English version of the name of a Portuguese king who attempted to colonize Angola in the sixteenth century before his army was humiliated at the Lukala River. Also like John Pedro, before arriving in Jamestown, Sebastian Cane spent some time in New England, where he sailed as a crewman on the ships of Boston merchant Robert Keayne, who traded with Jamestown. The surname "Cane" likely derived from "Keayne."

But unlike John Pedro, Sebastian, whose name was sometimes short-ened to "Buss," converted from Catholicism to become a Puritan, and he lived for several years in Massachusetts. How he became a free man (if he was ever enslaved) is not known but, at Dorchester, with his first wife, he owned a home and a plot of land on which he raised wheat. He also owned a sizable share in a fourteen-ton fishing vessel named the *Hopewell.* In 1656 Sebastian Cane put up his entire estate as security to redeem an African named Angola from slavery in the Keayne house-hold. The agreement had Cane paying the Keaynes sixteen pounds in wheat within a year for Angola's freedom. He made the payment on time and Angola was released.

As a sailor in the Boston-based Keayne fleet, Sebastian Cane fre-quently sailed to Dutch New York and to Jamestown. Jamestown had many more Africans than did New England, so, after his wife died, Cane sold his property and hopped on a ship bound for Virginia. Old Plantation Creek in Northampton County, where a number of blacks, free and enslaved, were concentrated, appealed to Cane, and he became a tobacco farmer. He married a twenty-three-year-old black woman named Grace, who was enslaved on the nearby Waltham-Vaughn plan-tation. This was the neighborhood of the Custis and Michael planta-tions, and Cane did business with these wealthy white Virginians.

After setting roots in the community, Buss Cane in 1666 harbored a black man who fled slavery on the Pigot-Littleton plantation. For this offense, the court ordered Cane to be whipped publicly with ten lashes. Four years later he died in Jamestown, and his will, witnessed by his free Angolan-American neighbor John Francisco and an Englishman, stated:

> As touching such transitory estate as God hath blessed me withal, I give and bequeath unto my beloved wife Grace Cane all my estate both in Virginia and elsewhere my debts being paid.

Black families of the first American generation, such as the free Cart-ers and the Canes, were part of a community that was bound by the experience of departing Angola on a slave ship, and in which blacks, natives, and whites of the same social-economic condition lived, inter-married, and helped one another. That help sometimes came in assisting runaways, and in the lowlying region of Tidewater Virginia, experienced African sailors like Buss Cane with knowledge of the Atlantic coast proved invaluable. In 1670, according to Douglas Deal,

> A group of white servants plotting to escape their Accomack County farms and flee to New England, put their trust in a black pilot named James to guide them there.

The underground work of the malungu community continued long after Jamestown ceased to exist. One of many examples was Mollie Goins, a free descendant of Mihill Gowen of Jamestown, who it is supposed was the son that John Graweere purchased from slavery in 1640. Mollie Goins married Leonard Grimes, the grandson of a white woman and a black man. The Grimes lived in the District of Columbia, where Leonard Grimes worked as a coach driver. Black coach drivers had a measure of mobility that gave them the opportunity to smuggle black runaways from Virginia to ships waiting to take them north. Mollie and Leonard Grimes helped a number of entire families get to freedom. They were eventually caught after it was discovered they helped a family of seven escape to Canada, and Leonard Grimes was sentenced to two years in prison.

After he served his sentence, Leonard and Mollie Grimes moved to Massachusetts, where they became ministers of the Twelfth Street Baptist Church of Boston, known as the Fugitive Church. There the Grimes played a significant role in the landmark case of the runaway Anthony Burns, when they arranged the purchase of Burns from the slaveholder. The Grimes were latter-day torchbearers of a cause championed by their ancestors. In seventeenth-century Jamestown, the first generation of the Angolan malungu communities had developed two methods to free slaves in Virginia: they bought their freedom with cattle, or they helped them run away. Almost two hundred years later, their free descendants were still on the front lines of the battle for freedom.

One of the continuing controversies surrounding early black America, however, arises from clear evidence that some free African Americans purchased Africans as slaves. Even in the same black families, slavery was a divisive issue: some of the black Carters, for example, held slaves even as other black Carters helped them run away. However, the wealthy black family most frequently cited as slaveholders were the Johnsons, one of the original Angolan families taken from the *Bautista* in 1619.

· 14 ·

*A*ngola Plantation

WERE SLAVE-HOLDING AFRICAN Americans like Anthony Johnson betraying their fellow countrymen, or were they continuing a centuries-old institution first established by their African forefathers in Africa? The issue is obscured by misperceptions. Slavery originated in English North America with the peculiar colonial development of "headrights" that encouraged Virginians to introduce foreign laborers into the colony in exchange for land. Headrights established Virginia primarily through cultivation rather than military conquest. But as the history of Virginia reveals, the headright system also served as the incubator of slavery from the very beginning of English-speaking America.

❀

THE YEAR THAT the Bantu of the *White Lion* landed at Jamestown, Galileo, silenced by the Inquisition and using a pseudonym, wrote *Discourse of the Comets*, which was presented to the Florentine Academy as a lecture by his pupil, Mario Guiducci. The best European cartographers were debating whether the entire North American continent, from east to west, could be crossed on foot in "eight or ten days journey." European soldiers still fought in metal breastplates and helmets, and the favorite recreations among those who could afford recreation were such medieval sports as the chase, archery, and tilting. Whitehall Palace had a jousting, or tilting, yard and, in 1619, crowds gathered amid fluttering banners to cheer as a galloping Prince Charles demonstrated his skill against the spinning quintain.

Complaining about the lack of qualified labor at Jamestown, Captain John Smith cited planters at the time who declared that a few farmboys who could hold a plow were more important to Jamestown than the dozens of "knights" who could "break a lance" who were living there.

Yet as long ago as that was, 1619 was not the first year that Africans set foot in the land now called Virginia. In fact, the Bantu were almost a century late. The first Africans came to Virginia long before the first Englishmen. They did not come from the Congo River but from the Niger River, and the plight of the Spanish conquistadors who brought them is a tale of repeated failed attempts to colonize the Middle Atlantic region of North America before the seventeenth century.

❖

JAMESTOWN, THE FIRST successful English settlement in America, was built by a Christian slave who ran away from his Muslim master. In 1602, Captain John Smith, then a professional soldier in the service of Austria, was fighting the Turks in Transylvania near the Black Sea when Muslim soldiers captured him and sent him as a slave to Istanbul. The Black Sea region of Eastern Europe had been the contested battlefield of Christian and Muslim armies from the time of the very real Christian Prince Vlad Dracula (1431–1477). After escaping Turkish slavery with, as he later claimed, the help of a beautiful Muslim princess, Captain Smith returned to England and entered the service of the Virginia Company of London with orders to plant an exploratory outpost in America. The Virginia Company, along with the old Plymouth Company, obtained from King James on April 10, 1606, a royal charter for North America that stretched from Long Island Sound in the north to Cape Fear at the thirty-fourth parallel in the south. (The Plymouth Company would become inactive three years later with the failure of the Popham colony.) The joint stock Virginia Company was made up of English investors who hoped to find gold and silver and a passage to the South Sea from Chesapeake Bay. In 1606, farming and planting were not on the Virginia Company's agenda. Sir Raleigh had disastrously tried agriculture with married couples at Roanoke twenty years earlier, and no one had yet located his settlers. The Virginia Company of London sent Captain John Smith not to plant potatoes, but to discover cities of gold in North America.

With about one hundred men and boys, Smith's expedition sailed from England in 1606 and crossed the ocean on the ships *Susan Constant*, *Godspeed*, and *Discovery* and then turned north at the West Indies. The voyage along the present-day Carolina coast took the explorers past the deserted English colony of Roanoke and the forsaken Spanish settlement of Santa Elena at Parris Island, giving them opportunity to contemplate the hazardous challenge before them. Leaving Cape Fear, the *Susan Constant* continued north and reached Chesapeake Bay, and turned into a large watercourse they named the James River. On a peninsula in the James River forty miles upriver from Chesapeake Bay, Smith and his men built Fort James upon the old ruins of an abandoned Spanish mission called Ajacan, founded some forty years earlier. Ajacan itself was built on an even earlier deserted Spanish plantation settlement called Tierra de Ayllón, founded in Virginia eighty-one years before John Smith arrived. Unlike the English colonists who built Fort James, the Spaniard Lucas Vasquez de Ayllón had not come to Virginia in 1526 to find gold. The Spaniard came with a force of men six times larger than the number with John Smith. And he came with a sensible plan to farm.

Lucas de Ayllón, the first European to attempt to settle Virginia, also brought the first Africans to the Americas. The Atlantic African slave trade began in fact as an extension of the ancient European trade that moved white slaves from the Black Sea to the Mediterranean. For generations, an old Italian banking family, the Marchionnis of Florence, from their trading outpost at Kaffa in the Crimea beginning in the 1380s, transported large numbers of white slaves—Armenians,

Bulgarians, Circassians, Georgians, and Tatars—for the production of sugar in Crete, Cyprus, and Sicily around the Mediterranean coast. The word *slave* comes from "Slav"—the ethnic name of these European people. The Marchionnis' vital "white slave" artery to and from the Black Sea was cut off from Europe in 1453, when the Ottoman Turks invaded and captured Constantinople (modern Istanbul). Muslims seized the Black Sea slave ports and began redirecting Slavic prisoners of war to Islamic markets as well as to markets in Sicily and Majorca in direct competition with the Florentine white slavers. Controlling the white slave route, the Muslims barred the Marchionnis from their Black Sea labor source.

At this time, Portuguese explorers sent by Prince Henry the Navigator were feeling their way southward down the coast of West Africa and beginning to export Africans from Guinea to the Mediterranean. Facing financial ruin in 1470, only twenty-two years *before* Columbus discovered America, Bartolommeo di Marchionni transferred the central office of his languishing white slave business from Florence, Italy, to Lisbon, Portugal, to exploit the growing numbers of Guinea captives from the upper west coast of Africa, just as Portugal was beginning to pour these Africans into manufacturing ports girding the Mediterranean. It would be a smart business move.

Twelve years later, Diogo Cão discovered the Congo River, and, a decade later, Columbus "sailed the ocean blue" to the Americas. In 1502, just ten years after Columbus's first voyage, a Spanish government official named Lucas Vasquez de Ayllón settled on the island of Hispaniola, east of Cuba, shared today by Haiti and the Dominican Republic, where he pioneered the Caribbean sugar industry. Ayllón had connections to the king of Spain and personally knew Christopher Columbus, his son Diego Colon, and Hernán Córtes in Hispaniola. His sugar plantations prospered with white workers but he needed more laborers to expand. He urged Spain to send more workers and, in 1510, King Ferdinand borrowed money from the Italian transplant Bartolommeo di Marchionni in Lisbon, to send to Hispaniola the very first Atlantic shipment made up exclusively of enslaved Africans. And

thus, because of Christian-Muslim conflicts in Europe, the Mediterranean sugar industry once manned by Marchionni-financed Eastern
European slave labor, relocated to the Caribbean where it was manned
by Marchionni-financed West African slave labor.

In 1521, just twenty-nine years after Columbus's discovery of America, Ayllón dispatched Francisco Gordillo on an expedition to explore
the present Virginia-Carolina coast, for suitable land and anchorage to
expand his sugar operation. Gordillo returned with a favorable report
and in 1526, upon securing permission from Spain, Ayllón loaded his
colonists, including the Guinean Africans he had sent for in 1510, into
several ships and sailed from Hispaniola to Chesapeake Bay. Upon
arriving, the Spaniard disembarked a large well-armed expedition of
horses, soldiers, priests, and African and European servants. Six hundred men strong, the 1526 Ayllón expedition to Virginia was exactly
the same size as that led by his friend Córtes in conquering the Aztec
Empire. The king of Spain had promised Ayllón the title of viceroy
of North America, but Virginia was not Mexico and Ayllón would not
achieve the success of Córtes.

The Algonquian, according to an English tradition, called the land
Wingadacoa and they defended it aggressively, immediately attacking
Ayllón's town of San Miguel before he could finish building it. After
just a few weeks, Ayllón died of sickness in the Great Dismal Swamp
of Virginia that would later kill so many Englishmen, and then the
grand Spanish invasion of North America, equipped with all the modern
weaponry and advanced European technology that the sugar baron had
amassed, came to a dead stop. Out of the original 600 Spaniards and
Africans who came with Ayllón, only 150 survived to straggle back to
Hispaniola in 1527.

Contrary to the Anglo tradition, Spaniards did not come to North
America only to look for gold. Transporting slaves, farmers, priests, and
soldiers, the Spaniards tried repeatedly for many decades to maintain
forts, towns, ranches, and plantations throughout present-day Virginia,
North Carolina, Kentucky, and Tennessee. Spain's failure seemed
inexplicable because the Algonquian were not as "advanced" as the

Aztec who, like Europeans and the Bantu of Central Africa, built great structures and empires. In fact, the more primitive way of life among the Algonquian was Spain's major obstacle in colonizing Virginia. Culturally, the Algonquian were not easily assimilated into the European agricultural system. The men were hunters, not farmers. They did not make iron, and so clearing and plowing land was a more time-consuming process, limiting the size of their maize, bean, and squash patches, and requiring that they supplement their diet by hunting and foraging. Also, when land became overused after a few years, the Algonquian moved their villages to another cleared area that had lain idle for some time. Having never domesticated animals, they had no prior experience in tending the cattle the Spaniards brought over. The Algonquian would not easily take to Spanish culture, remaining independent and threatening. And because they were not centralized in great cities under one leader like the Aztec, they were more difficult to defeat.

In addition, the land of the Middle Atlantic region was very different from that encountered by the Spaniards in Mexico. The first Spaniards came to North America hoping to farm, but they found an uncultivated vastness blanketed with forests, lakes, and marshes. Large European plantation projects did not thrive well in uncultivated wilderness. Thousands of Spanish soldiers and settlers led by de Leon, Narváez, de Vaca, Pardo, Coronado, and others marched inland and withered away. In Florida and Georgia, they were safe only within cannon range of their ships on the Gulf Coast and along the navigable rivers emptying into it. Spain sent Hernando de Soto, with soldiers and great ferocious hounds, as far inland as the Appalachian Mountains. But there was no great city to conquer in Kentucky, and no human god to capture and no permanent fields of maize to take over. The hostile North American nations they found in Appalachia and The Piedmont were not city builders, though there was much evidence of such a civilization along the Mississippi River in the mounds and clearings they sometimes discovered. Finding nothing large and cultivated to conquer, de Soto's terror campaign massacred entire villages and stole women and gained nothing but resentment and reprisals from local natives. Although they had nearly a century head start on the English, Spanish farmers and ranchers failed to establish a presence in the interior of North America beyond the Gulf Coast regions of Texas, Louisiana, Georgia, and Florida. Working on the theory that conquest was hampered by native hostility to rapacious soldiers, Spain, a few decades after Ayllón died, attempted to establish the mission of Ajacan exclusively made up of Dominican priests on the present site of Jamestown. Algonquian soldiers, led by a baptized native who had spent time in Spain, quickly descended on Ajacan and wiped out all but one of the priests who fled. Spanish soldiers returned and hanged some suspects and then abandoned Ajacan.

The year that Spain finally retreated from its headquarters at Santa Elena in the Carolinas was the same year Sir Raleigh sent the first English colonizers, all male, to Roanoke. Yet Raleigh's first expedition fared no better than those of Spain. The English soldiers failed within months due to native resistance and cyclical famine and returned to England. Then in 1587, Raleigh sent a second group of one hundred men, women, and children to settle Roanoke, but, delayed by the Spanish Armada invasion of England, Raleigh's relief ships found no survivors when they returned two years later. Similar English attempts by Popham and Georges to settle in the region of the upper Atlantic coast now known as New England, also failed. It seemed after a century of monumental flops that Europeans were not equipped to survive in Virginia. The land of Wingadacoa devoured whites by the thousands and swallowed all traces of their abandoned attempts.

At last in 1606 came the one hundred gold hunters sent by the Virginia Company of London with King James's blessings and led by Captain Smith. And they failed as Raleigh's settlers and the Spaniards before him. So many perished in the first few years that the founders of Jamestown actually set out to return to England only to be turned back in Chesapeake Bay by timely relief ships from England.

After a decade of stagnation and misery at Jamestown, the big turnaround began in 1616 when in desperation the Virginia Company shifted its focus from pursuing risky schemes, such as searching for phantom gold mines and rivers to the South Sea, to social and economic ventures intended to create a permanent colony of consumers, producers, and manufacturers with whom company investors hoped to trade. The firm began to think in terms of settler families and not just single male laborers or Indian fur traders. After a fruitless first decade of wildcat ventures, its investors had tired of pouring money into a bottomless abyss. The architects of change within the Virginia Company were Robert Rich, who wanted a refuge for Puritans and Separatists, and Edwin Sandys and allies like John Ferrar and the Earl of Southampton who, at King James's urging, set out to exploit the one thing, other than wool, in which England had a vast surplus—people. But to get English families to resettle in the harsh American frontier, the company had to offer inducements. Previously, it owned all the land but, in 1616, desperate stockholders offered private acreage to wealthy adventurers. These lands on the periphery of the company's holdings were known as private, or particular plantations. Those willing to risk their own capital were allowed to bring in workers to improve and cultivate the vast acres of raw land they purchased. The firm also started the system of headrights, offering fifty acres for each indentured servant the landowner brought into the colony. The headright system that was introduced in 1617 launched the real birth of Jamestown, and in the next decade a few large prosperous private plantations, such as Flowerdew, Piersey's Hundred, Denbigh, and Bennett's Welcome, began springing up along the rivers and creeks emptying into Chesapeake Bay.

After finishing their indenture on the plantations, those English peasants who had been brought in as headrights, received "freedom dues" from the planters in the form of seed corn, clothing, tools, and sometimes a few head of cattle. The company also gave each new freeman fifty acres of uncultivated land as a start-up package, to encourage them to stay in Virginia. Those former servants who accepted would in turn marry, have children, and import more workers to Jamestown, using the headright system. Small peasant farmers who exchanged their labor for land are to be credited for domesticating Wingadacoa, though at an incredible toll in human suffering between 1617 and 1660. England never sent an army of conquistadors to conquer Virginia in the seventeenth century.

Angolans arrived in Virginia in 1619 when Jamestown still teetered on the brink and seemed about to disappear like the many doomed Spanish and English colonies before it. Their arrival coincided with the Virginia Company's decision to change its course from seeking treasure to building communities and one of the first generation African Americans to benefit from the new reforms was among those stolen from the *Bautista* by the *White Lion* and the *Treasurer*, and taken to Bermuda. Two years later, Governor Nathaniel Butler of Bermuda shipped several of these Africans, including Antonio, Maria, and John Pedro, to Lord Rich in England, who in 1621 placed Antonio onboard the ship *James* bound for the Virginia plantation of the Puritan Edward Bennett. Several weeks later the Algonquian carried out the Good Friday Massacre of 1622, and Antonio once more narrowly avoided death.

Then, his future began to brighten. Maria arrived from England on the *Margaret and John* in 1622, and they were married on the plantation. As noted earlier, Antonio and Maria anglicized their names to Anthony and Mary, and took the surname Johnson. Between 1624 and 1634, they had four children, two girls and two boys. The couple's early life in Jamestown is obscure, but they probably worked on Bennett's plantation as slaves. Bennett lived in England, and his brother Robert and nephew Richard Bennett ran the Warrosquoke plantation. Two months later, in 1635, after a Puritan-led faction within the Virginia House of Burgesses thrust Governor Harvey out of office, the Puritan Richard Bennett, who would soon be governor under Cromwell, "loaned" Anthony and Mary to planter John Upton who listed them with thirty-three people whose transport he claimed in acquiring 1,650 acres for headrights on neighboring Pagan Creek. Since Anthony and Mary had lived in Virginia more than a decade by 1635, it is not clear if this was a fraudulent case of recycling headrights or if Virginia allowed headrights for transporting servants from one county to another. Whatever the case, it appears that Anthony and Mary Johnson never actually worked on the Upton plantation. Richard Bennett had ties to Edmund Scarborough, the most prominent planter in Northampton County on the Eastern Shore, and his daughter married Scarborough's son Charles. Apparently, the Johnsons and their four children were moved to Scarborough's land in the late 1630s as Bennett's wedding gift to his daughter, or perhaps to help Charles expand his headright claims for the three thousand acres he acquired on Pungoteague Creek.

But soon thereafter the Johnsons' status changed. Between 1647 and 1648, they acquired four head of cattle from area planters and, perhaps not coincidentally, soon after left plantation slavery just as the English Puritans defeated and captured King Charles I at Naseby. Royalist Virginia had no choice but to acknowledge Parliament's victory. Berkeley was ousted, and a Puritan was made governor of Virginia. It was during the Puritan era of the 1650s that Anthony and Mary Johnson were first documented as free, so Richard Bennett perhaps set them free to seal their loyalty to the still feeble Puritan government.

Settling on Old Plantation Creek as tenant farmers in a small Angolan American malungu community, the now-free Johnsons increased their herd as they also planted their own tobacco. In 1650, they acquired their first land in a remote stretch of raw wilderness north of Nandua Creek, which was to become part of Accomack County. Their first farm, 250 acres, was five times greater than the plots awarded white indentured servants upon their release. Cashing out tobacco and cattle, the Johnsons had obtained the patent for the land with five headrights, that is, by paying the passage of five English servants who were indentured to them. In 1652, the oldest son, John Johnson, obtained an additional 550 acres of land by paying for the voyages of eleven whites, male and female. The same year, the youngest son Richard Johnson claimed an additional 100 acres with two more white headrights. During this time they also purchased an African servant named John Gesorroro (also known as John Casor) and a black woman named Mary Gersheene.

The Jamestown Johnsons and other free blacks in the South who enslaved Africans were later condemned in hindsight as sellouts to European influences. In fact, Africans *in* Africa owned other Africans as slaves for centuries, before and after Anthony Johnson came to Virginia, and he was continuing a long tradition of his native homeland. He and Mary Johnson had themselves been enslaved by Africans in Angola and sold to Europeans. As under the precolonial Angolan system, Anthony Johnson allowed the enslaved Casor to raise cattle and crops so that he could eventually afford to purchase his release. But, under the *American* headright system, the method of land acquisition by bringing new laborers to the colony, increased the demand for laborers thereby driving up the price of slaves, including the price that enslaved Africans had to pay to free themselves.

That the affluent black Johnson family held two slaves in addition to several white servants, along with the fierce competition for laborers among white planters in Virginia, likely lies at the root of the trouble the family began experiencing. Because the Johnsons were the first to settle north of Nandua Creek, they were able to claim the best land in the area. The family was prospering and seemed to be in good standing with local white planters in the early years. But eventually the Johnsons were hit with several setbacks apparently motivated by the envy of a few white neighbors who arrived later and who coveted their prime land. A feud started between Anthony Johnson and two English neighbors, brothers George and Robert Parker, who had recently patented land next to the Johnsons. The conflict began shortly after what colonial records describe as "an unfortunate fire," destroyed the Johnson home along with most of their possessions, forcing the family to appeal to the court for relief from taxes, which was granted. Not long after the suspicious fire, George Parker, also a churchwarden, accused one of the Johnson sons, Richard, of "enormities contrary to the laws of God and man," alleging he lay with the family servant Mary Gersheene.

About the same time, a white man with the same name as Anthony's son John, attempted to steal his land after the sheriff had mistakenly delivered the black John Johnson's land patent to the white John Johnson. The patent was returned to the rightful owner only after Edmund Scarborough, the county's most prominent white planter and incidentally the county surveyor, set the record straight. According to Scarborough's testimony, the title would not have been disputed except for the confusion resulting over the identical names and the mistake of the Sheriff [who was not] able to distinguish whose [land] it was. [The] said Johnson, Joyner, hath no relation to the above mentioned patent, but that John Johnson, Negro, whose patent it is and for whom the Survey was made and by his purchased rights only taken up.

Scarborough, perhaps because of his family ties to the Bennetts, would remain a friend of the Johnsons throughout their ordeals in Northampton and Accomack counties.

As all of this was happening, Johnson's slave John Casor in 1654 protested to Jamestown authorities that he was wrongfully enslaved and that he had papers to prove he was originally purchased as an indentured servant. The Parker brothers spoke up on Casor's behalf but it later became apparent that they were not motivated by antislavery sympathies. The Casor case went to court at which time, exhausted by the feud with the Parkers, Mary Johnson and her two sons pleaded with Anthony to set John Casor free. Pressured from all sides, Anthony Johnson relented and promised to pay Casor freedom dues although Casor had never produced the papers proving he had been purchased as an indentured servant. Immediately Casor began to serve on the Parkers' plantation, which appears to have been why the Parkers intervened on his behalf in the first place. Becoming suspicious about their motive, Anthony Johnson had second thoughts, and the following year he sued the Parkers to have Casor returned to him. The court sided with Johnson and ordered the Parkers to return Casor and to pay all court costs on the finding that the white planters had enticed him to leave his master. Publicly rebuked, the Parker brothers retreated for a time.

Mary Johnson is almost forgotten by historians who have focused at length on the vast lands that her husband was able to acquire. After Anthony died, Mary Johnson allowed John Casor to purchase his freedom with the cattle he was allowed to raise. She guided the family for a decade after, was well regarded by blacks and whites alike, and served the community as an informal doctor. Mary Johnson represented a significant leap forward in the development of colonial Jamestown and indeed in all of English speaking North America. She and the women of the first generation, black and white, worked in the tobacco fields in the 1620s. They bore children in the 1630s; they became involved in family finances often as widows in the 1640s; and by the 1650s they established the foundation of advisors, informal historians, lay ministers, folk healers, godmothers, small financiers, adoptive mothers, babysitters, and midwives that was important in frontier social life. Jamestown was no longer a job but a community. Because of the contributions of the women settlers, colonial Virginia by the middle of the seventeenth century had become a place in which immigrants from across the Atlantic could live with some measure of happiness.

During this time, Anthony and Mary's son John Johnson moved north to take advantage of land opening in Maryland. In 1677, he acquired a tract of land in Somerset County for a plantation that he named Angola after the home country of his parents. This indicates that Anthony and Mary had reminisced favorably of their native homeland to their children, perhaps out of a growing nostalgia as racism increased in the colonies. After old Anthony Johnson died, the Accomack County, Virginia, court ruled in 1670 that his Virginia property should be escheated to the Crown rather than be passed to his family because he was "a Negro and by consequence an alien." The Parker brothers eventually acquired part of the Johnsons' estate.

The amazing life of Anthony Johnson covered the dramatic fall of Kabasa, the forced march to Luanda, the terrible voyage over the Atlantic on the *Bautista*, capture by pirates who threatened to throw him overboard at Bermuda, the Good Friday Massacre of 1622, freedom in Jamestown, the English Civil War, and success as a plantation owner. The Johnsons had many freeborn descendants and not a few fought in the American Revolution. One of them, the free Brutus Johnson, was a soldier who died while serving with General George Washington at Valley Forge.

Anthony's son John Johnson had migrated north up the Eastern Shore to the younger, more raw, and therefore more tolerant colonies of Maryland and later Delaware. Other free Africans, however, remained in Virginia. As the second half of the seventeenth century ended, these free black Virginians met increasing racism due in great part to the dramatic increase in the importation of enslaved Africans. As enslaved blacks were dehumanized through negative characterizations of Africans in general, free blacks from the earlier *Bautista* generation saw their rights gradually diminishing and grew concerned for the future of their children. Some, like the George family, took innovative steps to distinguish their children who had been born free in America, from newly imported black slaves from Africa.

America George

AFTER THE FALL of Kabasa in 1619, Mbande, king of Ndongo, fled with his remaining court to the Kindonga Islands in the Kwanza River. The Portuguese set up a puppet, António Correa Samba a Ntumba, as the new ngola, but later dropped him when the subjects of Ndongo refused to recognize his legitimacy. At his relocated throne in the islands, Ngola Mbande turned the tables on the Portuguese and hired the Imbangala general Kasa ka Ngola to defend him as he set up a government in exile. It was during this period that Mbande's half sister Nzinga emerged on the scene as a major player. Nzinga, also called "Jinga" by the Portuguese, has been made a modern icon of feminism and African nationalism and is frequently named among history's top ten greatest women who succeeded in male dominated societies. A tough negotiator who spent most of her life at war with one enemy or another, she persistently resisted European colonization and she would influence Angola longer than any previous ngola.

Her star first appeared in 1621, when her exiled half brother sent her and her sisters Kambo and Funji on a diplomatic mission to the Portuguese at Luanda. According to a Portuguese account written four decades later, in 1669, when the Portuguese viceroy at Luanda attempted to show authority over her by removing all the chairs but his own in the receiving room, she ordered a servant to kneel on all fours to provide her a seat so that she might meet him as a monarch. In much the same way, the Jamestown Africans were not intimidated by Europeans in 1619: more than a century had passed since Europe had first made contact with Angola and whites, and their customs and technology were no longer strange to the Mbundu and Bakongo people.

Furthermore, Angola's complex Iron Age social and political history gave West Central Africans the sophistication to deal immediately with Europeans on equal footing when the Portuguese arrived in 1482. After 130 years of experience with the Portuguese, it is not surprising that the first generation of Angolans delivered to Jamestown in 1619 were, within two decades, using English-style courts in Virginia to free themselves and their children; record their land, cattle acquisitions and transactions; and file lawsuits to protest unfair treatment.

Nor did religion present a difficult obstacle for the Angolans in interacting with the Jamestown settlers. Nzinga, like thousands of her countrymen, was exposed to Christianity as a child in the late 1500s. Priests such as the Jesuit Francisco de Gouveia had served in royal Kabasa by invitation of the ngola since the 1560s, and other missionaries came before him. John Pedro, Antonio and Issabella Tucker, John Graweere, Emanuel Driggus, and other Bantu who had converted voluntarily in Angola would, upon arriving in Jamestown in the early 1600s and with a responsible degree of discretion, seek out and join Virginia and Maryland churches. Portuguese governors in Angola had hired soba officers who were already Christian, or who agreed to be baptized and to baptize their soldiers. Many of the earliest African captives were young Angolan men who had previously fought in the Portuguese guerra preta in Angola as baptized soldiers alongside or, if Jagas, against Europeans. Such soldiers, when captured and shipped west in slave ships, made up a significant part of the African community in North America. These black soldiers were knowledgeable about close order attacks and how to counter them. Many had fought with muskets and explosives, worked on Portuguese plantations in Angola, and attended mass with European soldiers. It is therefore not unusual that, of the first generation at Jamestown, there exist accounts of Africans such as Philip Mongon, Francisco Payne, William Harman, James Longo, and John Pedro baptizing their children, owning firearms, and participating in colonial militias.

Merchants who were Spanish, Portuguese, Dutch, and Jewish were trading with the Bakongo and the Mbundu in the interior of Angola well before 1619. Italian priests were also active there. Additionally, Bantu envoys had visited cosmopolitan Italian courts; also, selected Bantu youths had been educated in Southern European universities and had returned to Angola completely Europeanized. At the royal court in Kabasa, Princess Nzinga since childhood had been exposed to European multiculturalism two decades before prisoners departed from Luanda on the *Bautista* in 1619.

That some first-generation Africans at Jamestown took white husbands and white wives was also not new. In their homeland, many of the Portuguese, Dutch, and Jews had given their sons and daughters in marriage to Angolans of the same social class, even among the aristocracy, producing an Angolan mestizo society several decades earlier.

❖

THE STRUGGLE BETWEEN Bantu iron kings, the Portuguese, and the Dutch for control of Angola continued to impact the black community at Jamestown after 1619, as more enslaved Angolans arrived over the next few decades. Therefore, Angolan history between 1625 and 1650 is important in the story of that first African-American generation.

The lives of the Angolan royalty read much like the lives and intrigues of European royalty of the same generation. Mbande was the son of Ngola Kiluanji by his chief wife, while Nzinga's mother was Kiluanji's Jaga concubine or lesser wife. Nzinga's personality, charisma, and ambition exceeded her station, however, and Mbande's advisors warned him that his half sister coveted his throne for her son in the traditional matrilineal succession. In response, the ngola had Nzinga's son assassinated, to promote his own heir. Mbande reportedly committed suicide in 1624 because of the disgrace over his escalating losses to the Portuguese, but some said Nzinga poisoned him in revenge for the death of her son. Before dying, he placed his son in the custody of his Imbangala commander. His heir did not long survive and Nzinga, who was accused by a rival in the young prince's death, took the throne herself as ngola of Ndongo despite opposition from Ndongo aristocrats who resisted a woman as king.

Nzinga had grown up in Kabasa with Jesuit missionaries, and she voluntarily converted and was baptized with her sisters at Luanda, where she received the Christian name Dona Anna de Sousa Nzinga. Her conversion made her agreeable as a possible Portugal ally when she crowned herself ngola in 1624. Governor Fernão de Sousa at Luanda presented her with the tempting offer of Kabasa as her royal city *if* she would accept a Portuguese colony in her realm. Portuguese acknowledgment would have strengthened her legitimacy with Europe but the attached strings would make her Sousa's puppet in the eyes of Africans, and in reality, a mere soba under Lisbon and Luanda. Before accepting the throne at Kabasa, she demanded that the Portuguese first close their fort at Ambaca until coming to terms with her. Governor Sousa refused.

So she remained in her island kingdom while continuing to strengthen her armies by extending refuge to Angolans drafted into the guerra preta. Christian Bantu soldiers knowledgeable about European weaponry and tactics rushed to her in numbers that alarmed the Portuguese governor. This created the legend of Anna Nzinga as an early emancipator. But, as someone who both owned slaves and sold hundreds of African enemies to the Portuguese and Dutch, such a title is dubious. Like her royal Mbundu predecessors, as well as King James in England and Weroance Powhatan in Virginia, Ngola Anna Nzinga presented herself as an absolute monarch. She extended an invitation to runaway slaves because of political necessity. By strengthening her army she increased her bargaining power with the Portuguese and her African rivals.

Colorful stories followed her. Ndongo was a cattle-herding kingdom with a male-dominated culture, and so Anna Nzinga was obliged to seek recognition as a king instead of as queen. In keeping with that kingship role, she retained a harem of male concubines whom she forced to wear female attire but allowed to have other wives. European chroniclers sensationalized her conduct as bizarre and unnatural, without understanding that she behaved like an Angolan nobleman to establish her legitimacy as a traditional Ndongo ruler. It was as a "king" of equal stature that she also dealt with opposing European powers struggling to control Angolan slave markets.

Early seventeenth-century Dutch New York, then known as New Amsterdam, rivaled Jamestown as a destination in North America for Bantu people shipped from Angola. Church baptismal records at that time show the most common surname taken by Africans in the Dutch colony was Van Angola. Through military and trade alliances with kingdoms like Kongo and Ndongo, the Dutch pressed hard to supplant the Portuguese in Angola in the early 1600s, as the Dutch West India Company set up trading posts along the major rivers and purchased hundreds of Bantu Jaga prisoners taken captive by the nanikongo and the ngola, to ship to farms and plantations in Dutch New York and also Dutch settlements in Brazil.

The Dutch profited by skillfully exploiting the ongoing conflicts between Portugal, intent on colonizing Angola, and the Bantu iron kings, intent on expansive conquest, centralization, and independence. The Angolan kings, in turn, pitted the Dutch against the Portuguese to resist colonization by either of the European countries.

Formed in 1621, the Dutch West India Company, with assistance from the Christian manikongo of Kongo, sent an armada of ships into the harbor of Luanda in 1624 and there destroyed the Portuguese fleet. Fearful of a Dutch takeover of this vital Atlantic port city, the Portuguese recalled their forces from the interior to shore up defenses on the west coast. The Dutch took advantage of their retreat to Luanda to make trade contacts upriver in Angola. Ngola Anna Nzinga met with the Dutch at this time, and they gave her a small company of Dutch soldiers as a token of their alliance. The Dutch captain was impressed with her and much intrigued with her military camp—the quilombo.

By 1626, the Portuguese, believing the Dutch military threat had subsided, sent a large army inland to crush Anna Nzinga in the Kindonga Islands and to install a king over Ndongo who would not make deals with the Dutch. This invasion and a smallpox epidemic forced Nzinga to retreat to south of the Kwanza River, toward the Kwango River. Though Governor Sousa had driven Anna Nzinga back, he had no success in setting up a king in her place. The sobas of Ndongo noted that the new Portuguese puppet, Ngola a Hari, was born of a slave mother and had himself been a slave of Anna Nzinga's sister Funji. Whatever charisma attracts loyalty in times of crisis swayed the once-dismissive sobas, who now insisted that the daughter of the great Ngola Kiluanji was the legitimate ruler of Ndongo. In the following years, Anna Nzinga lost nearly every battle she fought against the Portuguese, but she would not go away. When she returned to the river islands two years later, she found even more popular support and was further acknowledged as the true ngola of Ndongo by the influential manikongo of Kongo.

When Hari complained that Anna Nzinga was supplanting him in the peoples' hearts, the Portuguese attempted to send an army against her again. A renewed Dutch threat delayed the expedition for a while, but by 1629 the alarm had diminished and a new Portuguese-African army marched out against Anna Nzinga. Abandoning her fort, she retreated to Tala Mugongo near the Kwango River and prepared for the battle. May 25, 1629, ended with another Portuguese victory and, though Anna Nzinga escaped, Portuguese soldiers captured her two sisters. Needing to raise a new army, the ngola presented an alliance of marriage to the Imbangala general, Kasanje. He replied that he did not wish to be her "wife" and would join his army with hers only if she agreed to relinquish power, for there "could not be two lords in his quilombo." Her response to Kasanje was the same as to the Portuguese governor who sought to reduce her power. She turned him down.

In desperation, Anna Nzinga began to employ the cruel tactics of the Imbangala. To increase her notoriety and attract mercenaries and although baptized as a Christian, she reportedly began to lead bloody Imbangala ceremonial rites. She was also said by Portuguese chroniclers to have recruited the children of Africans slain by her raiders. This army, she placed under the command of her son Nzinga Mona while she remained in command of her loyalist Ndongo army. Some historians believe that her adoption of Imbangala tactics and ritual is evidence that she renounced Christianity. However, several Portuguese governors who professed to be devout Christians also employed Imbangala companies. Like the Portuguese, Anna Nzinga found these guerrilla tactics extremely successful and, by 1631, she had conquered the kingdom of Matamba to become its ruler and then returned to the Kindonga Islands on the Kwanza, to once again challenge the Portuguese for the rule of Ndongo proper. Embargoing the interior slave trade to get Luanda's attention, Anna Nzinga dispatched a Jesuit representative in 1637 to negotiate a new trade deal with the Portuguese governor.

The timing was ripe. The Dutch West India fleet returned to the coast of Angola and the new Portuguese governor at Luanda, Vasconcellos Acuna, was unable to send out a force against Anna Nzinga. Unable to fight two enemies at once, he proposed peace in 1640. Professing Christianity, Anna Nzinga received his envoy with the sign of the cross but she still refused to consider any commitment allowing the Portuguese to build a settlement in Ndongo. Allying with Kisanje, the Imbangala general who had spurned her marriage proposal, Governor Acuna began preparing a Portuguese expedition to strike not only Anna Nzinga in the Kindonga Islands but the pro-Dutch kingdoms of Mbwila and Kongo as well.

Once again the Dutch fleet, in coordination with the manikongo and the ngola, attacked the Portuguese. On August 26, 1641, the Dutch West India Company launched a full-scale assault, led by El Mulato's old pirate consort Admiral "Peg-leg" Jol, against the Portuguese stronghold at Luanda, catching the Portuguese army off guard as it marched inland to fight Anna Nzinga. Luanda fell and the victorious Dutch seized it, quickly consolidating alliances with Bantu kings and sobas chafing under Portuguese colonialism. The Dutch West India Company now controlled most of the slave exports from Kongo and Angola and would continue in power through most of the 1640s.

With the Portuguese removed from Luanda, Anna Nzinga returned as the recognized ngola of Ndongo and formalized a treaty with the Dutch that included a slave trade deal. It was during this time of Dutch aggressiveness on the Angolan and Kongolese coast, between 1635 and 1648, that Angolan captives began arriving in Jamestown from Angola by way of Dutch New York, Barbados, and also Providence Island, where Lord Robert Rich had set up a new colonial company and installed as his admiral the old pirate Daniel Elfrith.

❦

FOR THE ENGLISH of Jamestown, Dutch control of Luanda opened Dutch New York as a second source of Angolan laborers in addition to those provided by British pirates such as John Powell, Thomas Jones, Daniel Elfrith, Samuel Axe, Arthur Guy, and John Colyn Jope, who were preying on Spanish and Portuguese slave ships in the West Indies. Virginia governor William Berkeley was a great promoter of trade between the colony and Dutch Protestants, and he granted land in Jamestown to the New Amsterdam Stam merchant family to encourage Dutch consumption of Virginia tobacco. In fact, Jamestown was heavily settled by Englishmen such as George Yeardley and Nathaniel Littleton, who had previously served as English soldiers fighting in support of the Dutch Protestant Low Countries in their war against Spain. Jamestown was then far more pro-Dutch than was the English Parliament.

Tobacco plantations were flourishing in the 1630s, and prices were starting to climb in the colony. At this time, a healthy young African man cost twenty-seven hundred pounds of tobacco, valued at about £18 sterling, and an African woman was purchased for twenty-five hundred pounds of tobacco. Due to their resistance to European diseases and their advanced knowledge of dense farming, iron tools, and cattle, the Bantu of Angola were considered the most prized workers. In 1657, William Woolrich who leased the London/Africa/Virginia–based ship *Hopewell*, testified that the Africans "they took aboard at Calabar are not generally considered as good as those of Angola." By the 1650s, the premium price paid for an Angolan was £35 English sterling. High prices were an incentive to keep Africans as slaves for life.

Coming from Kongo and Angola by way of Dutch New York, successive waves of Bantu men and women soon joined the first

African-American generation at Jamestown. During the period of the Jamestown-Dutch mutual trade pact, Virginia planter Edmund Scarborough, like some of his neighbors, sailed to Dutch New York to purchase dozens of Angolans for his Northampton County plantation. Because of their common Bantu origin, the newcomers who arrived from Angola between 1635 and 1660 merged seamlessly with the Angolan malungu communities already established by the earliest Jamestown Africans who had arrived in 1619.

However, not all of the Angolans in Jamestown found equal access to freedom, as can be seen in the histories of Africans at the Littleton Plantation. Nathaniel Littleton came from a wealthy English family. As a young man he had served with the Protestant Dutch armies in the Netherlands, and he had ties with Dutch families in New Amsterdam. Littleton arrived in Virginia in 1635 with big plans. Settling on the Eastern Shore across Chesapeake Bay from Jamestown, he began importing white servants for headrights and thus acquired huge tracts of land. Along the way, Littleton also obtained fourteen Africans from Jeremiah Robinson and, through his marriage to the widow Anne Harmar, he acquired eight more Africans who had been purchased by her first husband, named Harmar or Hamor, in 1635.

The origin of the Bantu group at the Littleton plantation can be determined by some of their names, which are identical to the names of exported Angolans still legible in the old seventeenth-century Portuguese slave lists at Luanda. There was a man named Congo with his wife Cossongo and another woman named Pallassa on the Littleton plantation. ("Pallassa" was a popular Angolan name, for at the same time there was a black woman named Pallassa Van Angola in Dutch New York as well as another woman named Pallassa on the Stafford plantation in Jamestown.) These names and the typical Portuguese Christian names of their companions, such as Maria, Antonio, Pedro, Francisco, and Emanuel, identify the group of Africans at the Littleton plantation as Bantu people from Kongo and Angola. Though they likely did not all come from the same village and perhaps not even from the same kingdom or nation, they shared the same greater Angolan

Bantu culture. Congo and Cossongo still retained their African names in Jamestown, which indicates they had been forcibly baptized at Luanda and subsequently had forgotten their Christian names upon arriving in America. Congo, Cossongo, and Pallassa were among the eight Africans brought to Jamestown by the Harmars in 1635, possibly from Angola by way of Dutch New York. Africans with Portuguese Christian names joined them on the Littleton plantation in 1640. It is probable that this later group with Christian names had been captured during Dutch Protestant and Portuguese Catholic struggles for control of Luanda. These latter prisoners had long ago converted voluntarily in Angola and therefore they remembered their Christian names in America; some would eventually gain their freedom in Jamestown, unlike the earlier arrivals. Congo, Cossongo, and Pallassa. In fact, there is no indication in the colonial records of the seventeenth century of any African with a non-Christian name ever being set free in Virginia (though there are some cases in Dutch New York in the same era), indicating that, while not ensuring it, prior voluntary conversion to Christianity before coming to Jamestown significantly increased an African's chances of freedom in the colony.

Among the group with Christian names who arrived at the Littleton plantation were Pedro George, who was trained as a carpenter, and his wife Jone; this couple had a daughter they named Jane. The story of Peter George and his family reveals how Africans who were becoming free in the second half of the seventeenth century were beginning to experience increased racism at Jamestown.

After Colonel Littleton died, his widow Anne Littleton began thinking of her children Hester, Edward, and Southy Littleton and their inheritance. She bequeathed Jane George, then in her teens, to her son Southy. To eldest son Edward she left most of the Bantu. After 1663, Widow Littleton remarried planter Francis Pigot of Northampton County, and she brought Peter and Jone George and another black couple, Paul and Hannah Carter, with her as servants. Jone George died in 1676 while enslaved on the Pigot plantation, but her husband Peter survived her to gain his freedom that year on the condition that he would later pay Pigot ten thousand pounds of tobacco. Peter George rented land as a tenant farmer next door to another Angolan-American family headed by Emanuel Driggus and, by 1682, he had paid the amount to Pigot, for in that year Peter George was a freedman and the owner of a herd of cattle.

Peter George had as a neighbor an unscrupulous Englishman who exploited ethnic fears that were beginning to grow in the late seventeenth century. This less-than-friendly neighbor concocted a scam to bilk the prosperous freed black man. In 1688, Robert Candlin persuaded Peter George that "there was a law made that all free Negroes should be slaves again." Alarmed, George informed Sarah Driggus, Emanuel Driggus's daughter-in-law. She went to Candlin to question him further, and he told her "he would advise Peter George to make what haste he could away lest he should be stopped." As George hurriedly packed his worldly possessions into a wagon conveniently provided by Candlin, the white farmer assured him that he would oversee his estate in his absence. Candlin drove the heavily loaded wagon along with the black man's livestock to his own farm as Peter George, Sarah Driggus, and a few other free black Virginians fled into Maryland.

After three hard years starting over from scratch in Maryland, Peter George returned to Northampton County, Virginia, realizing he had been duped out of his property. In the meantime, Robert Candlin had died. So Peter George filed a lawsuit against Widow Candlin seeking his cattle and hogs. Three white men supported his suit and the Court ordered Candlin's widow to return the swindled livestock to Peter George.

The incident exposes worsening ethnic relations at Jamestown in the late seventeenth century and the subsequent economic decline of free blacks that would pressure many of them to take their families to other colonies. The brief era of tolerance was closing in the Tidewater region, though opportunities still existed on the frontier. After the death of his first wife Jone, Peter George married Mary Rodriggus of the Driggus family and two sons were born, Peter II and Samuel George. In 1702, after the freeborn Peter II and his cousins John and Johnson

Driggus were convicted of intimidating several white persons "in an insolent manner," he moved to Maryland and married a black woman named Mary and they had a daughter in 1705. This was the year that the colonies adopted the far-ranging restrictions known as the "Slave Code," which greatly reduced the rights of Africans and increased the difficulty for newly arriving Africans to gain freedom. As early as 1670, Jamestown had enacted a law that all later Africans arriving by sea "shall be slaves for their lives." Aware of the colonies' growing hostility to them and anxious to manifest their country of birth, black Americans attempted to distinguish their children born in the American colonies from Africans coming directly from Africa. For this reason, Peter and Mary gave their daughter the name "America George" to signify that she was born in America. A number of free black descendants of Peter George lived up to the name "America" as patriot soldiers in the American Revolution.

❖

IN HIS PROPHETIC play *Masque of Blackness*, King James in 1605 invited fictitious princesses of Africa to visit his new empire—an empire that a few months later claimed a significant large part of America. Among all of genuine African royalty, Anna Nzinga would rise to become one of the most historically important in the era that saw the birth of English-speaking America. The ngola would live to survive the Dutch expulsion and witness the return of the Portuguese to Luanda in 1648. Losing battles but winning wars, she ruled the kingdoms of Ndongo and Matamba until her death in 1663, three years after the restoration of the interrupted Stuart monarchy in England and the beginning of the rapid growth of slavery in America via the chartering of the Royal African Company by James's grandson. Her death caused a temporary disruption of African autonomy in Angola, as Portugal took over the country as a colony until finally withdrawing in the 1970s as one of the last colonial European powers to relinquish Africa.

Popular myth claims that Ngola Nzinga was buried in a garment of leopard skin clutching a fistful of arrows—as a show, it is said, of her resistance to colonialism and rejection of Christianity. In fact, at her own request, she died as Dona Anna de Sousa Nzinga and was buried in St. Mary's Church in Matamba in a Capuchin nun's habit, clutching a rosary.

Anna Nzinga's lifetime (1583–1663) represents the age of the first African-American generation. The true story of her life questions the myths and bigotry that have obscured the original founders of black America and reveals the relevance of both their Bantu and Christian background to their survival, contributions, and successes at Jamestown.

The name "Nzinga" appeared around the time of her death as a free surname in the first generation of African America, as also did the name of her sister, Kambo—the name of the African Cambon family at Jamestown. Captain Henry Fleet was an early pirate/explorer who settled in Jamestown after voyaging on Lord Rich's ships, the *Warwick* and the *Tiger*, that sailed down the West African coast and to the West Indies in the 1620s and later. Upon his death, his widow, Sharon Fleet married Lieutenant Colonel John Walker of Virginia and brought into that marriage a number of enslaved Africans, including Edward Mozinga. The name "Mozinga," or "Mozingo," is the form of the Bantu "Nzinga" found written in seventeenth-century Angola. Edward Mozinga eventually purchased his freedom in the customary Bantu way and entered into an apprenticeship with Colonel Walker that he completed in 1672. Mozinga was one of only a few Jamestown Africans who retained his African name as a freedman. He married a woman named Margaret and prospered. To the second generation, to his free sons Edward II and John, Edward Mozinga of Jamestown left his land, his cattle, and two guns. Americans descended from Edward Mozinga survive to this day with the original surname.

PART IV

THE FOUNDERS' LEGACY

*A*FTER NEARLY SIXTY years from the time that two pirate ships attack the Bautista, the first African-American generation is about to pass from the stage. But it will not go quietly. From 1619 to 1676, one generation has a brief opportunity to bestow freedom upon its descendants and their generations before the onset of nearly two centuries of slavery.

Just ahead, the original founders of African America, who in their youth saw Kabasa fall in flames, now fifty-six years later with dimming eyes witness the fiery destruction of Jamestown at the birth of the antislavery movement, and the creation of an American Jaga army of Angolans and Europeans battling against the entrenched royalist planter elite.

And then the final chapter reveals how the pirate lord, who brought the first slaves to English North America in 1619, also planted the first seed of a radical idea that would one day abolish slavery.

Jamestown Burns

LEADERLESS, THE PURITAN Commonwealth sputtered after the death of Cromwell. Some of the Puritan nobility, including Lord Robert Rich, had never consented to abolishing the monarchy, which, as a divinely ordained executive profession, had previously served the country reliably when held accountable to the law and to the people. So England in 1660 invited Charles II, grandson of James I, to return to the throne and restore the Stuart dynasty. Parliament still controlled taxes, so to raise royal revenue Charles II, among other things, that year gave the Royal African Company a charter to ship slaves directly from Africa. No longer would American plantations rely on freelance pirates raiding Spanish and Portuguese frigates for slaves. In 1660, slavery became a British industry, though the British did not bring slaves to England. England, and indeed all of Western Europe, had its own well-stocked native born labor pool of white peasants. Britain sold Africans to the faraway colonies to do jobs that English peasants did not want to do.

Between 1648 and 1681, the number of whites in Virginia increased by 5.2 percent, while the number of blacks in Virginia in the same time period increased by 10 percent, due in large part to imported Africans, all desperately desiring to be free. The older Angolan-American malungu families, those of the first Jamestown generation who had become free and who had built protective communities to assist each other, were now compelled to help enslaved Africans who, beginning in 1660, were arriving almost weekly on neighboring plantations from more diverse parts of Africa.

Also in 1660, the Quakers of Virginia, led largely by women, began to preach to Africans secretly in the forests, compelling Governor Berkeley to issue an order the following year forbidding whites and blacks from attending "unlawful assemblies":

> Whereas notwithstanding the King's most Excellent Majesties gracious pardon of all Quakers for the time before his said proclamation and the Right Honorable Governor's explanation thereof by both which it appeares that all Quakers are to be conformable to the Law as from publication thereof several meetings have been of the said Quakers in this Country especially by women whereupon his Majesty's said Governor orders that all women who should after publication of the said proclamation and explanation continue their said unlawful meetings & breach their schismatical and heretical doctrines & opinions should by their adjoining magistrate be tendered the oathes of Supremacy & allegiance & the refusees to be Imprisoned according to Law. And it appearing by 2 oathes taken this day in Court that several Quakers met the 25th instant in the woods amongst which were Mrs Mary Chisman and 2 or 3 Negroes belonging to her husband. It is ordered that the said Edmond Chisman & his wife have notice of the Governors said order & that she shall hereafter offend in the like kind that the said order be put in Effectual execution against her, and also that Mr Chisman restrain his said Negroes & whole family from repairing to the said unlawful Assemblies at his peril.

Many groups—freedom-yearning slaves, sympathetic free blacks and whites, exploited white servants, religious dissidents, and vulnerable small farmers on the neglected outskirts of colonial Virginia—were converging to spark a Jaga-style rebellion against the Crown colony's seat of government in Jamestown, which, under Berkeley and future governors, promoted the vision of the young British Empire centered in the royal city of London.

Africans, particularly Angolans, played a leading role in the first large-scale American rebellion in 1676, one century before the American Revolution. Six decades earlier, at the latter end of 1618, King James's chronicler William Camden had reported the sudden appearance in the sky of a comet visible in the constellation of *Libra* (Latin for "balance," or scales). Camden made this astronomical observation in noting the death of Queen Anne and the beheading of Sir Walter Raleigh that year, and he predicted a time of travail for the year ahead. The painful birth of African America was nine months away, for on December 7, 1618, as the corsairs *White Lion* and the *Treasurer* were preparing to leave for the West Indies, Camden reported the comet visible at the latitude of Jamestown. As the fireball blazed over Jamestown, the Imbangala torched Kabasa.

Nearly sixty years later, Virginians saw another comet in the latitude of Jamestown, coinciding with another burning city and the passing of the first African-American generation. Regarded as a great omen by Virginians at the time, this comet appeared

> every evening for a week or more, at southwest, thirty-five degrees high, streaming like a horse's tail west-wards, until it reached (almost) the horizon, and setting towards the northwest.

Thus began Bacon's Rebellion. The first spark that would consume Jamestown came shortly after the restoration of the old royalist Governor William Berkeley. Those who had remained loyal to the exiled Stuarts during the English Commonwealth once again dominated Jamestown and feasted on the spoils of incumbency with a vengeance. Governor Berkeley levied taxes on Virginia farmers to pay for a manservant and two horses for each of his cronies in the Virginia House of Burgesses. Representatives sitting on various committees were also provided free alcoholic refreshments along with expensive gifts and assorted perks. Charles II rewarded his faithful supporters with vast land grants in Virginia, dispossessing some with legal title. The new landlords had the power to grant land allotments, install sheriffs, redraw counties, and collect taxes in addition to those already imposed by the Berkeley legislature.

High taxes, falling tobacco prices, and slave unrest got the pot simmering. Small farmers on the edge of the colony complained of thefts and attacks by local natives, yet Berkeley, who was part of a trade monopoly with natives for animal furs, did nothing. Then in 1675 in Stafford County, a settler named Robert Hen was slain in his home by a small band of Doeg Indians. A party of farmers followed the trail of the raiders for miles, indiscriminately shooting any native they met along the way. When they reached the village of the culprits, the militia attacked all of its occupants and killed the king of the Doegs. Among the natives they attacked were innocent members of a delegation from the powerful Susquehannock nation that at the time was at peace with Jamestown. The Susquehannock retaliated, and the war even spilled over into Maryland where, at a peace parlay, settlers suddenly murdered five great Susquehannock kings. The natives withdrew and returned to Virginia, leaving a trail of bodies:

> Instead of the notched trees that were wont to serve as landmarks in the pioneer days, these infuriated Indians left behind them a pathway marked by gaping wounds upon the bodies of white men, women, and children. They swore to have still further revenge for the loss of their "great men," each of whose lives, they said, was worth the lives of ten of the Englishmen, who were of inferior rank, while their ambassadors were men of quality.

They attacked frontier farms on the Potomac and Rappahannock rivers, killing more than thirty settlers, but Governor Berkeley refused pleas from farmers to send the colonial militia to stop them. The governor further outraged planters when, in his trade with the natives, he continued to sell them guns and ammunition. Refused protection, settlers again took matters into their own hands:

Planters at Merchant's Hope Plantation in Charles City County on the James River, began to beat up drums for Volunteers to go out against the Indians, and so continued Sundry days drawing into Arms. The magistrates, either for fear or favor, made no attempt to prevent so dangerous a beginning & going on, and a commander and head seemed all that was needed to perfect the design and lead it on to success.

Into the leadership over the discontented stepped the energetic, charismatic, and well-connected Nathaniel Bacon, a planter and the first American populist. Bacon raised an army by promising freedom to every enslaved African and indentured Englishman who would run away and join him. This sizable force indiscriminately hit the innocent Nottaway and Nansemond peoples in a series of merciless attacks, and most of the native survivors moved away in fragmented bands.

Six months later, Bacon's campaign ceased being a war against natives and became a war of the colonial underclass against Jamestown's ruling royalist elite. Free black and white farmers, plus runaway Angolan fugitives, marched to Jamestown to protest government abuses and cast Berkeley and his favorites out of power. Governor Berkeley fled and, at the high point of the attack, Bacon's army, by then largely African, seized the colonial capital and burned it to the ground.

In the ashes of Jamestown, Governor Berkeley appealed to the Stuart king of England, who gave him a fleet to put down the Jaga rebels. Bacon died of natural causes at this time and the rebellion, though as powerful as ever, had no capable leader. The standoff remained a stalemate until Berkeley sent Captain Thomas Grantham, who blockaded and shelled a rebel garrison, forcing its surrender and capturing three hundred Bacon followers. But at the plantation of Colonel John West, he found the main garrison of four hundred armed African and English rebels, all runaway servants, impossible to take and, promising them freedom he offered a truce that he all the while intended to break:

> I there met about four hundred English and Negroes in Arms who were much dissatisfied at the Surrender of the Point, saying I had betrayed

them, and thereupon some were for shooting me and others were for cutting me in pieces. . . . I told them I would willingly surrender myself to them, till they were satisfied from His Majesty, and did engage to the Negroes and Servants that they were all pardoned and freed from their Slavery: And with faire promises and Rundletts of Brandy, I pacified them, giving them several Notes under my hand that what I did was by order of his Majesty and the Governor.

According to Captain Grantham, a company of mostly Africans and a few Englishmen still refused his terms:

Most of them I persuaded to go to their Homes, which accordingly they did, Except about eighty Negroes and twenty English which would not deliver their Arms.

Grantham tricked the remaining rebels into going aboard a sloop, with the promise that he would transport them to another camp down the York River. Another ship appeared bristling with guns and the rebels were trapped in the vessel, defiant to the end:

they yielded with a great deal of discontent, saying had they known my purpose they would have destroyed me.

The royalist elite returned and rebuilt Jamestown. They of course did not ignore the great number of Africans in the rebellion and took steps to prevent a future reoccurrence. Between 1619 and 1660, conflicts involving African slaves were handled individually in county courts. These local court rulings were not binding on all of Virginia, and therefore relations between planters and enslaved Africans varied. As previously described, some planters treated Africans as indentured servants and released them with freedom dues after a few years, other planters freed Africans in their wills, some allowed enslaved Africans to raise tobacco and cattle to purchase their freedom, yet others detested slavery and immediately freed Africans when they acquired them through marriage or inheritance, and the remainder held Africans in bondage for their entire lives.

After 1660, as the number of imported Africans dramatically increased, issues involving the status of Africans passed from the local courts to the colonial legislature, particularly as a result of Bacon's Rebellion. Still, universal slavery in the colony did not come in one day. In 1670, the Virginia legislature ruled that free African Americans could not own white servants. This law in effect barred African Americans from using the colonial headright system of importing English peasants to acquire land. That same year, Virginia passed a law declaring that "all servants not being Christians imported into this colony by shipping shall be slaves for their lives." This law mandated that all nonbaptized Africans being shipped to Virginia by sea were required to be permanently enslaved. Then in 1691, the Virginia legislature forbade the manumission of slaves unless the slaveholder transported them out of the colony. This law forced slaveholders who were inclined to free older slaves, to pay for moving them, their families, and whatever property they had accumulated, to the Carolinas. Faced with this large out-of-pocket expense, any slaveholder who wished to do so now had second thoughts about freeing his or her Africans. The Virginia legislature that year also outlawed mixed marriages and required that mixed children born out of wedlock to European women be bound as servants for thirty years. Because African men were able to raise livestock to acquire their freedom, more African men than women were set free. In addition, African men were frequently granted freedom earlier than African women, who were often freed after passing childbearing age. This male-female imbalance pressured some free African men to take European wives, usually English- or Irishwomen of the same social and economic class, because European women and their offspring could not be enslaved. By outlawing mixed marriage, the planter-controlled Virginia Assembly limited African men to marrying enslaved African women, and because slave status was defined by the status of the mother, their children were born enslaved even though the African father was a free man. As affordable land became available on the opening frontier, a free black man, as in the case of Mihill Gowen, had to decide to either leave his enslaved wife and child behind, or stay with them on the plantation and endure diminishing prospects. Gowen, for one, moved away with only his son and married an Englishwoman.

Another extremely critical stage in the development of institutionalized slavery came in 1705, when the colonial legislature banned the important but informal custom of slaves purchasing their freedom by raising cattle. In fact, the Virginia Assembly ordered that all cattle owned by slaves at that time immediately

> shall be seized and sold by the church-wardens of the parish wherein such horses, cattle, or hogs shall be, and the profit thereof applied to the use of the poor of said parish.

Finally, in 1723, the Virginia Assembly took the last step and banned outright the freeing of slaves, unless they had performed some notable public service, such as reporting a planned slave rebellion.

The curtain that opened on King James's welcoming *Masque of Blackness* in 1605 closed with the passing of the first African-American generation at Jamestown. The last actor, however, had not left the stage.

*R*oots of Abolition

T HE QUESTION OF *why* the Africans were taken from the *San Juan Bautista* four hundred years ago is ultimately as intriguing as *who* took them. The motive is intriguing because the pirates—John Colyn Jope, Daniel Elfrith, Samuel Argall, and Robert Rich—were also Puritans engaged in a battle of ideals. Was the taking of the first Africans a dark deed of avarice and greed, or an act of rebellion motivated by idealism? And if it was idealism, was the 1619 seizure of those Africans justified?

Robert Rich holds the answer to the first question. Though virtually unknown in America now, this Puritan lord personally launched and invested in more American colonies and ventures at the beginning than any other single individual. Did he colonize simply to amass wealth, or to spread important republican ideals that would take root in America? In April 1646, the second Earl of Manchester, Edward Montagu, complained against civil restrictions limiting free speech in England, despite "the power granted by Parliament to the Earl of Warwick for the American plantations." By "American plantations," Lord Montagu meant the colonies in both New England and Virginia. If the judgment of history is willing to portray the second Earl of Warwick simply as a pilfering pirate, it ignores the evidence that Rich not only pressed

Parliament to give Americans greater freedoms than those allowed in England but he also vacated a coveted family position with access to royal monopolies and privilege in the Stuart court, to risk his life and title to go to war against the tyrannical doctrine of absolutism.

Lord Rich's role in the *Bautista* piracy cannot be removed from the background of historical events at the time. Rome and Spain, the appointed defender of Rome, wanted to return England and the rest of Protestant Europe to the Catholic fold. In opposing absolute rule and the imprisonment of conscience, Puritans of the early seventeenth century saw two great enemies—King James and Rome. To Puritans, action, even rebellion, was required to stem what appeared to them to be a clear and growing danger. When the Spanish Count Gondomar, with James's consent, closed the republican Parliament for opposing the Spanish marriage, Lord Robert Rich, a Member of Parliament, attacked Spanish ships, one of which contained African prisoners.

The strongest reason to redeem the reputation of the second Earl of Warwick, from lawless pirate to idealistic Jaga, lies in a document that was written in a town that still bears his name in a colony he originally chartered. Becoming the first government anywhere in the world to ban African slavery, the general court at Warwick, Rhode Island, on May 13, 1652, during Rich's lifetime and by the authority he obtained for them from the English Parliament, enacted the following:

> Whereas, there is a common course practiced among Englishmen, to buy Negroes to that end they may have them for service or slaves forever; for the preventing of such practices among us let it be ordered that no black mankind or white being shall be forced to serve any man or his assignees longer than ten years. . . . And that man that will not let them go free, he or they shall forfeit to the colony forty pounds.

The political ideology that Rich and the Puritans derived from theology led them to rebel against absolute rule. That same ideology logically concludes that African slavery is just another form of absolute rule. Whether Rich himself had come to believe that slavery is wrong is unknown, though perhaps doubtful. But as a matter of conscience, he gave Rhode Island colony and dissidents like Roger Williams the freedom and authority to reach that conclusion.

After Charles I was beheaded, Robert Rich retired from public life. However, he bore the Sword of State at the inauguration of Oliver Cromwell and in 1657, his grandson married Cromwell's daughter, Frances. It might be presumed that he suffered with those of his rank who had overthrown and beheaded a king when, in 1660, the Stuart monarchy was restored. But Rich had never hated the Stuarts or the monarchy despite his republican views. Charles II acquitted him of regicide, and Rich died with honors in his old age.

Because of the resistance of Englishmen like Rich, the Stuart doctrine of absolutism abated in England but was carried across the sea in somewhat reduced form by royalist planters, who, beginning with the restoration of the monarchy in 1660, ascended to what would be a long rule empowered by the toil of slaves and protected by racist legislation. Though they dropped their monarchical sympathies in the American Revolution, the planter elite smuggled the last flickering vestige of European absolutism through the American Civil War with the enactment of Jim Crow segregation laws, until the U.S. Supreme Court doused the fire in the 1960s.

The second question, whether America's early struggle for religious and civil freedom justified the seizure of the *Bautista* Africans, is a difficult one in light of the many who followed them in chains, and the continuing reality of racial inequality. It is a question best answered by what we do now.

• BANTU GLOSSARY •

ANGOLA: The name of this West Central African country bordering the Atlantic Ocean is taken from the royal title ngola (iron maker) of the kingdom of Ndongo. Angola is one of a number of Bantu-dominated countries in Central and Southern Africa; it once contained three major Bantu nationalities and several iron-producing kingdoms or states that were first established by colonizers about A.D. 1000–1100. "Greater Angola" of the fifteenth century was larger than the present country. Europeans first visited Angola in 1482, ten years before Columbus sailed west. However, early historians Herodotus, Arrian, Pliny the Elder, and others cite ancient expeditions to circumnavigate Africa such as that sent by Pharaoh Necho (600 B.C.) and by the Carthagenian Hanno (425 B.C.) who may have described the Congo gorilla of Greater Angola. (See Pliny the Elder, *Natural History*, 6.200; Karl Müller, *Geographi Graeci Minores*, volume I; 1855 Paris; WFG Lacroix, *Africa in Antiquity* (Saarbrucken, 1998),.48–56, 380–84.]

BAKONGO: The Kikongo-speaking Bantu nation in the north of the older Greater Angola, composed of a number of kingdoms or states of which Kongo was the most dominant from the fifteenth century.

BANTU: A massive and successful town-dwelling, iron-producing, cattle-ranching, fixed-agricultural ethnic group that migrated into Central Africa about A.D. 1000. Many nations, kingdoms, and languages make up the Bantu ethnic group. In Angola, the dominant Bantu nations were the Bakongo, who spoke Kikongo Bantu; the Mbundu, who spoke Kimbundu Bantu, and the Ovimbundu, who spoke Umbundu. Each nation contained numerous smaller kingdoms. Bantu-rooted languages dominate over all other African languages in Africa today.

BUCKRAS: Angolan in origin, this describes whites, including underclass whites who were often employed as cowboys. Similar in meaning to *cracker*, a person who uses a bullwhip to herd cattle, the Angolan word *buckra*, and not the Spanish word *vaquero*, is the real origin of the word *buckaroo*, a wild cowboy. The Bantu, including descendants of prisoners from the kingdom of Ndongo, pioneered the seventeenth-century American cattle culture east of the Appalachian Mountains and carried it west after 1800.

DOGI: Bantu word for "small calf." It is the origin of *dogie* in the American West.

FUNJI: Porridge made from grain.

IMBANGALA: Now a settled people, the Imbangala were rootless bands of raiders of disputed origin who first appeared in Northern Angola in the late sixteenth century and who later offered their mercenary services to Portuguese governors and Angolan monarchs.

ITA: Kimbundu word for "war."

JAGAS: Bantu rebels, or "patriots," of conquered ministates who resisted loss of autonomy to larger superstates. They have been mistakenly identified with the Imbangala, who were roaming mercenaries with no state loyalties. When captured by Angolan superkings, Jaga rebels were enslaved, sold, and shipped overseas all over the world. Angolan Jagas were heavily involved in a number of rebellions in America, including Bacon's Rebellion and the Stono Rebellion.

KABASA: Royal capital city of the Mbundu kingdom of Ndongo, between the Lukala and Lutete rivers, built in the fifteenth century.

KALUNGU: The Atlantic Ocean bordering Angola on the west, and also to Angolans the spirit realm that "the eye could see but the feet could not walk."

KALUNGA NGOMBE: The god of the underworld who lived in the western sea.

KAZUMBI: Kimbundu word for "spirit," being from whence comes the word *zombie*.

KIJIKU: Kimbundu word for "slave" or "serflike dependent." The Portuguese called slaves *pecas*, or "pieces," for the sections of cloth first used as currency, and retained the word afterward.

KIKONGO: Language of the Bakongo nation of old Greater Angola.

KILANDA: Kimbundu word for "military officers."

KIMBANDA: Kimbundu word for "doctor" or "healer."

KIMBARI: Kimbundu word for "soldiers."

KIMBUNDU: Language of the Mbundu nation to the south of the Bakongo nation.

KONGO: One of the great Bantu kingdoms of the Bakongo nation in early Greater Angola. Kongo was first established as a federation of ministates by the first manikongo, Lukeni Lua Nimi, in the early fifteenth century. It had become an empire when the first Europeans visited Angola in 1482. Kongo voluntarily converted to Christianity in the sixteenth century but struggled to retain independence from Portuguese colonialism. The old kingdom of Kongo is spelled with a *k* to distinguish it from the current Democratic Republic of Congo.

KRAAL: Bantu word for "cattle enclosure," which became *corral* in America.

MBANZA KONGO: Sacred royal capital city of the kingdom of Kongo, founded on a mountain by Lukeni Lua Nimi who crossed the Congo River around A.D. 1400. It was renamed Sao Salvador around A.D. 1500, when the kingdom converted to Christianity under Lukeni's great-grandson.

MBUNDU: The nation of Kimbundu-speaking people in the Angolan highlands, composed of a number of kingdoms or states of which Ndongo was the most dominant. It likely evolved out of the Bakongo nation sometime in the past.

MALUNGU: Kimbundu Bantu word originally describing animist spirits. As used by Kimbundu-speaking slaves sent overseas, *malungu* carried the general idea of "shipmate" or "comrade who came by sea on the same ship." Portuguese influence altered the word to *melongo*, and as such later in Brazil this word also came to describe two infants nursed at the same breast regardless of blood kinship. In North America, *malungu* is the root of Melungeon. The Melungeons are a triracial people of whom a small remnant are still identified in Virginia, North Carolina, Tennessee, and Kentucky, though they have largely assimilated in larger cities. Melungeons descend from the first Bantu Americans of Jamestown who became free before the Civil War and intermarried with Europeans and Native Americans.

MANIKONGO: The Kikongo word for "king" is *mani* (from *mwene*), meaning "iron blacksmith" and is the title of the ruler of the kingdom of Kongo of the Bakongo nation. The first manikongo was Lukeni, who crossed the Congo River into Angola in the early fifteenth century and founded the city of Mbanza Kongo as the capital of the Kongo federation that eventually became an empire.

MBANDE: A Bantu word referring to the official boundaries of a kingdom or state.

NDONGO: The most powerful of the seventeenth-century Mbundu kingdoms of Angola. It was a large kingdom of cattlemen centered at the royal capital of Kabasa. Made up of many districts that had once been independent ministates, Ndongo, like the Bakongo kingdom of Kongo, was prone to civil war from intermittent Jaga rebellions.

NGOLA: Kimbundu word for "iron blacksmith," used as the title of the king of Ndongo. "Angola" is derived from *ngola*. The most famous ngola was Anna Nzinga, a woman of Ndongo's upper aristocracy who converted to Christianity and resisted Portuguese colonization as well as neighboring Angolan kings in the seventeenth century.

NGONGO: A double clapperless bell in every Ndongo district used to signal war.

NICEFO: Banana.

NZIMBU: Bantu word for the highly valued cowrie shell used as currency worldwide. In Angola, nzimbu shells were mined at Luanda. Europeans in the Atlantic triangular trade also bartered in nzimbu. Archaelogical excavations have yielded large caches of cowrie shells on American plantations, such as Monticello.

QUILOMBO OR KILOMBO: Bantu military camps, restricted to males. The quilombo also functioned as an academy to teach young men the art of war.

SOBA: Bantu official in the outlying districts surrounding the capitals of superstates. Sobas came from the royalty of ministates conquered by superstates and, as such, made up the lesser aristocracy in large kingdoms such as Kongo, Ndongo, and Matamba. The sobas coveted their lost autonomy and frequently rebelled or switched alliances to lead Jaga rebellions.

XI: Bantu word meaning "city."

• NOTES •

Author's Note

p. xvi   Concerning the identification: William Thorndale, "The Virginia Census of 1619," *Magazine of Virginia Genealogy*, 1995, citing the census listing "The Sums totall of all ye Persons, Cattle, Corne, Armes, Houses, and Boats Contayned in the generall Muster of Virginia taken in the beginning of March 1619," of which a subsection lists "Others not Christians in the Service of the English." Seventeen of the thirty-two nonwhites counted in the muster were African women. See "Copy of Population, Livestock Census," Microfilm 5963: Ferrar Papers, 1592–1637, Alderman, Library, University of Virginia. Despite Rolfe's claim to Edwin Sandys in January 1620 that the *Treasurer* left Jamestown without trading, in fact the ship had traded about half a dozen Africans to settlers, including those listed in the 1624–1625 Virginia census (which counted twenty-three surviving Africans in seven households) as "Antoney Negro," "Isabell, Negro," "Angelo, a Negro woman," and "Edward, a Negro." Furthermore, those named in the census as "Antonio, a Negro, "Mary, a Negro woman," and "John Pedro, a Negar" were Africans the *Treasurer* delivered to Bermuda in September–October 1619 after fleeing Jamestown, and who were later shipped individually to Jamestown. This census also noted the presence of the "twenty and odd" anonymous Africans whom George Yeardley and Abraham Piersey acquired from the *White Lion*. See "1624/25 Muster Database," Virtual Jamestown, Crandall Shifflett, 2000, at www.virtualjamestown.org/Muster/introduction.html.

p. xvi   However, in "An Early Virginia Census . . ." Martha W. McCartney, "An Early Virginia Census Reprised," *Quarterly Bulletin of the Virginia Archaeological Society* (1999); Jarvis and van Driel, "The Vingboons Chart of the James River," Virginia, Circa 1617, footnote 33, p.393, citing David Ransome, ed. of the Ferrar Papers. *William & Mary Quarterly*, 1997.

Preface

p.xvi   Languishing in obscurity: The "Black Mayflower" described here is the trivessel voyage of 1619 that brought the first Africans to English-speaking America, and is not to be confused with the so-called Black Mayflower ship *Elizabeth* that was used to take African Americans to Liberia, Africa, during the 1820s through '40s.

PART 1: THE FOUNDERS OF BLACK AMERICA LEAVE AFRICA

p. 1.   Riding a wicked storm: Cited in Peter Wilson Coldham, ed., *English Adventurers and Emigrants, 1609–1660*, (Baltimore: Genealogical Publishing Co., 1984), 12–13. John Martyn, as a crewmember of the corsair *Treasurer* participated in the attack on the slaver in July 1619, described the Spanish prize as an "Angola ship" during examinations taken in the case of *Robert, Earl of Warwick v. Edward Brewster*, from 29 January 1622 to 4 June 1624; see also High Court of Admiralty, *Examinations in Equity Cases*, vol. 44, as cited in Peter Wilson Coldham, ed., "Voyage of the Neptune to Virginia, 1618–1619, and the Disposition of its Cargo," [hereafter known as Coldham, "Voyage"] *Virginia Magazine of History and Biography* 87, no. 1 (January 1979); see also Engel Sluiter, "New Light on the '20 and Odd Negroes' Arriving in Virginia, August 1619" [hereafter known as "New Light"], *William and Mary Quarterly* 54, No. 2 (April 1997); see also John Thornton, "The African Experience of the '20 and odd Negroes' Arriving in Virginia in 1619" [hereafter known as "African Experience"], *W&MQ* 55, no. 3 (1998); see also W.F. Craven, *The Dissolution of the Virginia Company: The Failure of a Colonial Experiment*, (New York: Oxford University Press, 1932.)

p. 1.   Soon after the event: "Rolfe to Sandys, Jan. 1619/20," in Susan Myra Kingsbury, ed., *The Records of the Virginia Company of London* [hereafter known as *Rec. of the Va. Co.*] (Washington, D.C.: United States Government Printing Office, 1933). The Virginia Company of London had appointed John Rolfe as secretary-recorder of the Virginia colony at Michaelmas 1616 and, among other duties, charged him to record details of all ships arriving and departing Jamestown.

p. 2.   In a lost creek: A premature conclusion from historical evidence is based on testimony that the one-hundred-ton *Treasurer* rotted to pieces in Bermuda where, at the beginning of 1620, for example, the eyewitness John Dutton, a friend of her owner Lord Rich, described the vessel as so "weather beaten and torn as never like to put to sea ever again, but laye her bones here [in Bermuda]." John Dutton to Rich, January 20, 1619/20, *Manchester Papers*, PRO, 261; see Ives, *Letters from Bermuda*, 140. And in 1624, Captain John Smith, who was not an eyewitness, seems to support Dutton: "with the beginning of the New Year [1620] [Bermuda governor Nathaniel Butler] began his first piece of fortification, upon a Rock which flankers the Kings Castle, and finding the ship . . . stark rotten and unserviceable, he took nine pieces of Ordinance from her to serve other uses." On the other hand, a conflicting account has the *Treasurer* leaving Bermuda in bad shape and sailing to Virginia, where she was intentionally scuttled near Jamestown.

Coldham, who transcribed the 1623–1624 admiralty court testimony of one of the pirates, John Wood of Wapping, Middlesex, England, summarizes the statement that Wood gave under oath: "After the ship [*Treasurer*] returned *from Bermuda to Virginia* [italics added] she was taken into a creek where she was overturned and was sunk. Her company went ashore to live." [see Coldham, "Warwick v. Brewster," *English Adventurers and Emigrants*, 13] Why, and in which creek, she was scuttled, Wood did not say. Some of the pirates were captured by Captain Nathaniel Powell, who probably would not have ventured more than forty miles from Jamestown, and delivered to Governor George Yeardley for interrogation. [see Ives, "Draft Defending the Earl of Warwick," Ives, *Letters from Bermuda*, wherein Nathaniel Rich responded to the allegation that "this ship [the Treasurer] which formerly was complained of, was returned again to Virginia, where having cold entertainments (for they would not offer them a vessel of water), they soon departed in a very distressed estate, leaving amongst others of their company one principal member, master's mate or leiftenant behind them . . . who, though it were to be endangering of his own life, confessed that they had been robbing the Spaniard in the West Indies." The pirates probably scuttled the *Treasurer* in a creek of the James River between Jamestown and Chesapeake Bay, or near Warrosquoke or Elizabeth City, where Lord Rich had allies. There is a possibility that the remains of this infamous and historically important Black Mayflower vessel—which also kidnapped Pocahontas before carrying her to England in 1616, discovered a northerly course over the Atlantic to North America, intimidated Dutch New Amsterdam, and destroyed French settlements in Canada—could yet be discovered by modern archaeology within the Atlantic Coast area described.

Chapter 1: Masquerade

p. 3.   As James would inform: James to Parliament, March 1604, see C. H. McIlwain, ed., *The Political Works of James I* (Cambridge: Harvard University Press, 1918).

p. 4.   Among the first: "Penelope Devereaux Rich," *Oxford Dictionary of National Biography*: "In May, 1603, she was one of the noble ladies who went to the border to meet Queen Anne and escort her to London."

p. 4.   James introduced England: G. P. V. Akrigg, *Jacobean Pageant, or The Court of King James I* (Cambridge, MA: Harvard University Press, 1962).

p. 5.   To mark his coronation: Ben Jonson, *The Masque of Blackness*, entered in the Stationers' Register, April 21, 1608, The Stationers' Company Registers 1556–1842, Library, The Stationers' and Newspaper Makers' Company, Ave Maria Lane, London. At www.stationers.org/index.asp.

p. 6.   Queen Anne and her ladies: Jonson, *The Masque of Blackness*. For Jones's original sketches of the costumes and body paint for *Masque of Blackness* and its sequel, *Masque of Beauty*, see John Harris, Stephen Orgel, and Roy Strong, eds., *The King's Arcadia: Inigo Jones and the Stuart Court* (London: Arts Council of Britain, 1973).

p. 7.   James was exceptionally: James is quoted in Maud Stepney Rawson, *Penelope Rich and Her Circle* (London: Hutchinson & Co., 1911), 235.

p. 7.   In his confession: Robert Devereaux, second Earl of Essex, *An apologie of the earle of Essex against those which falsly and maliciously taxe him to be the onely hinderer of the peace and quiet of his countrey* (London: 1603).

p. 8.   Britannia, whose: Jonson, *The Masque of Blackness*.

p. 9.   According to Ben Jonson: See Jonson's introduction to *Masque of Blackness*.

p. 10.   Among the new books: Contemporary sources cited by William Shakespeare in *Moor of Venice* and by Ben Jonson in *Masque of Blackness* included Italian Cinthio, *Hecatommithi* (1565); *A Geographical History of Africa and of the Notable Things Therein Contained*, written in 1526 by the widely traveled Al-Hassan, and translated by John Pory (1600); and *Naturalis Historia*, by Pliny the Elder, translated by Philemon Holland (1601), which described the voyage of the Carthagenian admiral Hanno who reportedly circumnavigated Africa about 425 B.C. See *African Glory*, DeGraft-Johnson; *The Golden Trade of the Moors*, Bovill; *Masque of Blackness*, Stationers Register; and Amanda Mabillard, "An Analysis of Shakespeare's Sources for Othello," *Shakespeare Online*, 2000, at www.shakespeareonline.com/playanalysis/othellosources.html.

p. 10.   In Fez: Pekka Masonen, "Leo Africanus, the Man with Many Names," *Al-Andalus-Magreb, Revista de estudios árabes e islámicos*, 7–9, fasc. 1 (2002) 115–43. See also www.uta.fi/~hipema/leo.htm.

p. 10.   His journeys: Raymond Mauny, "Note sur les 'grands voyages' de Léon l'Africain," *Hespéris* 41, 1954, cited in Masonen, "Leo Africanus," *Al-Andalus-Magreb*.

p. 11.   Long before the birth: Also spelled Axum; see *Kebra Nagast*, written about the thirteenth century in Abyssinia, based on earlier oral traditions.

p. 11.   Seeking to enlist: See Prince Henry's contemporary chronicler Gomes Eannes de Zurara, *The Chronicles of the Discovery and Conquest of Guinea* (1444), trans. Raymond Beazley and Edgar Prestage (n.p.:1896), available through the Hakluyt Society, cited in Daniel J. Boorstin, *The Discoverers* (New York: Random House, 1983), 157. The legend of Prester John can be traced back to the early Church and a rumor spread by the Apostle Peter that Jesus had declared that the Apostle John the Beloved (*prester* is from "presbyter," meaning "preacher") would never die. See John 21:20–24. John sought to squelch the rumor to prevent any new gospel—such as the many late gnostic gospels—appearing in his name after his death, purporting to announce new revelations. The earliest Prester John legends placed him in the vicinity of the Euphrates River, India, or in Asia. The lost Christian kingdom of Aksum created speculation that Prester John was in Africa.

p. 12.   Retreating to the extreme: Zurara, *Chronicles* (n.p.: 1444), cited by Boorstin, *The Discoverers*, 221. Boorstin, commenting on Prince Henry's task to get superstitious sailors to use technology such as the compass, writes, "Since the inexplicable power of a magnetized needle to "find" the north smacked of black magic, common seamen were wary of its powers. For many decades the prudent sea captain consulted his compass secretly ... Still, in Columbus's day, a pilot who used the magnetic compass might be accused of trafficking with Satan. At Sagres, Prince Henry the Navigator combated such superstitions by accustoming his pilots to the everyday use of the compass."

p. 12.   At the time: Classical literature indicates that long before the time of Christ, fleets send by Asian and North African monarchs, as well as some Greeks, had attempted to circle Africa, and some had succeeded. Among the sources are Herodotus, Arrian, and Pliny. "Pliny the Elder records that the Greek historian Polybius sailed down along the west coast of Africa in ships lent to him by his friend Scipio Aemilianus when the latter was involved in the Third Punic War around 146 b.c. He may have seen Mount Kakulima in Guinea, which, Pliny says, the Greeks call 'Theon Ochema,' the Chariot of the Gods." [Ciaran Branigan, "The Circumnavigation of Africa," *Classics Ireland*, vol. 1 (Dublin, Ireland, University College, 1994), citing Pliny, *Natural History*, 5.9–10, 6.199–200, in F. W. Walbank, *A Historical Commentary on Polybius* (Oxford: 1979), 3:630–39.] And before this, in the early fifth century b.c., Carthage sent Admiral Hanno with a large fleet to found a new colony in Africa beyond what was then known. He was the first to describe "gorillas" in West Africa: "In this gulf was an island, resembling the first, with a lagoon, within which was another island, full of savages. Most of them were women with hairy bodies, whom our interpreters called 'gorillas.' Although we chased them, we could not catch any males: they all escaped, being good climbers who defended themselves with stones. However, we caught three women, who refused to follow those who carried them off, biting and clawing them. So we killed and flayed them and brought their skins back to Carthage. For we did not sail any further, because our provisions were running short." [Translated in Karl Müller, *Geographi Graeci Minores*, vol. 1, Paris, 1855, cited in Branigan, *Circumnavigation*.] See also WFG Lacroix, *Africa in Antiquity* (Saarbrucken: 1998), 48–56, 380–84; W. W. Hyde, *Ancient Greek Mariners* (London: 1947), 143–47. And before Hanno, the Egyptian Pharoah Necho II (615–95 b.c.) sent out a Phoenician fleet from the Red Sea, which circled Africa clockwise and returned to the Pillars of Hercules after three years, reporting the sun rising on their right as they sailed up the West Coast of Africa [Herodotus, 4.42, cited in Hyde, *Ancient*, 142]. Euthymenes of Massilia was another early explorer said to have explored the coast of Africa, but little is known of his voyage [Hyde, *Ancient*, 143]. King Xerxes sent another early Carthaginian explorer, Sataspes, who reached the southern tip of Africa, where he found a race of dwarves [Herodotus, 4.43, cited in Hyde, *Ancient*, 142]. Many of these early voyages were trade missions, details of which would have been closely guarded by the explorers and not published abroad. Furthermore, many of the places cited in the ancient accounts are difficult to identify. Claudius Ptolemy of Alexandria (second century A.D.) published the voyage of Hanno of Carthage, which remained the authoratative text for West African maritime exploration until Prince Henry sent the Portuguese south in the fifteenth century.

p. 12.   To initiate the quest: Zurara, *Chronicles*, cited by Boorstin, *The Discoverers*, 157. At the young age of nineteen, Henry with his two brothers took a fleet across the Straits of Gibraltar and captured the Muslim stronghold of Ceuta in Morocco, yet when he appealed to his father for permission to campaign through North Africa, he was refused. In a pique, Prince Henry left court life and the army and isolated himself at Sagres where he drew about him people knowledgeable about the sea, such as merchants, local fishermen, and Jewish and Muslim scholars. He may have consulted Arabic sources based on Herodotus, Arrian, and Pliny the Elder that described expeditions launched by Pharoah Necho in 600 B.C., as well as Phoenician voyages that had later rounded Africa. As prince, Henry held the office of the Grand Master of the Order of the Knights of Christ, once known as the Knights Templar. Banned by the pope on false charges of heresy and occult practices, the Templars had been reorganized and renamed in the country of their order's birthplace by Portugal's King Deniz in the fourteenth century. These banker-knights, once guardians of Jerusalem, had accumulated much lore about Prester John, and their evidence pointed to the heart of Africa. That was not all. While sacking Ceuta, Prince Henry was told that twenty days south of Morocco and over the Atlas Mountains flowed the Senegal River, where Muslim caravans went to barter in a curious custom, known as the "silent trade," with non-Muslim people whose language they did not know: Laying out separate heaps of coral, salt, and cheap trade goods, the Moroccan merchants retreated from sight. The local tribesmen of the river then came from hiding to pile up gold next to the trade goods and then they retired from view. The Muslims reemerged to accept the gold or reduce the heaps of goods. The tribesmen returned to either take the goods or reduce the piles of gold. The silent haggling continued back and forth until the two sides reached an agreement and departed. The gist of such stories indicated to Henry that the fabulous country of Prester John could be reached from the unexplored West Coast of Africa.

p. 12. Gomes Eannes de Zurara: Zurara, *Chronicles* (1444), in Boorstin, *The Discoverers*, 167. Citing Zurara to describe the capture of those Africans, Lerone Bennett Jr., *Before the Mayflower*, writes: "There, on a fateful day in 1444, Henry's men came upon the first large group of Africans. They tiptoed through the high grass and crept to the edge of the village and then, said a contemporary, 'they looked towards the settlement and saw that the Moors, with the women and children, were already coming as quickly as they could out of their dwellings, because they had caught sight of their enemies.' But [the Portuguese], shouting out '*St. James*,' '*St. George*,' '*Portugal*,' attacked them, killing and taking all they could.'"

p. 13. Without slavery: Charles-Louis Montesquieu (1689–1755), cited by Herbert Wendt, *It Began in Babel: the Birth and Development of Races and Peoples*, trans. James Kirkup (London: Weidenfeld and Nicholson, 1961; repr. 1963), 205. Montesquieu, who greatly influenced Euro-American ideas, in 1748 concluded that Africans had no souls and therefore there was no obligation to treat them humanely. His views on Africans were instrumental in the thinking of such people as French monarchist Joseph Arthur de Gobineau, who invented the Aryan myth; Thomas Jefferson; the nineteenth-century American race scientists Josiah Nott and Samuel Morton; and later, Adolf Hitler.

p. 14.   Upon Captain Cão's return: Zurara, *Chronicles*, cited in Wendt, *It Began in Babel*, 210.

p. 14.   The "lost" kingdoms: Zurara, *Chronicles*, cited in Wendt, *It Began in Babel*, 211.

p. 14.   Precolonial Angolans: Fernandez de Enciso,1518, cited by Sir Richard F. Burton, *Two Trips to Gorilla Land and the Cataracts of the Congo*, vol. 2 (n.p.: 1876); volumes 1 and 2 can be accessed at several sites on the Internet, including the Gutenberg Project Web site at www.gutenberg.org/etext/5760.

p. 15.   On our departure: Collected by Belgian missionary Père J. Van Wing and cited by Roland Oliver and Anthony Atmore, ed., *The African Middle Ages: 1400–1800* (New York: Cambridge University Press, 1981).

p. 15.   Their kindred: Precolonial Angolans did not build the stone structures that their Eastern Bantu cousins erected in Central Africa, because of differences in climate and terrain. Instead, they protected their towns and great buildings with stout stockades woven of logs and grasses that resembled the later palisades protecting Jamestown and Plymouth and even the wooden walls of sixteenth-century London. The explorer Burton found that the Angolan Bantu in their grass houses were adapted ideally to the tropical climate and compared their living conditions favorably with that of sixteenth-century Europe. He noted that "the Congoese is better lodged than we were before the days of Queen Elizabeth; what are luxuries in the north, broad beds and deep arm-chairs, would here be far less comfortable than the mats, which serve for all purposes." [Burton, *Two Trips to Gorilla Land*.]

p. 15.   Each state: John Thornton, *African Politics and European Conquest* [hereafter referred to as *African Politics*] unpublished, used by permission of author. For an expanded view of the Angolan State, see also John Thornton, *Africa and Africans in the Making of the Atlantic World, 1400–1680* (New York: Cambridge University Press, 1992). Angolans called their kingdoms/states *xi*. A king or queen ruled each xi from a large city, and a lesser aristocracy, the *makota*, oversaw individual royal districts with their towns and villages, while governors known as *sobas* administrated outlying provinces that had been small foreign kingdoms before being conquered. These states before 1482 were clearly defined by strict boundaries called *mbande*.

p. 16.   The town of: Jesuit Francisco de Gouveia to Jesuit General, 1 November 1564, in António Brásio, ed., *Monumenta Missionaria Africana* [hereafter known as *MMA*], 15:230–31, cited by Thornton, "African Experience," *W&MQ*. See also Thornton, "Mbanza Kongo/Sao Salvador: Kongo's Holy City," in *Africa's Urban Past*, eds. Richard Rathbone and Andrew Roberts.

p. 16.   They traded: Beatrix Heintze, "Unbekanntes Angola: Der Staat Ndongo im 16. Jahrhundert," *Anthropos* 72 (1977): 771–76, cited in Thornton, "African Experience," *W&MQ*.

p. 16.   Precolonial Bantu law: Van Wing, *Etudes Bakongo*. In addition to secular laws, the Bakongo nation, for example, enforced *nkondo mi Nzambi*, "God's prohibitions." The precolonial Bantu believed in a supreme creator god and in lesser spirits who were either good or evil. Nzambi Mpunga was the chief Bakongo deity. It was believed a *sumu ku Nzambi* (a sin against Nzambi) was specifically punished by a *lufwa lumbi* (bad death). Civil law included the Mbundu marriage pledge, in which a man paid a bridal price of cattle for a wife. The husband vowed to treat his wife kindly and she promised to be faithful. If she was not, the cattle were returned.

p. 16.   Wisdom and art: Joel Chandler Harris, *Uncle Remus, His Songs and His Sayings 1880*, ed. Robert E. Hemenway (New York: Penguin Books, 1982); Linda S. Chang, "Brer Rabbit's Angolan Cousin: Politics and the Adaptation of Folk Material," *Folklore Forum* 19 (1986): i, 36–50; James Mooney, *Myths of the Cherokee; and Sacred Formulas of the Cherokees* (see "Melungeons," reprinted and published in the nineteenth and seventh Annual Report, Bureau of American Ethnology (Nashville: Charles and Randy Elder—Booksellers, 1982); James R. Aswell, *God Bless the Devil! Liars' Bench Tales* (Knoxville: University of Tennesee Press, 1985; orig., Chapel Hill: University of North Carolina Press, 1940); James Mooney citing Swan Burnett's "Notes on Melungeons," in *American Anthropology*, (n.p.: 1889).

p. 17.   With their iron axes: T. H. Breen, *Myne Owne Ground: Race and Freedom on Virginia's Eastern Shore* (Oxford University Press, 1982), 71, quoting historian Charles R. Boxer, *The Dutch Seaborn Empire: 1600–1800* (New York: 1965), says of precolonial Angolans in Africa that they "practised shifting cultivation and the rotation of different crops. They knew how to work metals, including iron and copper, and they were fairly skilled potters. They wove mats and articles of clothing from raffia tissues or palm-cloth . . . They had domesticated several animals—pigs, sheep, chickens and in some districts cattle." They were also skilled in "using the hoe and the axe." The typical fare for an Angolan village family was a porridge called *funji* that had been prepared from cereal grains such as millet and sorghum, which were ground into meal and supplemented with yams and bananas (*nicefo*). [Thornton, "African Experience," *W&MQ*]. Their liquor, palm wine, was distilled from the sap of the palm tree, and which they drew without destroying the tree.

p. 18.   In the crowd: Christopher Columbus, cited in Samuel Eliot Morison, *The Great Explorers: the European Discovery of America* (New York: Oxford University Press, 1978).

p. 18.   In this Realm: Boorstin, *The Discoverers*.

p. 18.   He affirmed: Covilha, cited in Boorstin, *Discoverers*.

p. 19.   Astounded to see: Crew member of the da Gama expedition (1498), cited in Boorstin, *The Discoverers*.

p. 20.   Aided by Turks: Adrian Hastings, *The Church in Africa: 1450–1950* (Oxford: Clarendon Press, 1994); Aziz S. Atiya, *History of Eastern Christianity* (Notre Dame, Indiana: University of Notre Dame Press, 1968); Elizabeth Isichei, *A History of Christianity in Africa from Antiquity to the Present* (London: SPCK, 1995).

p. 20.   Sir Richard Burton: Richard F. Burton, *First Footsteps in East Africa, or an Exploration of Harar* (London: Tylston & Edwards, 1894). See also online, including at www.gutenberg.org/dirs/etext04/7ffea10.txt

p. 21.   This pope: Masonen, *Leo Africanus*.

Chapter 2: Jagas

p. 23. In his scathing: Letter of Dudley Carleton to Mr. Winwood (January 1605), cited in Stephen Orgel, ed., *Ben Jonson: The Complete Masques* (New Haven: Yale University Press, 1969).

p. 23. He [the Spanish: Letter of Dudley Carleton to John Chamberlain (1605), cited in Orgel, ed., *Jonson: The Complete Masques.*

p. 24. Contemporary historian: Arthur Wilson, *The history of Great Britain, being the life and reign of King James the First* (London: printed for Richard Lownds, 1653).

p. 24. Having first proposed: James I to Parliament, March 1608, McIlwain, ed., *The Political Works of James I*, trans. Meg Powers Livingston, see "Overthrown only by words': Transformative Language and Authority in 'A King and No King'" 1996 Southland Graduate Student Conference, UCLA, titled *Fighting Words; Seventeenth Century Rhetorics of Power.*

p. 25. When James threatened: James I to Parliament, March 1610, McIlwain, ed., *The Political Works of James I*, trans. Livingston, *Fighting Words: Seventeenth-Century Rhetorics of Power.*

p. 25. Struggling for supremacy: "James I, speech to Parliament, 21 March 1609–10, On Divine Right of Kings," *State Papers, Domestic, James I*, Public Records Office [hereafter identified as PRO], London.

p. 26. If popular: See Livingston, "Overthrown only by words," *Fighting Words.* Livingston: "[The] king's very struggles to assert control and to claim power, not only on the level of political policy but on this level of language, seem to come under a broad public scrutiny he obviously wished to avoid. Lee Bliss, Margot Heinemann, and Richard Dutton all discuss how the events of 1609–1610, especially James's clashes with Parliament over various issues, including his insistence on his divine rights, conspired to draw (mostly negative) attention to the king's language and policies. Beaumont and Fletcher's plays from this period, *Philaster* (c. 1608–09), *The Maid's Tragedy* (c. 1610–11), and *A King and No King* (1611), definitely explore these issues in ways which make me wonder how their subject matter made it through the period's censorship process."

p. 26. Complained James: James I quoted by R. W. Church in *Bacon, English Men in Letters* (New York: Harper & Brothers, 1884). See also, Jim Powell, "Edward Coke—Common Law Protection for Liberty" *The Freeman: Ideas on Liberty* (November 1997).

p. 27. Angola's precolonial: John Thornton, "African Political Ethics and the Slave Trade, Central African Dimensions," *The Winthrop Papers Project*, Massachusetts Historical Society, Millersville University, http://muweb.millersville.edu/~winthrop.

p. 27. The prevailing: Regarding misperceptions about Angolan attitudes and practices after the European arrival see, Thornton, "African Political Ethics," *Winthrop Papers*, citing a letter Álfonso wrote to the king of Portugal on 18 October 1526. Álfonso: "Sir, there is in our kingdom, a great obstacle to God. Many of our subjects crave the Portuguese merchandise which your people bring to our kingdom so keenly. In order to satisfy their crazy appetite they snatch our free subjects, or people who have been freed. They even take noblemen and the sons of noblemen, even our kinsmen. They sell them to white men who are in our kingdom, after having transported their prisoners on the sly in the dead of night. Then the prisoners are branded. The white men cannot say from whom they have bought the prisoners." (For the historiography of Álfonso's correspondences, see also John Thornton, "Early Luso-Kongolese Relations: A New Interpretation," *History in Africa* (1981)). Thornton observes of scholars who misinterpret Álfonso's letter as evidence that he opposed slavery and trade, that "To the degree that scholarship has noted that relatively few people were enslaved by direct capture by European marines, the African elite's attitude has still not been examined much, and then it has been singularly uncomplimentary. African rulers who cooperated with the Europeans are often characterized as sell-outs, greedy, and cynically exploitative, or alternatively, as so overwhelmed by European superiority in commerce, production, or technology as to have little choice but to go along with the slave traders from abroad. Yet these positions are probably not true. African leaders were not necessarily forced into the slave trade through their inabilities, or the inability of their country to prevent it, and neither were they necessarily simply cruel dupes of foreign traders who sold their own people out for short term gains. African leaders clearly participated voluntarily in the slave trade, but this does not mean that they did so without recognizing the ethical problems that the trade presented. . . . [All] the African rulers led societies that recognized an institution of slavery, and they accepted the legal possibility that an individual could have a bundle of rights over another person that surpassed those of any other community or the state. These rights moreover could be alienated to any other person by sale. This institutional framework made the slave trade possible, and smoothed its way along. Recognizing these features of African social structure certainly can explain why African leaders did not actively resist the sale of people as slaves, and it must be invoked in their defense when they are accused of being European dupes for doing so. But simply recognizing that the making, holding, use, and sale of slaves was legally permissible did not mean that the slave trade did not pose ethical problems for African leaders. They felt strongly that there were legal limits to who could be enslaved and when. In many cases they felt that the Portuguese and other Europeans violated these limits, and moreover that these violations were a manifestation of greed and pride, two serious political sins. The question was not with the institution of slavery itself, but in establishing a proper order of enslavement and an orderly slave trade." [Thornton, "African Political Ethics and the Slave Trade, Central African Dimensions," *The Winthrop Papers Project*, Massachusets Historical Society, Millersville University, http://muweb.millersville.edu/~winthrop.]

p. 27. Upon becoming king: Story collected in Angola by Capuchin priest Bernardo da Gallo (1710). See also John Thornton, "Origin Traditions and History in Central Africa," *African Arts* (Spring 2004). In his analysis of the conflicting origin stories of early Kongo, Thornton writes: "The earliest insights we have into the origin of Kongo were set in writing in 1588 by Duarte Lopes. Although Lopes was a Portuguese New Christian (converted Jew), and thus a foreigner to Kongo, he served as Kongo's ambassador to the Holy See at a crucial time, when the Vatican was considering making Kongo the seat of the first bishop on mainland Africa. As such, and as a 'fidalgo of the royal house' as the letter of credentials from Kongo's king Álvaro I states, Lopes was surely privy to the version of Kongo's history that circulated in the capital; as a trusted ambassador he must have presented it accurately in Europe. Lopes's written text is lost to us, but it formed the basis, along with his oral testimony, of Filippo Pigafetta's book, *Relatione del Reame di Congo et delle cinconvincine contrade* (1591). That source does not deal explicitly with the origin of the Kingdom of Kongo, but in asides that deal with the history of the provinces, it seems likely that the history of the country was conceived as something like this: The Kingdom of Kongo was formed when several independent provinces came together. The focus seems to have been on the voluntary nature of the original kingdom, thus a federation, although some of the provinces were conquered by force (Pigafetta, 1591: 37–38). This version of Kongo's history probably reflects the relatively decentralized nature of Kongo's polity in the immediately preceding period and the power of some of the provinces. The origin story and the politics changed when the next set of oral traditions was written down in the mid-seventeenth century. These texts were put together by European missionaries, first by the Jesuit Mateus Cardoso in 1624 and then by the Capuchin missionary Giovanni Antonio Cavazzi da Montecuccolo in 1668 (but probably also based on Jesuit sources, most likely the now lost chronicle of Joao de Pavia, composed around 1635). The Jesuits' mission, founded in 1619, was close to the royal family, and the Jesuits were deeply interested in Kongo's affairs, so that it seems likely that the missionaries' accounts are well-founded in the version that circulated at court. In these Jesuit-authored accounts, there is no mention of a federation. Instead the first king, Lukeni lua Nimi, is presented as a conqueror who came from the north, on the other side of the Congo River. In Cardoso's account, he was the younger son of a king, unlikely to succeed to power after his father, and seeking a new kingdom of his own. In Cavazzi's telling he commits a dreadful double homicide, stabbing his pregnant mother through the womb; then, gathering his followers, who are encouraged rather than repelled by this gruesome murder, he conquers Kongo. The version written by Cavazzi clearly engaged an already existing, contradictory historiography that included the emphasis, in Lopes's earlier version, on provincial privileges, but it characterizes these privileges as granted by the king only after conquest as an act of kindness. Thus the older tradition survived in the new. Political motivations most likely underlie this transformation of tradition. The two Kongo kings who dispatched Lopes to Rome, Álvaro I and II (together ruled 1568–1614), underwent a long process of centralizing authority, pushing their claims against provinces like Soyo and Mbata that did not easily cede their own claims. Cardoso, in his version, stresses that the king gave out the right to rule provinces, not for life but at the king's pleasure—clearly a slap at the concept of provincial federation that was implicit in the earlier tradition. The royal version thus represented the marching orders of a new order, determined to centralize power, revenue, and decision making at the court. Descriptions of the Kongo government during this period make it clear that the program was largely successful. Kongo centralization did not last, however. In 1665, following the death of King Antonio I at the Battle of Ulanga (Mbwila), the country underwent a long and disastrous civil war. Its proud capital of Sao Salvador was destroyed, and, in 1678, abandoned. Rival kings built fortified capitals in the north, east, southeast, and western parts of the country, but none were strong enough to overcome their rivals and restore the kingdom. Finally, toward the end of the century, Pedro IV, who made his base in the rocky mountain fortress of Kibangu east of the ruined capital, sought to unite the country by diplomacy. He sponsored or participated in several round-robin diplomatic efforts, working with Capuchin priests as intermediaries, and eventually managed to win unification in 1709. In 1710 two Capuchin priests produced two versions of Kongo's origin story, one old and one new. In the old story, told by Bernardo da Gallo [1999]: 46–47), Lukeni lua Nimi conquered the country to avenge an insult pronounced against his mother by a ferryman."

p. 27.   As the first manikongo: Thornton, *African Politics*. For more on early Kongo, see Thornton, "The Origins and Early History of the Kingdom of Kongo, c. 1350–1550," *International Journal of African Historical Studies* 31 (2001): 89–120.

p. 29.   The pope bestowed: Brásio, ed., *MMA*, cited by Thornton, *African Politics*. In 1508, the Franciscan missionary Rui d'Aguiar. while based at Mbanza Kongo, describing Álfonso I, wrote: "It seems to me from the way he speaks he is not a man, but an angel, sent by the Lord in this kingdom to convert it. For I assure you, it is he who instructs us. He devotes himself entirely to study, so that it often happens that he falls asleep at his books, and often he forgets to eat and drink in talking of the things of our Lord."

p. 30.   Administrators of: The indirect indictment of *civilizations* for allegedly failing to cope with an infusion of foreign culture and alien technology is at best, benignly racist. Angola, having successfully diffused European culture and adapted European religions through syncretism, remains distinctly African today as always. In fact, as a result of the millions brought in chains, Bantu culture and worship practices have significantly influenced mainstream America. Furthermore, for the argument that technological advances are geographical rather than genetic or cultural, see Jared Diamond, *Guns, Germs, and Steel: the Fates of Human Societies* (New York: W.W. Norton and Company, 1991). From the Fertile Crescent in the Middle East, ideas and innovations passed easily among Asians, Europeans, and North Africans in the Northern Hemisphere because they were geographically joined by the lateral landmass surrounding the Mediterranean. As related by Diamond, merchants, missionaries, scholars, soldiers, herders, and farmers could travel thousands of miles east and west on foot in the same climate from China in the far east, to Portugal in the far west.

Western European firearms, as one example, would not have existed had not the Chinese invented gunpowder. The horse culture arrived in Spain through Muslim conquest from North Africa and Arabia. Metallurgy, cattle, transportation, and such technology as windmills tended to radiate east and west from the Fertile Crescent because of geography and climate, and not because of any supposed superiority of European and Asian races. Though Central Africa was physically attached to that landmass, the vast desolate Sahara isolated the Bantu in the south from the latest technology in the same way that the Atlantic and Pacific slowed technological progress in pre-Columbian America.

p. 30. As early as 1514: Brásio, ed., *MMA*.

p. 30. Manuel I of Portugal for: Instructions given by King Manuel I to Gonçalo Rodrigues on a royal mission in 1509. See "Despacho de Gonçalo Roiz, 1509," Brásio, ed., *MMA*, 4:61, cited by Thornton, "African Political Ethics," *Winthrop Papers*. Álfonso gave Gonçalo Rodrigues fifty slaves in 1509 and within the year also gave more than 120 slaves to Fernão de Mello, donatory of São Tomé, and his relatives, as well as "many slaves" to King Manuel of Portugal that same year.

p. 31. As the manikongos continued to use: "Alfonso to Manuel, 5 October 1514," Brásio, ed., *MMA*, 1:312–15, cited by Thornton, "African Political Ethics." Thornton: "In describing a war he conducted against Munza, known only as a nobleman of the Mbundu region, around 1512 or perhaps 1513, Afonso's primary complaint about the conduct of the war was that Portuguese served him poorly in it. Many were reluctant to join him in the campaign against an opponent who, Alfonso maintains, had started the war by attacking the Kongo province of Mbamba. Alfonso's account makes it clear that he intended to be served by the people he captured as slaves, both at home, and to meet overseas expenses. Some he sent out to Portugal on his own account, some as gifts to the king or others, and some he retained in Kongo, presumably for local service."

p. 31. From that time: "Sebastião I to Gouveia de Sottomaior, 19 March 1574," Brásio, ed., *MMA* 3:120; "Garcia Simões to Luis Perpinhão, 7 November 1576," Brásio, ed., *MMA* 3:145–6; "Álvaro to Garcia Simões, 27 August 1575," Brásio, ed., *MMA* 3:127, cited in Thornton, African Politics.

p. 32. If Novais succeeded: Pero Rodrigues, "Historia da residencia dos Padres da Companhia de Jesus em Angola (1 May 1594)," Brásio, ed., *MMA* cited by Thornton, *African Politics*. Also to the Novais family would go hereditary titles, criminal and civil jurisdiction, ownership of the valuable *nzimbu* mines, and the right to appoint officials and to charter towns and collect taxes on commercial revenues including exported slaves.

p. 33. Upon taking office: "Garcia Simões to Provincial of Portugal, 20 October 1575," Brásio, ed., *MMA* 3:131, 138–9. The identity of this ngola is disputed in Ndongo tradition, given either as Quiloange Angola or Njinga Ngola Kilomobo kia Kasenda. See Thornton, "Legitimacy and Political Power: Queen Njinga, 1624–1663," *Journal of African History* 32 (1991).

p. 33. In particular: Rodrigues, "História," Brásio, ed., *MMA* 4:572; see also Mendes Castelo Branco, "Relação," *MMA*, 6:456, cited in Thornton, *African Politics*.

Thornton: "Dias de Novais was already complaining about the local Portuguese community in 1578 (see "Dias de Novais letter, 3 January 1578," Brásio, ed., *MMA* 3:295), and working, no doubt to end their influence at court in Ndongo. Jesuits were convinced that they eventually persuaded the king of Ndongo that Dias de Novais was up to no good, as Pero Rodrigues, the first Jesuit chronicler of the conquest, writing in 1594, recalled: 'in '79 the Governor was at peace with the King and aiding him in his lands,' when a Portuguese who was 'much trusted' met with the king and his councilors and advised them to kill the Portuguese (meaning, of course, Dias de Novais and the royal party, not his own group) and take their goods, then drive them from his estates."

p. 34.   Lately, following: Formerly, Ndongo, under Ngola Inene Kiluanji around 1515, would integrate conquered neighbors only loosely into its constitutional system, allowing them a good deal of autonomy. [See Beatrix Heintze, "Written Sources, Oral Traditions and Oral Traditions as Written Sources: The Steep and Thorny Way to Early Angolan History," *Paideuma* 33 (1987): 263–87] cited in Thornton, *African Politics*]. See also Thornton, "Legitimacy and Political Power: Queen Njinga, 1624–1663," *Journal of African History* 32 (1991): 36–38. Ndongo retained former kings as local governors, or sobas, of conquered ministates that it annexed as provinces. The sobas, though required to pay taxes to Ndongo, retained their lands and titles and the right to raise armies. [see Heintze, "Unbekanntes Angola: Der Staat Ndongo im 16. Jahrhundert," *Anthropos* 72 (1977): 777–80.] Only by allowing the sobas such leniency, could Ndongo count on their loyalty. This was not always effective and eventually Ndongo attempted to strengthen its hold on their loyalty by centralizing power at Kabasa, which instead created resentment among the sobas. The presence of Europeans in Angola was irrelevant to the Ndongo centralization attempt (Portugal and Ndongo had not then established formal contact), although the ngola did sometimes hire a few independent Portuguese mercenaries in his army. Instead, Ndongo was emulating the centralization model that its powerful neighbor Kongo had pioneered before the Portuguese arrived in 1482.

p. 34.   Novais's third army: Rodrigues, "Historia," Brásio, ed., *MMA*, cited by Thornton, *African Politics*.

p. 35.   The date of: Rodrigues, "Historia," Brásio, ed., *MMA*, cited in Thornton, *African Politics*.

p. 36.   Loyalist Ndongo troops: Rodrigues, "Historia," Brásio, ed., *MMA*, cited in Thornton, *African Politics*.

Chapter 3 : A Game at Chess

p. 39.   Though dutifully married: English definition of the Latin: "Elizabeth was King: now James is Queen." See Lady Antonia Fraser, *King James VI of Scotland and James I of England* (London: Weidenfeld and Nicolson, 1974). Much has been sensationally written of James's favorites, rumored to include Esmé Stuart, Robert Carr, and George Villiers—the first Duke and later Viscount of Buckingham. (Buckingham sued Samuel Argall in 1622 in *Buckingham v. Argall*. Buckingham also joined Lord Rich in 1620 in starting up the new New England Company.) It was further rumored that Henry Rich, the handsome brother of Robert Rich, had to be removed from his position as commander of the King's Guard to protect him from James's advances.

p. 39.   The sentiment: "Report on England presented to the Government of Venice in the year 1607, by the illustrious Gentleman Nicolo Molin, Ambassador there," Robert Ashton, ed., *James I by His Contemporaries, An Account of His Career and Character as Seen by Some of His Contemporaries* (London: Hutchinson, 1969).

p. 40.   In a satirical political: Thomas Middleton, *A Game at Chess*, ed., T. H. Howard Hill (Manchester: Manchester University Press, repr. 1997).

p. 40.   Though hissed: Arthur Wilson, *James I* (n.p.: 1653). Wilson, though an ardent parliamentarian and fiercely anti-Spanish, admired King James for being a man of peace: "The King desirous of the Title, *Pacificus*, did not only close with his own Subjects, but healed up also that old wound that had bled long in the sides of England and Spain, both being weary of the pain, both willing to be cured."

p. 41.   Portraying African: *The Cambridge History of English and American Literature* (1907–21), vol. 6, "The Drama to 1642," part 2, chap. 13; "Masque and Pastoral," 6; "Introduction to the Antimasque" (by Rev. Ronald Bayne), 23.

p. 41.   His immensely: Concerning Rich's athleticism and exploits at sea, see *The Court and Times of Charles I*, comp. by Thomas Birch, ed. R. F. Williams (London: Henry Colburn, 1848). During the battle to capture the Portuguese treasure fleet sailing from Brazil in 1626, it was said of the second Earl of Warwick by a member of the expedition that, he was "never sick one hour at sea, and would as nimbly climb up to the top and yard as any common mariner in the ship: and all the time of the fight was as active, and as open to danger as any man there." Also, W. F. Craven, "The Earl of Warwick—A Speculator in Piracy," *Hispanic American Historical Review* 10 (1930): 457–79.

p. 42.   Though [Rich] had: Wilson, *James I* (n.p.:1653).

p. 42.   The puzzle: The friendship between Robert Rich II and the Puritans *is* extraordinary when one considers the history of his ancestors. Among other things, his great-grandfather, the Lord High Chancellor Richard Rich, a particularly agile conniver, infamously betrayed Sir Thomas More and Lady Jane Grey, and, during the reign of Catholic Mary Tudor, burned at the stake a number of Protestants, at his home in Felsted, Essex (which he had been rewarded, ironically, after the dissolution of the Catholic monasteries). That same Chancellor Rich, with his own hands, personally racked and tortured Lady Anne Ascue until, by her own testimony, "I was well-nigh dead," for denying the doctrine of Transubstantiation, as recorded in *Fox's Book of Martyrs*.

p. 42.   Rich was described: William Drogo Montagu Manchester, seventh Duke of Manchester, *Court and Society from Elizabeth to Anne* (London: Hurst and Blackett, 1864).

p. 42.   Many of the lords: It probably didn't hurt Rich's relationship with the Puritans that the man who granted his mother, Lady Penelope, her at the time notorious and very rare divorce from his father, the elder Robert Rich, and then performed the subsequent marriage ceremony for her and Charles Blount, Lord Mountjoy, without the knowledge of King James, was William Laud, afterward Archbishop Laud, from whose vengeful hand young Robert would rescue a number of Puritans and Separatists. See *Oxford Dictionary of National Biography*, "Penelope Devereaux Rich."

p. 43.   In a letter: Cited in Kenneth Shipps, "Political Puritan," *Church History: Studies in Christianity in Culture* [quarterly journal of the American Society of Church History] 45, no. 2 (June 1976): 196–205.

p. 43.   Commenting: Edward Hyde, first Earl of Clarendon, *History of the Rebellion in England* (London: 1676, repr. 1888). In the informative funeral eulogy upon Lord Rich's death on 19 April 1658 at his estate of Leighs Priory, the minister summed up his habits and character: "Let me tell you that we have lost this day one of the best natured Noblemen in England, and one who had not only a good nature, but (as I verily believe) gracious principles, and religious inclinations and dispositions . . . He was bountiful and Prince-like in his hospitality and housekeeping. He was merciful and charitable to the poor members of Jesus Christ. I have often and often been his Almoner to distribute considerable summes of money to necesitous and pious Christians. He was a liberal and most loving master to his household servants, and hath given competent pensions to all of his old servants during life. In a word he was one who did not make use of religion for his owne private gaine and interest; he had no politick designs in professing godliness: his whole aime both by sea and land, both in Parliament and in private, was to be serviceable to Church and State, and in this particular he was a true Nathaniel in whom there was no guile; he was a countenancer of religion in the worst times: he appeared for God and for his cause and servants, when it was both dangerous and disgraceful in the eyes of the leading men of the Nation; he received Mr. Burroughs (that eminent Minister of Christ) into his family and protected him for a long while, till at last he was forced to fly out of the land. He was a very special friend unto that man of God of famous memory Dr. Sibbs. To summe up all in a few lines, as it is said of Socrates (as I remember) that he was so good a man that all that knew him loved him; and if any man did not love him, it was because they did not know him. So it may be said of the Earle of Warwick: All who knew him loved him, and if any man did not love him, it was because he did not know him."

p. 44.   According to historian: Craven, *Dissolution of the Virginia*, 126–27. See also Craven, "The Earl of Warwick—A Speculator in Piracy," *Hispanic American Historical Review* 10 (1930): 457–79.

p. 46.   Beginning in 1609: Helen C. Rountree, *Pocahontas, Powhatan, and Opechancanough: Three Indian Lives Changed by Jamestown* (Charlottesville: University of Virginia Press, 2005).

p. 46.   Argall ended: John Smith, *The generall historie of Virginia, New England & the Summer Isles, together with The true travels, adventures and observations, and A sea grammar*, vol. 1 (London, 1624).

| p. 46. | The scheme worked: William Strachey, *Historie of Travell into Virginia Britiania*, attributing Captain Samuel Argall in 1613, cited in Rountree, *Pocahontas, Powhatan, and Opechancanough: Three Indian Lives Changed by Jamestown*. See also Warner, *The Story of Pocahontas*, and William Broaddus Cridlin, *A History of Colonial Virginia: the First Permanent Colony in America* (Richmond: Williams Printing Co., 1922). |

p. 47. During her captivity: Smith, *The generall historie of Virginia*. Smith: "During this time, the Lady Rebecca, alias Pocahontas, daughter to Powhatan, by the diligent care of Master John Rolfe her husband and his friends, was taught to speake such English as might well bee understood, well instructed in Christianitie, and was become very formall and civill after our English manner."

p. 47. Her poised: The company, in its promotional campaign, perhaps took into account William Shakespeare's observation in 1613 that Englishmen, while callously refusing to donate one small coin to relieve crippled beggars, "will lay out ten to see a dead Indian," [Shakespeare, *The Tempest*], more so to see a live Indian princess who could sing English hymns.

p. 47. Introduced to King James: Smith, *The generall historie of Virginia*. Smith: "The small time I staid in London, divers Courtiers and others, my acquaintances, hath gone with mee to see her, that generally concluded, they did thinke God had a great hand in her conversion, and they have seene many English Ladies worse favoured, proportioned and behavioured, and as since I have heard, it pleased both the King and Queenes Majestie honourably to esteeme her, accompanied with that honourable Lady the Lady De la Ware, and that honourable Lord her husband, and divers other persons of good qualities, both publikely at the maskes and otherwise, to her great satisfaction and content."

p. 48. From what would: A meeting of Rich, Argall, and Rolfe necessarily occurred between June and October 1616 because this is the only window of opportunity the three would have to meet in England before the Michaelmas meeting of the Virginia Company in 1616, and before the piracy scheme went into operation in Virginia one year later. Details of the stay of Pocahontas in England from June 1616 to March 1617 has little interest to British scholars, and has been poorly documented by them to date; it is further obscured by questionable traditions cited usually for the promotion of American tourism in the United Kingdom. She was said, for example, to have visited Rolfe's ancestral home in Heacham, where the romantic couple allegedly planted a mulberry tree, the remains of which a tourist guide will show you though there is no record such a visit ever took place. Additionally, certain inns from old Plymouth on the road to London make claims of the "Pocahontas slept here" sort, even though it is more likely that the *Treasurer* took the Rolfes from Plymouth, Devon, to Southampton, by sea [see note "*Treasurer*" below]. Until further research illuminates the true story of Pocahontas's time in England, what little can be said with certainty is that, after a mysterious absence of nearly six months in England, Pocahontas and John Rolfe surfaced in London in November 1616 for an important meeting of the Virginia Company. Where, then, in England had the Rolfes spent that summer? It was only *after* their mysterious disappearance of several months that Lord Rich presented Argall and Rolfe to the company in November, for the offices of deputy governor and secretary-recorder. Rich's cousin, business partner, and part owner of the *Treasurer*, Lord Delaware shortly thereafter presented Pocahontas to King James at which time she attended a Christmas masque or two in December 1616/January 1617 and was entertained by the queen. At that time, Pocahontas, her child, and husband were living in the suburban Brentford, London, home leased by the bishop of London on the Earl of Northumberland's Syon House estate, where she was visited by a stream of curious gawkers, and where she and John Smith were reunited. She sat for a Dutch engraver about that time, and Ben Jonson claimed to have seen her leaving an inn, but little else is known for certainty. Even the cause of her death is a subject of wide speculation. This author concludes that, because Rolfe, who would become a key participant in Rich's schemes in Jamestown, arrived in England on Rich's ship with Argall, who would have reported to Rich immediately, and because Rolfe first appears in the records of their stay in England as Lord Rich's candidate for office, along with Argall, at the Virginia Company meeting in November 1616, therefore Rolfe spent some or all of his time in England between June and November in the company of Rich and Argall, probably at Leighs Priory in Essex, as they were hatching their piracy scheme for Jamestown.

That Rolfe was afterward implicated in the Jamestown schemes of Rich and Argall from 1617 to 1619 is well attested in primary documents and by his own testimony. In a letter sent from Jamestown to company president Edwin Sandys in January 1620, Rolfe both acknowledges that he was implicated in charges against Argall and Rich, and he defends the latter after he was recalled as governor: "[And] withall in conclusion cannot chose but reveal unto you the sorrow I conceive to hear of the many accusations heaped upon Captain Argall with whom my reputation hath been unjustly jointed, but I am persuaded he will answer well for himself. Here have also been diverse depositions taken and sent home by the *Diana*, I will tax no man therein: but when it shall come to farther trial, I assure you that you shall find many dishonest and faithless men to Captain Argall, who have received much kindness at his hands and to his face will contradict, and be ashamed of much, which in his absence they have intimated against him. Lastly, I speak on my own experience for these 11 years, I never amongst so few, have seen so many falsehearted, envious and malicious people (yea amongst some who march in the better rank) nor shall you ever hear of any the iustest Governor here, who shall live free, from their scandal and shameles exclamations, if way be given to their report." ["Rolfe to Sandys, January 1619/20" (In favor of C. Argal. That people ill-conditioned) Kingsbury, ed., *Rec. of the Va. Co.* 3].

See also the complaint of Lady Delaware against Rolfe and Argall presented to the Virginia Company on 10 July 1621 [Kingsbury, ed., *Rec. of the Va. Co.*]; the testimony of Captain Edward Brewster linking Argall and Rolfe to stolen goods in 1618 in a deposition taken 22 April 1622 in the lawsuits *Delaware v. Argall* and *Buckingham v. Argall* in which, futhermore, Captain Brewster along with kinsman Richard Brewster also swore that Rolfe, while colony secretary recorder in 1618, destroyed certain depositions injurious to Argall and withheld other depositions taken in Virginia [Coldham, ed., "Voyage," *Va. Mag. of Hist. and Biog* 87, no. 1 (January 1979): 47, 49, 58–59].

Note: *"Treasurer."* Regarding the route of Pocahontas after reaching England, the author thanks researcher Gynger Cook, who sent the following via e-mail: "Port Book: Port of Southampton, Customer, Overseas Imports and exports. Date Christmas 1615–Christmas 1616 from the list of Exchequer, Queens Remembrancer, Port Books part 2, 1565 to 1700 F. 315 which was copied April 20, 1960. 17 June 1616, in the *Treasurer* of Virginia 100 tons, John Hope Master, from Virginia, Sir Thomas Dale knight and company, *natives* [italics added], imported 2cwt pudding tobacco, valued at 112 pound (ie. each cwt contained 112 Lb valued at 10 shillings each pound.) This is the first occasion on which a ship's port of origin has been stated to be Virginia. In the light of an entry in the Acte of the Privy Council of England 1619–21 (v. Index: Ships: *Treasurer*), it seems that the ship was clearly the *TREASURER* of Virginia, rather than the *TREASURER OF VIRGINIA.* [Also, in a note for 4 December 1619, Privy Council Meeting, Star Chamber.] We also know the *Treasurer* arrived at the Port of Plymouth, England in June of 1616 when transporting Pocahontas and some of her tribe on the voyage she and her husband John Rolph [Rolfe] took to England." The *Treasurer's* records indicate that, after the ship arrived in old Plymouth in early June 1616, she took her passengers to Southampton one week later, meaning Pocahontas did not travel overland to London from Plymouth, but by sea on Lord Rich's corsair.

p. 49.   As the English historian: Samuel Rawson Gardiner, *History of England from the Accession of James I to the outbreak of the Civil War, 1603–1642* (London: Longmans, 1885, repr.1903).

p. 50.   According to Smith: Edward Arber, ed., *Captain John Smith, 1608–1631* (Westminster, U.K.: Archibald Constable & Co., 1895).

p. 50.   As one of Raleigh's: "Sir Walter Raleigh to Nathanial Rich, June 1617," regarding setting sail, ships, and the journey, 1 p., HMC 219, *Manchester Papers*; "James Hancock to Nathaniel Rich, 16 June 1617," *Manchester Papers*. Lord North, cousin of Lord Rich, represented the Guiana charter bestowed to Rich by King James.

p. 50.   Robert Rich believed: Dan Byrnes, "The Business of Slavery," *The Blackheath Connection,* see www.danbyrnes.com.au/blackheath/slavebc.htm. Following Raleigh's expedition to Guiana in 1617/1618, Robert Rich continued for another year to promote Guiana as a cloth manufacturing venture for the English Pilgrims exiled in Holland because of Guiana's access to dye sources. Byrnes: "In 1619, the Earl of Warwick took a prominent part in financing Roger North's Guiana expedition. . . . Warwick as organizer of the Guiana Company had wanted to settle there some of the separatists of Robinson's congregation at Leyden." Rich's participation in piracy, particularly the theft of Africans from a Spanish slaver in the summer of 1619, ended the Guiana scheme when King James ordered him to return the Guiana commission in the spring of 1620. Embittered by the confiscation of the *Treasurer*, and other actions by his enemies in the Virginia Company, Rich entered the New England venture.

p. 51.　　The Virginia Company, ecstatic: "Michaelmas term of the Quarter Court, November 1616," Kingbury, ed., *Rec. of the Va. Co.* Elected by the London Company at that session were Captain Argall, deputy governor; Captain Ralph Hamor, vice admiral; Captain John Martin, master of ordinance; John Rolfe, secretary and recorder.

p. 52.　　Governor Argall immediately: Michael Jarvis, Jeroen van Driel, "The Vingboons Chart of the James River, Virginia, circa 1617," *W&MQ* (April 1997).

p. 52.　　Later that year: "Governor Argall Proclamation, May 18, 1618," Kingsbury, ed., *Rec. of the Va. Co.* See also Gardiner, *History of England*; Craven, "The Earl of Warwick, a Speculator in Piracy," *Hispanic American Historical Review* 10 (1930); Cridlin, *A History of Colonial Virginia*; Byrnes in "The Business of Slavery" writes, "In 1618, Rich sent his ship *Treasurer* to plunder the Spanish West Indies; then he sought to use Virginia as a base for similar pirating. However, by 1620, Sir Edwin Sandys (1561–1629) and his circle intervened in this, and brought information to the Privy Council and the Spanish ambassador." [citing Brenner, "The New-Merchant Leadership of the Colonial Trades," *Merchants and Revolution*.]

p. 52.　　In London: James Howell, *Familiar Letters of James Howell* [Historiographer to Charles II] (n.p.: 1653, repr. Boston: Houghton Mifflin, 1907).

Chapter 4 : Into the Realm of Kalunga

p. 54.　　Later, as the Inquisition: Thornton, "African Experience," *W&MQ*, citing late sixteenth century routes mapped in Arquivo Nacional de Tore do Tombo, Lisbon, Inquisicao de Lisboa, 159/7/877, "Visita a Angola," fols., 23–23v, 28v, 54v–55v, 64–64v, 82–83,102v–103v. For more on the lives of these merchants, see Jose da Silva Horta, "Africanos e Portugueses na Documentacao Inquisitorial, de Luanda a Mbanza Kongo (1596–1598)," and Rosa Cruz e Silva, "As Feiras do Ndongo: A Outra Vertente do Comercio no Seculo XVII," in Comissao Nacional para as Comemoracoes dos Descobrimentos Portugueses, *Actas da Seminario: Encontro de Povos e Culturas em Angola (Luanda, April 5–6, 1995)* (Lisbon, 1997).

p. 55.　　The Portuguese missionaries: Catechismal literature was prepared for the growing Kimbundu-speaking Christian community by Jesuits who visited Ndongo in 1575, before the 1589 Battle of the Lukala. See "Practica para bautizar as adultos de gentio dos Reinos de Angola," MS, Biblioteca Publica e Arquivo Distrial de Evora, cited in Thornton, "African Experience," *W&MQ*. The Latin names of the Kimbundu-speaking Bantu Christians who arrived in 1619 in Virginia can be found in the 1624/5 Virginia Census cited in John Frederick Dorman, ed., *Adventurers of Purse and Person Virginia 1607–1624/5* [hereafter known as *Adventurers*], vol. 1 (Baltimore: Genealogical Publishing Co., 4th edition, 2004).

p. 55.　　According to Mbundu: See Ndongo traditions recorded by Cavazzi da Montecuccolo, in *Missione Evangelica al regno de Congo*, (c. 1665, updated to 1668), vol. A., book 2, p. 11–15, cited in Thornton, *African Politics*. For more, see Thornton, "Legitimacy and Political Power: Queen Njinga, 1624–1663," *Journal of African History* 32 (1991).

p. 56.   Andrew Battel: Battel is also sometimes spelled "Battell." The Portuguese assigned Battel and his musket to the Imbangala. He stayed with them and observed them closely for many months before escaping to the capital of Kongo and returning to England. See Andrew Battel, *The Strange Adventures of Andrew Battel of Leigh in Angola and the Adjoining Regions*, in Samuel Purchas, *Purchas, His Pilgrimes* (London: 1625), and *The Strange Adventures of Andrew Battel, of Leigh, in Angola and the Adjoining Regions*, ed. E. G. Ravenstein (London: 1901, repr. 1967). Battel had been one of a crew on an English privateer captured in India and was handed over to the Portuguese, who sent him to serve in Angola in 1599. Assigned to the Imbangala, whose ways he would later describe to his friend Rev. Samuel Purchas in England, Battel fled after two years (in 1603) to the Portuguese colony at Massangano where, as he recalled, "at this time there came news by the Jesuits that the Queen of England was dead, and that King James had made peace with Spain. Then I made petition to the Governor, who granted me licence to go into my country: and so I departed with the Governor and his train to the city of St. Paul . . . Then I purposed to have shipped myself for Spain, and thence homeward. But the Governor denied his word, and commanded me to provide myself within two days to go up to the Conquest again." After still more trying adventures, Battel escaped into the bush, made a canoe with two Africans, and sought to paddle upriver to the sea. "I was in great danger, because the, sea was great: and being over the bar I rode into the sea, and then sailed afore the wind along the coast, which I knew well, minding to go to the kingdom of Longo, which is towards the north." Finding passage with a friendly crew, in 1610 Battel returned to Leighs, in Essex, England. His tales of the *pongo* (gorillas) who sometimes seized villagers, was the first that England had heard of these animals of Angola.

p. 57.   He believed: The Imbangala informed Andrew Battel that they were originally from "Serra Leoa," Battel, *Strange Adventures*, ed. Ravenstein.

p. 57.   Described variously: For identification of the Imbangala and the Jaga, see Joseph C. Miller, "The Imbangala and the Chronology of Early Central African History," *Journal of African History* 13 (1972); also Jan Vansina, "Population Movements and Emergence of the New Socio-Political Forms in Africa," *UNESCO General History of Africa* (Los Angeles: 1981–1993), cited in Thornton, *African Politics*.

p. 57.   Battel reported: Samuel Purchas, *Purchas His Pilgrimage, or Relations of the World and the Religions*, ed. Ravenstein (London: 1617), book 7, chapt. 10, based on oral testimony of Battel.

p. 57.   Battel stayed: Battel, *Strange Adventures*, ed. Ravenstein.

p. 57.   The Imbangala had women: Battel, *Strange Adventures*, ed. Ravenstein; see also Cavazzi da Montecuccolo, *Missione Evangelica*, vol. A., book 1.

p. 57.   Battel observed: Battel, *Strange Adventures*, Ravenstein ed.; Thornton, "African Experience," *W&MQ*.

p. 58.   A Capuchin priest: No revulsion could be shown during the feasting on human flesh, according to their law. Montecuccolo, *Missione Evangelica;* Battel, *Strange Adventures;* Joseph C. Miller, *Kings and Kinsmen: Early Mbundu States in Angola* (Oxford, 1976); Thornton, "African Experience," *W&MQ.* Battel described the Imbangala "drinking, dancing, and banquetting, with man's flesh, which was a heavy spectacle to behold."

p. 58.   These moral deities: Thornton, *African Politics and European Conquest*, citing Montecuccolo, *Missione Evangelica.* See also António de Oliveira Cadornega, *História das guerras angolanas* (1680–1681), ed. José Matias Delgado and Manuel Alves da Cunha (Lisbon, 1940–1942, repr. 1972).

p. 58.   Their presence: Battel, *Strange Adventures*, ed. Ravenstein; see also Thornton, "African Experience," *W&MQ.* Thornton: "[The Imbangalas'] favorite pillage was palm wine taken from cultivated trees. Instead of tapping the trees and drawing small quantities of sap for oil or to ferment for wine, they cut down the whole tree. It gave no yield for ten days, then a small hole was drilled into the heart of the tree, which would yield about two quarts of sap a day for 26 days, when it dried up. By this method they destroyed all the palm trees in a region, and when all had been used up they moved on." The destruction of the palm trees was especially devastating to the Bantus. The tree sap not only produced wine but the palm fruit was dried and ground for bread, and the pulp rendered for cooking oil and cosmetics. The fibrous leaves of the tree were woven into baskets, sleeping mats, and silklike clothing and used to cover their roofs.

p. 58.   So great was: They generally rampaged in one region for about four months, until they had cut down all of the palm trees for wine, and then they moved on. See Battel, *Strange Adventures*, ed. Ravenstein; Thornton in "African Experience," *W&MQ.*

p. 58.   After devastating: Battel, *Strange Adventures*, ed. Ravenstein; Thornton, *African Politics*.

p. 59.   Then, Portuguese governors: For chronology of the Imbangala period, see Heintze, "Das ende des unabhängigen Staates Ndongo [Angola], Neue Chronologie und Reinterpretation (1617–1630)," *Paideuma* 27 (1981): 197–273; "Angola nas garras do tráfico de escravos: As guerras do Ndongo (1611–30)," *Revista Internacional de Estudos Africanos* (1984): 11–60, cited in Thornton, "African Experience," *W&MQ.* During nearly four hundred years of occupation in Angola, the Portuguese never won a battle without massive support from African soldiers using African battle tactics. The *guerra preta* (black army), recruited and led by sobas, became Portugal's main military strength in Angola. Before the forming of the guerra preta and before the Imbangala alliances, the majority of Africans exported from Africa were not captured by the Portuguese but purchased by them from Africans at *feiras* (markets), which sold prisoners taken in wars waged deep in the interior and far from Portuguese reach. European slave traders frequently sailed or trekked miles up the Congo River in the Maleba Pool area where Africans sold fellow Africans. The Jesuit missionary Pero Rodriguez observed in 1594 that the number of "slaves taken in war are nothing compared to those bought at *feiras* . . . at these *feiras* the kings and lords and all Ethiopia [Central Africa] sell slaves."

p. 59.   Dispatched by: Battel, *Strange Adventures*, ed. Ravenstein. As Portugal pursued colonization efforts, governor Rodrigues Coutinho, followed by Cerveira Pereira, received royal orders from Lisbon both to establish a colony on the coast in the region south of Luanda and to expel Protestant pirates who were looting Portuguese and Spanish ships in the area. See "Order for Conquest and Establishment of Government of Benguela, 14 February, 1614," Brásia, ed., *MMA*, 6:195–99, cited in Thornton, *African Politics*. Lisbon had not sanctioned the use of the Imbangala in colonizing Angola but did little to stop it despite vigorous protests from the manikongos, clergy, and settlers in Angola. Because they could pocket fees on exports, Coutinho, Pereira, and other opportunistic governors preferred to enslave and export Angolans rather than evangelize and colonize them. Imbangala raiders served them well.

p. 59.   Manikongo Álvaro II in 1617: "Álvaro III to Pope Paul V, 25 October 1617," Brásio, ed., *MMA*, 6:290.

p. 60.   Upon arriving: "Luis Mendes de Vasconcelos to Lisbon, 28 August 1617," Brásio, ed., *MMA*, 6:283–855.

p. 60.   Vasconcelos had ambitiously: De Vasconcelos, "Adbierte de las cosas de que tiene falta el gouierno de Angola, 1616," Brásio, ed., *MMA*.

p. 61.   In stunning abuse: Fernão de Sousa, "Guerras do Reino de Angola," (c. 1630); see Thornton, *African Politics*, and Thornton, "African Experience," *W&MQ*.

p. 62.   A hero of action: De Vasconcelos, *Arte militar. Dividida em tres partes* (Alenquer, 1612). Vasconcelos's war manual was referred to by Portuguese soldier Antonio de Oliveira de Cadornega in his *Historia geral das guerras angolanas* (n.p.: 1680, repr. Lisbon, 1972), cited in Thornton, *African Politics*.

p. 62.   Throughout the mountain kingdom: Thornton, "African Experience," *W&MQ*.

p. 64.   The Imbangala poured: Manuel Severim da Faria, "Historia portugueza e de outras provincias do occidente dese o anno de 1610 ate o de 1640 . . ." *Biblioteca Nacional de Lisboa*, MS 241, fol. 163v, cited in Thornton, "African Experience," *W&MQ*.

p. 64.   "As Vasconcelos: Manuel Bautista Soares, "Copia dos excessos que se cometem no gouerno de Angola que o bispo deu a V. Magestade pedindo remedio delles de presente, e de futuro, 7 September 1619," Brásio, ed., *MMA*, 6:370; Thornton, "African Experience," *W&MQ*.

p. 64.   Condemning the invasion: Soares, "Copia dos excessos, 7 September 1619," Brásio, ed. *MMA*, 6:369–70; Thornton, *African Politics*.

p. 65.   Vogado Sotomaior: Manuel Vogado Sotomaior, "Papel sobre as cousas de Angola, 1620," Brásio, ed. *MMA*, 15:476, 480, cited in Thornton, "African Experience," *W&MQ*.

p. 65.   He reported that: Sotomaior, "Papel sobre," Brásio, ed. *MMA*.

p. 65.   So great was: Manuel Severim da Faria, "Historia portugueza e de outras provincias (1620–1621)," cited in Cadornega, *Historia geral das guerras angolas*, ed. Delgado, 1:90. See also, Thornton, "African Experience," *W&MQ*.

p. 65.   Some estimate: Heintze, "Ende des Unabhangigen Staats Ndongo (Angola): Neue Chronologie und Reinterpretation (1617–1630)," *Paideuma*, 1981, revised in *Studien zur Geschichte Angolas im 16. und 17. Jahrhundert. Ein Lesebuch* (Cologne, 1996), cited in Thornton, "African Experience, *W&MQ*.

p. 65.   "Although many: Thornton, "African Experience," *W&MQ*.

p. 65.   In the fiscal year 1619: Heintze, "Ende des Unabhangigen Staats Ndongo, *Studien zur Geschichte Angolas*; Thornton, "African Experience," *W&MQ*; from Angola to Vera Cruz, see Contaduria, *Archivo General de Indias* Seville cited in Sluiter, "New Light," *W&MQ*.

p. 65.   Ndongo was a kingdom: David Birmingham, *Trade and Conflict in Angola: The Mbundu and Their Neighbors under the Influence of the Portuguese, 1483–1790* (Oxford University Press, 1966); cited in Thornton, "African Experience," *W&MQ*.

p. 65.   The Imbangala even: Soares, "Copia dos excessos, September 7, 1619," Brásio, ed. *MMA*, 6:170, cited in Thornton, "African Experience," *W&MQ*. See also "Practica para bautizar as adultos de gentio dos Reinos de Angola" (late sixteenth to seventeenth century), MS, Biblioteca Publica e Arquivo Distrial de Évora. Thornton: "By 1619, a Kimbundu-speaking Christian community existed in Angola, with its own informal catechismal literature, delivered by the Jesuit priests who had accompanied the first conquerors in 1575."

p. 65.   Prisoners: African names in the 1624/5 Virginia muster are cited in Dorman, ed., *Adventurers*, vol. 1.

p. 65.   Never in: Birmingham, *Trade and Conflict in Angola*; see also Heintze, *Studien zur Geschichte Angolas im 16. Und 17. Jahrhundert, Ein Lesebuch* (Cologne, 1996).

p. 66.   Their growing numbers: Heintze, "Gefahrderes Asyl. Chanzen Und Konsequenzen der Flucht angolanischer Skalven im 17. Jahrhundert," *Paideuma* 39, cited in Thornton, "African Experience", *W&MQ*.

p. 66.   Acuna was: Jose Antonio Saco, *Historia de la esclavitud de la raza africana en el Nuevo Mudo* (Havana: 1938), 2:96ff., Cited in Sluiter, "New Light," *W&MQ*.

p. 67.   Lisbon banker: Ana Hutz, *The Portuguese New Christians and the Traffic of Slaves for Spanish America (1580–1640)*, XXV Meeting of the Association of History Económica and Social Portugal, the Europe and the Mediterranean: Historical Economies and Societies, University of Évora, November 18–19, 2005.

p. 67.   Each asentista: Jose Antonio Saco, *Historia de la esclavitud de la raza africana en el Nuevo Mundo* (Havana: 1938), cited in Sluiter, "New Light," *W&MQ*.

p. 67.   In his negotiations: Records show that Acuna was forced to sell twenty-four male children in Jamaica to purchase medicine for the dying ship of slaves following the outbreak of disease, probably smallpox or dysentery. See Contaduria, AGI, cited by Sluiter, "New Light," *W&MQ*. Virginia records show that pirates took women as well as men from the *Bautista*. See the 1624/5

Virginia muster cited in Dorman, ed., *Adventurers*, vol. 1. See also John Thornton, "Cannibals, Witches, and Slave Traders in the Atlantic World," *W&MQ*, citing Joseph C. Miller: a "strong, healthy adult African male just off the boat they termed a 'piece,' or *peca* in Portuguese. The term derived from an expression employed in Africa very early in the history of slaving, when male adults sold allegedly for a single 'piece' of imported cloth."

p. 67.   The Bantu captives: Manual Bautista Soares, "Relacao," Brásio, ed., *MMA*. See also Thornton, "African Experience," *W&MQ*.

p. 68.   In the dark hold: Cited in Thornton, "Cannibals, Witches, and Slave Traders," *W&MQ*.

p. 68.   Jose Monzolo: Jose Monzolo (from Nzolo, a district of Kongo) was born into Christianity in the early seventeenth century and knew the catechism from his childhood in Angola. See Juan Manuel Pacheco, *Los jesuitas en Colombia* (Bogotá: Editorial San Juan Eudes, 1959), book 1. Jorge Palacios Preciado, *La trata de negros por Cartagena de Indias* (Tunja: Universidad Tecnológica de Tunja, 1973); cited in Thornton, "Cannibals, Witches, and Slave Traders," *W&MQ;* Thornton, "On the Trail of Voodoo: African Christianity in Africa and the Americas," *Americas* 44, no. 3 (Jan. 1988): 261–78.

p. 68.   African prisoner: Ottobah Cugoano, *Thoughts and Sentiments on the Evil Wicked Traffic of Slavery and Commerce in the Human Species* (in the following century, 1770). See also, Thornton, "Cannibals, Witches, and Slave Traders," *W&MQ*.

p. 68.   Since slaves on: At the beginning of the slave trade to America, Africans were generally purchased in Angola or Latin America by wealthy adventurers embarking on large projects for the first time. That is, they purchased laborers in batches for new and often large enterprises. For example, all of the "20 and odd" Africans delivered by the *White Lion* to Virginia in August 1619 were acquired by only two men—George Yeardley, the new governor of Virginia, and Abraham Piersey, the colony's cape merchant [see John Rolfe's letter to Edwin Sandys, January 1619, Kingsbury, ed., *Rec. of the Va. Co.*]—as they prepared to begin their plantations. And Piersey later purchased Yeardley's plantation. In the same era, even batches of white indentured servants, as many as sixty per lot, were frequently brought over from England to America on a single ship arranged by one planter seeking to begin or enlarge a single plantation, or one manufacturer about to begin an operation. Families with access to power, such as Yeardley, or to wealth, like the Littletons, Bennetts, Custises, Scarboroughs, etc., acquired shiploads or sent ships to acquire laborers in batches. Servants and slaves were usually acquired by the wealthy, who could afford several at one time. This changed somewhat in time as numerous former servants were set free to begin their (often small at first) farms or trades, and began to acquire small numbers of servants, often as few as one, of their own. In the case of Africans coming to America in the early seventeenth century, and particularly those who came from the fall of Kabasa in 1619, many were countrymen originally from a small region, who arrived on a single ship and remained together or near each other in the small colony of Jamestown. As will be seen, their common Angolan origin helped them easily build close-knit malungu communities in America in the early to mid-1600s, which would survive long after. Seventeenth-century Angola was in a peculiar circumstance, in that battles and wars—not the customary slave markets of diverse prisoners stocked by African merchants—that were fought among Portuguese and Dutch colonizers as well as the Mbundu and Bakongo kingdoms launched large numbers of close kinsmen and countrymen to the Americas, often together.

p. 68.   The word was *malungu*: Robert W. Slenes, *Malungu, Ngoma Vem!: Africa enco-berta e descoberta no Brasil* (Luanda, Angola: Museu Nacional de Escravatura, I.N.P.C., Ministerio de Cultura, 1995).

p. 68.   Upon arriving: Venture Smith, *A Narrative of the Life and Adventures of Venture, A Native of Africa* (New London, CT, 1798; expanded ed., Hamden, CT, 1896); Thornton, "Cannibals, Witches, and Slave Traders," *W&MQ*.

p. 68.   Of the two thousand: Archivo General de Indias, Contaduria 883, Seville, cited in Sluiter, "New Light," *W&MQ*.

p. 69.   As for the *Bautista*: Archivo General de Indias, Indiferente General, "Rela-cion," 2795, cited in Sluiter, "New Light," *W&MQ*.

p. 69.   Fearing the entire: AGI, Indiferente General, 2795, cited in Sluiter, "New Light," *W&MQ*.

Chapter 5 : Alias, the "Dutchman"

p. 70.   In Cuba: Saturnine Ullivarri, *Piratas y Corsarios en Cuba*, Renacimiento, "Isla de la Tortuga," Saturnino Ullivarri, *Piratas y Corsarios en Cuba* (Isla de la Tortuga Collection) (Seville, Spain: Editorial Renacimiento, 2004). Matthew Restall, "Black Conquistadors: Armed Africans in Early Spanish America," *The Americas* [Academy of American Franciscan History] 57, no. 2 (October 2000): 171–205.

p. 71.   Alhough the Jopes: *Visitations of Cornwall, comprising The Herald's Visitations of Cornwall, 1530, 1573, and 1620*, ed., Lt. Col. J. L. Vivian (Exeter: William Pollard & Company, 1887), 247–48. See also, Hugh Fred Jope, *Before the Mayflower* (Haverhill, MA: self-published, 1993, used by permission of author). According to the record of the College of Arms from the herald's visitation in 1620, John Jolyn Jope, of Merifield, in Cornwall, was the son of John Jope of Merifield and his wife Katherine, daughter of John Trenouth of Stoke Clymsland. His grandfather was Roger Jope of Meryfield, in Stoke Clymsland (will probated 1 March 1580) who married Jane, daughter of [. . .] Collyn. Their grandson, the Reverend/Captain John Colyn Jope, married Mary, daughter of John Glanvill of Launceston, on 16 May 1614. The exact date of the death of the captain of the *White Lion* is not known, but by the time Mary Jope died in 1632, she was a widow. See "Jope," in Vivian's *Visitation*, pp. 247–48, at www.uk-genealogy.org.uk/england/Cornwall/visita-tions/index.html.

With William the Conqueror to England in 1066, came one whose son, the Norman knight William deJope, landed at Plymouth, Devon, and settled a short distance away in Liskeard, Cornwall, around 1172 and became a mining lord, according to French records. English documents mention one of this family, William Jope, as Portreve of Liskeard, in 1410. Stoke Climsland, the home of John Colyn Jope, is a few miles from Liskeard. Hugh Fred Jope goes on to say, "The Reverend/Captain John Colyn Jope was born in Merifield, Cornwall in 1580. He came from an enterprising and prestigious family. His brother Roger was also a clergyman and wrote a sonnet to Queen Anne upon her death in 1619 which was printed and distributed throughout England at that time. In 1620, John Jope petitioned the Heralds for an Achievement of Arms (Coat of Arms) which was denied because he had ruffled some of the feathers in the Crown." In 1635, John Colyn Jope's nephew, William Jope, of Alfington (Alwington) near Sidmouth, Devon, a servant of the Prince of Orange, as an engineer hired by the famous Lion Gardiner, helped found the Puritan colony of Saybrook in New England. Cornwall-Devon presently holds the largest concentration of individuals worldwide (about one thousand) with the surname Jope, including those in Germany, France, America, and Australia. See also Hugh Fred Jope, *The Flying Dutchman* (Haverhill, MA: self-published paper January 10, 1993, used by permission of the author). There were conflicting views on the nationality of Jope and his ship at Jamestown in 1619. John Rolfe, the outgoing secretary-recorder for the colony, referred to the ship as "Dutch." However, the incoming secretary and president of the Virginia House of Burgesses, John Pory, described the mystery ship as "Flemish." See also the eyewitness testimony of Reinhold Booth [Coldham, ed., *English Adventurers and Emigrants, 1609–1660*, 181–82] who described the ship and her captain as "a Flemish man-o-war, the *White Lion* of Flushing, [Vlissingen] commanded by Captain Chope [Jope]." "Flemish" refers to Flanders, now in northwest Belgium near Ghent; Vlissingen is in the Netherlands. There is disagreement among these witnesses, however, Booth was an employee of, and both Rolfe and Pory were agents of, Lord Robert Rich, owner of the *Treasurer*, which consorted with Jope and the *White Lion* as pirates to take the Spanish slave ship *Bautista* in violation of the English-Spanish treaty of 1604. That neither Rolfe nor Pory identified the *White Lion* or gave the full name of Captain Jope, in clear negligence of their official duties, further indicates an attempt by them to conceal the event that occurred at the latter end of August 1619, to protect Lord Rich and Jamestown from allegations of piracy. Furthermore, there was additional reason to avoid naming the *White Lion*. A famous ship, she was previously owned by Charles Howard, Lord Admiral of England, as well as Francis Drake. [See John Cummins, *Francis Drake* (New York: St. Martin's Press, 1997), 145, 225; Garrett Mattingly, *Defeat of the Spanish Armada* (Boston: Houghton Mifflin Company, 1959); E. F. Benson, *Sir Francis Drake*, The Golden Hind (New York & London: Harpers, 1927); Sir William Monson, *Naval Tracts* vol. 1 (UK: Churchill, 1703), 124, 139; A. E. W. Mason, *Life of Francis Drake* (London: Hodder & Stoughton, 1941); Robert Milne Tyte, *Armada! The Planning, the*

Battle, and After (Wordsworth Military Library, 1998); Roger Whiting, *The Enterprise of England: the Spanish Armada* (Gloucester, UK: Alan Sutton, 1988); Bryce Walker, *Armada* (Boston: Little, Brown & Company, 1981); Ernie Bradford, *The Wind Commands Me: A Life of Sir Francis Drake* (New York: Harcourt, 1965); Jack Beeching, ed., *Richard Hakluyt, Voyages and Discoveries* (London: Penguin Books, 1982). See also C. K. Croft Andrews, "Sir Francis Drake and Captain James Erisey," *Devon and Cornwall Notes and Queries Quarterly Journal* 22 (1942–43): 255–57.] Andrews: "Drake ... assisted Captain James Erisey in 1585, when Erisey was raising money to fit out the *White Lion* for Drake's expedition of that year. On 6 September Erisey morgaged his manor of Pensignance in Gwen and Kea to Drake (of Buckland Abbey in the County of Devon, knight) for 220 pounds, the terms being that if Erisey failed to redeem the sum at Sir Francis's house at Michaelmas in 1586 the property would pass to Drake (Andrews, 'Sir Francis Drake and Captain James Erisey'). The manor did eventually pass into Drake's ownership because in 1595 he sold it to Richard Careew for 750 pounds (Indenture between Drake and Carew, 27 August 1595, West Devon Record Office, 277/11). . . . The deed, which I lately retrieved from a war-time dump of 'waste paper,' is signed by the mortgagor and by Roger Manwood, one of Queen Elizabeth's Justices, before whom it was acknowledged at Launceston on the 10th September, 1585." In 1614, John Colyn Jope married Mary Glanvill, daughter of John Glanvill of Launceston, at Launceston, about five miles from Jope's home of Merifield.

p. 72. It was about: From several testimonies it is clear that the *Treasurer* left Jamestown for the West Indies, via the Bermudas, about November–December 1618. See, for example, the deposition of John Martin taken in the case, *Delaware v. Argall*, 13 April 1622: "That true it is that this dept did goe in the shipp called the *Treasurer* from Virginia in the West Indyes, of which shippe Daniell Elfrith was Master or Captain, and saieth that the same Captaine Argall at his owne charge did send forth the said shippe, and from the tyme they went forth in the said shippe till they returned into Virginia they were about some ten months expired and spent." [Coldham, ed., "Voyage," *Va. Mag. of Hist. and Biog* 87, no. 1 (January 1979): 33.] See also letter of John Pory to Sir Dudley Carleton, September 1619, sent from Jamestown via the *White Lion* to The Hague, Lyon Gardiner Tyler, ed., *Narratives of Early Virginia 1606–1625* (New York: 1907); Kingsbury, ed., *Rec. of the Va. Co.*

p. 72. However, the *Treasurer*'s: In the eyes of King James, the *Treasurer*'s surreptitiously acquired foreign marque was never valid. Captain Edward Brewster, admittedly an enemy of Lord Rich and Governor Argall, gives perhaps the best description of the *Treasurer*'s Savoy marque: "Eight more of those forty two men [from Brewster's ship, *Neptune*] the deft [Governor Samuel Argall] did send and since force of them to go in the ship called the *Treasurer* into the West Indies to rob the king of Spain with a dead comission with a Blanke in it of the Duke of Savoy's, all which was performed [as by the testimony of the Virginia Company—deleted] by the taking of a ship which was brought to Virginia." Not only was the marque rendered obsolete by the cessation of hostility between Savoy and Spain in 1619 but, apparently, by stating that the marque was "Blanke," Brewster also claims that it did not identify by name the ship it empowered, in this case, the *Treasurer*. If so, it was a worthless letters of marque. [Concerning the admiralty hearing of the case, *Delware v. Argall*, 16 April 1622, see Coldham, ed., "Voyage," *Va. Mag. of Hist. and Biog.* 87, no. 1 (January 1979): 43.] The trustworthiness of Brewster's testimony is undermined, however, by his erroneous claim that the *Treasurer* brought a ship she had captured to Virginia in 1619. Brewster was in England at the time the *Treasurer* returned to Jamestown, therefore he was apparently repeating hearsay.

p. 72. Letters of marque: Sir Thomas Roe to the East India Company, London (1620), PRO.

p. 72. Prowling the West Indies: John Jope and Diego "El Mulato" Grillo were near-legendary privateering figures, and it is believed that other pirates later used their names and notoriety to conceal their true identities. When Grillo, for example, retired from piracy, another pirate took his name, followed by another, and then another. The surname "Jope" has been linked to the cursed legend of the Flying Dutchman. A pirate named Jope of Ghent was preying on English ships during the time of Prince John of Gaunt, father-in-law of Prince Henry the Nagivator, of Portugal, when a merchant named Laykensuder complained to Prince John that his ship had been attacked by this Jope in the English Channel. Hugh Fred Jope, of Haverhill, Massachusetts, wrote, "*The Virginia Chronicle* of March 1821 printed an article which stated that Captain John Jope of the *White Lion* had improvised a method which infuriated the captains of other vessels which consorted with him in that when the prize was sighted, he would launch a pinnace and strip it clean before the consorters could participate. It was this maneuver which earned him the reputation of the Flying Dutchman, according to the *Chronicle*. Further reference comes from an archaic publication called the *Flemish Archives of Classical Music*, by Hansel Voorhees of Amsterdam published in 1872 which states: 'Wagner has taken his obvious anti-semitism to new levels in *Der Fliegende Hollander* which he copied from [the Jewish writer Heinrich] Heine's *Memoirs of Herr Von Schnabelwopsky*. He assigned satanic symbolism to the lead role of his opera and imposed a curse which condemned him to sail the seas eternally until he met and married a good woman. Furthermore, it was common knowledge that the original Flying Dutchman was a Sea Beggar who sailed between Antwerpen and Cornwall under the Marque of William of Orange. His name was Johan Chope [John Jope], a man of the cloth and a gentleman also. Wagner's *Flying Dutchman* was indeed a finely finished work but alas, his so-called trip to the sea when he envisioned the particulars of this work differs greatly with the true events but is without a doubt, where the master got the idea and imposed creative license on it." [Hansel Voorheees, 29 June 1872.] Heinrich Heine had penned a satirical version of the Flying Dutchman after watching a now-lost romantic play about the title character in Holland. And even earlier legend links the immortally cursed Flying Dutchman and the surname

Jope [also written "Chope" and "Youpe"] with the Danite port of Joppa (modern Haifa) in ancient Canaan, named after Japheth, the son of the very first sailor, Noah, and the reputed father of the earliest Mediterranean sailors. In Greek mythology, the Ethiopian princess Andromeda, chained to a rock on the coast of Joppa to be devoured by a sea monster, was rescued by the hero Perseus, who slew the monster. The Red Sea, which is not red, is said to be called thus because the monster perished there on the coast of Ethiopia [Ovid, *Metamorphoses* 4]. Perseus married Andromeda and they founded Mycenae. All were made constellations, and one particular star was named Al Gol (the demon of the wood). A French story retold by Hueges Joppe (Paris, 1989) offers this origin of the name Jope: "La famille Joppe est originaire de Champagne, mais cette province ayant ete maintes fois ravagee au cours des siecles, beaucoup de documents qui auraient pu servir a en etablir l'histoire ont disparu. Aussi les renseignements sur la famille jusqu'au XVIIIeme siecle sont-ils assez rares, descous, et leur exploitation faite par Eduard (frere de Maurice) au XXeme siecle, complete par des traditions orales donne une trame serieuse, certes, mais qui ne satisfait pas entierement notre curiosite. Des les Villeme et Ixeme siecles on trouve en Champagne trace de Joppe sur des listes d'hommes d'armes. Ce nom de Joppe est certainement d'origine franque et voudrait dire 'qui appelle dans la foret.' On peut rapprocher cette signification du mot actuel 'japper' qui veut aussi dire jeter un cri ou un appel. Mais, par contre, il semble plus hasardeux de faire descendre Joppe du latin et de voir dans la premiere syllabe de notre nom celui de Jupiter: JO. Les Francs et particulierement les Francs Ripuaires avaient des cette epoque recouvert tout l'Est de la France actuelle et entre autres regions la Champagne qui, alors s'etendait sur une bonne partie de ce qui devint plus tard la Lorraine. Il n'est donc pas etonnant de voir apparaitre Joppencourt au Villeme siecle. Un 'court' etait une enceinte palissadee, demeure habituelle des Francs Alleutiers, simples guerriers qui en avaient possession en tenure libre. Et Joppencourt, petit village situe a quelques kilometres d'Audun-le-Roman, dans la region de Briey a ete fonde evidemment par un Joppe qui etait un bon soldat, un bon Champenois et un bon Franc." [HFJ, 1993]. The name Joppe or "Yappe" was first documented in France about 850, referring, according to the French, to an apparently disturbed individual who "shouted at the forest from the center of a field from morning to sunset." In 897, in the reign of Charlemagne "the yapper's grandson was recorded as William de la Jappe." Later, some of this family became early Protestants and fled Catholic France for Holland and Germany. The Protestant branch spelled the surname as "Jope," whereas the Catholic family retained "Joppe." [HFJ, 1993].

p. 72. Disappointed: Jope, *Before the Mayflower.* Regarding the nature of the consort, see also testimony in allegations brought by the Spanish ambassador against Lord Robert Rich, summarized in Coldham, ed., *English Adventurers and Emigrants, 1609–1660*, 181–82: "Reinhold Booth, of Reigate, Surrey, gent. aged 26. He has known Daniel Elfrith for 10 years. In 1619 the deponent went on the *Treasurer* [man-o-war owned by the Earl of Warwick of the Virginia

Company] to Bermuda from Virginia and at the end of June 1619 she was compelled while in the West Indies, to consort with a Flemish man-o-war, the *White Lion* of Flushing, [Vlissingen] commanded by Captain Chope [Jope] who threatened to shoot at the *Treasurer* unless Captain Elfrith complied with his wishes. Chope had permission to seize Spanish ships and in mid-July of 1619, he took 25 men from his own and Elfrith's ship and sailed away in a pinnace [a small, fast boat attending a larger vessel]. After 3 days, he brought back a Spanish frigate, which he had captured and out of good will toward Elfrith, gave him some tallow and grain from her. Immediately after this, the deponent departed from Bermuda, leaving the *Treasurer* and the *Seaflower*, [owned by Lion Gardiner] left Bermuda for England, 23 July 1620." Though Booth, one of the pirates of the *Treasurer*, intentionally withheld mention of the disputed Africans, others of his shipmates on that voyage revealed them. See testimony of Richard Stafford of Staplehurst, Kent, summarized by Coldham from the same depositions taken by the Spanish ambassador on 3 June 1620: "Daniel Elfrith whom he has known for five years, went as Master of the *Treasurer* in 1619 to the West Indies where he was in company with a Dutch ship. When the *Treasurer* brought into the Somer Islands 25 Negroes, the then Governor, Captain Kendall, suspected that they had been taken at sea from a Spanish ship and caused them to be put into a longhouse at St. George's Town. Some were then sold and others hired out by Captain Butler, now Governor." See also "Warwick v. Brewster," Coldham, ed., *English Adventurers and Emigrants*, 12–14; ref. Coldham, ed., "Voyage," *Va Mag. of Hist. and Biog.* 87, no. 1 (January 1979): 31–67; and the letters of John Rolfe (1620) and John Pory (1619), Kingsbury, ed., *Rec. of the Va. Co.*

p. 73.   The *White Lion* and: *Archivo General de Indias* (Seville), translated by Sluiter in "New Light," *W&MQ*.

p. 73.   Figuring ship capacity: *Archivo General de Indias*, Seville, 1619, account translated in Sluiter, "New Light," *W&MQ*, reads: "Enter on the credit side the receipt of 8,657.875 pesos paid by Manuel Mendes de Acunha, master of the ship *San Juan Bautista*, on 147 slave pieces brought by him into the said port on August 30, 1619, aboard the frigate *Santa Ana*, master Rodrigo Escobar. On the voyage inbound, Mendes de Acunha was robbed at sea off the coast of Campeche by English corsairs. Out of the 350 slaves, large and small, he loaded in said Luanda, (200 under a license issued to him in Sevilla and the rest to be declared later) the English corsairs left him with on 147, including 24 slave boys he was forced to sell in Jamaica, where he had to refresh, for he had many sick aboard, and many had already died."

p. 73.   The troubled voyage: See *Archivo General de Indias*, Indiferente General, 2795, in the "Relacion" cited by Sluiter, "New Light," *W&MQ*, which adds that Acuna was "robbed by corsairs on the coast of Campeche and from there the civil authorities transported them [the 147 blacks, to Vera Cruz] on the frigate [*Santa Ana*], master Rodrigo Descobar, who entered the said port on August 30, 1619."

p. 74.   The acting governor: Kendall was quoted in the Meeting of the Virginia Council, May 1623, ed. Kingsbury, *Rec. of the Va Co.* Kendall stated that, as acting governor of Bermuda before Butler arrived late in 1619, he first would not let the man-of-war with the Dutch license (the *White Lion*) dock at St. George's because he suspected that she, along with the *Treasurer*, had stolen Africans from a Spanish slave ship in the West Indies, but relented when her captain (Jope) claimed that he would throw fourteen Africans overboard because he did not have enough food and water to sustain them. According to the findings of the king's Privy Council, read to the Virginia Company at its dissolution in May 1623, "In the latter time that Capt. Kendall was Deputy Governor, there arrived at the Summer Islands [Bermuda] (vixt. In ye year 1619) a man of warr with a Commission from ye Prince of Orange by virtue whereof he had taken certain Negros in the West Indies: And being in great extremity for want of water and victuals and forbidden by Capt. Kendall to come into any of the said harbors, he gave him notice that he had fourteen Negroes aboard which he should be forced to cast over board for want of victuals and rather desired to bestow them upon Capt. Kendall for any small consideration which he should be pleased to give him: which was performed accordingly. . . ." After arriving in October 1619, the new governor, Nathaniel Butler, would claim that Kendall stole the Africans from the "Dutch" ship. This indicates that though Jope traded "20 and odd" Africans in Virginia, he had not sold all of his share of the *Bautista*'s stolen Africans at Jamestown when he left Chesapeake Bay in late September, and was still carrying fourteen Africans when he refreshed at Bermuda weeks later before sailing to The Hague to deliver John Pory's letters (dated 30 September) to Sir Dudley Carlton. Or, Jope may have first stopped at Bermuda and traded fourteen Africans from his cargo on his way inbound to Jamestown in 1619. The questionable legality of the *White Lion*'s attack on the *Bautista*, and the recent beheading of Raleigh, conflicted with Virginia's and Bermuda's great desire for laborers, and probably made everyone, including Kendall, Yeardley, and Piersey as well as their enemies Rich, Butler, Argall, Elfrith, Pory, and Rolfe, who had anything to do with the Africans, nervous about specific details of exactly how they were acquired. It is curious that upon reaching Bermuda the *White Lion* would be, according to Kendall, in "great extremity for want of water and victuals," after having just two weeks earlier traded "20 and odd" Africans in exchange for food in Jamestown, though not so if the *White Lion* stopped briefly at Bermuda while inbound to Jamestown. What is certain is that the *White Lion* traded most, if not all, of her share of the *Bautista*'s stolen Africans to planters both in Jamestown and Bermuda between August and October 1619.

p. 74.   For, as it happened: Count Gondomar was the son of Garcia Sarmiento de Sotomayor and Juana de Acuna. He married his cousin, Constanza de Acuna. Regarding the uproar in London in the summer of 1618, see William Camden, *Diary (1603–1623)*. A hypertext edition by Dana F. Sutton, University of California–Irvine, can be accessed at http://eee.uci.edu/~papyri/diary/1eng. In 1618, the previous year, as Raleigh returned to England from the disastrous Guiana expedition, William Camden entered the following in his diary: "June 9. A proclamation against Walter

Raleigh is published, in which he is rebuked for having violated his authority, entrusted him with a caution, by invading the Spanish King's territory in America in a hostile manner, and for having done his best to violate the peace confirmed between the two sovereigns. The King [James] disapproves of and disowns these things, and hence grants to one and all the power to make public what they know about this act, and that this man be dealt with according to the law, and they who are convicted of such a great crime be visited with exemplary punishment." James's proclamation against Raleigh further alienated the king from his subjects and enraged the English for years. James, a Scotsman, upon the instigation of a Catholic ambassador, had condemned their national hero for attacking the hated Spaniards. As for the *Bautista* piracy, a riding incident on a London street in 1618 probably spared Lord Rich from Raleigh's fate. The death sentence against Raleigh had enflamed the wrath of all London against King James and Count Gondomar, and that anger boiled over a few days later when Gondomar either accidentally or uncaringly trampled a child while riding through the city, an incident that set Londoners to rioting in the streets. Camden entered in his diary in 1618: "July 12, At London people are rioting against the Spanish Ambassador, since a little boy was accidentally injured by the Spaniard while he was riding." Londoners were known to rebel in their anger, and James was already unpopular before executing Sir Raleigh. So four days later, it was decided that Gondomar should temporarily leave England. Camden wrote: "July 16, Didaco Sarmiento, Count Gondomar, the Spanish King's Ambassador, has departed, entertained en route by Baron Teinham and Wotton. He set sail (with Priests released from prison at his request) on the 20th." Camden next recorded Raleigh's failed escape attempt from prison: "Aug 9, When Walter Raleigh was brought to London, he bribed his guardian Lewis Stukeley, and attempted flight with him. And, betrayed by I know not whom, he was intercepted on the Thames, fetched back, and clapped in the Tower." In fact, Raleigh had been betrayed by his kinsman, Stukely, (who, on another note, had served as custodian for Pocahontas's child, Thomas Rolfe, left in England after her death in 1617). Upon learning of Raleigh's escape attempt, King James was adamant about executing the aging privateer and punishing the mob that had attacked the Spanish ambassador's residence. Camden makes it clear that the London riot against Gondomar was linked to the arrest of Walter Raleigh: "Aug 12, Those who had rioted at the house of the Spanish Ambassador were called for questioning at Westminister City Hall in the presence of the Lord Mayor and certain delegates appointed to hear charges and determine penalties. Out of these the father of the injured boy and others were fined one thousand pounds, and imprisoned at the King's will. Walter Raleigh, examined about his flight, confessed that for the first time he had erred against the King in contemplating this flight." Camden's next entry reveals why the king persisted in punishing Raleigh and the rioters. James hoped that, by sacrificing Raleigh for the

St. Thomas assault, he could convince King Philip III of Spain to keep the treaty and proceed with the marriage between Prince Charles Stuart and the Spanish princess Maria: "Because of this man's [Raleigh's] daft plan for invading Guiana and the Londoners' riot against the Spanish Ambassador's house, not a few men thought that the hope of a marriage [for Prince Charles] with the Spanish King's daughter had been quite weakened. For he had not made the proposal for marrying his children into France and Spanish for any other reason than, by creating family alliances, to sever these kingdoms from the United Provinces and reduce them more happily to his command. The Chancellor and other Privy Councilors often met and examined Walter Raleigh." By executing the popular Raleigh, King James demonstrated to the Spanish monarch that he would go to great lengths to punish English pirates who dared attack Spanish ships.

PART II: THE FOUNDERS LAND AT JAMESTOWN

p. 77.   According to the traditional account . . . English settlers of Jamestown, Virginia: See, for example, the opening chapter of Lerone Bennett Jr., *Before the Mayflower* (Chicago: Johnson Publishing Co., 1966).

Chapter 6 : Unmasked

p. 79.   London was abuzz: Gardiner, *History of England from the Accession of James I to the outbreak of the Civil War, 1603–1642*, additionally notes: "In 1616, [Robert Rich I] had fitted out two vessels under the flag of the Duke of Savoy, and had sent them to the West Indies, from whence, after a cruise of eighteen months, they had returned laden with Spanish treasures." See also Jarvis and van Driel, "The Vingboons Chart of the James River, Virginia, circa 1617," *W&MQ* (April 1997).

p. 79.   William Camden: *William Camden, Diary (1603–1623)*, Sutton, ed., http://eee.uci.edu/~papyri/diary/1eng.

p. 80.   The widowed: For British Admiralty testimony in *Buckingham v. Argall* and *Delaware v. Argall*, see Coldham, ed., "Voyage" *Va. Mag. of Hist. and Biog.* 87, no. 1 (January 1979): 30–67. See also "Court of Virginia, July 10, 1621," Kingsbury, ed., *Rec. of the Va. Co.* In 1618, Lord Delaware and George Villiers (the first Duke of Buckingham) loaded the *Neptune* with sundry pots and potables they planned to sell in Virginia on the same voyage that Delaware was undertaking to bring Argall back to England. Buckingham remained in England. When several of the *Neptune*'s passengers, including Lord Delaware, became ill and suspiciously died during the voyage, Captain Edward Brewster, who was placed in charge of the ship, hailed the passing *Treasurer*, which Delaware partly owned with Lord Rich, to come to their assistance. Brewster transferred Delaware and Buckingham's trade goods from the stricken *Neptune* to the *Treasurer* and ordered the latter vessel to deliver them to Virginia. In so doing, Brewster interrupted Captain

Elfrith and the *Treasurer*, allegedly on a "fishing trip," from sailing secretly to attack Spanish ships in the West Indies. (Elfrith could not ignore the *Neptune* because Delaware was chief governor of Virginia and therefore his orders superceded those of Deputy Governor Argall.) The *Treasurer* indeed delivered the *Neptune*'s trade goods to Virginia and thus was forced to delay the Spanish raid because the sailing season had passed. In Virginia, Argall, irate that the *Treasurer* missed the Spanish raid, confiscated Delaware and Buckingham's trade goods in lieu of the pirate booty she would have gotten in the West Indies. See also Coldham, *English Adventurers and Emigrants 1609–1660*, for a summary of the testimony of Edward Withers of St. Katherine's Precinct, London, in the civil case of *Warwick v. Brewster*, 12. From 1620 to 1624, Buckingham and the widowed Lady Delaware, along with Captain Brewster, filed a series of lawsuits against Argall, Rich, and John Rolfe seeking to recover the value of Buckingham and Delaware's seized trade goods.

p. 80.   Lady Delaware was: In an upcoming book, the author links the assassination of Lord Delaware instead with the mysterious death of his guest Pocahontas, one year earlier.

p. 80.   A few weeks later: "*Earl of Warwick v. Edward Bruster* Concerning the Ships '*Treasurer*' and '*Neptune*,'" Admiralty Court, Instance and Prize, Libel 81, No. 6, Public Record Office (London: 1621), cited in Kingsbury, ed., *Rec. of the Va. Co.*,See also Coldham, *English Adventurers and Emigrants 1609–1660*, 12–14.

p. 81.   Upon clearing: Ibid.

p. 81.   The paper trail: Camden, *Diary (1603–1623)*, ed. Sutton. One week after Camden recorded Lord Delaware's death, he made the following entry: "May 13, 1618 John North, Baron North's brother, announced bad news to the King about the unhappy expedition of Walter Raleigh to Guiana, with his son killed in an assault upon a Spanish fortification, Keim dead by cutting his own throat out of grief, and the fleet scattered."

p. 81.   The corsair was: Kingsbury, ed., *Rec. of the Va. Co.*

p. 81.   Sandys controlled: *Abstract of the proceedings of the Virginia Company of London, 1619–1624*, prepared from the records in the Library of Congress by Conway Robinson, and edited with an introduction and notes by R. A. Brock (Richmond, VA: Virginia Historical Society, 1888–1889). Craven, in *Dissolution of the Virginia Company*, discusses suspicions by Sandys's rivals that he encouraged numerous small investors to join the company to increase his voting power.

p. 82.   Ten days before: Arber, ed., *Captain John Smith, 1608–1631*. See also the May 7 meeting of the Virginia Company at which the king's Privy Council stated that when the company determined to send Yeardley to Jamestown to replace Argall, "against which the said Earl [of Warwick] with other of his friends and followers having made great opposition but not prevailing, a course was tekn in fine to dispatch a Pinnace from Plymouth [England] to fetch away Captain Argall with his goods and booty before the arrival of Sir George Yeardley and his commissions. The said Sir George Yeardley by the persuasions (as is vehemently to be presumed

of Mr. [John] Pory whom the said Earl had lately confided unto Sir
Thomas Smith, then treasurer [president of the Virginia Company] for
the Secretary's place of Virginia) spending much time unnescesarily
upon our English coasts." Kingsbury, ed., *Rec. of the Va. Co.* In summary,
the king's Privy Council determined that Lord Rich had persuaded
then-company president Thomas Smith to name his agent John Pory to
replace John Rolfe as colony secretary, and that Pory delayed Yeardley
from sailing to Virginia while Lord Rich arranged a speedy ship to hasten
to Jamestown to rescue Argall.

p. 82. Sir Yeardley was forced: "John Delbridge to Edwin Sandys, April 29, 1619,"
Kingsbury, ed., *Rec. of the Va. Co.* Argall departed Jamestown for England on 9 April
1619, and Yeardley arrived in Jamestown from England exactly ten days later.

p. 82. Cushman described: William Bradford, *Historie of Plimouth Plantation* (n.p.:
1648). Text posted online by Caleb Johnson, 1998; can be accessed at
www.members.aol.com/calebj/bibliography.html.

p. 82. After coming ashore: The loot that Argall brought with him from Jamestown
included property he allegedly stole from the company during his administration. At the Virginia Company meeting on 7 May 1623 during which
shareholders were informed that King James would not renew their charter
of Virginia, the Privy Council mentioned Argall's loot: "[In the] Summer
1618 upon the clamor aforesaid, Sir Thomas Smith and Alderman Johnson
with diverse others of the Counsell addressed their letters to ye said Lord
Delaware lately gone for Virginia requiring him to send home Captain Argall
in quality of a Mallefactor and to sequester all his goods there for restitition to
ye Company; there was afterwards an order resolved in court that what goods
of Capt. Argall's should be returned for England should be likewise seized on
for the Company's use. Which order at, the said Earl's [of Warwick] request
was so far forth dispensed with as that his Lordship notwithstanding might
take out of his own part (intending so much as should belong unto him by
his right of partnership) upon promise to deliver the rest into the Company's
hands so far forth as should be his Lordship's power to perform it. The per-
formance of which promise is yet still expected, the said Captain having
returned all his goods from Virginia under other mens names and consigned
them into the other and great mens' hands, whereby the Company remaineth
still defrauded of the due restitution which they had so great cause to expect
from Captain Argall." Kingsbury, ed., *Rec. of the Va. Co.* In summary, Argall,
upon reaching England, mingled his goods with those of Lord Rich with
the company's understanding that Rich would later separate his goods from
those of Argall and send the latter to the firm. But Rich kept all of the loot.
The company was therefore unable to go to court to get what it considered its
stolen property from Argall unless it sued Lord Rich, which could not be done
without creating yet another scandal damaging to the firm's reputation—Rich
being the most prominent business partner in that venture.

p. 83. Instead, Lord Rich's friends: Craven, *The Dissolution of the Virginia Company.* See also "Extraordinary Meeting of the Virginia Company, May–June
1619," Kingsbury, ed., *Rec. of the Va. Co.*

p. 83. Such recriminations: "Sir Edwin Sandys. A letter to the Earl of Southampton, September 29, 1619," Kingsbury, ed., *Rec. of the Va. Co.* Sir Sandys later confessed to the Earl of Southampton that his handling of the *Treasurer* affair at the meeting had been "unsound." The furor that exploded following his public allegation against the Earl of Warwick rattled the confidence of investors who were already frustrated by their continuing financial losses in the failing colony. The horses were now out of the barn, and any hope that Sandys could discreetly appeal to Lord Rich died in the bitterly poisonous public confrontation.

p. 83. The prestigious stockholders: Mary Johnston, *Pioneers of the Old South: A Chronicle of English Colonial Beginnings* (New Haven: Yale University Press, 1918, repr. 1920). The Guelfs and the Ghibellines were the two opposing factions of Papacy supporters and German Holy Roman Empire supporters in the eleventh century. See K. Knight, online ed., *New Advent Catholic Encyclopedia*, at www.newadvent.org.

p. 83. Confronted in: Nicholas Hawes, an eyewitness testifying 16 May 1622, in *Delaware v. Argall*, and *Buckingham v. Argall*. See Coldham, ed., "Voyage," *Va. Mag. of Hist. and Biog.* 87, no. 1 (January 1979): 64.

p. 83. But Captain Brewster: Hawes, cited in Coldham, ed., "Voyage," *Va. Mag. of Hist. and Biog.* 87, no. 1 (January 1979): 64.

p. 84. Argall proved: The testimony of Argall's servant and eyewitness, John Craven. See Coldham, ed., "Voyage," *Va. Mag. of Hist. and Biog.* 87, no. 1 (January 1979): 65–66.

p. 84. Quickly realizing: Ibid.

p. 84. John Cushman: Cushman cited in Bradford, *Historie of Plimouth Plantation*.

p. 85. Sir Yeardley and: "Draft defending the Earl of Warwick," Vernon A. Ives, ed., *Letters from Bermuda, 1615–1646* (Toronto: University of Toronto Press, 1984), 148. In this preliminary defense, Robert Rich's kinsman Sir Nathaniel Rich, acting as his attorney, references Yeardley's allegations of the *Treasurer*'s exploit in 1619.

p. 85. Anxious that: Sandys to Yeardley, (1619), Kingsbury, ed., *Rec. of the Va. Co.*

p. 85. On June 21: Ibid.

p. 86. But without: This was one of many points that Nathaniel Rich pointed out in his defense of Lord Rich before the Virginia Company in 1620. See "Sir Nathaniel Rich in defense of the Earl of Warwick (1620?)," *Manchester Papers*.

p. 87. The widower: "John Rolfe to Edwin Sandys, January 1620," Kingsbury, ed., *Rec. of the Va. Co.*

p. 87. Rolfe also pointed out: Ibid.

p. 88. But Lord Rich's version: "John Dutton to Lord Rich (1619)," *Manchester Papers*.

p. 88. Or why Captain Acuna: Contaduria, Archivo General de Indias (1619), Seville, trans. Sluiter, "New Light," *W&MQ.*

p. 88. In describing the arrival: "John Rolfe to Edwin Sandys, January 1620," Kingsbury, ed., *Rec. of the Va. Co.*

p. 89. In the same letter: "Rolfe to Sandys, January 1619/20," (see "In favor of C. Argal. That people ill-conditioned") Kingsbury, ed., *Rec. of the Va. Co.*, 3.

See also complaint of Lady Delaware against Rolfe and Argall presented to the Virginia Company on 10 July 1621 [Kingsbury, ed., *Rec. of the Va. Co.*]; the testimony of Capt. Edward Brewster linking Argall and Rolfe to stolen goods in a deposition taken 16 April 1622 in the lawsuits *Delaware v. Argall* and *Buckingham v. Argall* [Coldham, ed., "Voyage," *Va. Mag. of Hist. and Biog.* 87, no. 1 (January 1979): 47] in which, futhermore, Captain Brewster along with kinsman Richard Brewster claimed that Rolfe, while the colony's secretary-recorder, also destroyed certain depositions injurious to Argall and withheld other depositions in Virginia in 1618. [Coldham, ed., "Voyage," *Va. Mag. of Hist. and Biog.* 87, no. 1 (January 1979): 47, 49, 58–59.]

p. 90.   Governor Yeardley had removed: "(John) Delbridge (Yeardley). A Letter to Edwin Sandys [1619] Written soon after April 29, 1619," Kingsbury, ed., *Rec. of the Va. Co.* Yeardley was certainly aware of Argall's continuing influence in the colony after he fled, for he wrote: "I make shift so well as I can to wade through being in many things by argument opposed by those by who I should be strengthened, the reasons indeed being that they themselves, some of them, have been partakers in Argall's actions . . . and they won with the love of his good liquor."

p. 90.   One of the group: William Evans's friendship with John Rolfe included the disposal of Lord Delaware's goods that arrived on the *Neptune* in 1618. See Coldham, ed., "Voyage," *Va. Mag. of Hist. and Biog.* 87, no. 1 (January 1979): 36, 37. On headrights and the appearance on William Evans's plantation in Virginia of the African named "John Graweere," see Surry County deeds in endnotes for chapter 10.

p. 91.   According to Pory: "John Pory to Dudley Carleton, The Hague, September 1619," Kingsbury, ed., *Rec. of the Va. Co.* This letter Pory sent to Europe onboard the *White Lion*, which ship he refused to identify in his letter to Sandys in January 1620.

p. 92.   Hither she [the *Treasurer*]: Pory to Carleton, September 30, Kingsbury, ed., *Rec. of the Va. Co.* The conspirators, including Argall, had agreed early in the *Treasurer* investigation to shield Lord Rich by letting Argall take the blame. Under Rich's protection, the king would have virtually have had to go to war to arrest Argall, and James was not warlike. See John Dutton's letter to Lord Rich (Document 261 of the *Manchester Papers*) informing him of the *Treasurer*'s arrival in Bermuda in September 1619: "All which being before proclaimed yours by Elfrith and Thomas Foster, Mr. Rich's Deputy, were so received, *the Governor and myself* (till we know how far your Lordship would be seen in the business, in regard she was in question ere we left England) *labored to control that received opinion, declaring it was Captain Argall's unworthy boldness to use your Lordship's name as a bolster to his unwarrantable actions,* [italics added] when you but only out of love, at his request victualled out such a ship, nor was it safe for any man from misreport to dishonor an honorable man; *though indeed I,* dealing with Elfrith and the Purser (who hath delivered in his book of accompts which is sent you by the Governor ([Nathaniel Butler]), *found plainly how your Lordship was engaged in the business,* [italics added] which though I saw, I sparingly confessed how easy a matter it might be fore Captain Argall, of whom you were so confident, to abuse so noble a nature in persuading things were that were not answerable. So that having drawn them almost to a seeming belief of what I said, I added that things standing as they did and Captain Argall standing bound to answer what [Sandys] should do, *that your Lordship not mentioned, might through yourself and noble friends clear the business for them, which made party you could not do.* " [Italics added.] In Bermuda, Dutton's defense of Warwick by blaming Argall was remarkably similar on several points to Pory's defense of Warwick to Carleton in September 1619, and to Sandys in January 1620, by blaming Argall in Virginia. Both Pory and Dutton were Rich's agents. The scheme was successful. Lord Rich and his friends managed to delay the Virginia Company's prosecution of Argall for three years until nothing came of it, the company folded, and Argall received a knighthood from King James. Rich, however, lost the *Treasurer.*

p. 92.   When Pory was caught: "James City, John Pory to Edwin Sandys, January 13, 1620," Kingsbury, ed., *Rec. of the Va. Co.*

p. 92.   Historian Alexander Brown: Alexander Brown, *The First Republic in America* (Boston: Houghton Mifflin, 1898).

p. 93.   After being alerted: "John Dutton to the Earl of Warwick, 20 January 1619/1620," Ives, ed., *The Rich Papers, Letters from Bermuda* (Previously cited, University of Toronto, 141–42. Dutton, in this letter to Lord Rich, reported that Captain Elfrith, after "some exploit undoubtedly upon the Spaniards," sailed to Virginia but, because he did not find there "the entertainment he expected," he fled to Bermuda where Rich had plantations also.

p. 93.   Lord Rich and his: Craven, *Dissolution of the Virginia Company*, 131–32, citing Acts of the Privy Council, col. I, p. 30. Craven states: "There had been a break in Spanish influence at James' court since 1618, but the pro-Spanish group was now reasserting its control. Lord Digby, England's ambassador at Madrid who was in London at that time, was so strong in his denunciation of acts of hostility to Spain that he appeared in the eyes of his opponents to be nearer "the King of Spaines ambassador in England," and the famous Count Gondomar was already on his way from Spain when Sandys appearerd before the privy council. Under these circumstances it is not difficult to understand the resentment with which Warwick regarded such treatment."

p. 94.   The Earl of Southampton: Craven, *The Dissolution of the Virginia Company*, 134–35. Craven: "Rich declared that in the summer of 1619 he had heard of Yeardley's intention to examine Elfrith's crew under oath, and had complained to Lord Southampton that this was unjust. Southampton apparently left the impression that he agreed with him, even going so far as to declare that it would be nearer the Spanish Inquisition than the law of England to make men thus accuse themselves, and he suggested that Sandys should be urged to instruct Yeardley to refrain from any such procedure. Sandys too had left the impresion that he agreed with Southampton, and this of course had aggravated the injury to Warwick. Rich went further to claim that the Company was not under obligation to report the affair. The requirement, as he interpreted it, was that upon complaint by any offended prince the company must make restitution as demanded by the king, and that if such restitution were not made in the allotted time the company would lose royal protection. Therefore, he argued, 'we were not tied to complain against our own countrymen.' Another grievance arose from the fact that Warwick had asked for the return of his ship and goods [including the Africans of the *Bautista*] to England and had offered bond to be answerable for them. Sandys, howerver, alleged that it could not be done without first acquainting the privy council, which Rich felt 'was a courtesy would not have been denied the meanest merchant in Town.' [Nathaniel] Rich in fact could see nothing but ill affection to the earl in the whole of Sandys' actions, and complained that, had they been able to prove this business, Warwick would not only have been, 'in the mercy of our own king, but must have been brought under the clutches of the king of Spain which perhaps would not have been removed till he had crushed him to pieces. . . . ' "

p. 94.   Astounded at: Lord Rich and Nathaniel Rich in his defense [*Manchester Papers*] cited in Craven, *The Dissolution of the Virginia Company*, 134–35.

p. 94.   Lord Rich protested: Ibid.

p. 95.   Referring to: John Fiske, *Old Virginia and Her Neighbors* (Boston: The Riverside Press, 1897).

p. 95.   Ordered by James: Cited in Lyon Gardiner Tyler, ed., *The Discourse of the Old Company, 1625, Committee of the Privy Council* (New York: Charles Scribner's Sons, 1907). See also "Privy Council Register, An Order concerning the ship *Treasurer* and its offenses against Spaniards," *James I*, IV, 433, PRO, London. Kingsbury, ed., *Rec. of the Va. Co.*; Alexander Brown, *The First Republic in America* (Boston: Houghton Mifflin, 1898), 358.

p. 95.   Grieved by: Cited in Robert Baldick, *The Duel* (New York: Barnes & Noble, 1996, by arrangement with Harold Ober Associates), 63–65.

p. 96.   Several days later: A letter discovered in 1867 in the Duke of Manchester documents written in 1623 by Chichester and published in *Notes and Queries*: "Noble Lady, I came yesternight hither from the Court and found here your ladyship's letters expressing your great care of your absent lord. I likewise received the declaration made by Sir Dudley Carleton [English Ambassador at the Hague] of his receipt of the lord's letters and several others from me written to prevent the meeting of the Earl and Lord Cavendish, and of his care and directions given for the stay of the Duel; of which and the way the Earl took to get into the Netherlands. I would have advertised your Ladyship this morning but as I was putting my pen to the paper I was called to a meeting of the lords at Whitehall: and inquiring of my noble friends what they had heard of the earl, Mr. Secretary Calvert told me that he [Lord Rich] went from England in a small boat laden with salt, appareled like a merchant; and being inquired after by force of letters written to Mr. Trumball [legate for his Majesty at Brussels], he was found and stayed at Gaunt. Mr. Secretary tells me that upon knowledge thereof he wrote to such of his friends there as would assuredly deliver it to tell his lordship that the King required him to make his return home; and thinks he is upon his way hither;

when he comes, I wish his lordship to repair to his own house and by some of his friends to make known his being there unto the Earl Marshall, and to receive his lordship's orders and directions before he come abroad; for the King expects information from his lordship before his Majesty will give further directions concerning the Earl or the Lord Cavendish. Now that your Ladyship knows that your noble lord is so near his return, you will I hope leave to disquiet yourself as you have done by reason of his absence. With my best wishes, I kiss your fair hands, and am your ladyship's humble and faithful servant, Arthur Chichester, Holbourne, the 12th of August, 1623, To the right Honorable and most worthy Lady, the Countess of Warwick."

p. 96.   He presented: As Lord Rich and Sandys clashed, Rich allied with John Martin, an influential Virginia Company investor with his own complaint against the company. Martin's brother-in-law was Sir Julius Caesar, a powerful member of the king's Privy Council. Rich, Martin, and others were able to put the petition alleging "scandals" against Sandys, Southampton, and Cavendish before the king, and the response from James was immediate. Cited in Craven, *Dissolution of the Virginia Company*, 119.

p. 96.   King James investigated: Tyler, ed., *The Discourse of the Old Company*: "Order of the Privy Council: Upon complaint of the Earl of Warwick and the principal adventurers in the plantation of Virginia and the Somer Islands, who with the Virginia Company were directed to attend the Commissioners for examination into grievances and abuses of government against an impertinent declaration, containing bitter invectives and aspersions upon the Earl of Warwick and others, styled his instruments and agents. Lord Cavendish, Sir Edwin Sandys, Nicholas and John Ferrar of the Virginia Company, the chief actors in the inditing and penning thereof to be confined to their several houses until further order, as guilty of a contempt of the commands of the Council Table." Both Southampton and Sandys had been placed under house arrest by King James in 1620, during a national crisis that almost hastened the approaching civil war barely more than a decade away. Sandys and his allies fought back. Nathaniel Butler, an ally of Lord Rich, forced his way into a company meeting held by the Sandys faction and revealed to Rich's brother that "they blurred upon my Lord of Warwick in the point of the *Treasurer* and according to their wont, were brawling, loud and violent." At this meeting, Sir Sackville blasted the absent Lord Rich and his party as "Traitors to the Company." [Kingsbury, ed., *Rec. of the Va. Co.*]

p. 97.   To evade: Nathaniel Butler, *The Unmasked Face of Our Colony in Virginia* (n.p.: 1622).

p. 97.   William Camden had: William Camden, *Diary (1603–1623)*, Sutton, see www.philological.bham.ac.uk/diary.

p. 98.   James accused: "A Court Held for Virginia and ye Sumer Ilands on Wednesday in ye Afternoone the 7th of May 1623," Kingsbury, ed., *Rec. of the Va. Co.* In addition to the Africans (men and women variously described as being between twenty-five and twenty-nine in number) brought to Bermuda onboard the *Treasurer* in September 1619, the findings of the king's Privy Council read to the Virginia Company on 7 May 1623 also noted that an additional fourteen Africans were delivered to Bermuda that same year by the so-called "Dutch" ship (the *White Lion*) [in addition to the "20 and odd" Africans that vessel had traded in Jamestown at the end of August 1619]. Former acting Bermuda governor Miles Kendall claimed that Captain Jope of the *White Lion* traded the fourteen to him in exchange for supplies, but that they were later forcibly taken from him by Rich's agent Nathaniel Butler, who arrived in October 1619 to replace him as governor: "Now upon ye arrival of Capt. Butler, [Kendall] was forcibly by him deprived of all his said Negroes upon pretence that they belonged unto the Earl of Warwick's ship called the *Treasurer* with which the said Holland man of war had consorted. This outrage by Captain Butler upon ye goods of his predecessor so contrary to all Law and forms of Justice and without any order for ought ever appeared, enforced Capt. Kendall to return into England and to exhibit his complaint to the Company against Captain Butler, where it pleased the said Earl [of Warwick] to make claim in open Court, that the said Negroes were his, as belonging unto his ship the *Treasurer* aforesaid, and to cross Capt. Kendall in his just demand, certain Articles of Complaints were exhibited against him without author to avow them, and without witness to prove them which being referred unto examination in the Sumer Islands [Bermuda] where he that did him wrong was also to be his Judge was the cause that for a long while he got no restitution. About Mid summer 1622, the Court taking consideration of the wrong done to Captain Kendall; and the Earl of Warwick referring to his Claim to the judgment of the Court, it was ordered that nine of the same Negroes should be delivered to Capt. Kendall, and the rest to be consigned to ye Company's use which the new Governor Capt. Bernard lately deceased was required by his Instructions to put in execution. After whose decease by a letter there produced as from the said Earl importing that the said Negroes should not be delivered unto the said Kendall and upon advantage taken of mistaking the Hollander's name, the said restitution is still deferred and the poor gentleman still languishes under the effects of most unjust oppression; So weak are the Company's orders in that Plantation [Bermuda] if they come once to be countermanded by and mandate from his Lordship [the Earl of Warwick]."

Upon arriving in Bermuda and after conferring with Captain Daniel Elfrith, who was still grounded there because Kendall had seized the *Treasurer*, Governor Butler rejected Kendall's claim that he had purchased the fourteen Africans from "a Captain of Holland having Commission from the Prince of Orange" and immediately moved the Bantu prisoners from Kendall's custody to the plantation of absentee owner Lord Rich, on the basis that the Africans in fact "belonged to a Ship called the *Treasurer* set out from Virginia by Sir Samuel Argall then Governor." When Butler had first arrived in Bermuda in 1619, he'd claimed that fourteen Africans were brought by a pirate called Kirby: "Daniell Elfrie, who came in the *Treasurer* when she touched here in her voyage from Virginia to ye West Indies . . . is the very same man, whom Capt. Kendall furnished out with our care in requital whereof, he presented him with thus in Negars." In the same letter, Butler stated, "We have all the *Treasurer*'s company [crew]: the 14 Negoors left by Kirby, ye Dutchmen of ye wrack . . . all extraordinary and unlooked for Guests." He added, "After the distribution of the Negroes, I was informed by divers of the *Treasurer*'s men that the Negroes that came on the Frigate were never of the *Treasurer*'s Company, nor did belong unto her; but were stolen from one Youpe [Jope], a Dutchman, who had been abroad in these partes." This document distinquished between the Bantu arrived on the *Treasurer* and a second, smaller group delivered or "stolen" from Jope of the *White Lion*. Kendall, in an effort to retrieve the fourteen Africans, had sent a letter to Edwin Sandys in London in January 1620, asking him to use his influence with the Bermuda Company so that he might lease the *White Lion*'s Africans for five years, saying that they were originally intended for Jamestown but "accidentally happened upon our coasts here." See also "Miles Kendall to Sir Edwin Sandys, 18 January 1619/20," Kingsbury, ed., *Rec. of the Va. Co.* In September 1622, James Butler, on behalf of his brother Nathaniel and Lord Rich, filed a lawsuit in the Court of Bermuda against Miles Kendall, demanding the return of the fourteen Africans that Kendall claimed he had acquired from the *White Lion*. On April 15, 1623, Kendall wrote to Edwin Sandys "about my negros, the which for the redeeming of I solely rely upon God and your self: and for the scandals I hope I have by the country sufficiently lay cleared unless Butler's sycophants do there falsely sware against me as formerly they have done." The Bermuda Company, made up of essentially the same investors in the Virginia Company, awarded Kendall nine of the fourteen, ruling they had been delivered to Bermuda by a "Dutch ship" (in fact, the *White Lion*), whereupon Lord Rich went to court to get them back, claiming the Africans were the legal prize of his ship (the *Treasurer*) and had not been purchased by Kendall from any "Dutch ship." King James cited the Africans acquired by Kendall from the White Lion as well as the other Africans taken from the Spanish slaver and delivered to Jamestown and Bermuda by the White Lion and the Treasurer, as evidence that, in its divisive feud with Lord Rich over the legal ownership of the Africans, the Virginia Company was derelict in its adminstration of the colony and was engaging in illegal trade with pirates who seized Africans from a Spanish slave ship in violation of his treaty with Spain, and on those grounds should be dissolved.

p. 98. Sandys and Cavendish: "James I. A letter to the Speaker of the House of Commons, April 28, 1624," State Papers, Domestic, James I, 163, no. 71, London, PRO, cited in Kingsbury, ed., *Rec. of the Va. Co.*

p. 99. According to: Craven, *Dissolution of the Virginia Company*, 127, 130, 140.

Chapter 7 : The Black Knight's Last Pawn

p. 102. The unavoidable fact: Britain's urban crowding was further aggravated by a disastrous new agrarian policy called Enclosure. To compete in the international wool trade, England in the sixteenth century began closing off common lands, on which village peasants had raised crops for generations, to make private pastures for the sheep of wealthy wool exporters. As a result, unemployed plowboys migrated to the cities by the tens of thousands, and in London made what one observer called a flourishing class of "sturdy beggars." Along with skyrocketing domestic unemployment made even worse by additional floods of white refugees pouring in daily from the Counter-Reformation wars on the Continent, Queen Elizabeth struggled with the blight caused by modern industrialization. King James, an avid hunter who preferred to spend most of his reign in the healthier atmosphere of the countryside, would describe London as a "filthy toun." Above that city's jungle of chimneys hung a perpetual cloud of thick black smoke so heavy that at times it created its own weather. Dodging carts and wagons in the manure-choked streets below, Protestant Dutch, French, and German refugees jostled elbow to elbow with native-born housewives, cobblers, coopers, farmers, apprentices, carpenters, clerks, seamstresses, bakers, sailors, actors, gamblers, vagrants, highwaymen, prostitutes, and cutpurses. Filth, overextended utilities, and unchecked migration bred disease and urban decay. Plagues killed thousands. Periodic fires destroyed entire city blocks and still no natural force could stem the unwanted tide of immigrants arriving in London daily.

p. 102.   Each prison: Geffray Mynshull, *Essays and Characters of a Prison and Prisoners* (n.p.: 1618).

p. 103.   His crew starving: "John Rolfe to Edwin Sandys, January 1620," Kingsbury, ed., *Rec. of the Va. Co.*

p. 104.   Sir Yeardley's will: See "Will of Governor Sir George Yeardley, 12 October 1627, proved 14 February 1628," Gerry Hammond, ed., www.genforum.genealogy.com/yardley. Hammond: "The witnesses were Abraham Peirsey, Susanna Hall and William Clayborne, Scr. A codicil, dated 29 Oct. 1627, was witnessed by the same scrivener. Commission to administer on the estate of Sir George Yeardley, late in Virginia, deceased, was issued 14 March, 1627–8, to his brother Ralph Yeardley during the absence of the widow, relict, Temperance Yeardley, in the parts beyond the sea, &c. Admon Act Book for 1628. From the Calendar of State Papers, Colonial Series (London: 1860), we learn that Governor Francis West and the Council of Virginia certified to the Privy Council, 20 December 1627, the death of Governor Sir George Yeardley and the election of Captain Francis West to succeed him in the government. In July, 1629, Edmund Rossingham sent in a petition to the Privy Council stating that he was agent to his uncle Sir George Yeardley, late Governor of Virginia, who dying before any satisfaction was made to the petitioner for being a chief means of raising his estate to the value of six thousand pounds, Ralph Yeardley, the brother, took administration of the same."

p. 105.   So when: Nell Marion Nugent, *Cavaliers and Pioneers: Abstracts of the Virginia Land Patents and Grants, 1623–1800* [hereafter known as *Cavaliers and Pioneers*], spons. by Virginia Land Office, Richmond, VA (Richmond, VA: Dietz Publishing Co., 1934, repr. Baltimore: Genealogical Publishing Co., 1963), vol. 1. Argoll Yeardley married Sarah, daughter of John Custis of Northampton County, Virginia.

p. 105.　Yet four years later: Edward D. Neill, "The Colony Under the Rule of Charles I and Charles II, 1625–1685," *Virginia Carolorum* (Albany, NY: Joel Munsell's Sons, 1886). See also British State Papers, Colonial Series, *Sainsbury Abstracts for 1629*, Virginia State Library, Richmond. See also T. H. Breen, *Myne Owne Ground*, 58. According to Breen, Jamestown settler Thomas Parks told guests at the home of Nathaniel Littleton that the late governor Sir George Yeardley "was no gentleman, at least he had not been one in England. In fact, he had worked only as a tailor in a '*Stall in Burchin Lane in London*.' " A contemporary, Chamberlain, described Yeardley as a "a mean fellow." Just before sailing to Virginia to become governor in 1619, James knighted Yeardley in Newmarket. The honor, according to Chamberlain, "hath set him so high, that he flaunts it up and down the streets in extraordinary bravery, with fourteen or fifteen fair liveries after him."

p. 106.　When Yeardley: Citing transcript from the Virginia General Court, 1625 [M. E. Lender and J. K. Martin, *Drinking in America—A History* (New York: The Free Press, 1982)].

p. 107.　A possible clue: "A Court Held for Virginia and ye Sumer Ilands on Wednesday in ye Afternoone the 7th of May 1623," Kingsbury, ed., *Rec. of the Va. Co.*

p. 108.　When Piersey died: British State Papers, Colonial Series, *Sainsbury Abstracts 1633*, "Abraham Piersey," Virginia State Library, Richmond.

p. 108.　Mathews, a Puritan: In a deposition taken on 27 April 1622, Samuel Mathews (then of "Arowttox in the Countrie of Virginia") testified that the "*Treasurer* came to land passengers in Virginia and then to trade and fish for the relief of the English colony in Virginia." See *Buckingham v. Argall* and *Delaware v. Argall* in Coldham, ed., "Voyage," *Va. Mag. of Hist. and Biog.* The *Treasurer* had in fact, *not* come to Virginia in 1618 to 1619 to fish, as Mathews well knew. Mathews's support of the Puritan leader Lord Robert Rich likely contributed to his future troubles with Gondomar's agent, John Harvey, over ownership of the *White Lion* Africans, as will be seen.

p. 108.　Coming from: See Thornton, "African Experience," *W&MQ.*

p. 108.　Ferrar wrote: David R. Ransome, ed., *Ferrar Papers, 1590–1790* (Cambridge, UK: Magdalene College, Microform Academic Publishers, 1993).

p. 109.　Native skills: When, for example, Jamestown planter Francis Pott was overwhelmed by debt in October 1646, he informed his nephew John Pott, who was overseeing his plantation, that as he was in the "saddest condition that ever I was in," John was to pay off his bills with tobacco, cattle, goods, and even land, only "reserving my said Negros or what you can of them; for I had rather part with any thing or all that I have besides, than with my Negroes." Northampton County, Virginia, records cited by J. Douglas Deal, *Race and Class in Colonial Virginia—Indians, Englishmen, and Africans on the Eastern Shore During the Seventeenth Century* (New York & London: Garland Publishing, 1993), 280.

p. 110.　The overburdened streets: Scholars generally agree that between 1607 and 1625, about seven thousand people had come from England and other parts of Europe to live in Jamestown, yet only one-seventh (twelve hundred men, women, and children) of the colony's population remained alive in 1625, according to the Virginia census of that year. See Dorman, ed., *Adventurers*, vol. 1.

p. 110.   The company would: Cited in James Truslow Adams, *The Founding of New England* (New York: Atlantic Monthly Press, 1921); H. E. Egerton, citing Garnett, in *Origin and Growth of Greater Britain* (Oxford: Clarendon Press, 1903), 107.

p. 111.   It was notoriously: Arber, ed., *Captain John Smith, 1608–1631*.

p. 111.   Ferrar, in 1649: David R. Ransome, ed., *Ferrar Papers, 1590–1790*.

p. 112.   Ferrar charged that: Peter Thompson, "William Bullock's 'Strange Adventure': A Plan to Transform Seventeenth Century Virginia," *W&MQ* 1, no. 61 (January 2004), citing Peter Peckard, *Memoirs of the Life of Mr. Nicholas Ferrar;* and *Virginia Impartially Examined;* and John Ferrar's authorship of *A Perfect Description of Virginia*.

p. 112.   Hoping to clear: "Sir Nathaniel Rich in defense of the Earl of Warwick, 1620," Kingsbury, ed., *Rec. of the Va. Co.* In June 1619, Sandys received a letter from Governor Yeardley in Virginia stating that the *Treasurer* was at sea on the orders of Lord Rich to engage in piracy against the Spaniards. Sandys put the matter before the Virginia Company, which advised Sandys to report the rumor to the king's Privy Council but with no direct reference to Lord Rich. This done, the "business was dismissed without prejudice to any," and the matter was dropped. Then in early 1620 just before Lent, Yeardley wrote Sandys that the *Treasurer* had returned to Virginia after fleeing to Bermuda in the previous year and that he had captured some of her crew who confessed that the ship had been robbing Spaniards in the West Indies. Yeardley informed Sandys that he intended to interrogate the captured crewmembers, "whereby the poor souls might be brought to accuse themselves capitally." Even Lord Southampton agreed that forcing them to implicate themselves was unjust when the victim (Spain) had not yet protested, and therefore the company decided that it would be foolish to "complain against our own countrymen." The firm instead moved to settle the matter quietly between Rich, Southampton, and Sandys, under the arbitration of Lord Zouch and the bishop of London; the rivals were then to enter "some Church in London" to "receive the Communion together in confirmation of their mutual accord." However, Sandys stunned Lord Rich by releasing the information to the Spanish ambassador and the king's Privy Council.

p. 113.   A week later: See "May 15, 1620," Meeting of the Virginia Company, Kingsbury, ed., *Rec. of the Va. Co.*, "Wheras this day was appointed by order of Court for hearing ye cause between Capt. Argall and Capt. Brewster, the said Capt. Brewster made his appearance and desired to be heard, but forasmuch as Capt. Argall was absent, and in his behalf was alleged that he desired to be excused in somuch that he was appointed to atend the Spanish Ambassador, the Court upon the request of the said Capt. Brewster deferred it till Friday afternoon next. . . ."

p. 113.   According to: "Extraordinary Court of the Virginia Company, May 23, 1620," Kingsbury, ed., *Rec. of the Va. Co.*

p. 114.   Made aware: Abstracts in the High Court of Admiralty (HCA), cited in Coldham, ed., *English Adventurers and Emigrants*, 1609–1660, 181–2.

p. 114.   Subpoenaed by: Coldham, ed., *English Adventurers and Emigrants, 1609–1660*, 181–2.

p. 114.   Samuel Mathews had been: See deposition of Richard Brewster taken on April 27, 1622 in *Delaware v. Argall*, Coldham, ed., "Voyage," *Va Mag. of Hist. and Biog.* 87, no. 1 (January 1979): 58. Testified Brewster: "Mathews came thither over [to Jamestown] as a servant to Sheriff Johnson of London and the deft Argall made him a Capteine and the said Mathews lived but a while in James Towne but went to live in Sherly hundred and there looked to some few men of the said Sheriff Johnson's and afterwardes went to a place called Harryhattock where the said deft [Argall] gave the said Mathews to command of men & made him Capteine of them." Argall in 1619 had promoted the Puritan Mathews from a lowly servant to captain, launching his start to wealth and power. Mathew's son would become governor of Virginia after King Charles I was captured and executed, when the Puritans held power in England.

p. 115.   Despite the lucrative: All of the country of England could fit between the Appalachians and the Atlantic, and this seemed the extent of the English curiosity of North America—their comfort zone. Englishmen, peerless at sea, seemed reluctant to venture into the unknown North American interior, unlike the French, Spanish, Angolans, Germans, Swedes, Norwegians, Scots, Irish, and Welsh. The first technically English subject to explore as far away as the Appalachians was a German, John Lederer, who complained that he could not persuade any Englishman at Jamestown to accompany him. Daniel Boone, James Mooney, and other Scots, Irish, and Welshmen were the first English subjects to travel through the Cumberland Gap into present Tennessee and Kentucky. Lewis and Clark, two Welshmen, were the first Americans to cross over the continent, sent by another Welshman, Thomas Jefferson. The first Baptist missionary to travel west of the Mississippi was a black man, Joseph Willis. The English covered the coast from New England to the Carolinas but rarely settled farther than a few hundred miles inland. The United States, though English speaking, is not an ethnically English country.

p. 115.   About this time: Cited in "A Paper read before the Maryland Historical Society, April 14, 1884," by Lewis W. Wilhelm, Johns Hopkins University, *Maryland Historical Society*, vol. 4 (Baltimore: Fund Publications, 1880–1884), 16–20.

p. 117.   The historian Herbert L. Osgood: Herbert L. Osgood, *The American Colonies in the Seventeenth Century* [hereafter known as *American Colonies*] (New York: Columbia University Press, 1904–1907), vol. 3, part 4, chap. 4, 96–102.

p. 117.   Many of the royal: Ibid.

p. 117.   John Ferrar recalled: Ransome, ed., *Ferrar Papers*; Thompson, "William Bullock's 'Strange Adventure,' " *W&MQ*.

p. 118.   Ferrar, who: Ibid.

p. 118.   To bypass: Osgood, *American Colonies*, vol. 3, part 4, chap. 4, 96–102.

p. 120.   The councilors: Ibid.

p. 121.   Sir, there: Ibid.

p. 121.   Then Mathews: Ibid.; see also Thomas J. Wertenbaker, *Virginia Under the Stuarts, 1607–1688* (Princeton University Press, 1914), and J. Mills Thornton III, "The Thrusting out of Governor Harvey: A Seventeenth Century Rebellion," *Va. Mag. of Hist. and Biog.*76 (1968): 11–26.

p. 122.   Harvey sailed: The Star Chamber, a kind of secret homeland security agency, was also used by the Tudor and Stuart kings to suppress political dissidents until abolished by the Long Parliament in 1641. See Samuel Rawson Gardiner, *History of England, 1603–1642.*

p. 122.   While Mathews: "For Joshua Mullard and Elizabeth his wife, widow of William Holmes, Gent. Deceased," *Examination in Equity Cases*, vol. 53, cited in Coldham, *English Adventurers and Emigrants 1609–1660*, 89.

p. 122.   Mr. Kemp: In 1639, Harvey turned over twelve Africans to George Menefie, one of Mathews's comrades who had sailed with him in 1637 to England to answer Harvey's charges. Morton, *Colonial Virginia*, vol. 1, 142; *Calender of State Papers, Colonial Series, 1574–1660*, 256. See also Nugent, *Cavaliers and Pioneers*, vol. 1, 128.

PART III: THE FOUNDERS SEEK FREEDOM

p. 125.   In the words: Georges Balandier, *Daily Life in the Kingdom of Kongo: Sixteenth to Eighteenth Century*, trans. Helen Weaver (London: George Allen and Unwin, 1968), 253, cited in Brown, *West-Central African Nature Spirits in the South Carolina Low Country.* According to Ras Michael Brown, the Bantu believed the spirits of their ancestors made their graves important to descendents who "hoped to receive blessings in return for the attention and landmarks of identity in that a person's country was where his ancestors were buried."

Chapter 8 : The First Martyr

p. 127.   Born in Angola: Regarding the early church in Angola, John Thornton, in e-mail message, used with permission of author. See also John Thornton, "Central African Names and African American Naming Patterns," *William & Mary Quarterly* 50, no. 4:727–42. Seventeenth-century records of names of exported African prisoners on file in Luanda reveal a mixture of Christians and non-Christians. Catholic priests arrived in Angola a century before the fall of Kabasa in 1618 to 1619, and many regions of Angola had converted prior to enslavement and colonization. Black Angolan Christians are documented as being captured by the Imbangala and sold to Portuguese, Dutch, and other European slavers. Thornton writes, concerning evidence of voluntary versus compulsory baptism as determined by Angolan naming patterns: "This is clearly revealed in John Pedro's name, which combined two first names. In central Africa it was a long established custom to give a child a given name and the given name of his father as a second element. Already in the sixteenth century this system was being applied to Christian names, resulting in such patterns as Joao Pedro, Manuel Afonso, Maria Joao, etc. These names are very common in Angola today as well, although the second name has now become a surname and is passed on along in that way. The patterns of naming that are revealed in New Amsterdam also fit this pattern. Joyce Goodfriend documented the pattern without realizing its Angolan roots. A good example is: Emanuel van Angola and Phizithiaen d'Angool married at DRC New Amsterdam, 16 February 1642. Son was Nicolaes Emanuel, baptized 22 August 1649, from the Reformed Church marriage registers. Note that Emanuel the father's name becomes the second name of Nicolaes."

p. 127.   Like Yeardley: See testimony of Richard Stafford in Count Gondomar's investigation of the Bautista affair in Coldham, ed., *English Adventurers and Emigrants* 1609-1660, 181.

p. 128.   However, Captain Elfrith: "John Dutton to the Earl of Warwick, 17 October 1620," *Rich Papers*. Dutton, Rich's agent in Bermuda, warned him that the *Treasurer*'s records directly connected the earl to piracy: "I, dealing with Elfrith and the Pursuer who had delivered in his book of accompts which is sent you by the Governor, found plainly how your Lordship was engaged in the business." The accounts to which Dutton referred were sent to Rich by Governor Butler on 9 October 1620, and contain details about the *Treasurer* and the fourteen Africans. ["Nathaniel Butler to the Earl of Warwick, 9 October 1620," *Rich Papers*]. Butler again referred to the Africans in another letter that year ["Governor Nathaniel Butler," *Rich Papers*]. Dutton also warned Rich "not to have any thing to do with Captain Kendall who is now come out, who your Lordship should find a very silly man, but a fitt instrument for Sir Edwin Sandys to use in the abuse of your honor if he be so inclined."

p. 128.   Butler wrote: "Butler to Warwick, October 9, 1620" *Manchester Papers*. See also "Gov. Nathaniel Butler to Sir Nathaniel Rich, 23 October 1620"; and "Governor Nathaniel Butler (early 1620?)," *Manchester Papers*. See also Craven, *Dissolution of the Virginia Company*, 134–35.

p. 129.   Bermuda, said: "Court of the Virginia Company, May 31, 1620," Kingsbury, ed., *Rec. of the Va. Co.*

p. 129.   Governor Butler organized: Coldham, ed., *English Adventurers and Emigrants, 1609–1660*, 15–16. See also Mendel Peterson, "Reach for the New World," *National Geographic* 152, no. 6 (December 1977).

p. 130.   As he had promised: "Barker v Nathaniel Butler, 29 Sept 1624," Coldham, ed., *English Adventurers and Emigrants, 1609–1660*, 15–16.

p. 130.   Five weeks later: The conclusion that John Pedro, Antonio, Maria, and other Africans were sent to Lord Rich in England in 1621 rests on several documents. First, Governor Butler in 1620 promised he would send them to Rich, in England, in one year. "Butler to Warwick, October 9, 1620," *Manchester Papers*. Since Butler himself had to flee Bermuda in 1621 to avoid arrest, he had no reason not to fulfil his pledge to his patron by leaving the Africans in Bermuda, where either the investigators of the Virginia Company or of the king's Privy Council would have found and questioned them regarding piracy allegations against Rich and Butler. Second, the ships that brought John Pedro, Antonio, and Maria to Virginia—Antonio in 1621, on the *James*; Maria on the *Margaret and John* in 1622; John Pedro in 1623 on the *Swan* (the *Swan* often confused with a Bermuda ship of the same name)—were all ships leased to Lord Rich or his business partners, and all sailed from England: the *James* and the *Margaret and John* sailed from London. See "Barker v Nathaniel Butler, 29 Sept 1624," Coldham, ed., *English Adventurers and Emigrants, 1609–1660*, 15–16. See also by ship listing at www.english-america.com/index, the Web site *English America—The Voyages, Vessels, People & Places*, compiled by Thomas Langford, 2003, citing the Virginia Muster, 7 February 1624/5 from *The Original Lists of Persons of Quality; Emigrants; Religious Exiles; Political Rebels; Serving Men Sold for a Term of Years; Apprentices; Children Stolen; Maidens Pressed; and Others Who Went from Great Britain to the American Plantations 1600–1700*, as recorded in the State Paper Department of Her Majesty's Public Record Office, England, ed. John Camden Hotten (London: Chatto and Windus, 1874, repr. New York: G. A. Baker & Co., 1931); Martha Woodroof Hiden, comp. and ed., *Adventurers of Purse and Person 1607–1625*, spons. by the Order of First Families of Virginia, 1607–1620 (Princeton, NJ: Princeton University Press, 1956); Nell Marion Nugent, comp., *Cavaliers and Pioneers; Abstracts of the Virginia Land Patents and Grants, 1623–1800*, spons. by Virginia Land Office, Richmond, VA (Richmond, VA: Dietz Publishing Co., 1934, repr. Baltimore: Genealogical Publishing Co., 1963); Peter Wilson Coldham, ed., *The Complete Book of Emigrants, 1607–1776* (Baltimore: Genealogical Publishing Co., 1988). The presence in 1623 of half a dozen Africans at Warrosquoke, Virginia, with the Latin names Francisco and Antonio imply they were either delivered by the *Treasurer* in 1619, or that they were first taken to Bermuda after the *Bautista* attack and then shipped by Butler to England in 1621 and later shipped by Lord Rich to Virginia at different times. Warrosquoke was originally settled by Lord Rich's allies and business associates, including Francis West and the Puritans Edward Bennett and Richard Wiseman, who placed over six hundred immigrants there. The enmity between Lord Rich and Edwin Sandys, Miles Kendall, and George Yeardley makes it unlikely that the Africans at Warrosquoke were from among the "20 and odd" Bantu acquired by Yeardley and Piersey in late August 1619. Furthermore, both Yeardley and Piersey placed all of those Africans on their own private and public lands and did not trade them to other planters. That the Africans from the *Treasurer*'s share of the *Bautista* booty were specifically sent to Lord Rich's sprawling estate of Leighs Prior in Felsted, England, is supported by documentation that Lord Rich also hid religious dissidents at Leighs Priory who were being persecuted by Archbishop William Laud. See endnote in chapter 2 citing Edward Hyde, first Earl of Clarendon, *History of the Rebellion in England*.

p. 131.   In 1621, Rich: Coldham, ed., *English Adventurers and Emigrants, 1609–1660*, 15. The *James*, sailing out of Bermuda, London, Southampton, and Virginia, was owned by Edmund Barker & Co., and from 1621 to 1622 was leased to Governor Nathaniel Butler and the Bermuda Company, in which Warwick was chief investor.

p. 131.   In 1618, King James: See J. W. Blake, "The Farm of the Guinea Trade," *Essays in British and Irish History in Honour of James Eadie Todd* (London: Cronne, Moody and Quinn, 1949), 86–106.

p. 132.   Angry that: "The Extraordinary Courte Held the 20th of March 1620," Kingsbury, ed., *Rec. of the Va. Co.* Lord Rich stopped attending Virginia Company shareholders' meetings in 1620. Ferdinando Georges (a.k.a. "Gorges"), along with Sir Nathaniel Rich, loyal kinsman of Lord Rich, assisted Samuel Argall in answering charges of piracy to the Virginia Company in 1620. Georges had been the admiral of Plymouth, England, in 1605 when Captain George Weymouth returned to that port city along with five captured Native Americans, boasting about the region now known as New England, and attracting Georges' interest. With friends, Ferdinando Georges, a thorough Englishman despite his Latinate name, managed to convince King James to grant the Plymouth, or North Virginia, Company, a charter for the northern part of North America at the same time he granted a charter to the Virginia Company of London in 1606. The regions of those two charters overlapped at present-day New York and Pennsylvania, and the two companies had to promise not to build a settlement within one hundred miles of each other. The first venture of the Plymouth Company, the Popham colony, failed in 1609, and the firm held its northern charter for six years in name only. In 1615, Georges sent John Smith to attempt a second venture in New England but it never got off the ground; Smith was unsuccessful in stirring interest in London in 1616, at which time he also reunited with Pocahontas. Georges then concentrated on exploiting the Cape Cod fisheries until 1620, when along with Robert Rich, Earl of Warwick, the Duke of Buckingam and the earls of Lennox, Southampton, and Pembroke, and other investors making up the Council for New England (a.k.a. the New England, or Plymouth Company), forty patentees in all, he got King James to reissue a new charter encompassing lands from present-day Quebec to Philadelphia, with broad monopolies, this new charter also being independent of the Virginia Company of London. The perquisite of New England fishing rights in particular angered certain of the Virginia Company and its investors, of whom a significant part were Members of Parliament who were already challenging King James on royal monopolies. The records of the Virginia Company show Sir Ferdinando Georges attempting to clear Lord Robert Rich and Samuel Argall of the African piracy charges presented by the Virginia Company while at the same time attempting to oust the Virginia Company from fishing in New England. Unable to place a Virginia Company–owned Jamestown-type settlement in New England (Lord Rich opposed company towns ruled from London and gave colonies freedom to run their own affairs), the Council for New England instead leased or sold land to various merchant ventures, such as the group that represented the Pilgrims. The council's loose, antimeddling, anti-Jamestown, "give them a free ticket and they will come" policy was successful. The Pilgrims had landed in New England in 1620 without permission and were actually trespassing for a few months until the Pierce venture group obtained permission for them to settle from the New England Company in 1621.

p. 133.   Lord Rich's grant: *Federal and State Constitutions Colonial Charters, and Other Organic Laws of the States, Territories, and Colonies Now or Heretofore Forming the United States of America*, compiled under Act of Congress of 30 June 1906 by Francis Newton Thorpe (Washington, DC: Government Printing Office, 1909).

p. 133.   Learning that: William Bradford, *Of Plymouth Plantation* (circa 1650), in William T. Davis, ed., *Bradford's History of Plymouth Plantation, 1606–1646* (New York: Charles Scribner's Sons, 1908). William Bradford reported that Weston urged the Pilgrims "not to meddle with ye Dutch [of New Amsterdam] [and] not too much to depend on ye Virginia Company."

p. 133.   In his memoirs: Sir Ferdinando Gorges, *A Brief Narration of the Originall Undertakings of the Advancement of Plantations Into the Parts of America* (London: 1658).

p. 133.   Pilgrim leader: Bradford, *Of Plymouth Plantation* (n.p.: 1650).

p. 134.   Lord Rich took: *State Papers, Colonial Series 1574–1660*, 17, 25.

p. 134.   Meanwhile, the Pilgrims: The first Pierce Patent was issued to the Merchant Adventurers group in 1620 by the Virginia Company of London. Because the Pilgrims settled beyond the Virginia Company's grant, the Merchant Adventurers in London requested a second "Pierce Patent" from the newly organized New England Council, which was granted in June 1621, authorizing the Pilgrim settlement in Massachusetts. As the Earl of Warwick and a principal investor in the New England Council, Lord Robert Rich, along with Ferdinand Georges, signed the Pilgrims' patent. Pilgrim William Bradford, as noted above, indicates that the Pilgrims knew what they were doing; they did not land at Cape Cod by accident, nor were they deceived by Thomas Weston to settle beyond the Virginia Company.

p. 134.   Having avenged: "Captain Thomas Jones," 17 July 1622, London PRO: "A motion was made in the behalf of Captain Thomas Jones, Captain of the [ship] *Discovery*, now employed in Virginia for trade and fishing that he may be admitted a freeman in this [New England] Company in reward of the good service he hath there performed. The Court liked well of the motion and condescended thereunto."

p. 135.   Rich bailed: "Rowland Golde v. John Burfitt," Coldham, ed., *English Adventurers and Emigrants, 1609–1660*, 11 and "July 29, 1640, John Couchman v John Beale," 107. Placed in command of Rich's ship *Discovery* in 1621, Captain Thomas Jones received a commission to fish in Cape Cod and to trade furs. The previous year as master of the *Falcon*, Jones delivered sassafras from Jamestown to England in a deal between Lord Rich and Captain William Tucker of Point Comfort, whose servants included the Africans Antonio and Isabella, who had been sold to him in Virginia from the *Treasurer* in August 1619. Tucker was the brother-in-law of Lord Rich's business manager, Maurice Thomson, who was listed as part owner of the *Falcon*.

p. 135.   According to: Edward Winslow, *Good Newes from New England* (n.p.: 1624). Text posted online by Caleb Johnson, 1998, can be accessed at www.members.aol.com/calebj/bibliography.html.

p. 136.   The Pilgrims soon: Ibid.

p. 137. By the winter: Thomas Morton, *New England Canaan* (n.p.: 1637).

p. 137. Edward Winslow: Winslow, *Good Newes from New England.*

p. 137. Safely at home: Ibid.

p. 138. Winslow, however: Ibid.

p. 138. He was there: Virginia Davis, *Tidewater Virginia Families–A Social History* (Baltimore: Clearfield Company, 1989). See also Mario Valdes, "The Patriss Family," PBS, www.pbs.org/wgbh/pages/frontline/shows/secret/june/april12.html.

p. 139. Captain West sent word: The 1624/25 Virginia Census cited in Dorman, ed., *Adventurers*, vol. 1; see also Davis, *Tidewater Virginia Families—A Social History.*

p. 139. Lord Delaware and: Despite the fact that Lady Delaware, the widow of his deceased brother Lord Deleware, was suing Lord Rich's agents Samuel Argall and John Rolfe for stealing her late husband's trade goods in 1618, Captain Francis West remained loyal to Rich, who was a powerful promoter of America colonization. Subpoenaed to testify in *Buckingham v. Argall* and *Delaware v. Argall* on 4 May 1622, Captain West stated that Argall's arch-foe, Edward Brewster, was, according to Coldham's summary of the transcription, "not well liked in Virginia because of his harsh dealings with the planters in former times." [Coldham, ed., "Voyage," *Va. Mag. of Hist. and Biog.* 87, no. 1 (January 1979): 62.] Immediately after testifying in 1622, West was made Rich's admiral for New England; he was also in possession of John Pedro, one of the Africans from Rich's *Treasurer.*

p. 140. It would be decades before . . . soldier at Fort Algernon: The 1624/5 Virginia Census, cited in Dorman, ed., *Adventurers*, vol. 1.

p. 141. Though Parliament: Gardiner, *History of England.*

p. 141. English peasants: Rich, cited by Gardiner, *History of England.*

p. 142. On July 3: Ibid.

p. 144. As John Thornton states: John Thornton, by e-mail, used by permission. Jesuit priests who came in 1575 translated a catechism into the Kimbundu language for the growing number of Mbundu converts, as they had previously for Bakongo converts in the Kikongo language.

p. 145. Jesuit Andrew White: Andrew White, *Relatio Itineris in Marylandiam* (Baltimore: Maryland Historical Society Fund, 1874).

p. 147. The High Court: Cited in Gardiner, *History of England.*

p. 149. Two of the Parliament: J. C. Long, *Maryland Adventure: A Story of the Battle of Severn* (Philadelphia: John C. Winston Company, 1956).

p. 150. The Protestants had: Long, *Maryland Adventure.*

p. 150. After Stone: William Eltonhead and family had moved from Virginia to Maryland. For Maryland notes and land records, see Maryland State Archives, including volume 0003, *Proceedings*, at www.djs.state.md.us/megafile/msa/speccol/sc2900/sc2908/html/search.

p. 150. Muskets flashed: Long, *Maryland Adventure*; Mario Valdes, by e-mail, used with permission; Davis, *Tidewater Virginia Families–A Social History.* According to Valdes, one account of the execution mistakenly listed John Pedro as a "German," a mistranslation of *[Ne]ger man.* Documents from Virginia and Maryland reveal only one John Pedro in the colonies before 1660:

the African John Pedro listed as a "Neger" in the muster of Francis West in 1624, who later acquired land in Lancaster County in the early 1650s. Furthermore, John Pedro of Angola was Catholic, and the likelihood that a German Catholic John Pedro had entered into the colony undocumented, only to fall at the Severn, is remote. The Puritans covered up much of what happened that day, to prevent Cromwell and Lord Baltimore from punishing them; in that process, the identity of John Pedro was deliberately obscured.

Chapter 9 : Two Save the Colony

p. 152.   The massacre: Rev. Samuel Purchas, *Hakluytus Posthumous or Purchas His Pilgrims* (London: 1622).

p. 153.   However, the English: John Smith, *The generall historie of Virginia*, vol. 1. One example of Jamestown settlers undermining Powhatan's authority is the treaty with the Chickahominie, soon after the kidnapping of Pocahontas, in which the natives agreed to be "New Englishmen," subject to King James: "When the appointed day came, Sir Thomas Dale and Captaine Argall with fiftie men well appointed, went to Chickahamania, where we found the people expecting our coming, they used us kindly, and the next morning sat in counsell, to conclude their peace upon these conditions: Articles of Peace. First, they should for ever be called Englishmen, and be true subjects to King James and his Deputies. Secondly, neither to kill nor detaine any of our men, nor cattle, but bring them home. Thirdly, to be alwaies ready to furnish us with three hundred men, against the Spaniards or any. Fourthly, they shall not enter our towns, but send word they are new Englishmen. Fifthly, that every fighting man, at the beginning of harvest, shall bring to our store two bushels of Corne, for tribute, for which they shall receive so many Hatchets. Lastly, the eight chiefe men should see all this performed, or receive the punishment themselves: for their diligence they should have a red coat, a copper chaine, and King James his picture, and be accounted his Noblemen. All this they concluded with a general assent, and a great shout to confirme it: then one of the old [Chickahominie] men began an Oration, bending his speech first to the old men, then to the young, and then to the women and children, to make them understand how strictly they were to observe these conditions, and *we would defend them from the furie of Powhatan*, [italics added] or any enemie whatsoever, and furnish them with Copper, Beads, and Hatchets; *but all this was rather for fear Powhatan and we, being so linked together, would bring them againe to his subjection; the which to prevent, they did rather choose to be protected by us, than tormented by him, whom they held a Tyrant* [italics added]. And thus wee returned againe to James towne." Though forced to a temporary peace by his daughter's abduction, Powhatan continued to seethe in anger over this and other blatant incidents of English usurpation of his kingdom.

p. 154.   Subsequently, he: Rountree, *Pocahontas's People*. Powhatan's successor, by Algonquian custom, should have been his brother Opitchapan. Powhatan's scheme to be succeeded by one of his descendants failed to overthrow tradition, and Opitchapan was made weroance instead, though he was overshadowed by the more forceful personality of Opechancanough.

p. 154. He refused: John Smith, *Travels and Works*, vol. 1:121–25.

p. 155. On the day: Smith, *The generall historie of Virginia*,. vol. 1. Citing Captain Nathaniel Powell as his source, Smith wrote of the Jamestown settlers' dissension over arming natives, that "Captain Yeardley (as acting deputy governor of Virginia, 1616–1617) had a Savage or two so well trained up to their pieces (firearms), they were as expert as any of the English, and one he kept purposely to kill him fowl. There were divers others (Englishmen) had Savages in like manner for their men. Thus we lived together, as if we had been one people, all the time Captaine Yeardley stayed with us, but such grudges and discontents daily increased among our selves, that upon the arrivall of Captaine Argall, sent by the Councell and Companie to be our Governour, Captaine Yeardley returned for England in the year 1617." A few months later, English settler Richard Killingbeck was shot and killed in an ambush by a native armed with an English musket. [Smith, *The generall historie of Virginia*, vol. 1; also Kingsbury, ed., *Rec. of the Va. Co.*]

p. 156: Futhermore, before: Smith, *The generall historie of Virginia*.

p. 156. Captain John Smith's: Ibid.

p. 156. After surveying: Ibid.

p. 157. Proclamations: "Governor Argall. Proclamations or Edicts, May 18, 1618," Kingsbury, ed., *Rec. of the Va. Co.*,

p. 158. Immediately upon: Rountree, *Pocahontas, Powhatan, and Opechancanough*.

p. 158. Algonquian military: Citing John Smith on the Algonquian custom of sparing women and children, see Strachey, *History of Travell*, 104–05. There is evidence that some of the Algonquian in 1622 spared about twenty Englishwomen whom they ransomed to the settlers. Some of these women felt they were better treated by the Algonquian than by the English, upon their return to Jamestown.

p. 159. According to Samuel Purchas: Purchas, *Hakluytus Posthumous or Purchas His Pilgrims* (London: 1622).

p. 160. All able-bodied: Elizabeth Arnett Fields, "African American Soldiers Before the Civil War," *A Historic Context for the African-American Military Experience* (Champaign, IL: U.S. Army Construction Engineering Research Laboratories, July 1998). Colonial records show seventeenth-century African Americans, such as John Pedro in 1625 and James Longo in 1685, enrolled in the militia. Slaves were not excluded from carrying arms and ammunition in Virginia until 1639. See Hening, ed., *The Statutes at Large*, vol. 1:226.

p. 160. Before the *Treasurer*: Antonio and Isabell arrived on the *Treasurer* in 1619 and were acquired by William Tucker, commander of Point Comfort. Between then and 1624, the African couple had a child and baptized him in the Church of England. See the 1624/25 muster of the "living and the dead" in Kingsbury, ed., *Rec. of the Va. Co*: household of William Tucker: "Antoney Negro and Isabell Negro and William theire child baptised."

p. 160.   Following the massacre: Hotten, *Original Lists*, 244.

p. 161.   Among the Virginia headrights: Northampton County Deeds and Wills (1645–1651), (1640–1645), (1645–1651), fol. 2, cited by J. Douglas Deal, *Race and Class in Colonial Virginia—Indians, Englishmen, and Africans on the Eastern Shore During the Seventeenth Century* [hereafter known as *Race and Class*] (New York and London: Garland Publishing, 1993), 325–26. Mingo had already been noted in court records by 1644, and Mongon by 1645.

p. 161.   Their Latin first names: There is little chance that Mongon and Mathews did not originally come from Angola. John Thornton and Linda Heywood by e-mail, used by permission: "Our contention is that until the English developed their own slave purchasing posts along the coast of West Africa all their slaves came from privateering on Portuguese ships, and these in turn almost all came from Angola. In *De Laet's History of the West India Company* (pub. 1644, a report on all the privateering activities of the West Indies Company from its foundation to 1638), all but one of the ships they took was from Angola." The possibility that William Hawley's three Angolans arrived in Jamestown after the *White Lion* Africans, however, cannot be completely discounted. Upon becoming king in 1625, Charles I of England, bitter that the king of Spain had refused him his daughter in marriage, approved letters of marque for privateers to attack Spanish and Portuguese vessels. Lord Robert Rich received such a letter from Charles at this time as did "Arthur Guy and others." See *Calender of State Papers, Domestic, 1628–1629*, for letters from admiralty fees collecter John Ellsey to Edward Nicholas, secretary to Charles's advisor, the Duke of Buckingham. Arthur Guy, commanding the one-hundred-ton *Fortune*, was issued a letters of marque on 28 July 1628, yet Ellsey stated at the time that Guy had already taken "an Angolan ship with many Negroes" off the coast of Luanda and delivered them to Virginia in exchange for tobacco he then brought to England. See also *Va. Mag. of Hist. and Biog.* 7 (1900), 265–66. Therefore, Guy had carried out the Angola piracy a year *before* receiving the letters of marque in 1628. See also McIlwaine, *Minutes of the Council*, 157–58, for the colony's account of Captain Guy's Virginia arrival and departure in 1627. (As documented in Kingsbury, ed., *Rec. of the Va. Co.*, Guy was linked with Rich as early as 1621, at which time he brought the ship *Warwick* to Virginia.) It cannot be ruled out that Mongon and Mathews were among an unspecified but probably low number of Bantu captives delivered to Virginia on the *Fortune* in late 1627. In addition, Mongon and Mathews may have arrived in Virginia yet another way. The English merchant George Menefie listed twenty-three Africans—"Negroes I brought out of England with me"—when he patented land for a plantation in 1638. See Morton, *Colonial Virginia*, vol. 1, 142 and *Colonial Series 1574–1660* (London: 1860), 256. Menefie had been a coconspirator with Samuel Mathews in 1635 in the "thrusting out of Governor Mathews" and had been forced to go to England with Mathews to answer Harvey's charges before the Star Chamber. While Mathews and Menefie were in England, Harvey raided Denbigh Plantation and made off with a small group of Africans held by Mathews. In 1639, Menefie received twelve Africans from Harvey. See Nugent, *Cavaliers and Pioneers*, vol. 1, 112. The surname of Domingo Mathews, indicates a connection of Hawley's three Africans to Samuel Mathews's Denbigh Plantation and therefore to the *White Lion*'s Africans of 1619. Less than three hundred Africans were present in Virginia by the time Puritan William Hawley arrived in 1641. The most likely scenario is that Hawley, after moving from Barbados to Virginia, obtained the three Africans directly or indirectly from the original group of *White Lion* Bantu (indirectly, meaning including their children born in America), who were held by the wealthy fellow Puritan Samuel Mathews in Virginia. Hawley then used the three Africans to acquire headrights in Northampton County in 1641.

p. 162.   Foster, however: Northampton County Deeds and Wills (1654–55), fol. 25, cited in Paul Heinegg, ed., "Mongom," *Free African Americans in North Carolina, Virginia, and South Carolina* [hereafter known as *Free African Americans*] (Baltimore: Genealogical Publishing Co. and Clearfield Company, 2001). Access at www.freeafricanamericans.com/; see also Deal, *Race and Class in Colonial Virginia*, 326.

p. 162.   Foster appealed: Northampton County Deeds and Wills, no. 5 (1654–55), fols. 25, 54, cited in Breen, *Myne Owne Ground*, 77, and Heinegg, ed., "Mongom," *Free African Americans*.

p. 162.   But in 1650: Northampton County Deeds and Wills, no. 3, (1645–51), fol. 217, cited in Breen, *Myne Owne Ground*, 77.

p. 162.   The Nanticoke were: Reverend Johann Gottlieb Ernestus Heckewelder (1743–1823), in *History, Manners, and Customs of the Indian Nations Who Once Inhabited Pennsylvania and the Neighboring States*, (n.p.: 1820, repr. in The First American Frontier Series (New York: Arno Press and The New York Times, 1971)).

p. 163.   Captain John Smith had: Smith, *Generall Historie*.

p. 163.   In their contact: Northampton County Deeds and Wills (1645–1651), fol. 217; see also comments in Deal, *Race and Class*, chap. 1 and p. 326, and endnote 7, pp. 333–34, citing Whitelaw, *Virginia's Eastern Shore*.

p. 163.   One year later: Northampton County Deeds and Wills (1651–54), fol. 33, cited in Heinegg, "Mongom," *Free African Americans*. Mongon signed a deed of jointure with her when wed, reserving her previous property for her and her children.

p. 163.   Within a decade: Northampton County Orders (1657–64), fol. 138; (1664–74), fols. 14, 28, 41, 54, 115; Orders and Wills (1674–79), cited in Deal, *Race and Class*.

p. 164.   In the role: Accomack County Deeds and Wills, 1663–66, fol. 92, cited in Deal, *Race and Class*, 328. Mongon credited the 426 pounds of tobacco Herrick owed him to a debt he owned planter John Stringer.

p. 164.   When brought: Northampton County Orders (1657–64), Heinegg, ed., "Mongom," *Free African Americans*.

p. 164.   In another court case: Northampton County Orders and Wills (1683–89), cited by Heinegg, ed., " Mongom," *Free African Americans*; Deal, *Race and Class*.

p. 165.   Describing the incident: Northampton County Orders (1683–89), 118–19, 320–22, cited in Heinegg, ed., "Mongom," *Free African Americans*; and in Deal, *Race and Class*, 331–32, citing Whitelaw, *Virginia's Eastern Shore*, 105, 220, 221, 227, 259, 260. Deal points out this kind of violence was also present in the higher classes, citing the English aristocracy in Lawrence Stone, *The Crisis of the Aristocracy 1558–1641* (Oxford: Clarendon Press, 1965), 233–34.

p. 165.   Another minor run-in: Northampton County Orders (1657–64), cited by Deal, *Race and Class*; Whitelaw, *Virginia's Eastern Shore*, 292.

p. 165.   In 1663: Northampton County Orders (1657–64), fols. 173, 175, cited in Heinegg, ed., "Mongom," *Free African Americans*; see also Breen, *Myne Owne Ground;* Deal, *Race and Class.*

p. 166.   In 1645: Northampton County Deeds and Wills (1645–51), fol. 2, cited in Heinegg, ed., "Mongom," *Free African Americans.*

p. 167.   Three descendents: Luther Porter Jackson, *Virginia Negro Soldiers and Seamen in the Revolutionary War* (Norfolk, VA: Guide Quality Press, 1944). See also Heinegg, ed., "Mongon," *Free African Americans.*

p. 167.   As a freedman: Northampton County Orders (1678–83), cited by Deal, *Race and Class.* Deal: "Mongon owned some livestock himself by 1666, when he had his mark registered in court. [Northampton County Deeds and Wills (1651–54)] Ibid., p. 6 at the end of the volume."

Chapter 10 : *That the Child Shall Be Free*

p. 168.   William Evans was: "John Rolfe to Edwin Sandys" (January 1620), Kingsbury, ed., *Rec. of the Va. Co.* Rolfe spelled "Evans" as "Ewins"; the name also appears in documents as Ewinns and Ewen [see below].

p. 168.   A few days: Kingsbury, ed., *Rec. of the Va. Co.*, vol. 4, "Extracts of all the titles and estates of land sent home by Sir Francis Wyatt, May, 1625," in the Territory of Tappahanna over against Jamest City, "Wm. Ewins 1000 planted; Virginia Land Office, transcribed in 1683 by clerk Edward Harrison, cited in Dennis Hudgins, "A Blizzard Hits Surry County!" *Virginia Historical Society Newsletter [VHS]*, September 2003. Hudgins: "In the first book of the Virginia Land office [transcribed in 1683 by the clerk Edward Harrison] William Ewins obtained an 1100 acre patent for land in then James City County dated 30 September 1643 in Patent Book 1, p. 904–905. This patent was obviously in error because the land was at the head of the western branch of Upper Chippokes Creek instead of on the James River. The patent was surrendered up and relinquished and the land later patented by Robert Mosely in PatentBook 2, and assigned to William Short on 29 October 1657 and repatented about 1671/72 by William Short, Planter, son & heir of William Short, in Patent Book 6. William Ewins' relinquished patent did contain a headright list which was partially reused in his later patent for his James River land." Among the headrights were "Michaell, a Negroe, Katherine his wife, John Grasheare a Negro, Mathew a Negroe." (Grasheare is variously spelled Graweere, Grasher, and so on) Evans's James River land in Surry, also known as the College Plantation, was patented in this timeframe: "part A—400 acres Tappahannah Territory patented 15 September 1619 by William Ewen; part B—1,000 acres Tappahannah Terr. Patented January 1621/22 by William Ewen; part C—1,400 acres James City County in Patent Book 2 dated 8 July 1648 by William Ewen, Merchant; part D—1,400 acres Surry County in Patent Book 7 dated 25 April 1689 by Mrs. Alice Stanford, Widow; part C—Patent Book 2, 8th of July 1648, Sir William Berkeley, Knight unto William Ewen, Merchant."

p. 169.   Michael and Katherine: Library of Virginia Microfilm Reel no. 113; Surry Deeds, Wills, & c. (1652–73), 154, cited in Hudgins, "A Blizzard Hits Surry County!" *VHS*. When later freed, the black Blizzard family became numerous in Virginia, and descendents survive to this day. Evidence indicates Evans sent Michael and Katherine to Virginia from England aboard the ship *Saker* in 1627 and 1628. Evans filed a lawsuit against the owners of the *Saker* at one point. See Coldham, "William Evans v. the Saker, 6 May 1619," *English Adventurers and Emigrants, 1609–1660*, 19. Among Evans's business associates were London merchant William Felgate and Maurice Thomson, the latter the business manager for Robert Rich. In June 1659, about the time that Michael died, he and Katherine had the following children: Rebecca, aged 20; Francis, 10; Amos, 7; and Susanna, 5.

p. 169.   At this time: Breen, *Myne Owne Ground*, 73. Breen: "It was not unusual, however, for great planters to allow servants or slaves small plots of land, and according to John Hammond, laborers customarily tended their crops on Saturday afternoons and other free moments. 'There is no Master almost,' Hamond explained, 'but will allow his servant a parcell of clear ground to plant some Tobacco in for himself, which he may husband at those idle times he hath allowed him.' . . . In fact, several blacks did quite well." Two African men bound to Bridgett Charlton brought in 1,220 pounds of tobacco for themselves in 1658, and 2,155 pounds the following year.

p. 169.   This custom played: H. R. McIlwaine, ed., *Minutes of the Council and General Court of Colonial Virginia* (Richmond, VA: Virginia State Library, 1924), 477. For a general discussion of early black Virginians' successes with livestock in the seventeenth century, see Breen, *Myne Owne Ground*, 81–85.

p. 170.   However, before: Tim Hashaw, *Children of Perdition: Melungeons and the Struggle of Mixed America* (Macon, GA: Mercer University Press, 2006).

p. 171.   When the Sweet-Cornish: McIlwaine, ed., *Minutes of the Council and General Court of Colonial Virginia* [hereafter known as *Minutes*], 477; see also William Walter Hening, *The Statutes at Large, Being a Collection of All the Laws of Virginia* (New York: Alfred A. Knopf, 1976), vol. 1, 552,.

p. 171.   Five months after: McIlwaine, ed., *Minutes*, 477.

p. 172.   Margaret had broken: Ibid.

p. 172.   The Angolan who adopted: Deal, *Race and Class*, 280, citing "Selections from Conway Robinson's Notes and Excerpt from the Records of Colonial Virginia," in McIlwaine, ed., *Minutes*, 477.

p. 173.   As for his son: Heinegg, ed., "Gowen," *Free African Americans*.

John Graweere's surname has been variously transcribed Graweere, Grasheare, Grasher, Gowen, and Geaween. The case for "Gowen" as the name borne by descendants of John Graweere is based on the various surname spellings of his supposed son, Michael Gowen, also transcribed as Mihill Gowree. See endnote section for Heinegg, ed., "Gowen" in *Free African Americans:* "The name Mihill Gowen appears like Mihill Gowree in the 1668 patent, but the 11, September 1717 inquisition refers to the same land as belonging to Mihil Goen/Michael Gowen." See "Michael Gowen" in "Gowen" section of Heinegg. See also "Patents Issued during the Regal Government," as documented in the *William and Mary Quarterly Historical Magazine 9*, no. 3 (1901): 139–44; Library of Virginia microfilm reel no. 113: "Surry Deeds, Wills &c (1652–1673)" and *Newsletter of the Surry County, Virginia Historical Society and Museum* for September 2003; and McIlwaine, *Minutes of the Council*, 477.

p. 173. Many of his descendants: "Major John 'Buck' Gowen," Arlee Gowen, ed., *Gowen Research Foundation Newsletter [GRF]* 2, no. 1 (September 1990). See also: "Zephaniah Goins Fought in Yorktown Campaign," Arlee Gowen, ed., *GRF* 5, no. 3 (November 1993).

p. 174. Some responded: Johnston County Judge William Bryan testified in court on behalf of Holiday Haithcock, who had been denied his application for a Revolutionary War pension in September 1834 simply because he was a free person of color. Cited in Heinegg, ed., "Haithcock," *Free African Americans*.

p. 175. But Driggus was: Northampton County Deeds and Wills (1651–54), 28, 114, cited in Heinegg, ed., "Driggers," *Free African Amerians*; Deal, *Race and Class*, 282.

p. 176. In his will: Northampton County Deeds and Wills (1655–68), fol. 8, cited in Deal, *Race and Class*, 290.

p. 176. After his wife Frances: Northampton County Orders (1664–74), fol. 75, 78, cited in "Driggers," Heinegg, ed., *Free African Americans*.

p. 176. Another descendant: R. M. Brown, *The South Carolina Regulators* (Cambridge, MA: Belknap Press, Harvard University, 1963), 29–31. In *Free African Americans*, Heinegg writes: "In the fall of 1770 [Winslow Driggers] escaped from jail in Savannah, Georgia, and returned to the area of the Little Peedee River in North and South Carolina where he continued his outlaw career. He was described as: *about six Feet; Complexion, black; Visage, pale, being much reduced by Sickness; Hair, black and long, generally cued.* The following year a band of ex-Regulators captured him at his hideout near Drowning Creek and used the provisions of the Negro Act as an excuse to hang him on the spot." [Clark, *Colonial Soldiers of the South*; Brown, *South Carolina Regulators*, 29–31, 103; Saunders, *Colonial Records of North Carolina*, 9:725, 771].

p. 177. Another Driggus descendant: Brown, *The South Carolina Regulators*.

p. 177. Around Chesapeake: Philip D. Morgan, *Slave Counterpoint: Black Culture in the Eighteenth-Century Chesapeake and Lowcountry* (Chapel Hill: University of North Carolina Press, 1998).

p. 178. William Ashworth was: Terry G. Jordan, *Trails To Texas: Southern Roots of Western Cattle Ranching* (Lincoln: University of Nebraska Press, 1981). See also W. T. Block, "Meanest Town on The Coast," *Old West* (Winter 1979); also A. F. Muir, "The Free Negroes of Jefferson and Orange Counties, Texas," *Journal of Negro History* 35 (April 1950); and "Ashworth, William," in *The Handbook of Texas Online*, www.tsha.utexas.edu/handbook/online/articles/AA/fas6.html.

p. 178.   These freeborn: Jordan, *Trails To Texas: Southern Roots of Western Cattle Ranching*; Block, "Meanest Town on The Coast," *Old West* (Winter 1979); Muir, "The Free Negroes of Jefferson and Orange Counties, Texas," *Journal of Negro History* 35 (April 1950).

Chapter 11 : Ties That Bind

p. 180.   To acquire his land: Surry County Patents 4:71–72, cited in Heinegg, ed., "Dale," *Free African Americans*.

p. 180.   A white widow: Bennett, *Before the Mayflower*; Heinegg, ed., "Dale," *Free African Americans*. According to Heinegg, "On 26 December 1659 Judah Hide authorized him (called Benjamin Dawl) to act as her attorney, and on 19 July 1660 he witnessed a deed from William and Alice Lea to William Heath, " citing [Haun, *Surry County Court Records* 1:146, 156].

p. 180.   John Doll acquired: Haun, *Surry County Court Records* 1:146, 156; DB 7:217, cited in Heinegg, ed., "Dale," *Free African Americans*.

p. 181.   James Doyal descended: Byrd, *Bladen County Tax Lists*, 1:6, 15, 44, 61, 95, cited by Heinegg, ed., "Dale," *Free African Americans*.

p. 181.   Tapley Dial married: The 1624/25 Virginia muster of the living and dead. See also Heinegg, ed., "Johnson" and "Dale," *Free African Americans*.

p. 181.   In the Carolinas: Hashaw, *Children of Perdition*.

p. 182.   That year: *Virginia Magazine of History and Biography*, 17:232, cited in Heinegg, ed., "Cumbo," *Free African Americans*.

p. 182.   He was freed in September of . . . John Graweere and Margaret Cornish: James City County Patents 6:39, cited by Heinegg, ed., "Cumbo," *Free African Americans*.

p. 182.   Cumbo, whose son would be a patriot . . . fined twenty shillings: Cited Heinegg, ed., in"Cumbo," *Free African Americans*. For who were soldiers in the War of Independence, see John H. Gwathmey, *Historical Register of Virginians in the Revolution, 1775–1783* (Baltimore: Genealogical Publishing Co., 1979).

p. 183.   Until the strict: Virginia Easley DeMarce, "The Melungeons," *National Genealogy Society Quarterly* 84, no. 2 (June 1996).

p. 184.   Molly's sister Sarah married . . . of April 23, 1793: Heinegg, ed., "Cumbo," *Free African Americans*.

p. 185.   The Cumbos fought: Heinegg, ed., "Cumbo," *Free African Americans*.

p. 185.   Many descendants: Gwathmey, *Historical Register of Virginians in the Revolution*, cited in Heinegg, ed., "Cumbo," *Free African Americans*.

Chapter 12 : Making Hay

p. 187.   Tony Longo was: Heinegg, ed., "Longo," *Free African Americans*. One writer (Deal, *Race and Class*, see note 3, p. 363) speculates that Nathaniel Littleton may have been connected to Thomas Littleton, a London merchant who governed the island colony of Nevis in the early 1630s, and raises the possibility that Antonio Longo was a "seasoned" African from the Caribbean. However, Nathaniel Littleton's service in the militia company of the Earl of Southampton in the Netherlands, along with Virginia's pursuit of trade with the Dutch of New York, as in the case of Littleton's neighbor Edmund Scarborough, suggests Littleton likely purchased Longo from Dutch traders out of New York. Longo's companions on the Littleton plantation had such Bantu names as Congo, Cossongo, and Phallassa, which "seasoned" Africans often did not have. The participation of Dutch Protestants as rivals of Portuguese Catholics in the Kongo-Angola slave trade in addition to Portugal's use of the Christian guerra preta against the Dutch and anti-Portuguese African states in Angola, opens the possibility that after 1630 the Dutch purchased or captured black Catholic combatants in Angola for direct overseas trade, and that Africans with Latin names such as Antonio Longo did not come to Jamestown from the Caribbean, but came directly from Angola.

p. 187. The surname "Longo": Angolans in America at this time sometimes took the names of their hometown districts, kingdoms, or the country of Angola itself. However, it cannot be said for certainty that Tony Longo's surname is based on the state name of Longo or Loango in (then) greater Angola. His granddaughter, Ann Longo, was later also called Ann Congo in one court case. [See Prince George's County, Maryland Court Records 91699–1705, 289a, 309b, cited in Heinegg, ed., "Longo," *Free African Americans*.] Therefore, as a surname, Longo may originally have been a corruption of Congo, for among the first Africans that Nathaniel Littleton acquired for his Northampton County plantation was a man named Congo, to whom Tony Longo may then have been related. [See "The Will of Ann Littleton of Northampton County, Virginia, 1656," Nora Miller Turman, Mark C. Lewis, eds., *VMHB*, 75, no. 1:11–13, cited in Deal, *Race and Class*, 368.] Congo and his wife Cossongo (from the Angolan district of "Kasanje") had two children who were not identified in the Littleton will.

p. 187. After obtaining: The evidence that Hannah was English is not direct, however, her son James was later described as a mulatto, and, as Deal points out, never as a Negro. [See Accomack County Orders (1690–97), 123a.] Furthermore, black women were listed as taxables, and Hannah was not listed as a taxable. [Northampton County Orders (1657–64), fol. 102, cited in Deal, *Race and Class*, 363, who additionally cites Nottingham, *Accomack Tithables*, 1–7.]

p. 188. In the course: Northampton County Deeds and Wills, nos. 7, 8 (1654–68), fol. 12., cited in Breen, *Myne Owne Ground*.

p. 188. Like his English: Edmund Morgan in *American Slavery—American Freedom*, 156–57; Breen, *Myne Owne Ground*, 94; Deal, *Race and Class*, 358; Heinegg, ed., "Longo," *Free African Americans*.

p. 188. Neene testified: Morgan, *American Slavery*, 156–57; Breen, *Myne Owne Ground*, 94.

p. 188. Tobacco prices: See Wesley Frank Craven, *White, Red, and Black: The Seventeenth-Century Virginian* (Charlottesville, VA: University of Virginia Press, 1971). According to Craven, there were good harvests in seven out of eight years between 1665 and 1672, following ten crop failures between 1645 and 1662. Virginia planters dealt with "three major crisis in which the colonists struggled none too successfully with the prolems arising from an over production of tobacco, first in 1639–40, next in the mid 1660s, and finally in 1682–83. The price of tobacco seems to have fluctuated though the period of the great migration (1650–1675) being better at its beginning than subsequently."

p. 188.   The magistrate relieved: Accomack County Orders 1666–70, 151–152, 154, cited in Deal, *Race and Class*, 358–359, 364. Deal: "Since 1646, justices of the peace had been authorized to take [poor children] from their homes and employ them in public workhouses, even when the parents, 'either through fond indulgence or perverse obstinacy, are most averse and unwilling to parte with theire children.' [Hening, Statutes, vol. 1, 336–7] In 1668 again, the employment of such children in public workhouses was authorized. Not until 1672 was there a provision for binding them out to other households."

p. 189.   Refusing to acknowledge: Accomack County Orders (1703–09), 68, 74, 98, 101a, 114, 114a, 122, 125, cited in Heinegg, ed., "Longo," *Free African Americans*.

p. 190.   Sholster later: Accomack County Wills and Orders (1682–97), 119, cited by Deal, *Race and Class*, 361.

p. 190.   On a nearby farm: Accomack County Wills and Orders (1682–97), cited by Heinegg, ed., "Longo," *Free African Americans*.

p. 192.   That year: Northampton County, Deeds and Wills, nos. 7, 8, (1654–68), pt. 2, fol., 12, cited in Breen, *Myne Owne Ground*, 84.

p. 192.   As a free black: Deal, *Race and Class*, 339.

p. 192.   Harman's neighbor: Northampton County Deeds and Wills (1651–54), fol. 165; Orders (1657) fol. 75, 138, 198; (1664–74), fol. 114, 125, cited in Deal, *Race and Class*, 339–340; Heinegg, ed., "Harman," *Free African Americans*. Deal: "Whatever Michael's view of the potential for trouble for stemming from slave-free black contacts on his plantation, he probably took a dim view of all the drinking. In his will, written some six years later, in 1678, he specifically requested that 'noe drinkinge immoderately nor shootinge may bee suffered at my funerall'" [citing Northampton County Orders and Wills (1674–79), 340].

p. 193.   Then the said Wilkins: Northampton County Orders and Wills (1683–89), 15–16, cited in Deal, *Race and Class*, 345–46, and Heinegg, ed., "Harman," *Free African Americans*.

p. 194.   Harman's black neighbor: Northampton County Orders and Wills (1674–79), 58–59, cited in Heinegg, ed., "Harman," *Free African Americans*; Deal, *Race and Class*, 340–41. Gray was imprisoned for beating his wife and drinking away the estate she had received from her deceased black husband. Northampton County court records: "29 July 1675, Whereas Amy the wife of Wm Gray hath complained to ye Court that her said husband hath made away almost all her estate and also hath in a grose manner beat her & abused her and she suspects that he intended to destroy what he can of that which is left & so to remove away and leave her upon the parish for relief . . . conveyed a mare from his plantation . . . sheriff take him into custody."

p. 195.   Whether Francis: Northampton County Orders and Wills (1689–98), cited in Deal, *Race and Class*, 344–45. Deal: "Madame Tabitha Custis lived a long and colorful life on the Eastern Shore. About fifty years old when the incidents mentioned occurred, she had already been married to two prominent planters before John Custis, and was to have a fourth wealthy husband, Edward Hill, after Custis died in 1696. She outlived Hill as well, and died in 1718 almost eighty years old. As the eldest daughter of Edmund Scarburgh, she probably had known the son of her father's friend and fellow justice, Robert Pitt, from the time she was a young lady. It is possible that the tales Frances Harman told about them, although declared false and scandalous by the court, had some basis in fact" [citing Whitelaw, *Virginia's Eastern Shore*, 968–71].

p. 195.   Nevertheless, free: See Heinegg, ed., "Harman," *Free African Americans*.

Chapter 13 : The Shirt

p. 196.   Whereas the only law: Hening, *Statutes at Large*. Rebellious indentured servants, not slaves, were punished in court by adding more years to their indenture. Since extra years could not be added to the term of a lifelong slave, to discourage disobedience slaveholders, rather than abolish slavery and offer Africans indenture, opted to attempt to curb rebelliousness in slaves through severe physical abuse—hangings, beheadings (as object lessons for others), whippings, mutilations, piercings, branding, etc.—all of which were already utilized in the criminal punishment of English malefactors in the seventeenth century. If the State could not be held responsible for the death of a criminal being whipped, for example, by similar reasoning the Virginia Assembly decided that private slaveholders should not be held responsible for deaths of slaves that occurred during punishment that the owners were allowed to mete out by law.

p. 197.   Their concerns: Cited in "Management of Slaves, 1672," *Va. Mag. of Hist. and Biog.* 7 (1899–1900): 314.

p. 198.   Their ancestors: Northampton County Orders (1640–45); *VMHB* 75:17–21; cited in Heinegg, ed., *Free African Americans*; Deal, *Race and Class*, 367.

p. 198.   Two blacks: Northampton County Deeds and Wills (1665–68), pt. 2; Orders (1664–74), fol. 14; (1674–79), cited in Heinegg, ed., "Carter," *Free African Americans*. See also Deal, *Race and Class*, 369.

p. 199.   The will: Northampton County Orders and Wills (1683–89); cited in Heinegg, ed, "Carter," *Free African Americans*. See also Deal, *Race and Class*, 369.

p. 199.   A black man named Caesar: : Northampton County Orders (1722–29), 146, cited in Deal, *Race and Class*, chapter 3 and 373 .

p. 200.   The *North Carolina Gazette* carried " . . . seen there several times": Cited in Bennett, *Before the Mayflower*.

p. 200.   One of Abel Carter's: Cited in Heinegg, ed., "Carter," *Free African Americans*.

p. 200.   Also like John Pedro: See Robert C. Twombly and Robert H. Moore, "Black Puritan: The Negro in Seventeenth Century Massachusetts," *W&MQ* (April 1967), cited in Deal, *Race and Class*, 317–18.

p. 201.   How he became: See "Fourth Report of the Record Commissioners of the City of Boston," *1880, Dorchester Town Records* (Boston: Rockwell and Churchill, 1883), 64, cited by Deal, *Race and Class*, 318.

p. 201.   The agreement: *Suffolk Deeds, Liber II* (Boston: Rockwell and Churchill, 1883), 64, cited in Deal, *Race and Class*, 318.

p. 201.   As a sailor: Cane previously sailed to Northampton County, Virginia, in 1652 and 1654 to pick up tobacco and gave depositions there. [Northampton County Deeds and Wills (1654–55)], cited in Heinegg, ed., "Cane," *Free African Americans*.

p. 201.   This was the neighborhood: Northampton County Orders (1664–74), fol. 89, 71, cited in Deal, *Race and Class*, 319.

p. 201.   After setting roots: Northampton County Orders (1664–74), fol. 29, cited in Deal, *Race and Class*, 319. For trading with Pigot's slaves—Thomas Carter, Peter George, or John Archer—he was imprisoned for one month. See also Heinegg, ed., "Cane," *Free African Americans*.

p. 201.   Four years later: Northampton County Orders (1664–74), fol. 89, cited in Deal, *Race and Class*, 320.

p. 202.   In 1670: Accomack County Orders and Wills (1671–73), 95, cited in Deal, *Race and Class*, 323–324.

p. 202.   Mollie Goins married: For the roles of Leonard and Mollie Grimes in the Underground Railroad, see Philip J. Schwarz, *Migrants against Slavery: Virginians and the Nation*, Carter G. Woodson Institute Series in Black Studies (Charlottesville: University of Virginia Press, 2001); for the genealogy of Mollie Goins Grimes, see Heinegg, ed., "Gowen," *Free African Americans*.

Chapter 14 : Angola Plantation

p. 204.   The best European: John Lederer, *The Discoveries of John Lederer, In three several Marches from Virginia, to the West of Carolina, and other parts of the Continent: Begun in March 1669, and ended in September 1670* (London: Printed by JS for Samuel Heyrick, at Grays Inne-gate in Holborn, 1672). Though Magellan had made his historic voyage exactly one century before *the Bautista* Africans came to Jamestown, there was at that time no known way of marking longitude, and even Francis Drake's later voyage, guarded as a state secret for many years by England, did not add the missing 40 percent of the Pacific Ocean by the time Jamestown was founded with King James's, as it would eventually be realized, impossible commission for Smith's expedition to follow Virginia's rivers to India. Cartographers, painstakingly putting the missing pieces of the globe together over the decades, were not much helped by the English American colonists who became more enthralled with tobacco than with what lay beyond the western horizon. Five decades after building Jamestown in 1607, the settlers had not yet ventured beyond the falls of the James River. In 1669, Virginia Governor William Berkeley commissioned a German immigrant, Lederer, to seek a passage from the colony to the Indian Ocean by exploring "into those Parts of the American Continent where Englishmen never had been." He became the first English subject to cross the Allegheny Mountains, and, in 1670, he reached the top of the Appalachians. Viewing the vastness to the west, Lederer wrote: "They are certainly in a great errour, who imagine that the Continent of North-America is but eight or ten days journey over from the Atlantick to the Indian Ocean: which all reasonable men must acknowledge, if they consider that Sir Francis Drake kept a West-Northwest course from Cape Mendocino to California." Still, even in 1672, many like Lederer believed that a shortcut to the Pacific Ocean could be found across North America. In the preface of his publication, Lederer, who had fled to North Carolina after alienating Virginians by accusing them of refusing to accompany him on the expedition, states, "My LORD, FRom this discourse it is clear that the long looked-for discovery of the Indian Sea does nearly approach; and Carolina, out of her happy experience of your Lordships success in great undertakings, presumes that the accomplishment of this glorious Designe is reserved for her. In order to which, the Apalataean Mountains (though like the prodigious Wall that divides China and Tartary, they deny Virginia passage into the West Continent) stoop to your Lordships Dominions, and lay open a Prospect into unlimited Empires." See the full text at: www:rla. unc.edu/archives/accounts/Lederer/LedererText.

p. 207. Facing financial ruin: David Brion Davis, "Looking at Slavery from Broader Perspectives," *The American Historical Review* 105, no. 2 (April 2000).

p. 209. Also, when land: Helen C. Rountree, *Pocahontas' People: The Powhatan Indians of Virginia through Four Centuries* (Norman, OK: University of Oklahoma Press, 1990).

p. 212. Two months later: Nugent, *Cavaliers and Pioneers*, vol. 1, 25.

p. 213. Cashing out tobacco: Breen, *Myne Owne Ground*, 11.

p. 214. A feud started: Heinegg, ed., "Johnson," *Free African Americans*; Breen, *Myne Owne Ground*, 13–15; Bennett, *Before the Mayflower*, 37–39; Deal, *Race and Class*, 221–22.

p. 214. According to Scarborough's: Heinegg, ed., "Johnson," *Free African Americans*. See also Deal, *Race and Class*, 220–21.

p. 215. As all of this: Breen, *Myne Owne Ground*, 13–15.

p. 216. In 1677: Ross M. Kimmel, "Free Blacks in Seventeenth Century Maryland," *Maryland Historical Magazine* 71 (1976): 19–25; "Anthony Johnson, Free Negro, 1622," *Journal of Negro History* 61 (1971): 71–75, cited in Breen, *Myne Owne Ground*, 17.

p. 216. One of them: See Heinegg, ed., "Johnson," *Free African Americans*.

Chapter 15 : America George

p. 218. According to a Portuguese: MSS Araldi, Cavazzi, "Missione Evangelica," vol. A, book 2; Francesco Goia da Napoli, *La meravigliosa convertione della Santa Fede da Regina Zinga* (Naples: 1669), cited in Thornton, *African Politics*.

p. 221. His heir: Fernão de Sousa, "Rellação de Dongo," 6 September 1625, *FHA* 1:199; Same to King, 23 February 1632, *MMA* 8:137, cited in Thornton, *African Politics*. Hari a Ngola, who had the support of the Portuguese for the throne, insisted Ndongo's constitution outlawed female succession and also claimed that Njinga had murdered her nephew. See Beatrix Heintze, "Das ende des Unabhängigen Staats Ndongo: Neue Chronologie und Reinterpretation (1617–1630)," *Paideuma* 27 (1981): 197–273.

p. 221.   But, as someone: See Thornton, "African Political Ethics and the Slave Trade," *Winthrop Papers*. John Thornton writes: "Nzinga's correspondence . . . reveals, as [*Manikongo*] Afonso's correspondence also does, that she was accustomed to a slave trade, that it was licit under her laws, as under Kongo's, and she both held and sold slaves as a matter of course. But like her Kongolese antecedent, she also felt that there were definite limits and rules about who could and could not be enslaved. Nzinga's initial letter, written within weeks after she assumed power and addressed to the governor of Angola, Fernão de Sousa, in 1624 is no longer extant, but it is clear from his summaries of it, that Nzinga was prepared to deal in slaves. In his summary, de Sousa noted that she told him that he should withdraw Portuguese forces from Ambaca, a town founded by Mendes de Vasconcellos as a forward base for his illegal wars of the 1618–20 period, as had been promised. If he consented to this, she would, 'make markets at Quicala where they are customarily made, and that she will order her [followers] to go to them and to carry pieces (slaves).' ["Queen Nzinga to Fernão de Sousa, c. dry season, 1624, in de Sousa to Government, 15 August 1624," in Beatrix Heintze, ed., *Fontes para a história de Angola do século* (Wiesbaden, Germany: F. Steiner Verlag, 1985–88), vol. 2, 85–6. See also Brásio, ed., *MMA* 7:249–50.] In the same letter, Nzinga asked that the Portuguese return her subjects who had been taken away by Mendes de Vasconcellos's campaigns, some were sobas, or local rulers whose lands were not under Portuguese authority, others were *quijicos* [*kijiku*], the serflike dependents sometimes called slaves in contemporary documents. ["de Sousa to Government, 28 September 1624," Brásio, ed., *MMA*, 7:256; "de Sousa to Government, 10 December 1624," Heintze, Fontes 2:117.] Not only did Nzinga hold slaves and other dependent groups, but she also sold slaves herself. In 1626, she wrote to Bento Banha Cardoso, the Portuguese commander at Ambaca, informing him that, 'I was sending some pieces [slaves] to the market of Bumba Aquiçanzo, Aire [Ngola Hari, a Portuguese-supported rival ruler of Ndongo] came out with his army, and robbed me of thirty pieces of those I had sent.' ["Queen Nzinga to Bento Banha Cardoso, 3 March 1625," quoted by Fernão de Sousa to Gonçalo de Sousa and his brothers, c. 1630, Heintze, Fontes 1:244–45.] She demanded an immediate restitution, as well as announcing the capture of some Portuguese soldiers. Much later in her life, Nzinga did not hesitate to continue in the slave trade, although in this case her cause was not simply economic gain. She was anxious to redeem her sister Barbara from captivity in Luanda, and to that end had to pay a ransom of slaves to the Portuguese for it. In a letter of 1655, she complained that this ransom was a high one, she had already paid 'infinite pieces' and was yet to get satisfaction. ["Queen Nzinga to Governor General of Angola, 13 December 1655," Brásio, ed., *MMA*, 11:524.] These slaves were war captives, for in a dramatic speech announcing her treaty of peace with Portugal in 1657, Nzinga thanked her soldiers for 'all the labor that you have suffered in the wars, and now in making slaves to ransom my sister.' ["Fr. Serafino da Cortona to Governor General of Angola, 20 March 1657," Brásio, ed., *MMA*, 12:108] Nzinga may not have had a philosophical difficulty with holding slaves or selling them, she clearly did have a desire to set limits to the exploitation of both forms of labor. This is clearly demonstrated in their willingness to harbor runaway slaves from the Portuguese, a telling point that often troubled relations between Portuguese Angola and its African neighbors. Nzinga's propensity to harbor runaways was the immediate cause of the first war between her and Portugal in 1625–26. Such concepts are fairly clear in a letter that Nzinga wrote to António de Oliveria de Cadornega, the Portuguese settler and historian, in 1660. Her letter was in response to one of his whose exact contents are unknown, but which complained that slaves that he had purchased through traveling commercial agents called *pumbeiros* had run away (or been stolen) in Nzinga's territory, and that she had not recovered them. She responded to his query by her own complaint, that the pumbeiros had not sufficiently inquired as to who was free and slave, and that many people who had been wrongly enslaved were now being harbored by her." ["Queen Nzinga to António de Oliveira de Cadornega, 15 June 1660," in Cadornega, *História geral das guerras angolanas (1680–81)*, ed. by José Matias Delgado and Manuel Alves da Cunha (Lisbon: 1940–42, reprinted 1972, Agencia Geral do Ultramar.]

p. 223.   He replied: De Sousa to Sons, *FHA* 1:345–46, cited in Thornton, *African Politics*.

p. 223.   In desperation: Cavazzi (1660–65), MSS Araldi, "Missione Evangelica," vol. A, book 2, fols. 84–85, cited in Thornton, *African Politics*.

p. 224.   Professing Christianity: Cadornega, *História* 1:193; MSS Araldi, Cavazzi, "Missione Evangelica," vol. A, book 2, fols. 44–46, cited in Thornton, *African Politics*.

p. 225.   In 1657: Coldham, ed., *English Adventurers and Emigrants, 1609–1660*, 171.

p. 226.   Along the way: Nora Miller Turman, Mark C. Lewis, eds., "The Will of Ann Littleton of Northampton County, Virginia, 1656," *Virginia Magazine of History and Biography* (January 1967); Nugent, *Cavaliers and Pioneers*, vol. 1, 28; Northamton County Deeds and Wills (1657–66), (1655–68), Northampton County Orders (1657–64), (1664–74), Orders and Wills (1674–79); Philip D. Curtin, "Epidemiology and the Slave Trade," *Political Science Quarterly* (June 1968), cited in Deal, *Race and Class*, 367.

p. 227.   After Colonel Littleton: Deal, *Race and Class*, 368–69. Will of Ann Southy Littleton, Northampton Co., widow of Nathaniel Littleton, 28 Oct. 1656: "To my younger son Southy Littleton all my land at Nandue as by a patent dated 1636 taken in his name, according to the bounds thereof and seven Negroes, viz, Robin and his wife Fallassa and her three sons, little Tony, and Jane the dau of Peter. To my dau Hester Littleton six negroes, viz, Congo and his wife Cossongo and her two children, Isaake the son of old Tony, and Besse the dau of Paul. My son Edward Littleton extr. Of the remainder of my estate, viz all my land at Magattey Bay, ten Negroes, three Irish Servants, and one English servant."

p. 228. Peter George: The disreputable Candlin had previously been accused of purchasing stolen goods from servants of the Custis family. Northampton County Orders (1678–83), Orders and Wills (1683–89), (1689–98); Torrence, *Old Somerset*, 492, cited in Deal, *Race and Class*, 376–77.

p. 229. As early as 1670, Jamestown had enacted " . . . slaves for their lives": Hening, *Statutes*, vol. 2, 283.

p. 229. A number of: Heinegg, ed., "George, " *Free African Americans.*

p. 230. In fact: Thornton, *African Politics.*

p. 230. Upon his death: Heinegg, ed., "Mozinga," *Free African Americans.*

p. 230. The name "Mozinga": E-mail from Linda Heywood and John Thornton: "In the seventeenth century, Kikongo was pronounced a bit differently from today, as evidenced by the usage in the catechism of 1624 and the dictionary of 1648. In particular, the class marker in Bantu class 1 was pronounced more fully as mu- and since then (in the eighteenth century) it was gradually elided until it became a nasal, as it is today. Hence today's spelling of 'Nzinga.' In fact, in seventeenth century renderings of this name it was spelled Mozinga. This is one of the few cases in America where we have a personal name (not an ethnic name) from central Africa."

PART IV: THE FOUNDERS' LEGACY

Chapter 16 : Jamestown Burns

p. 233. Between 1648: Evarts B. Greene and Virginia D. Harrington, *American Population Before the Federal Census of 1790* (New York: Columbia University Press, 1932), 136–37.

p. 234. Also in 1660: York County Deeds, Orders, and Wills, vol. 3, 125, 26 August 1661, cited in Heinegg, ed., *Free African Americans.*

p. 235. Six decades earlier: See "1618," Camden, *Diary (1603–1623),* ed. Sutton.

p. 235. Regarded as: Cited in Mary Newton Standard, *The Story of Bacon's Rebellion* (New York: Neale Publishing Company, 1907).

p. 236. Among the natives: Standard, *Bacon's Rebellion.*

p. 236. The natives withdrew " . . . ambassadors were men of quality: Ibid.

p. 236. Refused protection: Ibid.

p. 237. Bacon raised: Ira Berlin, *Slaves Without Masters: the Free Negro in the Antebellum South* (New York: Pantheon, 1974).

p. 237. But at the plantation: Cited in Standard, *The Story of Bacon's Rebellion.* See also Breen, *Myne Owne Ground,* 27.

p. 239. In 1670: Hening, *Statutes at Large,* vol. 2, 280.

p. 239. That same year: Hening, *Statutes at Large,* vol. 2, 283.

p. 239. The Virginia legislature that year also: Hening, *Statutes at Large,* vol. 3, 86–87.

p. 239.   As affordable land: York County (VA) Deeds, Orders, and Wills, "Manumission of Mihill Gowen," vol. 3, 16, October 25, 1657 and 26 January 1657/8. Also cited in Heinegg, ed., "Gowen," *Free African Americans*. Mihill Gowen was the young African servant of Christopher Stafford, who directed in his will that Gowen be set free when he came of age. Stafford's sister, Amy Barnhouse, complied with his wish in 1657. However, during Gowen's service for Barnhouse, he fathered a child by her black slave Palassa, or Prossa. Amy Barnhouse set Mihill Gowen free and let him take his young son, but she kept Palassa enslaved.

p. 240.   In fact: Hening, *Statutes at Large*, 3:459–60.

p. 240.   Finally, in 1723: Hening, *Statutes at Large*, vol. 4, 132–33.

Chapter 17 : Roots of Abolition

p. 241.   In April 1646: Edward Montagu, *Manchester Papers*.

p. 242.   Becoming the first: Cited in Anne Farrow, Joel Lang, Jenifer Frank, *Complicity: How the North Promoted, Prolonged, and Profited from Slavery* (New York: Ballantine, 2005).

• ACKNOWLEDGMENTS •

T HE AUTHOR WISHES to thank Arlee Gowen, John K. Thornton, Linda M. Heywood, Paul Heinegg, David Randall, Curtis Christy, and Park Ranger Kirk D. Kehrberg of Historic Jamestowne, as well as the staff of Warwick Castle in England, for their support and contributions to this research.

It was the author's very great privilege to communicate with Hugh Fred Jope, USAF Major (ret), of Haverhill, Connecticut—twice captured and held as prisoner of war in the Philippines during World War II. The research that Major Jope graciously provided before his recent passing affirmed at last the identities of the long-sought anonymous Dutch man-of-war and her mysterious Captain John Colyn Jope of Stoke Clymsland, Cornwall, England, who brought the first Africans to Jamestown and English-speaking America in 1619.

· INDEX ·

• ABOUT THE AUTHOR •

T IM HASHAW IS a seventh-generation Texan who attended seminary and went into journalism. He is a descendant of George W. Hashaw who was a Confederate cavalryman in E Company of the Seventh Texas Mounted Regiment during the American Civil War. While researching his family genealogy the author discovered two African ancestors who appeared mysteriously in Jamestown in the early seventeenth century. Hashaw has won several investigative awards, including the National Radio and Television News Directors' award for best investigative journalism. He has also worked with Crandall Shifflett to place primary documents online at the Virtual Jamestown Web site, detailing the arrival of the first Africans in America. This project and Mr. Hashaw's contributions resulted in a seminar conducted in 2006 by Professor Shifflett at the University of Virginia, to research the earliest Africans at colonial Jamestown. He is also the author of *Children of Perdition: Melungeons and the Struggle of Mixed America*, which tells the later history of the descendants of the founders of African America at Jamestown in 1619.